## ADVANCE PRAISE

"A most compelling collection of historic facts regarding the origin of Islamic militancy and its devolvement to the current anti-Western jihadist terrorists—told in a most readable form. The thorough scholarly research by Don Sharpes, coupled with his on-the-ground personal experience, lay out an irrefutable foundation to counter those today who seem to be blinded by political correctness and are in denial that the Western Civilization is literally in a war for survival against the modern extremist followers of Mohammad. The reader should pay serious heed to Sharpes' conclusions!"
Major General Albert B. Crawford, US Army retired.

"Knowledge and understanding between Muslims and Non-Muslims, as well as convincing expert interpretations, have been mostly unsatisfying. Don Sharpes' book "Allah's Warriors" selects the theme of militancy and develops through history, scholarly analysis, and personal experiences a convincing interpretation of the current Islamic world. This book will reward thoughtful readers and help develop a rational basis on which co-existence between the Islamic and non-Islamic world can be possible."
Prof. Dr. Karlheinz Rebel, University of Tubingen

"In *Allah's Warriors* Don Sharpes provides an historical analysis of how and why the oppositional code of the Koran "speaks to" modern Muslims of all ages. His research on and in Muslim countries, conducted since the 1980s, reaffirms the view that the Islamic world hinders social and economic development with its resurgent orthodox fundamentalism. Sharpes argues that educators in Islamic countries have a critical role to play in indoctrinating extremists; he expresses hope that Western educators too might shape a thoughtful counter-agenda through use of this timely and insightful book."
Lyn Corno, Teachers College, Columbia University

"With his extensive knowledge of Islamic history and its religious dogmatism, Professor Sharpes illustrates how Islamic militancy through the centuries has inculcated in Muslim radicals a hatred of all other religions, Western countries, their people and values, and anything having to do with Israel and Judaism. He makes the compelling argument that today's militant Islam will, for perhaps years to come, overwhelm, and to an extent dominate, moderate elements in Muslim countries and continue to radicalize more and more youth. He sees little hope for any Palestinian-Israeli detente so long as Arab majorities dogmatically disdain and reject Western or Israeli proposals for political or economic solutions to this historic impasse."
Michael Condon, Retired CIA Officer

"In a word, this is an impressive book, reflecting a solid scholastic background, thorough research, and most of all, familiarity with the area and the complexity in dealing with this threat."
Col. Tim Geaghty, Retired Marine Commander

## SELECTED BOOKS BY DON SHARPES

*Our Divided House, Anti-Government and Radical Movements and the
Failure of Unification (CreatSpace/Amazon)*
*Handbook of International Studies in Education* (Ed.) (Information Age
Publishing, 2010)
*Outcasts and Heretics, Profiles in Independent Thought and Courage*
(Lexington Books, 2007)
*Sacred Bull, Holy Cow, A Cultural Study of Civilization's Most
Important Animal* (Peter Lang, 2005)
*Lords of the Scrolls, Literary Traditions in the Bible and Gospels*
(Peter Lang, 2004)
*Advanced Educational Foundations, The History, Philosophy and
Culture of Schools* (Routledge, 2002)
*Advanced Psychology for Teachers* (McGraw Hill, 1999)
*International Teacher Education Perspectives (Editor)* (Routledge,
1988)
*Curriculum Traditions and Practices* (Routledge, 1988)
*Education and the U.S. Government* (St. Martin's Press, 1987)
*Improving School Staffs* (American Association of School
Administrators, 1974)
*Strategies for Differentiated Staffing* (McCutchan Publishers, 1974)

# ALLAH'S WARRIORS
# The Global Islamic Militancy
# Movement

## Donald K. Sharpes

Vulcan Publishing
CreateSpace, a Division of Amazon
2012

4

ISBN: 97980615609102

Published by Vulcan
CreateSpace, A Division of Amazon
2012

# TABLE OF CONTENTS

# ACKNOWLEDGMENTS

To those of my friends who heard my ideas respectfully but who may not have always agreed with them, I salute: Ron Bright, Dick Bartunek, Gaylord Brockway, Sorrel Coven, Ted Crow, Gordon Fiala, Dick Hawkins, J. D. Helms, Lou Holtzman, Richard Hunt, Bill Luke, Dick McDaniels, Mike Morrison, Joe Nessim, Harold Sacks, Jim Plowman, Bill Oakes, Skip Schnierow, Tom Tull, Chuck Summers, the late Bob Gambill, Bob Kellogg, and the late Col. Charlie Scarborough.

I am indebted to scores of my Muslim students over the decades from Iran and Palestine, and my female students at Zayed University in Dubai, especially Ayesha Hamza Juma, Seham Ibrahim Mohammed, Batool Hassan Abdullah and Nooreya Yousef AbdulRahman for their participation in my research and translations. To my academic colleagues in Kuwait, Bahrain, and Oman (you know who you are), thank you. To my dear Iranian friends, Setayesha Afshordi, and my Egyptian friend Samir Dos, thank you for the time enlightening me.

To colleagues who offered advice or encouragement or both, I thank Professor Bassam Tibi, University of Goettingen, Germany, Dave Berliner, Ursula Casanova and Gene Glass, Arizona State University; Lotte Rahbek Schou and Peter Widell, Aarhus University; Julia Christmas Nishibata, Miyazaki International College, Japan; KarlHeinz Rebel, Professor Emeritus of Tubingen University; Witold Tulasiewicz, Cambridge University; and Stefan Hopmann, Professor at the University of Vienna. To Lyn Corno of Teachers College, Columbia University, who graciously agreed to review and comment, I am appreciative. I am especially grateful to Mike Heim for his photos of American soldiers in Afghanistan. I am indebted to Mike Condon, former CIA officer, and John Steinbacher, President of Summit Associates. I am indebted to Steve Pappas for his contributions to Islamic Sufi mysticism and especially articles on Ibn 'Arabi.

I am grateful to colleagues and supporters at the American University of Beirut, especially Karma El-Hasan, Director of Institutional Research, and Robert Myers, Director of the Center for American Studies and Research, who invited me in November/December 2009 to give lectures. I am also very indebted to Rami Khouri, Director of the Issam fares Institute for Public Policy and International Affairs at the American University of Beirut and a frequent spokesperson on Middle Eastern affairs for the international media.

I would have gratefully requested my multiple Islamic colleagues in several Middle East countries to write a favorable preface or endorsement, but with such a request would have knowingly placed them in potential social jeopardy with other Muslims because of my honest perspective of the militant aspect of Islam. I cannot avoid my convictions based on conclusions from history and current affairs and neither can they. I had to give them all a pass so as not to endanger their communal and social standing.

Thanks to those publications that permitted me to publish in part articles that originally appeared in their pages: *The Scottsdale Tribune, The*

*Arizona Republic, The Salt Lake Tribune, Politiken* (Denmark), *Padagogisches Handlin* (Germany), *The Jordan Times* (Amman), *Emeritus Voices, The Journal of Value Inquiry, Journal of Education for Teaching*, and the 2010 volume I edited for Information Age Publishing, *Handbook of International Studies in Education.*

And to those institutions that allowed me to represent my views on this topic I am indebted to: Arizona State University for luncheon talks to the Emeritus College; the Semitic Museum at Harvard University where I gave three lectures on this topic in the summer of 2005; The Stanford Phoenix Club that allowed to address Islam and the West for the Stanford and Ivy League community in Phoenix in May 2009; Fox 10 News in Phoenix where I appeared several times in interviews speaking about Iraq and Islam; and to my colleagues at The American Educational Research Association, and the International Studies Group I served as president from 2007-2010.

# ABBREVIATIONS

| | |
|---|---|
| AS | Air & Space |
| ASC | American Scholar |
| AR | Arizona Republic |
| AM | Atlantic Monthly |
| BJ | Berlin Journal |
| BAR | Biblical Archaeological Review |
| CJDS | Canadian Journal of Development Studies |
| DSA | Defense and Security Analysis |
| EC | The Economist |
| FA | Foreign Affairs |
| FOR | Fortune Magazine |
| GU | Guardian |
| JNES | Journal of Near East Studies |
| IHT | International Herald Tribune |
| IQ | Islamic Quarterly |
| JFQ | Joint Force Quarterly |
| JICI | Journal of Intelligence and CounterIntelligence |
| JET | Journal of Education for Teaching |
| JSS | Journal of Strategic Studies |
| JVI | Journal of Value Inquiry |
| LT | The London Times |
| MEJ | Middle East Journal |
| NYT | New York Times |
| NYTBR | New York Times Book Review |
| NYRB | New York Review of Books |
| NYTM | New York Times Magazine |
| NY | The New Yorker |
| RUSI | Royal United Services Institute Journal |
| SS | Security Studies |
| SF | Social Forces |
| SUR | Survival |
| SCR | Studies in Conflict and Terrorism |
| TWQ | Third World Quarterly |
| USNWR | U.S. News and World Report |
| TN | The Nation |
| WP | The Washington Post |
| TSJ | The Wall Street Journal |

# PHOTOS

*Ingentes animos augusto in pectore versant.* (Virgil)

(Powerful spirits turn sacred in the heart)

# PREFACE

Allah loves those who fight in His cause united in one column, like the bricks in one wall. (*Koran* 61:4)

Repeated news reports and profiles of young Muslim men in America and Europe confirm that threats from Islamic radicals are persistent, longstanding, and global. Concerned citizens are unaware of how extensive and historically prolonged has been the challenge of Islamic militancy, the story of some young Muslim men willing to extirpate non-Muslims to atone for past or perceived grievances. Since 2001, there have been 14 terrorist-related attacks in New York City alone.

Amine el Khalifi, 29, must have thought it was a go. He had his MAC-10 gun, a vest full of nails, and was ready to explode his suicide device at the U.S. Capitol in Washington, DC. But it was all a con by the FBI. He had been convinced that an undercover agent was an al-Qaeda operative supervising his terrorist attack. He was arrested in February 2012. Unemployed Amine had entered the U.S. on a tourist visa in 1999 and never left.

Jose Pimentel, 27, a U.S. citizen living in Manhattan, was arrested months earlier, in November 2011, for plotting to bomb post offices, police stations and returning veterans. Pimentel was in the process of assembling pipe bombs with instructions from *Inspire*, the online al-Qaeda web journal.

In July 2011 a U.S. Muslim serviceman, Pfc. Nasser Abdo, was arrested in Killeen, Texas as he was planning to target military personnel near Fort Hood army base, scene of one of the most outrageous killings on domestic soil in military history by Maj. Nidal Hassan. Abdo was found with guns and bomb-making materials in his motel room. The previous year he had been granted conscientious objector status because of his religious beliefs.

Also in July 2011, Omer Abdi Mohamed, 26, of Minnesota, was arrested and admitted being part of a conspiracy helping Somali terrorists murder, main and kidnap others in a foreign country. Omer recruited Somali young men and, among other activities, bought them airline tickets to travel to Somali to fight as members of the al-Shahbab terrorist group.

In September 2011, Norway charged three men with conspiracy to commit terrorism in connection with a cartoon controversy. They were all Muslim with different ethnicities: a Uighur from China, an Iraqi Kurd, and an Uzbek, all living in Norway. In the same month six Muslim men living in Birmingham, England were charged with plotting terrorism and suicide bombings in England.

This study is a comprehensive look at Islamic militancy, exploring the historical and social roots of Islamic fundamentalism that bred men like Osama bin Laden and the cells and individuals of al-Qaeda and similar groups that carry on Islam terrorist cause. I seek to enlarge the context of Islamic militancy to show the comprehensive scope of the challenge facing the West.

Arabs invaded the Middle East, North Africa, Egypt, Persia, Spain and Gaul, and the later Ottomans subjugated the Balkans until the sultan's army was defeated outside Vienna in 1683. Arab Muslims only want everyone to remember the Crusades as an historical narrative and not their own invasions and conquering of peoples and countries in previous centuries. The West will be perennially engaged with the Islamic world as a part of its global outreach and have to grapple with Islamic militancy for the rest of this century.

September 11, 2001 really did change the world's worldview, not just America's. It was clear that retribution would be coming, but against whom? Modern wars had always been against nation states or empires. To attack a loose confederation of active terrorists funded by a psychopathic fanatic, Osama bin Laden, who had cohorts in several Islamic countries seemed equally mad.

So American officials conveniently declared a "war on terror," because they didn't know where threats might exist, even in the U.S. The Bush Administration, bowing to the public's instinct for revenge in 2001, decided to attack the one country, Afghanistan, really not a country at all as much as it is unrelated groups of tribal entities harboring al-Qaeda militants. Then, because of arrogance and a hasty impulse to restore what they believed was America's tarnished image, the U.S. attacked Iraq in anger only to discover that America's image became even more blemished, and the invasion a colossal miscalculation built on deceit and surprising naivete about democracy for the Arab world. It was the first pre-emptive war in American history. The Obama Administration had to exit ungracefully in late 2011 after a decade of blunders to preserve the minimum of a sloppy foreign invasion divorce settlement.

The Islamic terror threat is global. What do the following countries and regions have in common—Nigeria, Sudan, Somalia, Chechnya, Dagestan, the southern Philippines, Indonesia, Yemen, Afghanistan, Pakistan, to name a few? Answer: they are all countries with active, separatist Islamic movements. These are not Presbyterians or Methodists, Hindus or Sikhs, Catholics or Lutherans. Only Islam seeks its own religious form of government exclusively and finds authorization in the Koran to use violence to attain it. The militant wings of Islam today employ the same violent strategies of murder and mayhem on behalf of their religion and to establish a Caliphate similar to that of the Ottoman Turks.

From 2001 to 2008 there were 527 terrorism charges in the U.S., about a third that number in Europe, resulting in 319 convictions, with additional trials pending. The per-capita Muslim arrest rate in the U.S. is two and a half times as high as it is in Europe. By September 2011 there were 30 terrorist attacks and plots by homegrown jihadists on U.S. soil since 9/11. This does not speak well for the argument that improved socio-economic conditions or better cultural relations will solve the problem. Terrorism is un-related to the economics of the perpetrator. [1] Al-Qaeda is weaker after Osama's death but still operating.

The Guantanamo Files exposed by *The New York Times* through WikiLeaks and an anonymous source revealed a chilling account of a father and Muslim militant cell operating in New York City. In 2011, Saifullah Paracha, 63, the oldest prisoner in Guantanamo who worked with Khalid Shaikh Mohammed the planner of 9/11, and his son Uzair, now held in a federal prison, were both part of a small team of al-Qaeda operatives planning new attacks in the U.S. They planned attacks using biological, chemical and nuclear weapons, aircraft attacks on the west coast, and explosives in heavily populated areas in New York. Saifullah came to the U.S. from Pakistan on a student visa when he was 26 years old to attend New York Institute of Technology and stayed to become a small businessman and worked as a travel agent in New York City for thirteen years. The father and son cell is one example of the growing face of militant Muslim extremism just in the U.S.

France and America in the 18th century revolted against a traditional autocratic enemy in the form of unbridled and capricious monarchy. One way to understand the rage of Islamic radicals who oppose the West is to revisit the origins of the French and American Revolutions. In the 18th century the plebeians in France and America almost universally opposed monarchs, Louis XVI in France, and George III in England. The opposition was indicative of a rising sense of the sovereignty of the people and not the autocracy of kings, a collective consensus of people who sought their own form of government, and who had a growing and profound distrust of royal inheritance. We easily sympathize with this emergent idea of the sovereignty of the people in the West since we are the heirs of these political revolutions that overthrew kings and spawned republics and representative democracies.

The Arab world has never experienced such political transformations until the Arab Spring when several countries revolted against dictators. Instead, the majority of nations experienced a colonial paternalism that, having liberated its own people from royal autocracy, imposed it on economically challenged peoples in Africa, Asia and the Middle East. Although it appeared that many of these countries did not have the intellectual capital to develop new designs for governance, they uniformly revolted against colonial administrations. Having obtained freedom from colonial oppressors and exploiters, they often reverted to one-man, tribal, party or military rule, in many cases simply an extension of their historical legacy. Since World War II Asian countries adopted more secular forms of European and American parliamentary democracies. But in sub-Saharan Africa and much of the Middle East—including North Africa and the Levant and Persian Gulf—one-man, military or tribal autocracy is still the prevalent norm even as masses challenge that political ideal.

Muslim extremists see the situation as a reinstatement of lost or misplaced values. The hardcore Muslim world has always rejected the western secular, political and cultural model. Extremist groups like al-Qaeda seek to totally destroy the western world. Terrorism and federal government debt, of ten issues surveyed by the Gallup Poll, tied in 2010 as the issues Americans say are most threatening to the future wellbeing of the U.S.

The unequivocal call to a return to Islamic values is a return to radical fundamentalism. It is a page torn from European history a thousand years ago when the combination of the Reformation, Enlightenment, the scientific revolution and capitalism challenged the dominance of Christian imperatives.

The fear is heightened when news of captured individual terrorists is known. Khalid Aldawsari, 20, who came to America as a college student to study chemical engineering, was arrested in February 2011 at Texas Tech in

Lubbock and charged with the use of a weapon of mass destruction for planning attacks on potential targets like former president George Bush's Dallas home and various dams. He had been planning such *jihad* attacks, and had the technical knowledge to carry them out, for years prior to coming to the U.S. From 2008 to 2010 more than two-dozen Muslim Americans have either joined or sought militant group training with groups abroad. About 50 Americans, from a variety of socioeconomic backgrounds, have been charged with terrorism-related offenses during that period.

My initial study of Islam became in the late 1970s. A few years ago Islamic fundamentalism had a negative connotation in the West associated with inflexibility and conservative morality and theology. Today, it is associated in the West almost exclusively with fanatical extremism, though many have voiced optimism for its more positive accommodations. Generalizations about the Islamic world or any peoples or civilizations are hazardous. But books and articles beginning in the late 1970s revealed how Islamic scholars were becoming more isolated.

The First World Conference on Muslim education was held in Jeddah at King Abdul Aziz University in 1977 attended by 313 Islamic scholars from throughout the world. The number 313 is symbolic—it is the same number of soldiers that Mohammed had at the battle of Medina. The central theme of that conference was that the faith of Islam was to govern all education and learning. Western educational ideals typically distinguish between secular and religious education. Islamic scholars henceforth re-affirmed that Islam would make no such distinction. After 1977, I rarely saw another Arab scholar at professional meetings in Europe or America.

I continued my inquiry as a postdoctoral fellow at the Institute of Development Studies at the University of Sussex in 1984-85. I examined statistics on educational trends, and looked specifically at teacher training and higher education in 16 Islamic countries. What I found then was startling. There were wide disparities in higher education enrolment patterns, especially for teachers. I found that the average population growth rate was at about three percent, that the average adult literacy rate was 44%, the average teacher to student ratio was 1–68, and the average higher education enrolment at nine percent. I asked, "How can a country, or group of religiously oriented nations boost its economy if it is lacking skilled personnel and qualified teachers?" None of these figures or trends was encouraging for long-term national or regional socio-economic development. The ratios have not changed much in the intervening decades.

But the more disturbing trend I found in the mid-1980s was that there were more than four times as many higher education students enrolled in religion and theology, not subjects conducive to economic development. There were only 2% enrolled in math and computer sciences. Brazil at the time had approximately the same number of teachers and students enrolled in secondary school teacher training as did all the Islamic countries with a combined population four times higher than Brazil's. The Islamic world of the Middle East was not cultivating its personnel resources for productive economic development. Petroleum production was the only saving resource holding several Islamic countries stable economically.

Since then I have continued to gather evidence from reports, scholarly reviews, books, websites, and scores of personal interviews, many with Muslim scholars, journalists and academics. I have Muslim friends and colleagues in Europe and the U.S. and in Kuwait, Bahrain, Oman, the United Arab Emirates, Pakistan, Syria, Lebanon, Jordan, Egypt, Indonesia, Azerbaijan, Iran and Turkey. Collecting evidence required sorting and analyzing which material from readings, personal experiences and interviews was relevant. I selected the Koran, the sacred book of Muslims as one central point of reference for the movement toward militarization and violence. I also present findings from my own research conducted with colleagues in Europe since 2006.

I have been studying Islam for more than a quarter century and have lived and worked in Malaysia, Cyprus, Dubai, Lebanon and Indonesia. I have also enjoyed tea and Arab hospitality with Bedouins in their tents in the deserts of Jordan. I have taught Iranian exiles, Palestinian refugees, Turkish Muslim school administrators, and done research in Malaysia where my children attended Muslim schools. In 2002 I taught at Zayed University, an all female college in Dubai, the United Arab Emirates. Many of my colleagues sought to portray Islam as a peaceable and inherently benevolent religion, as if it were an at-large humanitarian, welfare society. It is, but only for other Muslims.

The logic of religious zealotry is not that its propositions are rational, but that the believer invests such intense emotions in its defense, and is willing to die to uphold its premises. The enemy of Islam is not only obnoxious and loathsome to fundamentalist Muslims, but an enemy of God. As the world has become more complicated, and economically and socially globalized, religious fundamentalism has retreated into convenient, traditional explanations for understanding the world as a perpetual struggle. In Islam that movement has retrenched into militancy, into fighting against a cultural tsunami that confronts ancient, traditional religious beliefs.

Ali Allawi in *The Crisis of Islamic Civilization* (2009) defined Islam as a formerly great civilization the West does not fully understand. [2] He wrongly poses the dilemma between Islam and the West as a philosophical conundrum between individualism and collectivism, between personal freedom and communal authority. It is a false comparison. The tacit assumption of Islam with militancy within its religious tenets is unacceptable in any civilization. Granted Islamic countries have been the victims of colonial imperialism, but so have other repressed non-Islamic countries, as the USSR demonstrated. It is not the religion of Islam that is impugned but its unhesitating acceptance of violence in its doctrine. The criminality of a few terrorists is linked intimately to the communal legacy of Islam, a quintessence embedded in the Koran and which thus infects the whole culture.

At this writing in the transitional march among some Arab countries toward a mild form of democracy the possibility of political instability is real, as is the potential rise of Islamic fundamentalists dominating the political agenda, and dedicated militants carrying on a war with the West. In the meantime, Middle Eastern peoples want to keep America at a distance while embracing the ideals of free speech and expression, the right of peaceful assembly and financial transparency in their countries, except in Iran, the 400-pound Islamist gorilla in the West and Israel's diplomatic dining room.

Protests began in the streets of Tunis, Tunisia in January 2011 and quickly migrated to Egypt, Bahrain, Jordan, Yemen, Libya and Syria. The nearly simultaneous uprisings toppled Ben Ali, Tunisia's leader, Egypt's Hosni Mubarak after days of protests by hundreds of thousands, and Ali Abdullah Saleh of Yemen. Political fault lines will follow these disruptions, possibly fracturing into clan or tribal borders, or even civil war and national or sectarian divisions.

It's amazing how the pattern of history among autocrats reacts with repetitive similarity to protests to its regime. First, comes the public denial, then the blaming of foreigners and interferers, then the media is at fault, then everything will return to normal, or maybe the constitution will be revised, if only the protesters will go home. No one seems to realize, with the genie out of the bottle analogy, that there is no more normal. Reform will be more traumatic because it has been repressed for so long, as if fear and intimidation would last among the populace forever.

The West had all but ignored autocracy in the Arab world, instead treating it as a vast enterprise of fueling stations for its insatiable petroleum energy consumption. But protests have erupted nearly everywhere in the Arab world, triggered by the force of street protestors in Tunisia, Egypt, Libya, Bahrain and Syria because of the absence of freedoms, the lack of jobs, the suppression of women's rights and all forms of artistic and personal expression. The transition from totalitarian autocracy will clearly create footholds for extremists in the confusion and possible anarchy as some Arab countries try to move closer to democratic ideals while avoiding more dictators.

Who will come out of the shadows of autocratic suppression to try to form states? Will it be political leaders who favor secular or Islamic rule? Will the Muslim Brotherhood take control of political vacuums to establish an Islamic state in Egypt? Will fundamentalist or militant groups grab control from weak leaders and create clerical theocracies antagonistic to democracy such as exists in Iran? Al-Qaeda type militants will attempt to take advantage of political confusion in several states to establish a base for furthering its aim of creating Islamic states.

Amidst these transformative movements, factor in the foreign policy directives. The U.S. will want to maintain some military presence in the Middle East to counter possible incursions, and to have a counterbalancing power influence to Iran. Saudi Arabia will seek to hold on to a Sunni balance from the dominance of Shiite Iran. Turkey will want stability among Kurds on any of its borders with Syria, Iraq or Lebanon. Egypt will want to play a moderating role in the region. Israel, alone or with the help of the U.S., will monitor activities antithetical to its interests on its borders and within the occupied territories. In such an unsafe, volatile and fragmented neighborhood, Muslim militants may be able to thrive and even find sympathetic nations to house them, especially if new governments cannot find a path between dictatorship and anarchy.

The West has slowly over two hundred years built political systems reducing religion as an influence in law and public policy. American religious beliefs intrude in matters of abortion, prayer and the influence of government in any religious policy that conflicts, or appears to conflict, with governmental agendas. With rare exceptions—Turkey, Indonesia and to some degree Syria, Lebanon and Egypt—the Islamic world has not yet begun this process of secularizing its government so that a dominant religion does not force its policies on minorities. [3]

What is abundantly clear is that minorities and especially Christians are living in fear in Arab lands as they become victims of sectarian violence. Iraqi Christians have fled in the thousands since the 2003 invasion. Over 93,000 Coptic Christians have fled Egypt since March 2011 and another 150,000 were expected to leave by the end of 2011. [4] Lebanon's Christians fear continuing alienation and disenfranchisement as they hold loosely onto a fragile and eroding power base. Islamic militancy is not just directed at the West but at anyone not a Muslim. Releasing the iron fist of a dictator in any Arab country also releases sectarian religious frenzy.

Conservative values are prevalent in many countries, including the U.S. But the expansion of particular religious values places restrictions on democratic states, whether predominantly Muslim or not, that also seek to preserve the rights of minorities who do not necessarily endorse the same values. Events in the Arab and Islamic world will always be contentious and turbulent. Nevertheless, the militancy embedded in the doctrinal scripture of the Koran makes confrontation with the West inevitable and makes western posture to Islam perennially vigilant. [5] This book is an exploration of that challenge to the western world.

Jordanian Bedouin Children

# INTRODUCTION

Later I realized the prejudices and hatred that Muslims harbor against
almost all non-Muslims are not the result of any misinterpretation of the
teachings of the Qur'an, but is because this book teaches hate and
encourages prejudice.
(Ali Sina in his testimony in Crimp & Stevenson, 2008, p. 54)

The Koran was composed in the sultry sands of Arabia, one of the most inhospitable, moonscape places on earth, written in Medina and Mecca close to the coastal waters of the Red Sea, and has since energized a billion plus people. It is a collection of one hundred and fourteen chapters or *suras,* and is one of the most influential sacred books in history because it was reported to have been transmitted by the angel Gabriel. Mohammad dictated messages to his scribes over the last twenty-three years of his life. Passages were written on leather, parchment, bones and palm leaves and then squirreled away in several different kinds of receptacles with no organizational method of identifying in what order each revelation was transcribed, or for any special care taken for their preservation. These dictated revelations were assembled years later in decreasing length, from longest to shortest, which means that the Koran is the history of its transcription and revelation in reverse order. [1]

The Koran, the perfect, timeless word of God for its believers, is couched in the lyrical poetry of Arabia. Its prose abandons logic in organization and presentation. It is filled with dull dialogue, fragments of stories and violent imagery. You can find in it maddening inconsistencies of tolerance and intolerance, passages advocating peace and war, forbidding suicide but encouraging death against infidels.

The Koran does not tell a story, offers no history or sermon, and yet has a repetitive intensity that inspires. Those partial to its creed believe it is the greatest book ever written, that it holds all truth, and that its sacredness comes from the holiness believers confer on its text because they are the words of Allah. The words of any sacred scripture cast a spell on believers, emboldening them to excessive fervor and to extraordinary feats. More objective readers, and not necessarily the most skeptical, find that its passages rise occasionally to poetry matching biblical passages, but that it is a prosaic repetition of Jewish Torah prescriptions with more vivid descriptions of heaven and hell. Its value is that it is the first Arabian prose literature that undoubtedly contributed to the increased literacy of the peninsula.

A few Muslim intellectuals believe the Koran has to be interpreted in its historical context but that its laws can change with the times. Followers of the *Salafi* Muslim school on the other hand, like the followers of austere Protestant sects, believe there can be no contemporary application. The majority of Muslim scholars over the centuries have emphasized the Koran's timeliness and that its legalistic code speaks to all ages. Many modern Muslim women seek equal rights but their democratic movement contradicts a thousand years of Islamic legal scholarship and practice. A combination of fierce belief in monotheism, and prescribed rituals of prayer and fasting—belief in one God, and prayer and fasting were all borrowed from Judaism—together with a militant spirit, would guide successive disciples. For nearly fourteen centuries the Koran inspired its faithful, provided indispensable and unifying rituals for its adherents, and reputedly sanctified some of its devout. But it has also emboldened many extremists, sanctioned by the militant revelations of Allah with a fanaticism fueled by intense piety to wage war.

According to Sayyid Qutb's (1906–1966) influential book *Milestones*, Islam is not merely a religious belief but a declaration of freedom of people from servitude toward others and by this he means all other political systems. Islam as a way of life means to abolish all systems and governments based on human rule and the servitude of one person over another. Muslims believe that there can be no civil or secular government separate from Islam. This merger of religion and the state is comparable to the historical parallel of Catholicism and medieval civil order when the whole of Europe was under the sway of the Holy Roman Empire. The Pope commanded kings.

However, there is in Islam a transformation from the simplicity of the beliefs of this ritualistic religion toward a disturbing movement of bellicose violence that has been endemic in its scripture for centuries. Even the Sikhs, founded by the prophet Nanak in the early 16th century in northwest India, a cross between Islam and Hinduism, carry a legacy of militarism. The men are not allowed to cut their hair and carry with them at all times a small knife representative of the sword of Islam.

Mohammed exhorted his followers to wage war on non-Muslim tribes. In the Koran's scriptural directives radical Muslim fundamentalists find all the cause they need to declare terror on unbelievers. "Muhammad is God's Apostle. Those who follow him are ruthless to the unbelievers but merciful to each other." (*Sura* 48:29). Saudi school texts state that loyal Muslims should "consider the infidels their enemy." Such a statement is a repetition of what exists in the Koran. Here are the most recurrent phrases from the Koran advocating animosity towards non-Muslims.

When you meet the unbelievers in the battlefield, strike off their heads. (*Sura* 47:4)

And fight in the way of God with those who fight with you . . . (*Sura* 2:190)

And slay them whenever you come upon them and expel them from where they expelled you." (*Sura* 2:191)

When the sacred months are over slay the idolaters wherever you find them. (*Sura* 9:5)

A collection of similar passages can be found in the following *suras*.

- Kill unbelievers wherever you find them. (2:191)
- Murder them and treat them harshly (9:123)
- Fight them (unbelievers) (8:65)
- Humiliate them (9:29)
- Slay them if they are pagans (9:5)

- (Unbelievers) will have a great punishment in the hereafter (5:34)
  Strive against the unbelievers (25:52)
- Unbelievers belong to hell (66:9)

Most Muslims would not take these statements literally. Indeed, Twenty Imams affiliated with the Islamic Supreme Council of Canada issued a *Fatwa* in January 2010 declaring the attacks on Canada and the United States by any extremist would be an attack on 10 million Muslims living in North America. This is the first *Fatwa* by the Muslim clergy declaring attacks on Canada and the United States as attack on Muslims too. [2] Similarly, a Munich Imam, Hersham Shashaa, has tried to dilute the enthusiasm for radical Islam among young Muslim men. A number of Europeans imams have denounced suicide missions and terrorism.

Esposito and Lalwani contend that Islam, especially American Muslims, is badly compared to terrorists which is only true in this sense: that like many other religious people they do not know well their own scripture. Most Americans surveyed by *The Washington Post* said they had an unfavorable view of Islam. Few Americans and few Muslims likely do not know that the Koran specifically permits violence to infidels, and that means anyone not a Muslim. Most Muslims are indeed peaceful and have integrated successfully. But for those inclined to violence or who are exceptionally devout can find in the Koran all the scriptural authenticity they need to practice violence against those they perceive as non-Islamic.

But for devout fundamentalists, criminally inclined, or psychologically disturbed Muslims who seek violence as a means against non-Muslims, and certainly foreign soldiers on Arab soil, such scriptural sanctions lend all the divine authority needed to carry out violent acts. No religion can prevent someone from hating. But Islam theologizes hate and loans divine scripture as authenticity.

The current global proponent and witness for the violence in Muslim ideology is Ayaan Hirsi Ali, born in Somalia in 1969. She left her arranged marriage and family, immigrated to Europe and was elected to the Dutch Parliament. Her best-selling memoir *Infidel* (2007), and her 2010 study *From Islam to America*, outraged many throughout the Muslim world, but are no more provocative than the message I suggest in these pages. Islam is imbued with violence and encourages it. As a young girl she was taught with violence, how to perpetuate violence, and to wish it for the infidel, the Jew and the American Satan.

The Koran has no lessons on love, hope, justice, or morality. Its claims about what we today know from science reveal the ignorance of the era (certainly not of an all-knowing God) and the illiteracy of its author. If you are righteous—which means if you believe in Allah and his prophet—and even if you kill in his name you are still righteous—then you will get unlimited sex in the celestial afterlife, something only people like Hugh Hefner enjoy in this life.

Mohammad again and again urged his followers to engage in implacable war, especially in several passages in *Sura* 2. Sophists might think these passages metaphorical. But because they are repeated so often in the Koran there can be no doubt they were meant literally, especially because Mohammad engaged in raids and war himself and put his enemies to death. The Islamic sword became sanctified. No other religious leader so declared that war against him and the faith's enemies was justified. For the last decade of his life Mohammad was essentially a military commander, as far removed from a Buddha, Jesus, Gandhi or Martin Luther King as is possible and still be called a religious leader. Gods like Yahweh and Shiva can be vengeful, but prophets are not supposed to be God's appointed executioners.

On the other hand, if you can imagine the Byzantine world of the fourth century when Christianity was installed as the only authorized Roman state religion, then it's possible to partially understand what Islam is undergoing today as its grapples with other religions and the influences that contravene its scriptural principles. Islamists, those believers who are at war with the West, are totalitarian and anti-democratic. For Muslims, Islam is a faith that knows no constraints and has no limitations. Fundamentalists will scrutinize the Koran for tips on how to solve every imaginable dilemma in medicine, economics, or diplomacy because they believe that their sacred literature contains all truth and the answer to all problems.

The 1979 Iranian Revolution that overthrew a despotic regime and installed clerical rule, and the 1989 conquest of the Soviets in Afghanistan in 1989, both galvanized the Muslim world. Suddenly, through political revolutions and military actions against invaders, Muslims everywhere felt empowered to overthrow other regimes and oust invaders and occupiers. Armed conflict and violent attacks on Western targets found an ideological home in literal meanings of Islamic militancy, a rejection of secular, modern politics by elevating *jihad* to the pinnacle of religious belief, but thereby also devaluing the coin of Muslim religious legitimacy. Islamic warfare has been continuous since 632, always territorial and political. Its modern form of terrorism is an extension of this same Islamic imperative. *Jihad* is not new and never rests. Like North Korea, it is in a permanent state of militarism.

The common perception is that Islam is in the throes of losing its religious and spiritual equilibrium by engaging or encouraging a militaristic movement of activists and sponsors that will in the long run destroy many of its adherents, threaten whatever religious culture it believes it has, and damage its global spiritual appeal. The more truthful fact is that militancy has always been an integral component of Islamic belief. Its toxic rhetoric is an opiate against real or perceived enemies.

For example, Scott Roeder shot Dr. George Tiller, a Wichita abortion physician, as he handed out church bulletins on Sunday, May 31, 2009. On January 29, 2010, a Kansas jury deliberated for just 37 minutes before returning a guilty verdict of first-degree murder. Scott Roeder admitted his guilt, which was never in doubt. What was doubtful was whether his culpability would be mitigated because of his fevered religious outrage against legal abortion. Democracy is undermined when vigilantes can believe that they are protected because of the strength of their moral convictions. But this is not true in the Islamic world where the moral code is the legal code, and when killing is approved under certain conditions.

Since the Koran legitimizes violence it cannot ever be expunged or re-interpreted. Thus, it's not just about how long a man's beard is, or whether or not Muslim women are hidden behind veils (forbidden in France beginning in April 2011) and bulky clothes, or Shiites can pray to saints like Imam Reza, or Dervishes can find mystical visions in music and dances, or whether or not mosques can display minarets.

Clearly, not all Muslims are terrorists. But every member of al-Qaeda is a Muslim. Even journalists captured in war zones, like the Norwegian Paul Refsdal, face the choice of beheading or conversion. And members of the Muslim Brotherhood are sympathetic to violence and the creation of a global Islamic state. Therefore, the threat is global and not limited to theaters of war. Although U.S. efforts have somewhat marginalized al-Qaeda, its reach is still significant and its havens expanding into Yemen, Somalia and other parts of Africa, and the North Caucasus. The future danger is with franchise groups, and second and third layers of regional militant groups and grassroots individuals, that borrow the more virulent ideology. Internet chat rooms and cafes are the *modus operandi* of the operational and tactical communication of Muslim radicals.

I distinguish between a growing conservatism in the Islamic world, exemplified by increased devotion and traditional wearing of headscarves for women from this more troubling militancy trend. My study is not a McCarthy style Witch Hunt for secretive terrorists hidden in government agencies, or veiled racism against a particular religious group. It is an examination of an expanding extremist movement in Islam that most Muslims do not follow nor sympathize with. Militants can include brainwashed Pakistani peasant boys recruited to kill, as they did in the Mumbai massacre in 2008, or individuals or bands of Islamic terrorists arrested annually in Europe, or self-recruited psychologically disturbed loners like Army Major Nidal Malik Hasan, or intended *jihad* suicide bombers like Umar Farouk Abdulmutallab, the Christmas Day, 2009 attempted airline bomber.

A 2006 Gallup poll found that those who sympathize with terrorists constitute only a small minority and that they least admire "narrow minded fanaticism and violent extremism." [3] The education of militants I discuss in this book does not imply just a formal education in violence, although that also occurs in Islamic schools and military-like training camps, but to a belief in an ideology of militancy that can be self-taught.

There is of course a history of grievances the Arab world has with the West. Imperialism prompted many of the outrages of Islamic peoples towards European nations who partitioned the Ottoman Empire after World War I in 1918, carving out chunks of desert that would become Lebanon, Iraq, Jordan, the Persian Gulf emirates and the simmering and controversial lands of Palestine. Muslims have not forgotten the acid consequences of colonialism and have used its dark abuses repeatedly as an excuse for badgering the West, neglecting to note its own religiously–justified militant excesses in subduing that part of the world. Most Arab states have dynastic ruling families—or in the case of non-Arab Iran, a clerical oligarchy—that they hold in Islamic confession and that persecute minorities, have cosmetic parliaments, and restrict freedom of expression.

Dante's description in *The Divine Comedy* over the gates of hell might apply to anyone who sought to live permanently under Islamic rule in the Middle East: "Abandon all hope you who enter here."

Muslim extremists have now moved beyond the aftershocks of 20th century warfare to plague the West with a new form of rage and militancy aimed at randomly terrorizing non-Muslims. I explore this transformation, a movement toward militancy that has always been present in Muslim scripture and history, and explore a few examples and motives of those who pursue its radical goals. I classify as radical fundamentalists those of Muslim faith who endorse, support, encourage or do violence to other Muslims or non-Muslims. Their individual justification, often with state sponsorship, is the Koran's concept of *jihad* and the goal is military training or its sponsorship and support. [4]

Of the 44 global terrorist organizations listed by the U.S. Department of State, 30 are Muslim groups. The half century-old battles between Israel, its Arab neighbor countries and the Palestinians, and between India and Pakistan over Kashmir—plus the separatist movements in The Philippines, Chechnya, Thailand, China, Sudan and Somalia—testify to long-lasting, intractable conflicts. Besides ongoing wars, there are little known struggles in places like Kabardino-Balkaria, a region bordering the Caucasus Mountains between Russia and Turkey where Islamic extremist groups have military camps.

Islamic terrorists are not like Buddhist Shaolin monks, the spiritual warriors who defended their temple against raiders and who invented Kung Fu fighting. Nor are they freedom or resistance fighters, though they may think they are protecting a homeland. There have been similar nationalistic terrorist groups—the IRA in Northern Ireland; the PKK in the Kurdish part of Turkey; the Tamil Tigers in Sri Lanka, the ETA in Spain's Basque country—but nothing like this warlike religious movement that seeks to destroy everything not in accordance with Islamic thinking.

America too has had its homegrown terrorist movements, like the Ku Klux Klan (KKK) in the time of Reconstruction after the Civil War in 1866, and the Black Panthers and the Weather Underground in the 1960s. Movements like the White Supremacist groups or Neo-Nazi National Socialist Movement skinheads have been similarly racist, exclusionary and violent.

A literal *jihad* is an essential factor in Islam, not a pious footnote that means struggling against oneself as many Muslims claim. Conservative Muslims may not practice or condone violence against infidels but may not condemn it either. They seek government reform toward Islamic political change and social justice and this almost invariably means rule by *sharia* law.

Some are misguided and confuse respect for religious values with the presumed benefits of a rival legal code. [5] *Sharia* (meaning "path") law is a religious law, derived from the Koran and the *Hadith* (teachings of Mohammad and religious leaders) and governs behaviors in most Islamic states. Its laws governing domestic issues like marriage and divorce are not as controversial as its criminal codes that allows for legalized honor killings, requires the cutting off of limbs for theft, flogging, or blood money for murder, or prohibitions against drinking of alcohol. The Koran notes that the rule of *sharia* law, the civil code, and the belief in Islam, are one and the same. *Sharia* in Islam is everything that God has legislated for mankind, including principles of belief, morality, human relationships and principles of knowledge, and it is good everywhere and for all time.

No religious code, not canon law or *sharia* law, can be a substitute for, or be integrated into, U.S. law. This is not about respect for ethnic or religious values—as illegal displays of the 10 Commandments, debates about abortion, or prayer in school testifies—but an acknowledgement that secular law rules all. The 1st Amendment solidifies the prohibition against the establishment of any religion, including religious laws.

The radicalism and extremism I describe is primarily an aberration but a growing discriminatory movement opposed to international beliefs adopted December 10, 1948. The *UN Declaration of Human Rights* notes in Article 2: "Everyone is entitled to all the rights and freedoms set forth in this Declaration, without distinction of any kind, such as race, color, sex, language, religion, political or other opinion, national or social origin, property, birth or other status." Additionally, the *UN Declaration of Human Rights* notes in Article 18: "Everyone has the right to freedom of thought, conscience and religion; this right includes freedom to change his religion or belief, and freedom, either alone or in community with others and in public or private, to manifest his religion or belief in teaching, practice, worship and observance."

For a Muslim to convert to another religion means apostasy, to say unflattering things about the Prophet means blasphemy, and both invite death. [6]

Islam does not have a complicated doctrinal message. According to a 2009 report of the Pew Forum on Religion and Public Life, America is experiencing an increase in blending Christianity with New Age and Eastern beliefs like reincarnation, mystical experiences, or encounters with ghosts. Instead of such a mishmash of traditional beliefs, superstition, psychic energies, fantasy and mythology that characterizes some American beliefs, Islam is a simple message that Mohammad enforced on all the towns in Arabia he conquered in the last decade of his life after he had assembled 30,000 soldiers to forcibly convince polytheistic unbelievers. Islam's message against unbelievers and infidels has been resoundingly clear from the last days of Mohammed and followers and disciples ever since. [7] As Wafa Sultan, an Iranian psychiatrist, notes:

> Islam has made itself inaccessible to the influences of the outside world . . . It has fought against every innovation, doubting its appropriateness and legality. Its relationship with the world that has surrounded it has been characterized by aggression rather than mutuality and reciprocity. No notable change has taken place inside Islam since the moment it came into being. [8]

The obligation to impose Islam, violently if necessary, is not a distortion. Nor is it a radical interpretation of a few extremists. It is mandated by the Koran and reflected in all classical scholars, like Muhammed bin Ismail bin al-Mughirah al-Bukhari (died 870) who has 199 references to *jihad*. Radical Islam, that part of the religion that encourages violence, is a non-centralized movement that lacks a national government and has a religious identity without a national consciousness. It is equivalent to the imposition of orthodox Christianity in medieval Europe prior to the establishment of nation states.

The concept of heresy in Islam has become fluid. Because there is no clerical hierarchy each individual can decide who is a heretic or apostate. The revolutionary interpretation is that radicalized Muslims are leveling the accusations of *kafir*, apostate, against Arabic civil authorities. Members of militant associations in Egypt, Iran, Algeria and elsewhere have declared rulers as having abandoned Allah's law by importing western customs thereby abandoning Islam. Therefore, in their thinking secular rule is illegitimate and they are no longer obliged to obey or believe orders or decrees. It thus becomes the militant's duty to resist and attempt to remove such rulers. In the minds of radical Muslims, heresy is intimately linked to civil disobedience, conspiracy, and revolt against the state. The 1979 attack on the Grand Mosque in Mecca, where hundreds were killed, is one example of this ideology. The enticement has proved a powerful recruitment tool for disaffected Muslims, regardless of educational or socioeconomic status.

Additionally, Islamists who promote and practice violence to infidels believe that only they can save Islam by murdering those not of their religion. The policy of mayhem is a deliberate attempt to defeat the modern western spirit with weapons of self-destruction, a policy that elevates suicide, that many radical Muslims call martyrdom, as the protector of religious prestige. Adherence to this passionate religious intensity and martial addiction exposes the lifeless ideology advancing it. The irrational exuberance for death and martyrdom shows resolve but is ultimately fatalistic. It is a method of punitively damaging a western, secular image that will be self-defeating.

Islam has rabid clerics who pursue policies that revive emotional attachment to religious slogans, and preach anti-Semitism and anti-western propaganda. Their message is simple and direct, without nuances or subtleties, powerfully emotional but without intellectual rigor or seasoned thought. There is no need for theological mysteries or explanations, nor even literacy to convey its meaning. This radicalized Islamic movement is as bankrupt of ideas as it is poisoned with religious hostility. Yet radicalized Muslims are expected to find salvation in opposition and sulking resentment.

Westerners who feel optimistic about a cultural interchange are also going to be disappointed. Islam is not prepared to accept modernity as the West defines it. If the West tries to impose its social values on Muslims it risks the predictable response of Islamic fear of western cultural domination. Islam must undergo its own religious reformation, cultural renaissance and enlightenment before it can embrace modernity. One response has been to "Islamize knowledge," a reaction that assumes that all formal knowledge comes first from a sacred text and must be somehow reconciled with revelation. For the moment, too many Islamic young—confused, distracted, disengaged or feeling disenfranchised—have retreated into the age-old response of Islam to all encounters—*jihad* militancy as a way of resolving psychological and cultural conflict, a response that has the backing of numerous religious clerics.

In western societies the aim of a liberal education is to alter mindsets and worldviews, to disrupt presumptions, to critique facile opinions, to challenge absurdities. Western education favors individualism, that people should be able to think for themselves, to break free from life's stereotypes and discover their own values and prescriptions for living. Orthodox Islamic societies and some Islamic governments almost universally reject this philosophy. The tradition of educating the individual is lacking in orthodox Islamic countries. The purpose of education is to indoctrinate the religion, as it once was for Christendom in medieval Europe. I have observed this non-subtle form of religious instruction in grade school classrooms in the Middle East.

Islam has become so institutionalized and permeated the culture so thoroughly that challenging it is dangerous. Intellectual and political movements based on the rights and liberties of the individual have not occurred in Islamic countries, not even uniformly in Turkey or Egypt, the most secular of Islamic countries.

In the view of most Muslims, the foreign policy of the United States in the Middle East and Arab world—the naked and unquestionable support of Israel, the failure to help the Palestinians achieve statehood, the intervention in the internal affairs of Arab states, and the location of military bases, and, the final insult, raw military invasion—are some of the primary causes and recruitment tools for Islamic militants.

Consider the following slogans, altered from American military recruitment phrases, to show how ingrained is the language of our military recruiting phrases and how patriotic the feelings they symbolize.

> Be strong. Be Muslim strong.
> The Few, the Proud, the Islamic bombers
> Above all, the Martyrs

I modify these phrases to show how advertising images can encourage the emotion of patriotism and can be a powerful recruitment tool for adventurous youth to enter military service. Instead of killing for your country you can kill for your religion. To understand this military difference from different cultural eyes, just substitute the word "Islam' for "patriotism" as a western recruiting tool to feel the pull of emotion toward a worthy military cause. Many in the West can differentiate between nationalism and religion. Few in the Islamic world make this distinction.

The late Samuel Huntington reminded us in his 1996 book *The Clash of Civilizations and the Remaking of the World Order* that the reshaping of the world order in the future would be aligned with culture, ethnicity and religion and that globalization would result in more conflict not less. [9] He fingered Islam as the most likely source of conflict with the West. The "clash" is certainly separated by one or more oceans, and possibly one or more planets. Many in the West do not believe in Huntington's prediction. But all Muslim militants do.

I believe there is both a clash within nations and between nations, religions and civilizations. Unquestionably, there are eruptions between Hindus and Muslims in India as there are between Hamas and Fatah in the Gaza strip. But that does not militate against Hamas, for example, wanting to destroy Israel and the U.S. even while it fights against Fatah and its own people for power. There are too many examples of struggles within Islamic countries like Pakistan that are also a part of larger struggles of Muslim groups like al-Qaeda against infidels everywhere. After 9/11, Huntington's theory became more prescient, and subsequent engagements become not just a clash of civilizations or religions but a battle between modernity and barbarity that will define the 21$^{st}$ century. And it is instructive to recall—lest we become overly optimistic about the outcome of the struggle—that the hordes of barbarians led by Alaric at the gates of Rome in 410 conquered one of the greatest civilizations ever in the world, and immediately plunged Europe into the Dark Ages for over seven centuries.

None of the western ideologies imported into the Islamic world—nationalism, socialism, Baathism, a secular political party whose ideas were borrowed from Nazi socialism, or limited democracy—brought unity to Muslim peoples. Imperialism was a description reserved by Arabs for the West, who obviously forgot that the Ottoman Empire was Islamic. In fact the political system of Arab countries is autocratic and despotic, and its history the essence of subjugation. So it must be, the argument goes, that Islam must return to its militant roots and mobilize its people to re-establish its legitimate place among nations in a unified Islamic state, the Caliphate. [10]

All Muslim terrorists characterize themselves as modern *ghazis*, soldiers and defenders of Islam, which is what Mohammad was. Devout Muslims believe everything he did, chiefly raiding and thieving, was inspired by Allah. Modern Muslim terrorism, including murder, deceit and theft, is not a perversion of Islam. It is central to its global mission of conquering the world. Nonie Darwish, daughter of an Egyptian martyr, notes: "Conquering the world for Islam is the stated goal that emanates from powerful, ruling Islamic clerics throughout the Middle East, whether it is the Wahabbis of Saudi Arabia, the mullahs of Iran's Islamic Revolution, the Muslim Brotherhood of Egypt, the Taliban of Afghanistan, or the followers of Osama bin Laden." [11]

Those who believe their principles are sacred because they reputedly come from sacred sources will always have a following. But when they believe that such principles are eternal, good for all time and all people, they will be met with reserved skepticism. All human convictions are subject to relative truth. The presence of multiple religions is itself a witness of diverse paths from and to the spiritual. There are many reasons like insanity or a pathological disorder that can lead one to fanaticism. But religious infallibility has often been the chief cause.

The 2006 report *Militant Ideology Atlas* contains information about the most vocal and influential thinkers in the *jihad* movement who, through preaching and propaganda outlets, spread the militant movement's aim and practices. [12] They carry their beliefs as baggage, a religious appeal uncomplicated with metaphysics or abstract imagery, except in the Prophet's descriptions of the paradise of heavenly oases to which they believe they are entitled as followers. Such extremists may have been western educated but are intellectually impoverished as a group, seeking vengeance with a twisted sense of aggrieved justice, using Islam as a cloak over criminal behavior. They know not the art of compromise and, with the confederacy of the religious clan, have used the sword, gun and explosives instead of internationally recognized law to avenge their wronged sense of honor and morality. They claimed they acted from honor but their worth is besmirched by wounded pride, a crude religious code of justice, and militant methods of revenge, traits that have been a legacy since the desert origins of their religion.

Jordanian Bedouin

# PART I
# MUSLIM RADICALIZATION

## CHAPTER ONE
## ISLAMIC MEDIEVAL VALUES:
## A MILITARY HISTORY

Until the modern era, the pecking order of Arab survival—after eating lamb and having sex, and the camel, horse, and falcon—was Islam, consisting of oaths of allegiance to Allah and his Prophet, and the prescribed behaviors of prayer, the giving of alms, fasting, and the pilgrimage to Mecca. These rituals totally governed peoples' lives and habits. But even more than religious enthusiasm, I want to show in this and the following chapters the militancy that Islam has historically been compelled to endorse, and how still today it drives many of those committed to its cause. "The worldview of committed jihadists is no less expansionist today than it was in the time of the Prophet Mohammad." [1]

Men of all religions must have been bored from weaving baskets and taking out the trash from their walled towns, tents and crusader fortresses. Crusaders carried their gonfalons of feudal allegiances and crosses as ensigns of divine protection and emblems of holy war, and descended on the lands of the Middle East like famished locusts. The advantages of bringing home stolen plunder to the wife and kids must have been worth the perilous risks. Theological assurances easily justified rapine, as disputants argued that God was always on their side, and could usually find scriptural passages to convince the skeptical. The application of force and brutality became the final arbiters of issues.

Arab invasions everywhere in the $7^{th}$ through the $10^{th}$ centuries are touted as the advancement of Islam and the glories of Allah. The beginnings of Arab history and the origins of Islam are filled with raids on caravans and Arabian towns opposed to Mohammad, and attacks on non-Muslims (*dhimmi*). The Prophet carried out at least twenty-seven raids in his lifetime and the principal aim was to acquire booty. A fifth of the total went to Allah's messenger, Mohammad. So raiding, theft of the enemy's possessions, and killing were permitted. Following the example of the Prophet, when a Muslim kills a non-Muslim he has the right to despoil him. The Prophet in effect canonized theft and murder as religious rights.

In December 623 Mohammad sent a coded messages to eight of his followers to intercept a caravan with orders to plunder it. Here is what he wrote: "Go forward to Nakhlah in the name of the Lord, and with His blessing! Proceed with those who accompany you . . . lie in wait for the caravans of the Quraysh." [2] As a result of Mohammed's designated raiding parties on those he believed unfaithful to him and his message, the following prophecy was revealed:

> But when the forbidden months are past then fight and slay the Pagans
> wherever you find them, and seize them, beleaguer them, and lie in wait
> for them in every stratagem (of war) . . . (*Sura 9:5*)

Thus, from Mohammed's quest for revenge against his own tribe by raiding the trade goods of a caravan of Abu Sufyan, one of his most feared opponents, we have a command from Allah for the justification of theft. This successful raid in 624, with fewer than 300 Muslim converts against about 950 men with 700 camels and 100 horses was led by Abu Jahl, Mohammad's uncle who was killed in the raid. Because the Muslim won after they were outnumbered by about three to one, this victory is heralded as a milestone in Islamic history. Since God himself was supposed to have been instrumental in the victory, the pattern of divine guidance and approval was forever stamped in Muslim history and military consciousness.

The medieval Arab concept of governance was to use the sword and take money. Returning to the 7th century in the history of Islamic conquests is to enter an era of bloody subjugation similar to the barbarian invasions of the Goths into the Roman Empire, the violent European sprees of the Vikings, or the Asiatic rampages of the Mongols in the 13th century. The historical comparison between Viking and Muslim raiders is instructive because the origins have martial and religious parallels. The way to become wealthy for Viking and Muslim warriors, as it would be for the Mongols, was to steal. For Vikings it helped to have as companions the gods of Odin and Thor, themselves warriors, and Odin's Valkyrie virgin daughters who would bear you willingly to Valhalla. For Muslims, it helped to have the assistance of Allah who would insure military victory and help you slay all non-Muslim enemies. And when the so-called Muslim martyrdom of death came, it was beneficial to have virgins to comfort you in the afterlife. The mythical tradition, documented through literature, augments the legend and shows have widely dispersed ethnic groups believed in overlapping cultural themes.

About the same era, from the 8th to the 11th centuries, as Islam was expanding its territory with raids throughout the Middle East and North Africa, the Vikings, composed of warriors from Denmark, Sweden and Norway, then with undefined borders, were also raiding Europe. They captured what is today the Baltic States, Belarus and parts of Russia, Yorkshire and Essex in England, eastern Ireland, northern Germany and France. They eventually settled in Normandy until their descendant William continued the raiding tradition and overran England in 1066. The Normans occupied Palermo in 1072 and all of in Sicily in 1091. This series of Viking expeditions was occurring during the same three-century period as Islam was bludgeoning an adjoining part of the world. [3]

The parallel raiding cultures of Islam and the Vikings in the late Dark Ages shows how these two geographically dispersed groups exemplified overlapping themes of plundering, militaristic and vengeful gods, and idealistic virgins to symbolize and encourage respective marauding mentalities. Today's Muslim suicide bombers not only carry on this cult of murder and death, but they await the legendary blessings of the godhead, while they consort with virgins to rationalize violence. It isn't clear if this gender consortium tames or energizes militant tendencies. The intervening centuries have not diminished the belief by radicalized fundamentalists in an all-encompassing worldview of conquering the world for Islam in the name of Allah. Some illiteracy, ignorance of history, and massive doses of superstition help fuel the fanaticism.

Although Islam originated in violence and still bespeaks violence, we have seen it is not singular in the pursuit of militancy. Each civilization and era has violence in its history that from time to time emerges to engulf its enemies. Human nature, not any one ethnic or religious group, has aggressiveness in its genetic composition. But when the scriptural or mythical god becomes the principal champion of violence against opposing gods and unbelievers, he permits votaries to go on Dionysian indulgences of murder with divine authorization.

The radicalized Islamic fundamentalist believes that orthodox doctrine, combined with a repudiation of the West and its values, is divinely guided, without error, and not subject to alternative interpretations. Although there are modernists who accept that Islam must be re-shaped for survival and progress, the radical Islamic movement is on the ascendant and combines traditional religious consciousness with intense moral purpose, and drowns out, when it does not arrest, imprison or kill, moderate spokespeople.

Once unified under Islam, Arabs poured out of the land of frankincense, camels, camel caravans and nomadic pastoralists, perhaps to avoid desert boredom but certainly to kill, an activity in which they became proficient. Even during the lifetime of Mohammed, Arabs became good at raiding caravans. Now they would become good at raiding whole nations and killing votaries of other religions who resisted their impositions.

Let's explore the early history of the years following the death of Mohammad and analyze how this desert religion made such startling military advances. The conquistador mentality of many Islamic believers is still alive and a large and integral part of the Muslim legacy.

## The Years of Arab Conquest

Remember your Lord inspired the angels (with the message): "I am with you: give firmness to the Believers, I will instill terror into the hearts of the Unbelievers: you smite above their necks and smite all their finger-tips off them." (*Koran* 8:12)

I quote the passage above to point out that the "smiting above the necks" gave authenticity to beheading, still the most practiced form of killing authorized by the Koran. Of course two of Henry VIII's wives, Anne Boleyn and Kathryn Howard, endured a similar fate, as did aristocrats in the French Revolution. A statue of Saddam Hussein was left standing after the Iraqi invasion by U.S. forces in 2003, but even the statue's head was decapitated.

Abu Bakr, a faithful companion to Mohammad and his immediate successor who gave his daughter Fatima to Mohammad as a wife (Mohammad's only surviving child was also named Fatima), died a natural death months after Mohammed. In 633 the armies of Khalid, the Islamic general, and Abu conquered Oman and Yemen with great slaughter, and united all the dissident tribes of the Arabia under the banner of Islam. After Mohammed's death the tribes had decided to quit paying taxes, according to Al-Fakhri the medieval statecraft writer. Once these tribes were declared apostates for this tax revolt, they were marked for extermination unless they reconverted, which understandably many did.

Under the generalship of Khalid who had united all the tribes, Arabs defeated the Byzantines under the Emperor Heraclius, thus opening up all of Syria to Muslim domination. The defeat of the Greek Emperor Romanus IV in 1071 at Manzikert in Armenia by the Seljuk sultan Alp Arslan opened Anatolia and all of Asia Minor to Islamic occupation, began the slow decline of the Byzantine Empire, was the root cause of the Crusades, and converted the entire Middle East to Islam.

Less than five years after Mohammad's death, the Muslim army was camped near Yarmuk at the corner of today's borders with Syria, Israel and Jordan, about 30 miles northeast of the Sea of Galilee. Within a hundred years they would be in central France, at Poitiers. The Arabs had force-marched from Iraq in 634 and had captured towns throughout the Jordan valley. According to contemporary accounts, their battle formations and tactics at Yarmuk were conventional. Muslims fought more effectively over six exhausting days to secure victory in formidable terrain with plunging cliffs and ravines that lead to the Yarmuk River, a tributary to the Jordan River. The Arabs pursued the Byzantines back into the mountains of Anatolia. By 638 both Damascus and Jerusalem had succumbed to Arab military might.

The successors to Mohammed were both the religious leaders and the commanders of the standing Arab armies. The murder of the caliphs—usually by beheading, beginning with Othman, and later with Ali, Mohammad's adopted nephew and son-in-law—would become a regular occurrence. The murder of Othman exposed Arab violence capable of turning on fellow Muslims and on the designated religious leader. Othman was the last Arab and Islamic leader to reside in Medina, the city of the Prophet.

The Koran provided no rules for how to select successors to the Prophet, so each death of a caliph was hotly disputed, usually by a relative, and often by the death of a rival. Muawiya (602–680), born the son of Abu Sufyan, had been Mohammed's scribe and a late and reluctant convert to the Prophet's mission after Mohammed's conquest of Mecca. He served in the Arab armies in Syria, and was appointed Governor at Damascus under Othman. He enlarged his power base when Ali was named caliph in Medina. Muawiya used the rumor that Ali was responsible for the death of Othman to fuel his claim that he should be caliph and not Ali.

The armies of Ali and Muawiya confronted each other in today's Iraq, in what came to be known as The Battle of the Camel near Basra. No conclusive military engagement resulted there or elsewhere, and negotiations continued until Ali was assassinated in 661, an event that allowed Muawiya to claim the caliphate without opposition. This rivalry divided Muslims into Sunni, the followers of Muawiya, and Shia, devotees and followers of Ali, as the rightful heir. This division survives as the deepest religious chasm between Muslims. When the grandson of the

Prophet, Hussain, attempted to reclaim the caliphate from Yezid, Muawiya's son then reigning in Damascus, he too was killed in battle in 680 at Karbala, the Iraqi site of one of the holiest Shiite shrines. Seventy years after his death, Muawiya's body was unceremoniously disinterred and his remains scattered.

Within eighty-two years of the death of the Prophet, and, like nomadic army ants in search of prey, Arab Islamic soldiers in rapid succession captured the Middle East, South Asia, North Africa, and parts of southern Europe and Spain. They found both Byzantine and Persian empires bankrupt, exhausted from wars against each other, and paralyzed by internal discord. The Byzantine Roman legions were not what they had been under the days of imperial Rome and under military emperors like Vespasian, Titus, and Trajan. The Goths had utterly exterminated a Roman army at Adrianople in 378 when cavalry charges emerged as the revolution in military tactics. The rival monarchies of Roman Byzantium and Persia became the victims of an enemy they had come to despise emerging from the desert sands.

But the Arabs failed to take Byzantium in 674 and again in 718. Had they succeeded in capturing the capitol they would have unquestionably been victorious throughout the Balkans and possibly Italy and into Eastern Europe. At the time, the political fragmentation of the European barons reduced any possibility of an organized defense against an Islamic threat. Western Europe only gained strength when the Arabs decided to move eastward into Baghdad and beyond.

The invading Arab hordes were generous to those who capitulated, but brutal to those who did not. Beheading was the usual outcome for recalcitrant opponents. The killing often took days, when the Arabs decided not to take the wives and children as slaves and ship them back to Arabia. In 808 in Toledo in Spain, the former Visigoth capitol, some Christians had been rebelling against Muslim rule. The Amir al–Hakam decided to rid the city of this sedition. He invited all the leading citizens of the city to the castle for a banquet. As each guest entered, he was beheaded and his body thrown into a large ditch dug the night before for this purpose. Several hundred were thus slaughtered in this manner. This effectively quelled the revolt. [4]

Islam had discovered its true vocation. The new religion was stamped with the signature of the sword. Its militant purposes were exposed in the last years of Mohammed. The message that the religion was steeped in blood and conquest, partly a tradition of Arab tribes, was not lost on objective observers, nor was the understanding that to survive one had to be militarily victorious. It also helped, as it does today to Muslim militants, to be religiously fanatical. The passage of the centuries, and the plurality of secessionist movements throughout the world, in places like The Philippines, Chechnya, Bosnia, Somalia, Pakistan, and collective global terrorist attacks, has not depreciated this message.

As a current example of militancy against other Muslims, on Friday October 3, 2008, suicide bombers targeted Shiite worshippers as they emerged from mosques in Baghdad on *Eid al-Fitr*, the end of the fasting month of Ramadan, killing scores of Muslims. This series of brazen bombings revealed the depth of hostility of one Muslim sect over another,

Sunni against Shiite, and insensitivity toward a Muslim feast day. The unleashed Sunni/Shiite violence became a daily occurrence in Baghdad and throughout Iraq after the American invasion and after the occupation ended.

After initial Arab conquests, governance presented unique problems for the conquerors as they had no administrative experiences, no truck for compromise, and no understanding of democracy. Arabs were nomadic peoples, naturally ferocious, unused to urban life. After having conquered the Semitic world and the better part of the lands of Persia by the eighth century, loath to rule and settle down to governing, they began fighting each other.

There is no word for "state" in Arabic. The idea of providing for, and controlling, large tribes and religious and ethnic groups with differing customs and languages was foreign to Arabs who only knew the laws of family groups, kinsmen, tribes, and clans. The Middle East today, and Afghanistan and Pakistan, still functions with the leadership model of a tribal chieftain and clan leader. It is unaccustomed and uneasy with secular state control or the messy mechanics of democracy. The earliest caliphs were religious leaders operating as tribal chieftains fighting over lands and resources, as today they still are in Saudi Arabia, Afghanistan, Iraq and Pakistan.

After the year 656 rival Arab groups sought the assistance of non-Muslims to retain governmental power. As descendants of nomads they had extensive experience in raiding but none in ruling. Except for the Koran the Arabs had no civil code, no police, no judiciary, and no laws except *sharia*. The blood feud and simple reprisals, against culprits or relatives, substituted for codes of justice. Among Muslims retaliation is a moral right; among Christians, it is a sin.

Once the Arabs subdued a region they had extensive supply lines stretching across hundreds of miles. To secure their communications and supplies they formed agreements that included the Persians, for example, to supply the Arabs with food and accommodations to all traveling Arabs. The Arab conquerors killed anyone who assaulted an Arab. And for any acts of aggression against Muslims, all previous agreements were forfeit and the offending city of country reduced to slavery. Thus did the Arab conquerors provide for the safety of their long supply caravans. [5]

The subjugated Semitic peoples of the Middle East were mostly squabbling Christians of varying sects, denominations and heresies—Coptic, Chaldean, Syrian, Armenian sects, and Arian, Monophysite, Nestorian and Donatist Christian heresies, scattered Jews, and Zoroastrians. They reluctantly accepted Arab rule instead of the despotic and discriminatory Roman and Byzantine authorities. Many Christians were converted to Islam in order to avoid paying a head tax on non-Muslims. Minorities either accepted without equivocation subjugated status and the supremacy of Islam and paid their discriminatory taxes, or they were put to the sword. Their conversion was more about paying less in taxes to the conquerors and less about the niceties of theology. The threat of death resolves many religious arguments but generates new animosities. The thought of imminent death holds reason ransom and carefully thought-out creeds in impotent disregard. With few exceptions, the subtleties and passions of theology invariably succumb to the glint of the sword, the bullet or the bomb.

In these centuries, non-Muslims, who at the time were also non-Arabs, had certain restrictions placed on their citizenship, probably not more burdensome than those by any conquering zealots. Non-Muslims had to pay a penalty tax for their religious persuasions. When too many were converted to Islam tax collectors complained that revenue was lost. Christian churches had nearly all been destroyed, including the Church of the Resurrection in Jerusalem, and its treasures redistributed to Muslims. No new churches could be built, though some could be repaired, and no church bells rung. Christians had to wear only certain clothing, never green, could not ride a horse only a donkey, not wear shoes but only to walk barefoot, stand aside when a Muslim walked by, and not run pigs through the streets, though some claimed this was in fact a reference to Christians. Caliphs, since they were absolute despots, might ignore the customs of their predecessors and kill individuals or groups who displeased them, certainly a Muslim who became a Jew or Christian.

The ruling Umayyads (634–750) gave themselves to pleasure when they should have attended to administration. They alienated citizens, forgot to pay soldiers when the booty from pillage was depleted, neglected agriculture, taxed the country mercilessly, and trusted corrupt ministers. Some parts of the Middle East still honor this neglected heritage. The first few centuries of the descendants of soldier Arabs had no knowledge of service but were good at practicing autocracy, tyranny and terror, and certainly deceit. Contemporary tactics in some Muslim heads of state—like the late Idi Amin in Uganda, the deposed and executed Saddam Hussein in Iraq and Muammar Qaddafi in Libya, Hafez al-Assad in Syria, Omar al-Bashir in Sudan—have not changed tactics.

The Umayyads (634–750) attempted to destroy all the descendants of Ali, son-in-law of the Prophet. The Abbasids (750–1258) attempted to destroy all remnants of the Umayyads. By the end of the Umayyad dynasty in 750, the new Abbasid dynasty relocated the capitol from Damascus to Baghdad under the ruthless Abu-l-Abbas Abdallah, who named himself *al-Saffah*, or Shedder of Blood. The thirty-seven rulers in Baghdad of the Abbasid Caliphate, once they had consolidated the growth of Islam and ceased killing rivals and each other to determine who would succeed as caliph, began promoting a flowering of science, philosophy, medicine, architecture, calligraphy, art and literature that rivaled any age at its apex and lasted over five hundred years.

By the time of the Abbasids the Caliph government had abandoned the remnants of tribal democracy and preferred the Persian governing mode of a benevolent monarchical despotism. They had decided to settle in the land of the Babylonians because it retained the mighty rivers of the Tigris and Euphrates and an intricate system of irrigating canals, perfect for agriculture. The fourth Abbasid Caliph, Harun al-Rashid (763–809), a patron of learning and the arts, is better known in the West because of his role in the stories Scheherazade tells in *The Arabian Nights*, or *The Thousand and One Nights*, and is based on his life at court. [6]

The Abbasid caliphs were named after Mohammed's uncle, Abbas, who converted to Islam in 629. His descendants established this second dynasty.

The government had no constituent assemblies, no aristocracy, and no clergy. Their turbulent reigns were punctuated by assassinations, palace coups, brother-heir-apparent killings, followed by years of anarchy, revolts and regional uprisings. The Abbasid dynasty lasted until 1258 when the Mongols began a new global campaign of terror, destroying Baghdad. Mongols emulated the first bloody Arab conquests as models for massacre in the 13th century, though they likely did not know predatory Islamic history. [7]

In 711 Muslim troops largely composed of newly converted Berber irregulars, and with coordination with the caliph in Damascus, crossed the Strait of Gibraltar, vanquished the Visigoth King Don Rodrigo, and began the conquest of the Iberian peninsula ending Christian rule. Muslims remained in Spain for the next 781 years until defeated in Granada by Ferdinand and Isabella in 1492. They named their conquered land Andalusia, Al-Andalus, or the Land of the Vandals, though the residents were actually Visigoths. The Muslims must have assumed that all barbarians are alike.

The caliphs had no emperor to help assemble leaders and resolve doctrinal differences, as Constantine did for quarreling Christians in 325. On the other hand, religious belief was largely embedded in ritualistic practices, and had few or no theological distinctions to sway or confuse its believers. Caliphs were leaders of both the religion and the government, the equivalent of King and Pope of the Muslim world. Infidels and heretics were often tolerated for their special skills, but more often than not extirpated because they were not Muslim. Caliph Mahdi (775–785) began an inquisition against infidels (*zindiks*), as the dual-god Manichees in Persia were then known. [8] Under the mad al-Hakim, the Fatimid ruler of Egypt (985–1021), a renewed persecution of Jews and Christians began, and the destruction of churches and synagogues, including the Church of the Resurrection in 1009, certainly a contributory cause for the Crusades. Al-Hakim was assassinated when he was just thirty-six after proclaiming, like Caligula, that he was a god.

Like al-Hakim, Mahmud (1000–1030) of Ghazna (near today's Kabul in Afghanistan) led about seventeen expeditionary raids into India, plundered Hindu shrines, using the pretext of destroying idolatrous statues, and exposed the tepid defenses of India's semi-feudal culture. Mahmud's pillaging and carnage prepared the Ganges Plain for future Islamic invasions that eventually subdued all of northern India in succeeding centuries to Mogul rule. When not engaged in raids and military incursions, Muslim rulers everywhere had cruel and abbreviated reigns, periodic assassinations, racial and religious strife, class and civil warfare and insurrections. Their political rule was characterized by disorder, occasional madness in the ruler, and revolts among subjects. The only political unity seemed to have been when they joined ranks, banged drums, and went on murderous campaigns.

Muslims killing Christians is not just an historical footnote. In late 2008 hundreds of Christians were fleeing Mosul in northern Iraq where they had lived for nearly 2,000 years because of a string of killings targeting them. About 500,000 Christians had once lived in Nineveh province. By 2009 there were less than 100,000 Christians, with about 50,000 in Mosul in an area where Assyrian and Chaldean villages and monasteries were erected during the time of Mohammad.

The evidence for Muslim hatred of other religions engulfed Christians living in the city of Gojra in central Punjab. More than a hundred Christian homes were looted and torched on August 1, 2009 by a rampaging crowd estimated as 20,000, culminating in several days of rioting against Christians who comprise less than five percent of Pakistan's population. The rioters were fueled by a rumor that Christians had somehow defiled the Koran, as it turns out a spurious accusation. A cleric had filed a blasphemy charge against a Christian family that justified the sectarian violence. The police did little to stop the rioters.

A call for *jihad* became a way of unifying the faithful and of acquiring new lands for restless caliphs. Having subdued the Middle East, the descendants of the Arabs did something they had never done before: the soldiers of the desert braved the waters of the Mediterranean by building a navy and becoming sailors. They conquered Corsica in 809, Sardinia in 810, Crete in 823, Malta in 870, and all of Sicily by 902. Now known in Europe as Saracens—for unknown reasons named after Sarah, the wife of Abraham—they easily plundered Rome in 846 and burned the monastery of Monte Cassino in 884. The Germans under Emperor Louis II had to descend from Germany in 866 to expel them from the Italian peninsula. [9] No central military force existed to repel their strength especially when Viking raids were ravishing northern Europe. Feudal European chieftains had neither the capacity nor will to unite and form a national army. Arab recruits enlisted in the armies and navies of Islam on the promise of booty from conquests and enticing treasures in the afterlife.

Soon after the Arab conquests were consolidated in the tenth century, a new threat to Muslim unity arose in south central Asia. The Seljuk Turks, coming from the region of today's Uzbekistan, embraced Islam about 965. The Turks then entered western Asia in the second half of the 11th century and formed an alliance with Islam like Arab armies three centuries earlier had with Persians. Christianity had waned in Asia Minor and the loss of religious and political unity prepared the way for the Ottoman triumph, and alerted Europe to the threat of more Muslims on its eastern frontiers. Whole regions of south central Asians converted to the new religion of Islam, as the Ukrainians had converted to Christianity when Vladimir decided for its religious allures in Kiev in 988.

The Seljuk Turks assumed the military campaign under the banner of Islam, crushed the Fatimids in Egypt, regained Asia Minor, and threatened the Byzantine Empire and the diminishing pockets of Asian Christianity. All this prepared the way for the military counter-offensive known as the Crusades. Antioch fell to the Crusaders in 1098 and Jerusalem in 1099. The massive walls of their fortifications, like that of the Crac de Chevalier in Syria, could not secure the infamy of Crusader reputations. Eventually the Ottoman Turks would conquer Byzantium in 1453 and forever end Christian and Roman rule in Asia Minor.

The Arabs, together with the newly conquered Berbers of North Africa, had completed the conquest of Spain by 714 and had pursued their Spanish victories over the Visigoths northward across the Pyrenees into Gaul. They seemed unstoppable. But Charles Martel (688–741), or Charles the Hammer, the illegitimate son of Pepin, Duke of the Franks and father of Charlemagne (742–814), who laid the literate foundations of modern

Europe, defeated the Saracens between Poitiers and Tours in October 732, exactly a century after the death of Mohammad, in one of those crucial military victories that determine the fate of millions for centuries. It had taken the Roman legions two centuries to occupy Spain. The Muslims conquered it in five years.

The Saracen army of Abd ar-Rahman had been pursuing the army of Eudo, Duke of Aquitaine, but discovered a new army in its path. The Duke's army was then fleeing northward after being routed by the Saracens in the vicinity of the Garonne River and the Dordogne region near Bordeaux. When Abd ar-Rahman discovered that another Frankish army was in front of him he halted to determine its numerical strength. Charles Martel waited on the edge of the forest for a week. On the morning of the seventh day Abd ar-Rahman decided to attack but ran headlong into a Frankish army better equipped and trained than his informant spies had indicated. The infantry army of the Franks stood transfixed, equipped only with battleaxes, and they cut down the Muslim cavalry, horse and rider, with unmitigated ferocity. Moreover, the Arabs were carrying all their captured booty. As the Franks approached the carts carrying the loot, the Arabs stopped fighting to defend their treasures, and suddenly the tide of battle turned. A lance killed Abd ar-Rahman, and his army quarreled through the night about whom they should elect as the new leader. By morning the Arabs and their cohorts had fled southward back into Spain. The Muslims by this time had been fighting everywhere for a hundred years. Arabs conquered Sicily in 827 and ravished the French Riviera throughout the 9th century. Europe might today be speaking Arabic had the Islamic armies not been defeated in central France.

Niccolo Machiavelli in *The Prince* gave voice to intrigue and cruelty for political stability for Italian regional rulers. Islam needed no such written advice from scholars. It had the Koran and Mohammad's example to incite its undeterred warlike activities.

Nevertheless, the Carolingian legacy that Charlemagne expanded was as religiously intolerant as Islam was, and more intellectually impoverished. The university at Cordoba predated the first European university at Bologna by more than a century. Europe at the time was ruled mostly by barter trade and had no cities that exhibited marks of an established civilization, no libraries, no literate elite, and few monks. No European city or leader could hold a candle to the civilization the Muslims created in Spain, and held intact until 1492 when Muslims were expelled and Spain re-united under Ferdinand and Isabella.

In the intervening centuries Europe transformed itself through intellectual revolutions, and granted individuals constitutional rights and used trial processes to adjudicate party conflicts. The Islamic world relied on *fatwas* from clerics to declare death to those it considered blasphemers, like the novelist Salmon Rushdie in modern times, and even condemnation of countries like Denmark and Sweden for publishing satirical cartoons about Mohammed. For Muslims, a country's leaders are supposed to control the social behavior of individuals. In the West, a country's leaders are to protect individual rights.

# The Caliphate:
# The Flowering of Islamic Culture

*cujus regio ejus religio*

The enjoyment of wealth constricts religious ardor. Yet when disaster comes—whether for Jews during the Babylonian captivity or the Roman destruction of Jerusalem, or among Visigoth Christians in Spain, or Muslims in 1492—it is said to arrive because of inattentiveness to the observances of the faith. But when conquest is complete, and hostile warfare is quiescent, human genius can work its wonders unencumbered and often be sponsored and patronized by the king or caliph. Between about 750 and 1258, the Islamic world witnessed such a civilized surge in scholarly, aesthetic and practical activities. [10]

While Europe descended into the Dark Ages from the sixth to the twelfth centuries, Arab astronomers invented the astrolabe used successfully by European explorers. Muslim scholars introduced the decimal system into Europe about the twelfth century. Algebra, almanac, zenith, zero and scores of similar terms are Arabic in origin and are now an integral part of scientific and mathematical thought. Muhammad ibn Ahmad Abu al-Khwarizmi, in *Keys of the Sciences* (976), noted that if no number appears in the place of tens that a little circle should be used to "keep the rows." This circle was called *sifr*, or empty. The English word cipher comes from it. Latin scholars translated *sifr* into *zephyrum* that Italians shortened to zero. So while Europe was busy fighting off marauding raiders like the Vikings, the Islamic world basked in world of unprecedented aesthetic and intellectual refinement. Islamic culture, promoted also by high intellectual achievements in Jewish culture—where it was allowed to flower as it was not in Europe—reached its zenith from the eighth to the fourteenth centuries.

Christians, Jews and Persians were all protected merchants sharing in the production of consumer goods across the Abbasid Caliphate. Arabic words like traffic, tariff, caravan and bazaar were absorbed into English commercial use. We derive the word "check" based on the Arabic *sakk* for credit extended to medieval Arabic traders. Arabs brought the orange tree from India before the tenth century, cultivated cotton (muslin), made linen (*damask*) in Damascus, quarried gold, silver, iron and marble, dove for pearls in the Persian Gulf, and raised handicrafts to the level of industry unknown in Europe until the sixteenth century.

The Arab mathematician al-Haitham, known in the West as Al-Hazen (965–1040), born in Basra in today's Iraq and educated in Baghdad, spent much of his career in Cairo. He discovered the laws of refraction and wrote *The Book of Optics*, the most influential book in the Middle Ages. It transformed mathematics and painting in Europe. Al-Hazen recognized that we see an object because it reflects a cone of rays to the eye and this angle of rays determines size and distance, or, in other words, perspective, an idea that reinvigorated Renaissance painting. Albrecht Durer used a sight rod to paint and sketch. The grid paper is now standard for math, architectural drafting and engineering. Al-Hazen correctly calculated the height of the atmosphere, about ten miles he said, based on the angle of the refraction (about nineteen degrees) of the light that reaches us after sunset.

Mevlana Jelalludin Rumi (1207-1273) was a renowned Sufi Islamic poet. His name means "the one who loves" and his poetry about life and love make the unseen appear in the ordinary. He taught and helped the poor in his early life until one day in 1244 he met a vagabond dervish, one who danced in a religiously inspired, mystical way, and who disappeared suddenly, presumably killed by jealous rivals. Soon after, Rumi began writing poems that speak about Christian, Jewish and Muslim leaders, about prophets, drunks and donkeys, Greek and Muslim philosophers, and about love. "Gamble everything for love/If you are a true human being." [11] Admired by the Sufis, the religious mystics, Rumi was captured by Hollywood and promoted by entertainers and romantics as his poetry gained in popularity in the late twentieth century.

In architecture, Muslims contributed the pointed arches and the minaret, later to become the bell-towers of Christian churches and watch towers like the campanile in Venice. The Alhambra in Granada is the epitome of a breath-taking explosion of shape, pattern and color, the highest expression of architectural achievement of Arab civilization in Europe. I can testify that the most exquisitely beautiful building in the world is in Agra, India, the marbled Taj Mahal, a mausoleum for both the Sultan Shah Jahan's favorite wife, Mumtaz Mahal and himself. Abdul Malik built the Dome of the Rock in Jerusalem in 691, and Mansur built the Al-Aqsa Mosque near the Dome of the Rock in 770. They are two of Islam's holist shrines and stylistically and historically two of the world's architectural marvels.

A hard core of culture had conquered the descendants of the Islamic sword. Muslim scholars found the leisure to think and create. Supported by the patronage of caliphs, they pursued studies unimpeded by occupational necessity. Poets were especially prized and rewarded. And who can forget the Arabian adventures of Sinbad the Sailor, *Alladin's Lamp*, and *Ali Baba and the Forty Thieves* in *A Thousand and One Nights*? Nicolai Rimsky-Korsakov's (1844-1908) *Sheherazade* is a composition of lyrical and melodic delight based on inspiration from the exotic adventures of *The Arabian Nights*.

Islamic scholars and artists, stretching from Delhi in India to Cordoba in Spain, were superior to Europeans in architecture, engineering, navigation and geography, mathematics and astronomy, medicine, horticulture, crafts, metallurgy, calligraphy, literature, music and philosophy—just about every field of knowledge. Arabs doctors divided hospitals into wards for different diseases, still used today. Arabs first used the magnetic needle for navigation and invented the astrolabe. Al-Birundi accurately determined longitude and latitude. Avicenna's work, an encyclopedia of medical knowledge, was required of all medical students in Europe until the seventeenth century.

Islamic horticulturalists brought the orange (an Arabic word) from India to the Mediterranean, and the cultivation of sugar cane, a major crop in the American trade route from the Caribbean. Crusaders returned to Europe with sesame, cloves, rice, melons, dates, lemons, pepper, ginger and coffee––all unknown in Europe. Islamic artists raised woodcarving, glassblowing, jewelry making, tile-glazing, pottery and rug-making to new aesthetic and precision levels. Arabs gave the West the guitar in all its various forms.

There were also setbacks based on preserving the faith. In 1150 Caliph Mustanjid at Baghdad ordered all philosophy books burned. In 1194 Emir Mansur in Seville did the same and forbade anyone even to study philosophy. By 1200 speculative inquiry had almost totally expired in Islamic empires and independent thought suppressed when not actively assaulted. One could acquire an extended fundamentalist reputation for piety by burning non-devotional, scholarly books.

> Whoever of you apostatizes from his religion, will die a heathen . . . Their actions will be defeated in this world and the next. These are the people who will remain eternally in hell fire. (Koran, *Sura* 2:217)

The first modern seminaries of learning, always associated with religious learning, began in the Islamic world. The comparative leisure of the Muslim world, unlike Europe where raiders like the Vikings brought a complete halt to the promotion of arts and letters, contributed to an Islamic cultivation, a flowering of intellectual activity similar to the Renaissance in Europe.

In the year 825, about 300 Kerouan people settled along the river in the city of Fez in Morocco. They built a mosque with a roof of bright green tiles which still stands today in the old section of the city I once visited. It is reputed to be the world's oldest center of learning, dating from 857. The library at Fez contains 30,000 volumes, including a 9th century copy of the Koran. Religious study would take precedence over secular learning in the Middle Ages throughout the Moslem, Jewish and Christian worlds, while the debate over religious versus secular learning continues in every age.

By the 9th century there were active Muslim learning centers, later to emerge as formal colleges, in Cairo and in Cordoba where religious instruction blended with secular knowledge embodied in the writings of ancient Greeks and Persians, literature not then available in Europe and lost after the collapse of Roman civilization and the barbarian invasions of the Goths. Islamic universities as centers of learning, whose entire curriculum was theological and based on the Koran, had a two hundred year educational head start over Europe.

Islamic, Jewish and Christian scholars lived and transacted business in cities like Toledo, Seville and Cordoba where trade intersected and ideas and books became the principal commodity. Jewish scholars borrowed from Islamic scholars; Islamic from Jewish; Christian from both Jewish and Islamic, and all drew their inspiration from a re-discovered Aristotle promoted by Averroes. They lived in proximity but they certainly did not live in multicultural harmony, sharing the same territory but not the same religion, values or culture.

Arab culture during the time of the caliphs did help create modern civilization. But contemporary Arabs have no response to why that historical level of civilized reality has not been sustained. Why have all the sciences that once flourished been repudiated and abandoned? The typical Arab apologist response is to retreat into victimization using the curse of western imperialism as the cause of its cultural backwardness. Because of

Islamic repressive governments, independent freedoms and creative expressions have been curtailed. But festering humiliation and incessant blaming of the West for all internal problems has not advanced Arab competitive economic, scientific, aesthetic or literary agenda. Fundamentalism will not accept any foreign cultural accretions that might diminish its puritanical message, and keeps Arab culture focused backwards, away from the impact of globalization, and focused on scapegoats like the Jews for its lost or misplaced cultural identity.

But if the Muslim world basked in a soft glow of learning during the medieval era, Europe lingered in a gloom of intellectual detachment and inertia. Ironically, it was the Crusades that opened the eyes of Europe to the refinements of the Arabs and the Oriental world, and caused everyone to wonder how Europeans had so long stagnated in metaphysical and theological ennui, and before soap and detergents were invented. Luxuries competed with heresies as the principal trade goods. Paper from Egypt quickly replaced expensive parchment, though without necessarily sparing the lives of sheep. The printing press appeared like an explosive device churning out relatively cheap pamphlets and books. The study of alchemy did not yield gold, but the experiments would lead to chemistry. Fear of the unknown was replaced with a curiosity about the natural world and a natural quest to find answers to troubling questions.

Islamic culture had been built on the militarism of the sword and almost exclusively on the Koran, and only in part on the underlying culture of conquered peoples. Islam in Arabia was a culture of poverty and ignorance, not enough to sustain itself or regroup cultural losses after the Mongols laid waste lands and peoples. Fundamentalists said that if truth is to be found only in revelation, then why is there a need for any other kind of knowledge? Once Islam, always suspicious of secular learning, was faced with a revival of its destroyed civilization, it reverted to a discountenance and rejection of all sciences and arts and fell backwards and in upon itself, and into exclusive reliance on religious doctrines and practices. For the fundamentalist and extremist, new knowledge changes nothing.

The multicultural civilization of medieval Islam was able to flourish because of several factors. First, the conquered lands already possessed an unbroken cultural life dating from the ancient civilizations of Babylon, Egypt, Persia, Syria and Greece. The Byzantine Empire helped preserve some forms of knowledge. Arabia had no such cultural history. Second, the new language, Arabic, itself offered a unifying structure for governance and dissemination, both religious and commercial. Once whole national identities were brought together, a peaceful interlude allowed people of genius to display their talents.

The conquered peoples of the Middle East and North Africa, prior to the Arab invasion, had been careless of defense, neglectful of military tactics, and had less allegiance to a leader who might rally them to defend their homelands. If Christians did not accept the more perfect revelations of the Prophet of Islam, they might be spared further humiliation by the payment of a tribute that entitled them to the privileges of retaining their rituals and worship. Thus, Muslims rulers profited from the existence of other religions, except in North Africa where Donatists, Vandals and Moors, or Berbers, had virtually abandoned Christianity because of differing theological hostilities. By 749 there was no longer a need for Muslim to levy a tax on Christians as the majority of the population had converted to Islam.

The swords of Islam cut through the bickering discussions of canonical and heretical Christians over the persona, virtues, and divine attributes of Jesus. The quibbles of theology fell victim to the religious passions of Arab militias and their cavalry. Survivors hailed the Arabs reluctantly as saviors after they had rid the region of Christian despotism, having already savaged the land and depopulated resistant inhabitants in the literal and only meaning of *jihad*.

But for the Muslim world, a destructive force that as they themselves had once unleashed was about to engulf them.

## The Mongol Destruction

As with so many flowering cultures that have succumbed to invasion, internal factors, usually weak leadership combined with a weakening of economic diligence, corrupts the civilization before external forces reduce it to obscurity and possible dismemberment. The Mongols would show how easily weak leadership could be overcome. As the wealth of Islam and the Caliphate grew, its arrogance became bloated and its military ardor faded. The civilization anchored in Baghdad became itself ripe for conquest.

The profusion of Islamic culture was curtailed by the destruction of Baghdad by the Mongols in 1258, the burning of over five hundred years of scholarly inquiry, and the butchering of the populations of cities that resisted capture. The collapse of the caravan trade and urban life stagnated all commerce and culture and reduced the empire of the Middle East to subsistence living and a scavenger lifestyle.

Temujin, later known as Genghis Khan, was born in 1167 in Mongolia. [12] By 1203 he had unified all Mongolian tribes, and in 1215 captured Peking that inaugurated the rule of the Manchu dynasty. Not content with eastern Asia, he trekked across the Russian steppes to capture today's Kazakhstan. His brother Hulagu Khan (1217–1265) conquered Persia, eliminated the Abbasid Empire, and destroyed Baghdad in 1258, at the time a city of one million inhabitants. He then took Aleppo and Damascus. His advance into Egypt was broken by the bravery of the Mamluks, the descendants of mercenary slaves from the region of the Black Sea. Genghis' son Ogedai completed the conquest of Russia in 1237, and by 1241 his soldiers swam in the waters of the Adriatic off the Dalmatian coast.

The Mongol venture southward and westward was not prompted by a search for warmer climes, or to enjoy a respite from bulky fur clothes, but because of an arrogant insult from an Islamic ruler. Honor, not a search for a hot spa, brought the Golden Horde out of its barren, wind-swept, wintry hideout in Karakoram in central Mongolia to engulf east, west and south Asia. The Mongols lived in yurts, moveable, sturdy tents to accommodate their nomadic lifestyle, and were quick to learn how to raid to increase livestock existence. Once abroad, they got used to marauding, murder and wholesale theft, just as the Arabs had centuries earlier. The unhygienic odor of approaching Mongols might have been enough to overcome a city and make its inhabitants relinquish arms.

The Mongols destroyed everything they could not carry back to Mongolia. They massacred whole urban populations, raped at will, and burned what they couldn't carry. The result was imperial devastation—schools were burned, teachers killed, libraries set afire and centuries of accumulated wisdom in books went ablaze. Irrigation canals, the lifeline for agriculture in the deserts, were choked with debris, trade was disrupted, agriculture destroyed, and governments annihilated. The Islamic world never fully recovered from the Mongol devastation.

A quote from Robert Payne's *The Holy Sword* (1959), and his observations based on years of study and living among Muslims, is as relevant as when it was written over a half century ago.

> Today with the Arab world awakening at last after centuries of sleep, it is more than ever necessary to come to grips with the Arab mind. There is a sense in which they are more dangerous to our peace than the Russians . . . [this was composed in the late 1950s] We have good reason to study the Arabs and probe into their ways of thought, for they have conquered the world before, and may do it again. The fire lit by Muhammad still burns brightly, and there is every reason to believe that the flame is unquenchable. [13]

Modern day terrorism uses suicides as the weapon of choice for the weak and the cowardly afraid to face an adversary helmet to helmet. It is still the historical weapon of the descendants and disciples of Islam, the military preference for groups like al-Qaeda and individuals to confront the secular and infidel West. Could the sword, gun or explosive be tamed by the supposed impartiality of religion? The Koran and the history of the Arab mentality, the armies of Islam, the Crusaders and the Mongols argue otherwise. The passions of religion are not neutral. Human nature is the root cause of vengeful and murderous tendencies. When sanctioned by religious authority, and granted perquisites in the afterlife by its proponents, it exacts a fearful price on victims and perpetrators alike.

# Chapter Two
# Turks, Ottomans
# And Muslim Hegemony

Soon after the Arab conquests were consolidated in the tenth century, a new threat to Muslim unity arose in south central Asia. The Seljuk Turks, coming from the region of today's Uzbekistan, embraced Islam about 965. The Turks would change the face of the Middle East for nearly the next thousand years. Their rule would continue the pattern of militancy embedded in Islam.

They entered western Asia in the second half of the 11th century and formed an alliance with Islam like Arab armies three centuries earlier had with Persians. Christianity had waned in Asia Minor and the loss of religious and political unity prepared the way for the Ottoman triumph, and alerted Europe to the threat of more Muslims on its eastern frontiers.[1] Whole regions of south central Asians converted to the new religion of Islam, as Ukrainians had converted to Christianity in Kiev in 988 under Vladimir.

From 1071 to 1243 the Turks, forced to become nomads because of Mongol movements into South Asia, migrated into Anatolia in what is today eastern and central Turkey in order to find fresh pastures and to win victories against the infidel where small communities of Greek and Byzantine Christians lived. Advancing through the country that would become their namesake, they depopulated smaller towns, deflowered females, and forced the defeated to accept their religion under threat of death by scimitar.

The Byzantine Emperor Alexis I (1048–1118) at Constantinople was alarmed enough by the potential invasion of the Turks to send urgently for aid from the West. In 1195 Pope Urban II gave a rousing speech at Clermont in France that set men on the long march to rescue once Christian lands, including Jerusalem, from Muslim control. The ragtag First Crusader army that arrived to rescue Christendom was so devoid of civility and, legend has it of cleanliness, that Alexis refused to let the horde enter the city.

By 1280 the Turkish warrior class was led by Ertugrul whose son Osman (1258–1326), father of the Ottoman Empire, was ready for wider victories.[2] He crossed the Sea of Marmara from Bursa, established residence in Gallipoli, and annexed Macedonia, Bulgaria, northern Greece and Serbia. The Turkish victory at Manzikert reduced the Byzantine Empire to the vicinity of Constantinople and allowed the Turks to encircle it, and begin to invade Balkan Europe. Many Balkan Christians suddenly became vassals and janissaries of Islam, and Europeans everywhere grew more apprehensive.[3] The beginnings of the Ottoman Empire, the Caliphate contemporary Muslims seek to re-create, were forming with these Balkan conquests, long before the actual capture of the Byzantine capitol.

The janissaries were taken from a manpower tax on Christian communities in the Balkans. Each household had to yield a young son in a forced levy in lieu of a monetary tax into the Ottoman Empire's elite army corps—just like the Taliban does today in western Pakistan. All were indoctrinated into Islam. The most capable were educated in palace schools and apprenticed to officers. All served in the infantry and were trained in the use of the latest firearms and battlefield artillery. As a standing army ready to engage in battle anywhere, anytime, they were the finest army in the world and usually defeated any hastily assembled and ill-trained European army. Hence, the education of Muslim warriors is through conscription or conversion and training in the martial arts. Soon other marauders were become converts and continue the practice of raiding and destruction.

## Tamerlane:
## The Merger of Mongol and Turk with Islam

The Turks under Timur (1336–1405), descendants of the Mongols and the results of intermarriages with locals, were short, ugly, and illiterate, the consummate image of conquerors in this besieged age. Timur was himself 5' 7", tall for a descendant of Mongolians. He had a wide forehead, short, thick eyebrows, and thick, straight reddish-gray hair. He had a long moustache, a moderately long beard cut in a wedge-shape. His visage remains undefined but I would guess he looked a little like Sitting Bull or Geronimo on a good day, or one of Francisco Goya's painted caricatures.

The rugged band of Turkish Mongolian nomads Timur led in incessant battle, and populated themselves through industrious polygamy, as neither in Mongolian culture or Islam were boundaries placed on the number of women—but only four wives at any one time—or concubines a man might have. Timur led by example with his own seraglio. He had eight known wives and countless concubines, some possibly acquired in raids. Like King Henry VIII, he had one wife killed for suspicion of unfaithfulness. [4] In addition, he acquired four wives of his rival and one-time friend and colleagues, Hussein, whom he had killed.

Timur's soldiers were extremely skillful with bow and arrow shooting unerringly from their horses. Their cruelty was boundless. In two of his early thieving expeditions Timur lost the third and fourth fingers of his right hand and was wounded in the heel and so limped the rest of his life. Hence he was Timur-i-Lang, Timur the Lame or Tamerlane. Although it would be brazen and over-reaching to claim that all barbarians like Timur did so because of religious ideology, he is another example of how illiterate vandals used Islam to validate their ambitions and lust for power. His entire life is filled with duplicity, assassination, raids, invasions, war and preparations for war, the kind of action anti-hero found in movies and video games. His predatory assaults took him from Uzbekistan, where he was born, to today's Afghanistan, Iran, Iraq, Syria, Georgia, Russia, India and Turkey. He besieged and massacred the populations of Baghdad, Damascus, Herat, Aleppo, Ankara, and Delhi, among lesser towns.

The wrath of Timur in his displays of slaughter exceeded the mythical but well-known wrath of Achilles in Homer's *Iliad*. But Timur's barbaric campaigns ran with real, not poetic blood in his multiple massacres. In avenging a revolt in Isfahan in today's Iran he massacred 70,000 people. Leaving the buildings intact, he built a monumental tower of all the dead men's skulls.[5] Timur learned from Mohammad that he could use religion as a justification for conquests, and he built mighty mausoleums for worthy Sufi sheiks, often eliciting from them endorsement for his urban raids.

According to one of his biographers, "his religion served frequently to further his aims."[6] It is an entrenched feature in Islam that for those so disposed to violence it is possible to engage in criminal activities and still be a good Muslim. Such an individual need not be prudent in choosing one's superstitions and simply follow divine commands about savagery toward infidels literally.

> While Timur posed as a Mongol [he was ethnically Turkic] and an upholder of the Yasa, the great law code of Chingis [Genghis Khan], the Sharia or Muslim law code was not displaced. It was Muslim divines who accompanied Timur and his troops, who fanaticized the latter and proclaimed Timur's victories.[7]

Timur found causes to wage *jihad* even against his fellow Muslims: because they were too tepid in their faith, or that they tolerated Hindus, or that he labeled them as heretics. Though he used Islam when it was convenient for him, he was one of Islam's worst enemies. Not to show too much preference to his own religion, he slaughtered Nestorian Christians, Hindus and Zoroastrians in equal numbers and without the necessity of Islamic sophistry or clerical or scriptural legitimization.

Timur is entombed in a mausoleum in Samarkand—a major city along the ancient Silk Road where countless South Asian sultans are entombed—near where he was born, revered by visitors today as if he were a renowned statesman instead of the vicious cutthroat he was. He was a warrior soldier and the commander of warriors whose purpose, in the hardened trait of both Mongolians and Muslims, was to capture cities and all their possessions, and then to slay the inhabitants. Timur lived for a ceaseless military campaign, only lingering long enough in his grandiose tents to replenish supplies and his armies' energies for the next urban raid or suppression of a tribal uprising. His strength was in unifying an odd collection of tribes, often warring with each other, into an army of conquest. His extended family and personal followers, many from his early days of thievery, were loyal and dependent on him and constituted an elite ruling class, though that is a generous description of this rampaging murderous band.

Timur was the epitome of a latter-day Osama bin Laden, embodying the same qualities of military governance and brutality toward enemies. Many of his soldiers were conscripts picked up along the journey to battle, or the sons of nearby tribal rivals held as hostages and forced to march with his troops so as not to cause trouble while he was away. Today's Taliban or al-Qaeda members are conscripted because they live in the region of the struggle or are afraid to display disloyalty to the cause. For every gun-toting soldier there is a guide, a currier, a watchman, a servant, a cook, and financial sympathizer who support the movement that many propagandists classify as civilians in this struggle.

While Timur was subjugating Islamic countries in the east of Asia, Turks were plaguing Islamic countries in the west of Asia. Turks and Mongols absorbed and modified a variety of cultures, a medley of languages

52

and peoples while upholding the substratum of Islam, the sole unifying force of all Asiatic regions except China, India and (at the time) Southeast Asia. The Mongolian nomads of the steppes had joined the Arab nomads of the Middle East in the same religious identification. Though western Asians had a mosaic of cultures, languages, dynasties and unruly tribes, the world for them was essentially divided between Muslim and infidel, as, in many places, it still is.

## The Fall of Constantinople in 1453

The 160,000-man army of the Turks under Mehmet II (or Mahomet 1432–1481) conquered Constantinople in 1453, the crown jewel of eastern Orthodox Catholicism, and Constantine XI, the last emperor of the Roman Empire. After having his three-year old brother drowned in his bathtub, and marrying his mother off to a slave, Mehmet II thoughts turned to the siege of Constantinople.

The feckless and disunited Europeans were unable to agree to send reinforcements to Constantinople because of political rivalries and lack of money to support navies abroad. Sultan Mehmet had resorted to diplomatic invitations about conditions of surrender of the city in that summer of 1453. The choices left to the Greeks were: surrender of the city, death by sword, or conversion to Islam. The choice of hardcore Islamic radicals today to western infidels is not much different, except in weaponry—total surrender to Islam or death by suicide bombings. [8]

Mehmet first built a fortress east along the Bosporus that cut off all supplies from Black Sea ports hoping to starve inhabitants. After seven weeks of Turkish bombardments using 1,200-pound cannon balls, the residents rang church bells, paraded through the streets with icons and relics on their shoulders and uttered audible prayers. The constant battering rattled the crockery and the frayed nerves of the inhabitants. Greeks and Italians living in the city prepared to die for faith, country or sovereign as indeed they did in the hours when the Turks broke through the walled defenses. Muslim forces were urged on by Koran assurances of spending immortal youth in the gardens of paradise and the embraces of black-eyed virgins. Truly, piety is enhanced by the promise of bountiful booty. Their shouts, whoops and yelps as they charged the fortress city camouflaged their multiple linguistic accents but revved passions. After allowing his troops to pillage the city for three days as their reward, Mehmet the pederast kept the fairest sons and daughters of the aristocracy for his personal seraglio.

The Sultan's word and code of honor was valueless. His example, from an eyewitness account below, illustrates two perennial traits toward infidels—lying and beheading are both are acceptable.

> After the city had been captured, the Sultan made proclamations that those who had houses in Constantinople should tell him and he would have them assigned to them . . . But instead of letting them have their houses, the Sultan had their heads cut off . . . [9]

Mehmet offered freedom and military commissions to youth willing to convert. Converting to Islam assumes that a devotee can be convinced to overthrow one set of superstitions, or none, for another without psychological damage deserving of either drugs or therapy. For the less devout, and when offered the choice of conversion or death, apostasy is preferable to religious intransigence.

In subsequent campaigns Mehmet added Serbia, Greece, Bosnia, Wallachia (today's Romania), and Albania to the empire. Islam forcibly incorporated new lands through the sword and cannon and imposed its religion upon vanquished peoples. After renaming the city Istanbul (from the Greek "into the city"), the conquerors were known as the Ottomans and their empire spanned half the world for the next five centuries.

By the 16th century the Sultans had adopted, like Henry VIII in England, the mantle of the sword and the tiara, the uniform of the commander-in-chief and the robe of the chief cleric, and led conscripted armies and the faithful into battle. Popes in Rome were more terrified of the Turkish incursions into the Mediterranean than they had been of Martin Luther's theological machinations. Islamic warrior power projected into the Mediterranean along North Africa and controlled major land and sea trade routes. Their efficient war machine used the latest cannon and musket technology, had capable administrators in its governance and peerless logistical support. It had slaves at its disposal and used Christian mercenaries, the janissaries, as its lead infantry.

If you substitute the name of the commander Mohammad for that of the Ottoman Sultan, you will find the same military mentality that existed in the 7th through the 17th century in Islam—a supremacist ideology, the use of conscripts and slaves in military service, the constant training of soldiers, the absolute authority of the general (or imam), and the perpetual warlike vision and thirst for conquest. Among the militant extremists camps of the Taliban and al-Qaeda in Afghanistan and Pakistan, and in Gaza, Sudan, Chechnya and Somalia, not much has changed in the nature of the leadership, recruitment of young men into military training, dedication to warrior Islamic causes, and the fight for land and against the infidel.

That imperial rule, the caliphate or sultanate, is what contemporary Muslim radicals seek to revitalize through global domination. But in order to accomplish that hegemonic or colonial goal they have to acquire old territorial claims such as the Ottomans once enjoyed, a concept once favored politically by Egypt's Nasser as Pan-Arabism. Then they have to eliminate or convert infidels, just like in the old days under the murderous khans, caliphs and sultans.

## Suleiman the Magnificent (1494–1566)

Sultan Suleiman Khan assumed the sultanate in 1520, a critical time in European history. The young pope, Leo X, formerly Giovanni de'Medici, reigned in Rome. Charles Habsburg had just been crowned as Charles V, Emperor of the Holy Roman Empire. Henry VIII had just married Catherine of Aragon, Charles' aunt. Martin Luther had published *On the Liberty of a Christian Man* that challenged the authority of the Pope and the King. [10] The flammable religious controversy known as the Reformation—the rise of Protestantism in Europe, Anglicanism in England, and disgust with the corruption in the Papacy and its hated taxes—distracted European monarchs

54

from the overt, militaristic proclivities of the Turks amid political divisions among themselves.

Under Suleiman the Ottoman Empire reached its zenith because of invasions into central Europe, into a Habsburg Empire convulsed with religious chasms in Christianity. Unlike Europe, Suleiman and his whole empire was organized solely for war. Islam is a reign of dogma as authoritarian as was medieval Catholicism. It is a binding chain heavier than the one Rousseau claimed was holding back humanity. When it coalesces its ardent and misguided followers it seeks to destroy whatever it brands as apostate or infidel.

Suleiman's military motivation may have been in part revenge for the loss of Andalusia, Granada and the exotic fortress of the Alhambra on January 6, 1492. King Ferdinand and Queen Isabella drove both the Muslims and Jews from Spain, after enduring the dominion of those they called Moors for 728 years. This ethnic and religious national cleansing allowed the king and his illustrious queen to let the Genovese Christopher Columbus the opportunity to sail west, a journey that resulted in Spain becoming a military conqueror, greedy aggrandizer, and ethnic exploiter. The Spanish were no less domineering than Muslims toward the conquered people of the Americas, and bequeathed to the varied populations their language, culture and assorted diseases. Indeed, they seemed to have inherited the martial and subjugating spirit of their Muslim ancestors.

In the summer of 1521 Suleiman led his army out of Constantinople and marched north to attack the heart of central Europe, adding the Balkans to the empire and establishing a dominion among the Hungarians. In 1522 with 300 ships and 200,000 men he attacked the island of Rhodes, then held by the remnants of the Knights of St. John who had been expelled from Jerusalem and the eastern Mediterranean in previous centuries. In a gracious wartime gesture, he offered to let the Knights escape to Crete and eventually Malta where descendants still reside. Rhodes became the Ottoman Empire's first sea base.

He attacked Europe again in 1529 and rattled the city walls and nerves of the army assembled in Vienna. But because it was autumn and the snow and rains had begun, and horses lacked water and forage, he was forced to retreat the 700 miles back to Constantinople reaching the city in mid-December after losing men and horses to the weather and poor military planning.

Suleiman could not tolerate peace, a cruel symptom of Islamic warriors. He brooded over Malta, reasoning that if it were Muslim the whole of the Mediterranean would be safe for imperial travel and Muslim forces could terrorize southern Europe. So in April 1564 he sent a fleet of 150 ships and 30,000 soldiers to seize it from the Knights. The Turks won a skirmish losing 6,000 but captured the fort of St. Elmo. The Maltese were so incensed over the killing of Christian prisoners that they decapitated Muslim prisoners and shot their severed heads by cannon into the Muslim camps. Turkish forces lost the battle to superior defenses and the old Maltese warrior La Valette in 1565. (The capitol of Malta is Valetta). Sulieman then aged 72 could not retire on a military defeat so he rode with 200,000 men through the Balkans past Sofia and Belgrade, and on November 6, 1566 as he lost 30,000 men, died himself. His beleaguered army in defeat bore his body back to Constantinople.

Sultan Suleiman lived a long life and survived the intrigues of the harem and the connivances of potential heirs and enemies. But his magnificence for the sons of Islam comes from his acquisition of most of southeastern Europe and his dedication to the militant tenets of Islam.

## Lepanto and Vienna

And mine, two hundred (galleys):
But though they jump not on a just account—
As in these cases, where the aim reports,
'Tis oft with difference—yet do they all confirm
A Turkish fleet, and bearing up to Cyprus. (Shakespeare, *Othello*)

If rivalries aren't about religion, they are most certainly about trade, commerce and money. By the middle of the 16th century Venice was Queen of the Adriatic and parts of the Mediterranean. Her chief rival was the Sultan in Istanbul and his mighty armies and navy that sought new wars for territorial acquisitiveness, to feed the needy soldiers and new converts, and to satisfy the demands of Islam. By 1500, the Ottoman Empire was attempting to make permanent inroads into the Carpathian and Balkan Mountains and turning toward the major cities of Eastern Europe with the clear intention of conquering as much territory as possible.

Venice, the sensible commercial empire, preferred diplomacy to war and paid tribute to the Ottomans when it was commercially advantageous. Besides Venice, France, Spain and the Habsburgs from time to time concluded separate treaties with the Turks. It was rare for Europe to unite against the Ottomans so envious, religiously divided and suspicious were the different European nations toward each other.

But when the Turks threatened Europe's territorial, trade and religious interests by overrunning Cyprus and massacring the population of its capitol Nicosia, and when Pope Pius V became alarmed over the threat to Christendom and not just commercial interests, Europe formed a shaky alliance known as the Holy League to turn back its common enemy. The alliance included Protestant states not anxious to conclude any agreement with the Pope. Spain was reluctant to defend Venetian interests, and France never did join the campaign.

What united Europe against the Turks finally was not the conquest of Venetian Cyprus, but the siege of Famagusta, the heavily walled and fortified Cypriot city on the eastern coast. [11] Famagusta held out for months, once re-supplied by corsairs accompanying Venetian merchant ships. But it eventually succumbed to incessant Turkish bombardment. A peace treaty with the Turks and between Lala Mustapha and the Venetian Marcantonio Bragadin was negotiated for the city's surrender. But after three days the Turks reneged and then humiliated and killed the elderly Venetian commander and all prisoners. News of the abrogation of an honored oath and treaty, and the despicable death of the opposing commander, convinced the Venetians that diplomacy with the Turks and the Sultan could never be a satisfactory resolution. Shipbuilding began in earnest while the Venetians enlisted the help of European states. The loss of Famagusta and the indiscriminate killing of the captives united Europe in disgust and revenge.

Europe's cooperation, hesitatingly approved by wary states, assembled ships in Messina, Sicily under the command of Don Juan of Austria, the bastard son of the late Holy Roman Emperor Charles V and the half brother of Felipe II of Spain. The fleet sailed into Greece's Bay of Patmas near Lepanto on October 7, 1571 where it encountered the Turkish fleet. The Turks had slightly more men, more ships, but a lot less cannon. The galleasses were larger ships with mounted artillery and they bombarded the Turkish galleys mercilessly and disrupted the fleet's formations. Each side had enough personnel to fill the largest football stadiums.

Don Juan's ship the *Real* headed straight through the center of the defenses for Ali Pasha's fleet ship the *Sultana*. Spanish troops eventually boarded it, then beheaded Ali Pasha and hung his head from a pike. Demoralized at this loss of their leader, surviving Ottoman ships withdrew. Accounts vary, but the Holy League lost about 50 galleys and had 13,000 casualties. One of the wounded was the novelist Miguel de Cervantes, author of *Don Quixote*. The Turks lost 210 ships and 25,000 killed. Over 12,000 rowers who were Christian slaves in Turkish ships were freed. [12]

Undeterred, within a year the Turks had rebuilt their depleted navy, imitating the building of the heavy galleasses of Venice, and began again ravaging the coasts of southern Italy and Sicily. Meanwhile, the Spanish, not to be outdone in territorial expansion by the Ottomans, began its own conquest and conversion of the Americas giving Christianity an equally bad name. As the Islamic empire remained intact, the Spanish, French and English began building new empires in the newly discovered Americas.

On September 11, 1683 the army of Jan III Sobrieski, King of Poland, arrived at the gates of Vienna with 60,000 Polish troops and German and Austrian allies to defeat the 250,000-man army of the Grand Vizier, Pasha Kara Mustafa. Ottoman armies had already overrun all the Balkan states and Hungary. The defeat of an Islamic army by a Christian army saved central Europe from Muslim domination, a significant date in the history of both civilizations. Al-Qaeda terrorists deliberately chose September 11, 2011 for revenge. Suleiman had failed to capture Vienna in 1529, so 154 years later another sultan would attempt a second siege in order to ravish the heart of religiously fractured Christian Europe. [13]

The sultan began a military campaign to assault Europe, a classic clash of civilizations between two empires, the Habsburg and the Holy Roman Empire against the Ottoman. He traveled a thousand miles from Istanbul to attack Vienna. The Sultan appointed his Grand Vizier, Kara Mustafa, as supreme commander of the Turkish forces. The assembled quarter of a million soldiers left Edirne (formerly Adrianople) on March 31, 1683 and reached Vienna nearly on July 14th, after inconveniently slaughtering 4,000 inhabitants of a nearby village, a foretaste of what the 11,000 Viennese citizens could expect.

The divisions within Europe between Catholic and Protestant were wide and deep, unlike the Ottoman Empire, unified against all infidels. Pope Innocent IX knew the danger posed by the Ottomans and tried to rally squabbling European states to unite against the Turks. But mobilizing an army to fight a known enemy abroad was more difficult than allowing soldiers to nurture mutinous thoughts at home with potential conspiring usurpers, usually members of the royal family. And that is if malcontents among the peasantry did not incite rebellion among state rulers, as they certainly did in France in the following century during the reign of Louis XVI.

The vicissitudes of war are always unpredictable, and the Turkish advance toward Vienna was no exception. Ottoman commanders had to victual troops, camp-followers and animals on the march daily, prepare camps, find water, and maintain morale as they moved through hundreds of miles of terrain, some of it hostile. The Viennese counterparts had to thwart the advance, estimate the numbers of the opposition, destroy bridges and guess at points of attack and retreat. Inferior intelligence reports, poor planning, incorrect defense counter-movements, complacency, lack of the proper equipment and supplies, failure to install messenger services, and military incompetence led to skirmish defeats and deaths. That was in addition to the scourge of all soldiers—dysentery—and the indispensable, timely receipt of payment in currency not credit for services. The defensive Viennese army as it wandered the countryside, and guarding its own supplies, couldn't often locate the enemy or reconnaissance detachments. Weather, accidents and incompetence still witness the ruin of wartime objectives.

There was panic in the smaller towns in a 25-mile circumference of Vienna as burghers fled, refugees went on the move, and peasants who remained prayed, but became victims of savagery from marauding bands of soldier scavengers. Most nearby villages were sacked for provisions. Should the preference be to protect the Emperor and the court, keep the regal valuables safe, store in more supplies and ammunition for Vienna, or erect more defenses? Messengers were urgently sent throughout the empire for troops. Some principalities responded, but wanted the Habsburgs to pay in cash for soldiers' food, pay and animal forage.

In the old days it was acceptable to find a virgin and throw her in a volcano to see if that would placate the divinities. But this was Catholic Austria. Jesuits had been consulted and found wanting in decisiveness and practical solutions. The forces of Islam were on the march and at the gates to conquer and convert by the sword. Emperor Leopold, meanwhile, was safely ensconced in Passau, about 100 miles up the Danube from Vienna.

In 1683 Louis XIV in France conspired against the Austrians to acquire parts of Germany. He attempted to bribe the Polish Diet that had to give its permission before the Polish King could rescue the Austrians. But the Pope's bribes were bigger than the French king's so the Polish consented. King Jan Sobrieski (1629–1696) marched his troops to Vienna arriving in September 1683 when the city had been under siege for weeks and was on the verge of capitulation. Sobrieski charged at the front of his cavalry into the Turkish flank and utterly routed the massed siege forces.

The Turks had no experience in dealing with a military problem that would be known to western forces, namely that of defense from a relieving army while besieging a garrisoned city. The Turks had neglected to fortify the outer lines of its camp. The combined forces of Europe swept the field, gained the day, rescued the city and celebrated with prayers in the churches and feasts in the banqueting halls. The Turks managed to flee *en masse* but not before decapitating Pearl of Loveliness, one of Kara Mustafa's concubines who had indiscreetly refused to accompany him back to Istanbul. As panicked Turks fled on the return journey, Mustafa ordered the beheadings of all officers who had disagreed with him on military strategy. Mustafa then fled to Belgrade to escape his disgruntled troops where the Sultan had him executed on Christmas Day, 1683. The Islamic crusade had come to an end, until the Turkish genocide of Armenians in 1915, and the vengeful events by Muslim terrorists in September 2001.

## Turkish Nationalism and the Armenian Genocide

Valiant Othello, we must straight employ you
Against the general enemy Ottoman. (Shakespeare, *Othello*)

According to population figures, 1,256,000 Armenians, who lacked full Ottoman citizenship, lived in the Ottoman Empire in 1915. By the end of 1916, only 284,157 remained. According to Turkey, the result was not genocide but the putdown of an Armenian revolt whose people were openly supporting Russia in its war against Turkey. But the Arabs in Saudi Arabia also revolted against the Ottoman Turks in 1915, yet there was no genocide of Arabs.

Forgetfulness and denial became the hallmarks of a horrific historical event—Ottoman Turkey's holocaust of its Christian citizens. Azerbaijan also borders Armenia but its nominally Muslim citizens were not harassed by the Turkish military. The Ottoman Empire was ruled for centuries by an Islamic theocracy in which it presided over large geographic swaths of western Asia and viewed people of ethnic or religious differences, like Armenians or Kurds or Christians, as ethnic or alien threats. The Christians of Turkish Anatolia in west central Turkey were also killed or forced to immigrate.

The internal conditions that allowed for the creation of the Republic were determined by the internal wars that were fought in Anatolia . . . developed on the basis of religious clashes. As a result of these clashes, which reached their apex with the Armenian Genocide, the Christian population of Anatolia was either annihilated or expelled from Anatolia. [14]

Viewed in the long history of Islam, the Armenian Genocide is not an aberration. Both Germany and Turkey lost heavily in World War I. Turks sought to regain national pride by enjoying a rejuvenated martial psychosis by wrecking vengeance on traditional scapegoats within their purview: Christians. [15]

There may have been extenuating circumstances for Turkey, such as the national humiliation of the slow territorial erosion of the Ottoman Empire by the early twentieth century, or the threat from a Christian Europe, or the fear of a separatist revolt among Armenians. But whether in Hitler's Germany in the 1930s and 1940s, Mao's China in the 1960s, Cambodia of the Khmer Rouge in the 1970s, Rwanda in the 1990s, or the Darfur region of the Sudan under Omar al-Bashir, genocides are internationally acknowledged crimes against humanity.

Atrocities and mass murders can and have occurred in every century and culture. Genocides are more rare, but have no special topography or ethnic group. They are a human phenomenon peculiar to no creed, nationality or group. On the other hand, the Armenian Genocide follows an historical pattern of Muslim domination, as brutal as the rampages of the Mongols or the socio-pathological killings by Nazis.

Hitler had his dreaded SS or Storm Troopers. Mao Tse-Tung, the peasant revolutionary responsible for the deaths of 70 million Chinese, who never took a bath or shower in his 27-year reign, had his corps of teenagers, the Red Guards, who carried out slaughters during the so-called Cultural Revolution. [16] Pol Pot and Foreign Minister Ieng Sary with hired thugs created a slave society in the 1970s by killing a quarter of Cambodia's population. Omar al-Bashir in Sudan created the *Janjaweed* militia in the twenty-first century to execute his elimination of the non-Muslim Arabs in the Darfur region of Sudan. During the Armenian massacre, the Ottoman army created a separate felonious gang, composed mostly of released prisoners, who carried out genocide orders from the regular army.

Thus, the history of the Ottoman Empire, like the history of the Arabs after they converted to Islam, is built on military conquest and the elimination of opposition and non-Islamic religious affiliation. The historian Arnold Toynbee (1889–1975), based on his personal collection of documentary evidence in 1916, has an even more unflattering comparison of Turks as descendants of nomads who built the Ottoman Empire on military mercenaries, the elite military corps of Christian slave children reared as Muslims to serve the Sultan, the Janissaries (corrupted in language from *yeni cheri*, or "new soldiers"). [17]

In short, the Ottoman Empire and its leaders planned and executed genocide against members of its own population then attempted to deny allegations of its atrocities. In March 2010 the U.S. House Foreign Affairs Committee by a 23 to 22 vote condemned this genocide.

After the total collapse of the Ottoman Empire at the end of World War I in 1918, Mustafa Kemal, hereafter known as Ataturk, "The Father of the Turks," emerged as the leader of a party that created modern Turkey in 1923. Kemal, the successful general turned beneficent despot, introduced radical social changes.

He abandoned the lunar calendar, forbade polygamy, the fez and religious instruction in schools, made Sunday the new holy day, and Romanized the Turkish script. Most important, he amended the Constitution to remove the statement that Turkey was an Islamic state and a caliphate. No state had ever previously renounced its religious symbols and substituted such sweeping western modalities, including its language. Kemal literally created nationalism from Muslim oligarchy and advanced a reluctant Muslim population into forced western modernization. [18]

The Turkish democracy that emerged has been fragile in the intervening century as the military played a dominant role in the state's power structure. It still tries to maintain a delicate balance between secular governance and a Muslim majority that seeks greater Islamic rule. Military coups occurred in 1960, 1971 and 1980, though power was returned to civilian rule shortly afterwards. In 1997 the military again intervened to engineer the ouster of a pro-Islamic government. A tide of Islamic fundamentalism lies just below the surface of the façade of Turkish democracy, kept in check only by the Turkish military and its support of secular principles. [19]

The Tomb of Tamerlane in Samarkand

# CHAPTER THREE
# INDOCTRINATING MUSLIM
# EXTREMISTS

Islamic militancy has emerged as the greatest threat to Western security
since the collapse of communism.
(Willy Claes, Secretary General, NATO, February 1995)

Now that we have reviewed the history of Islamic violence over the
centuries, let's explore in this and the follwing chapters some anecdotes
about Muslim extremism and how the education in the militancy in the
Koran has shaped the behavior of so many Muslim youth.

The effort among Islamic religious zealots and their militant
organizations is to recruit young men primarily through appealing videos,
and to instruct them in the techniques of guerilla warfare. It is exclusively a
military objective, and a stunted education of youth, but true to Islamic
religious ideals. Recruits are all convinced of the righteousness of their
cause and are willing to die to achieve the delights of a Muslim paradise.

The substitution of the reigious knowledge of the Koran devoid of other
educational content has intellectually impoverished whole populations and
helped incubate a culture of militancy. Mixed with religious fanaticism and
hatred for the values of the West, school instructors throughout the Islamic
world have created a corps of militant students, filled with Islamic fervor.
They were once largely ignorant of the knowledge of the developed world
but have realized its vales and accomplishments through social networks
and the global media reach. Islamic schooling in general is the medium for
fomenting hatred of the West at the expense of secular knowledge. By
learning about the militancy in the Koran, new recruits can even become
self-educated in the *jihad* movement.

Although some American mosques and Muslim organization often
reject violence they cannot compete with the lure of Islamic *jihad* on the
Internet or with *jihad* videos. Prominent clerics have helped inspire the
militancy movement and been recruiters for al-Qaeda. Radicalized Muslim
youth want validation for what they already believe. Clerics, functioning as
Internet Imams, tell them that *jihad* is not only permissible but a religious
obligation. Like people who find physicians who will prescribe the drugs
they need, radicalized Muslim youth will find imams who will convince
them of the righteousness of militant decisions.

Recruiters for al-Qaeda and associated extremist groups in Europe,
Africa Southeast and South Asia try to spot raw talent in mosques and
*madrassas*. Where possible militant groups will use pamphlets, DVDs and
videos just like any other recruiting organization. If a candidate is found
acceptable—and this usually means highly devoted to Islam—he is sent to a
military training camp, usually in Pakistan where he undergoes a series of
psychological, physical and religious tests. The military training comes
courtesy of military trainers, usually Pakistani, as do the weapons.

Foreign recruits, like the disillusioned follower, the Long Island 26-year old Bryant Neal Vinas, a.k.a. Bashir al-Ameriki his *nom de guerre*, and a convert to Islam, journeyed to Pakistan, initially to search for a wife, but where he joined al-Qaeda. He was captured in Peshawar and his story reveals how al-Qaeda evaluates and trains its foreign applicants. He pleaded guilty in January 2009 to receiving al-Qaeda training and conspiring to kill American soldiers. Vinas joined the U.S. army in 2002 but washed out in training. He converted to Islam in 2004 and decided to conform to the Salafi sect, one of the most fundamental of Muslim beliefs, and attended the local mosque in Selden, Long Island. In 2007 he went to Lahore, Pakistan and soon found his way to al-Qaeda training camps. He travelled with militants into Afghanistan. Soon, al-Qaeda began recruiting him for suicide missions. But first, he needed specific training.

Between March and July 2008 in Waziristan province in Pakistan he underwent three courses. The first was the uses of weapons—the AK-47, machine guns and a pistol. The second course was a two-week exercise in explosives that also included how to make suicide belts. The third course was in rocket-propelled grenades. There were other courses in this terror school that included forgery, poisons, and advanced bombs, but he did not participate in any of these advanced courses. Al-Qaeda officials kept evaluation documents on all trainees. Vinas trained with several Belgium and French men charged with terrorism in Belgium. His testimony was used in their trial. Vinas' testimony also led to drone air strikes on al-Qaeda camps, and to the arrests to two senior al-Qaeda operatives.

The root causes of recruitment of Islamic militants are as varied as the disciplines cited to explain them. Embedded in all such theories are the sociological dimensions of poverty, ignorance, social cohesion, group movements and the psychological ideas of male bonding, devotion and loyalty to a divine cause, psychological trauma or neurological deficiencies. The single most important aim of Islamic recruiters is to test for the depth of devotion to Islam. Trying to dissect militant motives is not totally fruitless, but guessing individual motives and their application to all who have joined radicalized groups is speculative.

It is an ancient dilemma—the extent to which religion, and by implication God—should judge misconduct. The story is as old as Aeschylus' *Oresteia* and Euripdes's *Orestes* when the goddess Athena, representing Zeus, stands in judgment of the trial of Orestes for matricide, the killing of his mother Clytemnestra, who had had his father Agamemnon murdered for sacrificing his sister Iphigenia in order to obtain a favorable wind for sailing to Troy. Athena insists on a trial by jury, in a nod to the democratic process and the West's chosen position to curb the excesses of endless rounds of tribal or family revenge. After a tie vote by the human jury, the goddess Athena votes to acquit. Aeschylus reminds us that the divine must yield to civil law, and let humans decide justice without divine intervention.

Iran overran the U.S. Embassy in Tehran in 1979 and took American diplomats as hostages and held them for 444 days, one of whom was a friend of mine. [1] Iran approved of the taking hostages ostensibly because of American interference in Iran in 1953 when the CIA installed the Shah of Iran. The intervention of U.S. marines in Lebanon to quell an uprising during the Reagan Ad-ministration further damaged American prestige. The bombing of the U.S. Embassy in Beirut and the attack on the marine barracks in Beirut on April 18, 1983 killing 241 Americans and 57 Frenchmen, and the bombing of a U.S. compound in Saudi Arabia on October 23, 1983 confirmed hatred for the U.S. [2]

Were these attacks on the U.S. in the Middle East the work of a few misguided extremists, or a signal that there was a wider circle of coordinated attacks against U.S. targets? The attacks on the Twin Towers in New York first in 1993 and again on September 11, 2001, the Madrid train bombings in 2004, the London subway and bus bombings in 2005, the downing of passenger airlines, the derailment of trains and metro bombings in Moscow, confirmed, if it had not registered previously, that the West, and not just America, was in a sustained conflict with a determined Islamic enemy. It soon became clear that in the Islamic world militant extremism was the mainstream.

Polls have shown a near universal hatred in the Arab world for the U.S. and its allies, including Denmark and Sweden for satirical cartoons. Americans readily admit to the strength of evangelical Christians—those who figuratively carry a gun on one hip and a Bible on the other—to set the political agenda and to support messianic candidates with money and votes. Unquestionably, religion is a primary force in the recruitment of Muslim young men and a few women to die for what they believe are blasphemies to their religious beliefs.

T. E. Lawrence (Lawrence of Arabia) wrote about the Arab mentality in the early 1920s after his experiences as a British army officer fighting on their side against the Ottoman Turks.

> In the very outset . . . was found a universal clearness or hardness of belief, almost mathematical in its limitation, and repellent in its unsympathetic form. They were a dogmatic people, despising doubt . . . They did not understand our metaphysical difficulties, our introspective questionings. They knew only truth and untruth, belief and unbelief, without our hesitating retinue of finer shades. [3]

The difference is that Arabs, who in Lawrence's day trained their hatred on the Ottoman Turks under caliphate rule, and, needing the British to support them in their rebellion against the Turks, have since turned their hatred to the West in general and America in particular. It is pure resentment: a kindergarten of folly for the unimaginative. Nevertheless, there is a process of indoctrination that begins with the very young.

## Formal and Informal Education in Militancy

Every Muslim child is taught on entering school that the Koran embodies all knowledge. Every child is taught that Islam represents all truth and everything else is falsehood, and that only Islam has a monopoly on good values. Children are instructed that anyone not a Muslim is an enemy and that the West represents licentiousness, weakness and ignorance, the kind of ignorance known as *jahiliya*, the ignorance that existed before Mohammed. If somehow a child does not receive multiple instances of this message, it will certainly be repeated in the *madrassas*, mosques or Arab media. Additionally, a Muslim child will not only receive a thorough education about his or her faith but some Muslim men will again get religion, so to speak, in their twenties and prepare to sacrifice themselves to the cause of eradicating infidels. I have been in Arab elementary schools in several Arab countries and observed not only the comprehensive curriculum focused on Islam and the Koran but the installation of hatred, discrimination and bias instilled in the youngest of children.

There are educational differences within Arab states, but they are marginal. There are certainly more schools to accommodate population growth. But academic performance remains low. Books, literature, reading and the thirst for knowledge are not a part of popular culture. Not only are students not generally taught much useful knowledge in schools, some Taliban militants actually attack schools and kill teachers. Four teachers, one a native Somali who was in his 70s, and three foreign teachers were murdered by Islamic insurgents on a raid at an English-language school in south central Somalia in April 2008. [4]

Palestinian children are fed doses of Islamic propaganda of terrorist activities, hatred for Israel and Jews, and fantasy images of virgins waiting for suicide bombers in the afterlife. Elementary school children are taught that suicide martyrdom is the highest honor for a Muslim male. They are taught to praise terrorists like Dalal Mughrabi who killed 12 Israeli children and 25 adults in a 1978 bus hijacking, and "to finish his journey." They regularly chant, "I have let my land drink my blood, and I have loved the way of the *shahada* (martyrdom for Allah)." [5] These are not skills that promote typical civic values or occupational preparedness.

Suicide bombings originated with Hezbollah in Lebanon in the early 1980s and its practice quickly spread until it became a global dimension with unprecedented numbers in Iraq from 2003 onward. Suicide bombings are high profile, tactically efficient and mechanically simple. [6] Suicide bombings attract funds and recruits. Individual suicides find comfort in popular approval among devout Muslims and in collective political success. These so-called martyrs enjoy an exalted elite status equivalent to sainthood. Families may also benefit financially from their death. [7]

Kristen Rouse was a first lieutenant in the Army National Guard who served in the 10th Mountain Division in Afghanistan. One day in April 2006, the Taliban attacked a primary school in Afghanistan just east of Asadabad. The school was in an open courtyard outside a mosque where boys and girls attended together. The first rocket hit the children directly as they sat in class. A second rocket exploded nearby. Seven children were killed and 34 wounded.

Young schoolchildren are not immune from the wrath and folly of the Taliban and its misguided fanaticism against the mixing of genders, even with innocent primary schoolchildren. The Taliban routinely burn schools, assassinate teachers, and maim and dismember children whose actions they disagree with. Girls should not be educated at all, according to them, and should only learn to memorize the Koran.

Phoenix native Hassan Abu-Jihaad ("Father of *Jihad*"), formerly known as Paul Hall before his conversion, is a relevant case. Hassan had been a U.S. Navy signalman sailor on board the *USS Benfold* before he was honorably discharged in 2002. He sent classified national defense documents in 2001 to a web site in London that openly espoused war with the U.S. He sent details about the composition of the navy battle group and how the formation would pass through the Strait of Hormuz in the Persian Gulf. Prosecutors called him a traitor for providing information that duplicated the bombing of the *USS Cole* in Yemen that killed 17 sailors, an event that he praised. He was convicted in 2009 in New Haven, Connecticut for a maximum of ten years in prison.

A Saudi man, Abd al-Rahim al-Nashiri, also accused of plotting the Cole attack, after his capture in 2002, was finally brought to a military trial at Quantanamo naval base in Cuba, the first terrorist to be tried under new rules after the 9/11 attacks.

Some actual and potential Islamic terrorists devote themselves to *jihad* because of indoctrination during formal schooling, some because of a later conversion because of a cleric, recruiter, relative or friend, and some through self-conversion. The number may be small compared to the overall Muslim population but the danger from their devotion and activities is real and global.

## Educating Against the Enemy

Radical militant Islamic fundamentalism, as I have pointed out, opposes any interpretation of the social contract other than its own. It rejects secular values that in democratic societies unite pluralistic religious traditions in law and equity. But the Muslim threat is not localized in any one country. It is global, better organized, has far more recruits, and is more lethal.

Ayaan Hirsi Ali, born in Somalia, left the husband assigned to her, became a refugee in Holland and was elected to the Dutch Parliament. She was condemned to death when she renounced her Islamic faith and became an international spokesperson for the dangers of militant Islam. This is what she said about her schooling.

> And then we were shown pictures of dead people. Bloodied, killed, large numbers of corpses in ran. And she said this is what the Jews are doing to Muslims; this is what the Americans are doing to Muslims. [8]

Muslim terrorists are not alone in murderous activities for their beliefs. Eric Rudolph bombed abortion clinics in the U.S. and sought to kill abortion doctors. Ted Kaczynski bombed developers of technology. Timothy McVeigh blew up hundreds of innocent civilians in Oklahoma City to get even with the U.S. government for perceived wrongs. David Koresh in Waco, Texas led gullible people to their death in pursuit of a misguided religious vision. Similarly, Jewish fundamentalists reject most expressions of secular behavior and seek a land held in dispute to be righteously theirs in holy covenant.

It is always hazardous to generalize about the Islamic world since cultures and nationalities differ tremendously from Morocco to the South Asian Moluccas. Radical clerics and militants have shouted down conciliatory voices of Islam. The enemies of political Islam have been quickly targeted by extremist clerics whose opposition includes:

- Local political elites who only pretend to be good Muslims

- Nationalists who propagate ethnicity at the expense of Islam
- Secularists who want to separate religion from politics
- Democrats who believe that it is the people not God that is the foundation of legitimacy
- The West, the source of all the above ideas

The intellectual elite in the Muslim world, including Islamic educators who are lulled by the fervor and dedication of religious politics, not only have failed to cultivate a professional accommodation with the West but have become more isolated. They have staunchly defended the orthodoxies of the Muslim nation, like the army and the church, rather than questioning the motives, ambitions and repressive operations of their national institutions. The culture of dogmatism, the rejection of everything western, the stereotyping, the prejudice—all have bred a contagious intolerance.

Arab intellectuals have been cowed into Islamic submission and have become puppet spokesmen of clerics and leaders. There is a legitimate fear to speak out against the nation state, ruler, emir or religious leaders, as is certainly true today in Iran. Independent voices are paralyzed. Challenging Muslim authorities places one's life in jeopardy. The crowds that gather to shout spiteful slogans have been fuelled by religious demagoguery. Islamic orthodoxy has purged most expressions of secular education and has intellectually isolated its diverse peoples. Many Islamic educators respond like politicians with a set speech, rarely seeking to understand more than their simplistic slogans and inflexible logic provides, viewing all problems with America through the prism of its relationship with Israel and imagined Zionist threats.

One tactic of young men to gain entrance to western society is to entrap and humiliate Christian women. Many of these young men are paid fees for converting Christian women to Islam. The idea is to entrap women into conversion by whatever means and then to humiliate them and their families so that Christians in general will be dishonored. Ahmed Awny Sahlakamy, a former Egyptian Muslim who courageously converted to Christianity, relates this and others stories. [9]

There is no typical profile for an Islamic militant recruit. The 9/11 hijackers came from middle class, educated backgrounds, as did the Glasgow airport and intended London disco bombers. Al-Qaeda recruits may come from disaffected or troubled young men in any country, and they may not meet in mosques or *madrassas*, but in health centers or social clubs, or simply become enthralled with a *jihad* website. They might be rich, like bin Laden, a middle class professional like Qutb, a criminal, or poor like any member of the Taliban.

Physicians like the Glasgow bombers, or like Major Nidal Hassan, the Fort Hood killer psychiatrist, or like Humam Khalil Abu Mulal al-Balawi, the Jordanian physician who blew himself up with seven CIA employees in Afghanistan, had sworn the Hippocratic Oath, that code of medical ethics that all physicians swear to uphold, "to do no harm." Their religious alliance trumped their sworn oaths to protect.

Richard Reid, the so-called "shoe bomber," son of a Jamaican father (himself a criminal) and an English mother, spent three years in a British prison, where he converted to Islam, for his conviction of over 50 burglaries in south London. He is now in the federal Supermax prison in Colorado serving a life sentence.

The most notorious criminal in the al-Qaeda camp was Abu Musab al-Zarqawi, a high school dropout from Jordan who began his career as a juvenile delinquent. Criminal records are not a disqualification for membership in the highest al-Qaeda circles, and in fact may be regarded as a badge of honor. He was covered in embarrassing tattoos that he tried to remove with hydrochloric acid. As a criminal, he came to *jihad* effortlessly. He was lodged in a Jordanian prison where he recruited other felons and drug addicts. He returned to Afghanistan, was convicted again *in absentia* in a Jordanian court with 47 other co-conspirators for plotting to blow up a Radisson Hotel in Amman. He made his way to Iraq as the al-Qaeda leader. He was killed in an air strike near the city of Baqubah on June 8, 2006 when two 500-pound bombs destroyed the house where he was staying.

Recruiting terrorists in prison occurs everywhere, and was a problem in Porong Prison near Surabaya, Indonesia where I visited in the summer of 2011. Among the 1,327 prison inmates are 27 convicted terrorists. Before a new warden arrived in 2010, inmates moved freely in Block F where terrorist inmates were housed in supposed isolation. Prisoners find the terrorists' piety and devotion to *jihad* inspiring and a few are converted after they modify lives to follow the prescriptions of the Koran more faithfully. [10]

Such is the kind of criminals and social rejects al-Qaeda recruits. Roughly 30,000–40,000 American prison inmates convert to Islam each year. Recruiting from the raw, incarcerated underbelly of society is practical because prison is a ripe climate for terrorism, as many have the same gang mentality they had on the streets, and the men are largely illiterate with broken spirits and little hope. A call for *jihad* for such desperate men seems like a worthy source of inspiration and a token reprieve that licenses violence.

If they are already Muslim they have time to read and reflect more on the central militant message of Islam. If they have loose religious beliefs they can become Muslim converts. But if they are criminally inclined, this tendency, together with the militancy of Islam, combine to make their conversion a high potential for terrorism, as it did for the four ex-convicts arrested in a bombing plot in Newburgh, New York in May 2009. Imams as chaplains in prison will steadfastly claim they reject any discussion that Islam radicalizes inmates, but the evidence suggests otherwise.

The more heinous fact among Islamic extremists is that children are recruited to act as suicide bombers. British officials noted in December 2008 that a boy believed to be about thirteen carried out a suicide mission that killed three British troops in southern Afghanistan. The Taliban's educational curriculum is to induce young boys, not old enough to be real soldiers, to carry out death wishes on purported Islamic enemies of the adults. Apparently, there are too many adult cowards so the Taliban has to recruit children and convince them of the justness of their cause. [11]

Thousands of Iraqi Shiite recruits enlisted to become members of one or more Iranian militia had been trained in Iran to fight in Iraq. Once inside Iran, recruits were met by guides at several locations before being flown to Tehran where they resided in apartments outside the city where training exercises were conducted. They were selected based on minimal qualifications. They had to be able to read and write, not a universal aptitude among Arab men. One captured leader described the selected attributes of recruits as having physical stamina, being mature and responsible, open-minded, having organizational skills and were not a disciplinary problem. These recruits were selected and trained for use against coalition forces in Iraq. The logistics were all arranged, as they traveled in special vehicles in order to cross the border, either legally or illegally, and stayed in safe houses in or around Amara north of Basra before crossing into Iran. Iranian border guards, when recognizing drivers of special vehicles, would simply wave the van (often a Land Cruiser) through without inspecting it. [12]

| MUSLIM PRISONERS AS A PERCENTAGE OF NATIONAL POPULATIONS | | |
|---|---|---|
| | Percent of Muslim Population | Percent of Muslim Prisoner Population |
| Belgium | 2% | 15% |
| Holland | 6% | 20% |
| France | 5% | 60-70% |
| England | 3% | 11% |

Source: J. Lefkowitz. (May 5, 2008). *Terrorists Behind Bars.* www.nefafoundation.org

The training of militias by Iran consisted of a variety of basic military operational skills including weapons familiarity for about three weeks. Advanced courses included the use of sniper procedures, roadside ambushes, explosives, guerilla warfare tactics and kidnapping. A typical advanced military tactic was to ignite a roadside bomb on one vehicle in a coalition convoy. Once the convoy stopped or slowed down, the support team then targeted the other vehicles with mortars and rocket rounds while another team fired small arms and rockets. If possible, one team would kidnap anyone not killed in the target vehicle.

Another goal of the training program was to create a special elite force whose members would become instructors and pass on their knowledge to other recruits. But most importantly, the Iranian military camps also had religious instruction as a mandatory part of every day's training.

Recruits for these camps come from a variety of the disaffected, altruistic and gullible mostly from Europe. Many came from criminal groups, some through Internet sites, *jihad* websites, others through friends and mosque referrals. They enter the program by handing over their passports and adopting a new identity, which, if they are ever captured, makes it difficult to identify them.

Recruiters are harder to locate and bring to justice. Mamoun Darkazanli, born in 1958 in Aleppo, Syria, joined the Syrian Muslim Brotherhood. Together with fellow Syrian Mohammad Zammar, they operated an al-Qaeda cell in Hamburg, Germany where they recruited Mohammad Atta, the lead 9/11 terrorist, and Marwan al-Shehhi. The al-

Qaeda cover was a company called Tatex Trading, run by a long time backer of Syria's Assad family Abdul Matin Tatari. There were only two shareholders. One was Mohamad Majed Said, head of Syria's security service from 1987–1994.

U.S. intelligence services were not aware of Darkazanli until 1993 when a suspect in the African bombings, carrying fake passports and counterfeit money, was found with his phone number in Hamburg. A few years later, Darkazanli received a deposit of $250,000 from the Twaik Group, a Saudi conglomerate with $100 million in holdings. Twaik is a front organization for Saudi intelligence with direct ties to Prince Turki al-Faisal. Darkazanli received funding from several Middle Easter sources and was responsible for recruiting hijackers for the 9/11 suicide bombings.

Darkazanli met in Spain on July 6 with several future 9/11 hijackers to finalize attack plans. On September 24, 2001 the U.S. froze assets of at least 27 individuals and organizations, including Darkazanli's individual and corporate accounts. By September 17, 2003 a Spanish judge had issued an indictment against Darkazanli alleging he belonged to and supported an al-Qaeda cell in Madrid and assisted the 9/11 hijackers. He was arrested in Germany on October 14, 2004 where he had been living openly. He could not be convicted of terrorism because German laws against terrorism were not passed until 2002, and he was released. German law prohibited his extradition to Spain because he was a German citizen.

The West needs to address its suppositions surrounding Islamic extremists. First, many are highly educated and not socio-economic bottom-feeders. Second, their parents are not always the source of their commitment to Islam. Third, they may or may not be a part of a larger network. But most important, their singular motivation for wanting to kill westerners is their Muslim faith. Hence, the only condition for their extremist views is their excessive belief in the vengeful passages in the Koran and clerical interpretations favoring violence to non-Muslims and rarely other extenuating circumstances.

The argument can be that anyone who commits a suicide bombing or murder in the name of religion is criminally insane and therefore not fully culpable. However, Muslim believers do not have the same religious perspectives as other faiths. Major Hassan was very likely suffering from psychotic episodes. But Islam gave him the legitimacy to murder non-Muslims regardless of his psychological state of mind.

It's easier to think of individuals as acting alone when each may be just one bomber in a larger conspiracy. Is it better to wait until a plot unravels and is near action so that authorities can collect all necessary evidence? Arresting suspects and disrupting a plot before any terrorism occurs prevents an attack but may be premature enough not to yield anything except circumstantial evidence, perhaps not enough for a court conviction. During *Operation Crevice* in England, officials arrested several suspects, five of whom were convicted, but others had to be dismissed for lack of convincing evidence. Some of those acquitted individuals eventually bombed the London subway on July 7, 2005. Counterterrorism officials must constantly balance the need to gather sufficient evidence with preventing attacks.

The terrorist war has its own trainees. Al-Qaeda has unified young recruits worldwide who seek to become soldiers in a war against the West, exporting its military and weapons' training throughout the Islamic world wherever it can obtain a toehold. The locally armed group *Ansar al-Islam* armed in the villages in northern Iraq, and Muslim mercenaries fought in Bosnia and Kosovo. Such groups had a mobile curriculum for fighters coming from diverse Islamic countries. They carried passports from multiple countries, with instructors and textbooks in weapons use, assassination, guerrilla attacks, suicide bombings and the use of poisons.

Islamic educators infected the young with militaristic values, anti-western propaganda, and the worst stereotypes of western culture, all under the blessings of religion. This hostility is actively sponsored by state regimes like Sudan, Pakistan, Iran, and the Palestinian Authority, or ignored or passively condoned though controlled, as in Egypt, Syria and Indonesia. The resurgence in Islamic orthodoxy and fundamentalism, which under the guise of education fosters hatred and terrorism, has silenced moderate voices of Islamic educators. Courageous Islamic intellectuals, novelists and journalists, including those in voluntary exile or speaking out against religious dogmatism, have often been assassinated if they haven't sought permanent exile. The absolutism of the clerical stranglehold on most intellectual life, and the universal condemnation of all western values and political policies, including western religions, discredits the non-violent message of Islam.

Muslim ideology is fed on slogans and militancy is more pervasive than even a decade ago. All Muslim governments are faced with ideological challenges to their educational and social systems. Islamic fundamentalism looks backward to when the Muslim faith was revealed in order to refute polytheism and rarely forward to any accommodation with the West.

Islamic peoples often have misperceptions of the western value of free speech in a democratic society. Conversely, the West has misperceptions of Islam as misogynists, opponents of democracy, and as a haven of terrorists. This cultural divide, bolstered by Islamic political rigidities, the lack of a broad civic education, a precipitous rise in population, endemic poverty and growing illiteracy, and the West's ignorance of Islamic history and culture, is widening.

Islam may be chief motivating factor in Islamic terror attacks but the Islamic world in general is deficient in overall educational and cultural development, as the following section illustrates.

## The Erosion of Muslim Educational Achievement

This ubiquitous religious radicalization has curtailed the quest for academic achievement. Muslim religious indoctrination in a few countries has superseded science, math, the social sciences, art and humanities. The result is a deepening intellectual impoverishment. The decline in literacy rates is in addition to the rapid increase in population combined with a lack of national financial resources to fund quality educational programs.

Trawling through data about the Arab world reveals a very bleak set of economic and social conditions. There is widespread under-development and stagnation in all sectors—infrastructure, investment, trade, and education. Manufacturing exports from the Arab world are below those of The Philippines, with less than a third of the population. The greatest social transformation has occurred in communications. Until the Emir of Qatar, Hamad bin Khalifa, introduced *al-Jazeera* television in 1996 that broadcasted hard-hitting reports and news from the Arab world, Arabs had been uninformed about even real events and people from their region.

Arab illiteracy is three times higher than in Latin America and the Caribbean. One third of Arab men are illiterate and one half of Arab women. But because of lack of educational opportunities and fundamentalist religious resistance to secular learning, most will remain uninformed.

According to the *Arab Human Development Report* in 2002, studies of educational achievement levels throughout the Arab world remained low on average compared to all developing countries. Illiteracy is higher in Arab countries than the international average, and higher than in developing nations. The illiteracy was about 43% in 1980, but in 1995 was more than 60% and increasing. The majority of Arab illiterates are women and the enrollment of women in schooling is lower than that for males even while there have been rising education expenditures.

The more recent *Arab Human Development Report 2009* did not reveal any improvements. [13] Arab countries continue to face enormous challenges because of environmental degradation like water shortages and desertification. But the most damaging statistics are social, beginning with the combination of high population increases, more than double in 35 years––395 million by 2015 from 150 million in 1980—and stagnating economic growth that includes crippling unemployment (about twice as high as the rest of the world), excessive levels of poverty, and inequalities in wealth. There is negligible investment from Arab countries in scientific research and development and the knowledge industries that derive the economies of the developed world.

Greece at a population of fifteen million, buys more books than all Arab states combined. Until recently the Arab world existed in a largely nomadic, peasant society and had no recourse or access to a literary, philosophical or scientific history. Their sole education then, and largely still now, came from the *Koran* and the *Hadith*. [14] Rigid adherence to the religious past may be a balm for the faithful but is an albatross for innovation and adaptation to modernity.

The region's recent investment is higher education promises optimism in the knowledge economy. More than a dozen American and two Australian universities have centers in Doha, Qatar. Dubai in the United Arab Emirates houses 32 branches of foreign universities. Saudi Arabia's King Abdullah University of Science and Technology opened in late 2009 with a royal investment of $20 billion.

The challenge of Islam is to permit civic discourse that might question the more extremist and radical tendencies. In many countries, however, this could erupt into riots and civil discord. Intellectuals, where they exist at all, are trapped within state tyranny and public ignorance. Novels are banned, books condemned by religious zealots, and the government, currying the favor of such organizations, connives in the condemnation leading to a sterility of discourse. Arab TV stations are generally not kind to western views. Ironically, access to universal communication channels has democratized Islam and permitted all viewers and listeners to compete for various interpretations of Islamic ideas, even those challenging home governments. This does not mean, however, that there will automatically be more liberal interpretations of the Islamic message, as the radicals have active bloggers and are skilled at tapping into anger and resentment.

For example, the following is the main educational objectives of Saudi Arabia according to data from UNESCO.

> The general goals of education in the Kingdom of Saudi Arabia are: to have students understand Islam . . . to plant and spread the Islamic creed; to provide the students with the values, teachings and ideals of Islam; to equip them with various skills and knowledge; to develop their conduct in constructive directions; to develop the society economically and culturally; and to prepare the individual to be a useful member in the building of his/her community. [15]

The stated essential educational goals are religious and not academic and the other ambiguous values have no specific scholastic attainment levels such as reading or cognitive proficiencies, or scientific or historical literacy.

PISA (Program for International Student Assessment) reports on science literacy among fifteen year-olds in 57 educational jurisdictions. The average U.S. science literacy PISA score in 2008 was at 489 below the international average of 500. Finland had the highest score at 563. Several Islamic countries scored significantly lower on these science tests as the Table shows. The average score for participating Islamic countries in the PISA project is 382, far below average. As educational performance is directly related to future economic progress, low achieving science scores does not portend economically well for many Islamic countries. [16]

---

**PISA SCIENCE LITERACY SCORES**
**FOR FIFTEEN YEAR-OLD STUDENTS**
**IN PARTICIPATING ISLAMIC COUNTRIES**
**(AVERAGE SCORE FOR 30 COUNTRIES = 500)**

| | | | |
|---|---|---|---|
| Turkey | 424 | Jordan | 422 |
| Indonesia | 393 | Tunisia | 386 |
| Azerbaijan | 382 | Qatar | 349 |
| Kyrgyz Republic | 322 | | |

Source: U.S. Department of Education, 2008, NCES

---

These results from international tests correlate directly on human capital and the effects of education, individual earnings, and the general economy. Education is a part of the global economic competition and the Arab and Islamic states are lagging behind. Saudi Arabia's compulsory schooling is only six years. Women are routinely denied the rights men have. The widespread increase in levels of poverty and decreases in schooling achievement has led to further disempowerment of women.

A World Bank study placed the economic dislocation of the Middle East in stark perspective. These combined countries, except for Israel and Turkey, exported fewer manufactured goods than Finland with five million people. Half of Saudi Arabia's population is under twenty years of age and unemployment for the 20–24 year olds is approaching 50%. The Saudi government is deeply in debt. At its current rate of spending it will be insolvent when the oil reserves run dry.

Arab countries have the highest rates for illiteracy and the lowest number of research scientists. There are over 200 universities in Arab countries. But a series of annual China studies of the best 500 universities in the world has not included any from the Arab world. None of the arguments about American imperialism can be attributed to this economic and social retardation. Nevertheless, knowing more about the West through advanced communications has made some citizens of Islamic countries more aware of their economic deprivations and more resentful of the West. The defeat of Arab armies in 1967 and 1973, and Islamic powers in the first Gulf War against Iraq in 1990-1991, and the Iraq war in 2003, revived the humiliation and anger toward America and gave rise to the likes of Osama bin Laden and his recruits. Directing the anger of the people to an external enemy, instead of the autocracy at home as the Arab Spring did in 2011, is a political tactic that seems to retain the power model of most Arab countries while providing new recruits for the fight against the West.

With the exception of oil, the Middle East is marginal to the world's economy. Its impact culturally, however, is now beyond prediction, even though it offers few intellectual challenges to command respect. The combined Gross National Product of the Organization of Islamic Conference states is roughly that of France. Looked at another way, and absent oil, the GNP of all twenty-two Arab countries is equivalent to the GNP of Spain, and less than one-half of Italy.

Oil has helped the Arab world rise above subsistence economies. Saudi Arabia was a self-contained trading zone and the settlements along the Persian Gulf states were all fishing and pearl diving villages until the middle of the 20th century. The educational, economic, creative, social and political differences between the West and Islamic countries are transparent. Disaffected Muslims look for someone to blame for present failures and future insecurities and to enlist in a campaign, an army like al-Qaeda or a neighborhood terrorist cell, to vent frustrations and to channel aggressions.

It is easy to blame the West for a variety of evils based on ignorance, the rambling sermons of clerics, and rumors and innuendos—the verbal lifeblood of the Middle East. This obviates the need to castigate autocracies for the lack of innovation and civilized progress. The imposition of religious rule in Iran under the Ayatollah Khomeini in 1979 did not create a new fundamentalism. It revived an ancient political system the West rejected centuries earlier—theocracy.

Impressionable youth, and a few middle-aged men and woman, receive healthy doses of anti-American and anti-Semitic sentiments and the monstrous brutality of the West against Muslims. In a behavioral sense, they are brainwashed, as they receive no education in critical thinking skills. There are bookshelves in *madrassas* but no books except the Koran.

Trainers cynically bombard zealous minds with repeatable slogans and packaged ideas until they all sound mantra-like in their denunciations.

It is estimated that roughly 100,000 were trained with Osama bin Laden, with help from Pakistan military intelligence services, when he had camps in Afghanistan beginning in 1989. Most of them are more than likely still active, hired killers playacting murder in the name of venomous religious ideas.

In conclusion, the introduction of widespread technological change, combined with political independence, freedom of movement, and the expansion of human freedoms has caused widespread social disruptions in Islamic communities. Islam has a broad-based appeal to young Muslims that cuts across racial and ethnic barriers. But Islamic fundamentalist core believers who find absolute reliance on religious beliefs as the single source of intellectual discovery will not advance the cause in promoting increasingly essential educational achievement goals for Muslim youth.

Is there a difference between a radicalized young man who chooses to die commandeering an airplane packed with innocent people into a building killing thousands from a person who walks into a hotel restaurant on a religious holiday and blows herself up killing scores of unaware diners? Martyrdom is neither a euphemism nor an excuse for terrorism. Ahmed Kiftaro, the Mufti or chief cleric of Damascus defends suicide bombers as the only available means of opposing Zionist weapons.

Suicide bombers intent on killing wantonly and randomly are not freedom fighters, soldiers or martyrs as they claim, but terrorists. The difference is not merely in the meaning of the words but in the nature of the behavior. The cult of indifference of life is now solidly embedded in the mentality of the radicalized young who are glorified and honored for this ignoble distinction. States funding the families of these martyrs with stipends for the death deeds are reimbursing contract murderers.

A movement that kills in the name of God has begun a nihilistic course that refutes all basic religious values. It is a political system that rewards death for religious purposes, that has failed to fulfill the economic needs of its people and fed its resentment, and is morally bankrupt. How do you combat an army that marches to the revelation of a God and Prophet that calls for your annihilation? Besides brute military force, how do you dialogue with an enemy sworn to your destruction and your way of life because it does not conform to its view of faith? Is it possible to confront a Muslim enemy—as terrorist, insurgent, militant or radical fanatic—without also confronting the insidiousness and violence inherent in Islam? This is not just a philosophical puzzle. It is the 21st century's most disturbing and exasperating predicament.

So having studied the inculcation of militant behavior it's time to ask how such individuals develop such a perspective. The next chapter describes multiple instances of planned but not always executed Islamic terrorism.

# CHAPTER FOUR
# ISLAMIC AVENGERS

For Hades holds men mightily to a strict
Accounting down below the earth;
He sees all things, inscribes them
Within the book
Of his remembering.  (Aeschylus, *Eumenides*, 314-18)

What prompts a young man with education credentials and/or skills that would allow him to have a productive career to turn to *jihad* and plan to kill innocent civilians? Apart from obvious psychotic tendencies, the single most overriding constant among these murderous plotters is that they are Muslim, and that they have become radicalized in the militancy of that specific religion that encourages them to kill those who are not Muslim.

The number of jihadists captured, a few of which I describe in this chapter, demonstrates the extensiveness and intensity of imbibed militancy, and also the success of police and Homeland Security prevention tactics. The series of planned terror attacks by individual and cell groups targeting civilians is horrendous and the motivation for such atrocities is not that difficult to detect. [1] This chapter synopsizings some of them.

Sami Osmakac from Kosovo was arrested in Florida in January 2012 for planning to bomb nightclubs, destroying bridges and shooting police officers in and around the Tampa area. He made a video of himself with an AK-47 and a handgun, typically of those who record their impending misdeeds.

Rezwan Ferdaus, 26, of Ashland, Massachusetts, an American citizen, was arrested in September 2011 and charged with plotting to blow up the Pentagon and the U.S. Capitol building using three remote-controlled drones filled with explosives. Rezwan, who has a physics degree from Northeastern University in Boston, planned to commit "violent jihad" against the United States. He also attempted to provide detonators, explosives, and other logistics help to al-Qaeda in Afghanistan.

Just these two terrorists illustrate that in America the threat of Islamic militancy is real and ongoing.

## Islamic Avenging Recruits

A Muslim has no country except that part of the earth where the *Shari'ah* of God is established . . . a Muslim has no nationality except his belief which makes him a member of the Muslim community in *Dar-ul-Islam*; a Muslim has no relatives except those who share the belief in God . . . [2]

Recruiting young men and women to become fighters or suicide bombers is only part of the indoctrinated military effort. The motivation to join the struggle against the West is not patriotism or nationality but following the kind of ideology Qutb wrote in the 1960s that has fueled Islamic fervor. Those who buy into his vision of total devotion and submission, like Hamas, al–Qaeda or the Taliban, are hooked into the message that leads to murderous militancy.

Take the case of Ahmed Omar Abu Ali. He was born in Houston in 1981 of parents who were naturalized citizens from Jordan. He grew up in Falls Church, Virginia, and was valedictorian of his Islamic school. He went to college in Saudi Arabia and in 2002 joined an al-Qaeda cell based in Medina. With others he discussed numerous possible terrorists attacks in the United States after establishing a sleeper cell, and even a scheme to assassinate President George W. Bush. He was arrested by Saudi officials in 2003 and jailed for 20 months and confessed. He was extradited to the U.S. and convicted by a federal court in 2005 of conspiracy and attempted presidential assassination with evidence supplied mostly by Saudi intelligence. In June 2008 a federal appeals court upheld his conviction.

We may never know nor understand the actual reasons for Ahmed Omar Abu Ali's turn to violence on behalf of his faith. But despite the potential illegalities of foreign rendition, or using foreign governments to keep possible terrorists in prison, the threat of self-classified Islamic soldiers is persistent. We may think that their devotion and dedication to their faith are misguided, but violent tendencies, some untrained and untamed, are unquestionably, according to them, divinely inspired.

Daniel Boyd, 39, a convert to Islam, a former American soldier and son a Marine, received training from Islamic radicals in Pakistan. He lived as the father of a typical family in America with a wife, Sabrina, and five children. Two older sons joined him in a terrorist cell. They lived in rural Willow Springs, North Carolina about 20 miles south of Raleigh. Boyd and his two sons, Zakariya, 20, and Dylan, 22, were among seven men—except for one, all American citizens—indicted with supporting a *jihad* movement in foreign countries including Israel, Jordan, Pakistan and Kosovo. The group had stockpiled automatic weapons, had practiced military tactics in the summer of 2009, and had plans to engage in a suicide attack.

Abu Khalid Abdul-Latif imagined killing military recruits at a processing station south of Seattle, and practiced using his M16 rifle in an abandoned warehouse with his co-conspirator Walli Mujahidh. They wanted to be sure that the weapons fired automatically. The hand grenades would help maim more potential military recruits. As they prepared to leave the warehouse after firing a few rounds, FBI and law enforcement agents arrested them. Plans to attack a military installation had been underway for some time but the plot was revealed when the man who sold them the weapons reported it to the Seattle Police Department. Alert civilian vigilance helped lead to another potential deadly attack on military personnel on U.S. soil. [3]

On Wednesday night, May 20, 2009, four ex-convicts were arrested in Newburgh New York for conspiring to bomb two Jewish synagogues with C-4 explosives and of planning to fire a surface-to-air missile to shoot down military aircraft. James Cromite, 44—with a record of 27 previous arrests, about half of them for drug offenses—Onta Williams, 32, David Williams IV, 28, (no relation), and Laguerre Payen, 28, all converts to Islam while in prison, were arraigned on terrorism charges. It is easy to ascribe the profiles of these confused young men—except for Cromite, the eldest and the leader—as in need of professional therapy. But the plot they hatched is too chilling and outrageously violent and perverse.

Jamal Ahmidan, a Moroccan fugitive living in Spain, with his brother and cousin, ran a small business that he combined with dope peddling. He murdered his accomplice in an armed robbery. He spent time nearly three years in a Moroccan prison, but was deported in 1993 and found his way to Spain when he continued to deal drugs. When Spanish police surrounded the apartment building on April 3, 2004, where Jamal, the second-in-command leader of the Madrid bombings (March 11, 2004), and six of his co-conspirators stayed, the terrorists greeted them with machine gun fire. As police blew off the lock and threw tear gas into the apartment, Jamal and his fellow terrorists detonated 20 kilograms of explosives. A Spanish anti-terrorism officer, Francisco Javier Torronteras, was killed together with all terrorists. Later, the buried body of Officer Torronteras was excavated, mutilated and burned.

Suspected terrorists might have had legitimate grievances, or have experienced discrimination and injustices, or harbored resentments. But unquestionably they felt called by Allah to renew their faith and eliminate un-believers, or, at a minimum, they lost faith in their own community's response to secularism. They probably felt as if the western countries where they lived would never accept them as authentic citizens so they decided to join a group they knew would accept them willingly as soldiers.

Elite warriors in democratic militaries are more thoroughly recruited and trained. The best recruits for the Navy Seals, the Green Berets, the Israeli commandos and other special operation units in national militaries, are selected for superior athletic abilities and special biological genetic advantages. They are tested in unusual physical conditions, like extreme cold, freezing water, and torrid heat, and exposed to environmental conditions normal humans do not easily endure. Most men do not function well under extreme bodily stress like high temperatures, loss of bodily fluids, or heavy weights simulating the carrying of special equipment. They have to perform with speed and accuracy in defending against an enemy and in hand-to-hand combat. They must be mentally tough to survive extreme conditions and then perform tasks accurately, like quickly assembling a gun and then shooting the potential enemy with a paint bullet, all after a long exposure to freezing water.

Islamic militants, on the other hand, are motivated by selected passages from the Koran, and are usually told they will be killed in whatever operation they undertake, so they do not need to learn to survive. Militant videos, CDs, and especially tapes of beheadings, Internet websites, and access to manuals are the reinforcement tools of hatred for potential and active recruits.

## Allah's Avengers

Najibullah Zazi, 26, is another example. First comes the lie. "Why," the suspect says, "are you investigating me as a possible al-Qaeda affiliate? I am only a shuttle bus driver trying to see friends in New York from my home in Denver." When explosives-making notes, evidence of the purchase of bomb-making ingredients, cell phones, backpacks and other troubling materials were discovered in four residences of his Afghani friends in

Flushing, Queens in New York during a raid in September 2009, counterterrorism officials begin intense questioning of several suspects.

Officials discovered that Zazi had had explosives training in a camp outside Peshawar in Pakistan in contact with al-Qaeda operatives, although initially he denied this. Zazi bought acetone, hydrochloric acid, and hydrogen peroxide—the signature bombing ingredients of al-Qaeda operatives, and the same ingredients used in the London subway bombings in 2006 that killed 52. The proper combination of these chemicals can be used to manufacture triacetone triperoxide, commonly referred to as TATP. It is relatively easy to make but unstable. In order not have explosive residue found in his apartment, Zazi rented a hotel room in Denver to experiment with his home-cooked explosive ingredients. Agents trained in forensics found acetone residue above the stove. As evidence accumulated of a terrorist attack, Zazi was arrested in Denver, charged with preparing explosives to detonate bombs, and transferred to Brooklyn for trial.

Zazi was a perfect recruit for al-Qaeda. He was born in eastern Afghanistan but raised from childhood in Queens. He spoke English and was an American citizen living in New York. He spent five months from August 2008 to January 2009 in Peshawar, Pakistan ostensibly to visit his wife but where he also received training in weapons and explosives in a military camp. In March 2009 he ran up over $50,000 in credit card debt and declared bankruptcy.

In February 2010 he pleaded guilty to terrorism charges in a federal court to a plot to explode homemade bombs in the New York subway system in a suicide attack so he could achieve martyrdom.

Also arrested was Imam Ahmad Wais Afzali, 38, a police informant who had originally cooperated with FBI officials but apparently alerted Zazi to surveillance and then repeatedly lied to authorities about conversations he had with Zazi. Afzali, born in Afghanistan of a wealthy family, who came to the U.S. as a boy and became an imam in Queens, was convicted and ordered to leave the country. Zarein Ahmedzay, 25, also an Afghani native who attended high school with Zazi, was arrested and charged as an accomplice in the New York suicide subway bombings. According to authorities, the group was urged to carry out these attacks by two senior al-Qaeda leaders in the tribal areas of Pakistan who were later killed in drone attacks.

Within days, additional plots surfaced. A 19-year-od Jordanian national in the U.S. illegally, Hosam Smadi, attempted to bomb a Dallas skyscraper, the 60-story Fountain Place. Michael Finton, 29, a convert to Islam while in prison from 2001 to 2006 for aggravated robbery, was arrested in Springfield, Illinois accused to trying to detonate a bomb at a federal courthouse. Federal agents, long monitoring him, had neutralized the bomb.

Adis Medunjanin, 25, a confederate of Zazi (they attended high school together), a Bosnian-born naturalized citizen who had received military al-Qaeda training with him in Pakistan, was arrested in Queens after crashing and fleeing his vehicle. He was indicted a few weeks after Zazi of conspiring to commit murder in a foreign country. Zarein Ahmedzay, 24, another plotter, a Manhattan taxi driver, was charged with lying to federal investigators.

Betim Kazui, 21, from Brooklyn, was arrested in Kosovo with attempting to make war on American overseas military personnel and conspiracy to commit murder and providing support to terrorists. Betim,whose family was originally from Kosovo, may be a typical young male recruit to Islamic militancy. As a boy he was not particularly religious and played football in high school before dropping out. He later finished his high school equivalency degree and then became more interested in the Koran and grew increasingly religious. He decided to go to Egypt to learn Arabic but while there tried to contact al-Qaeda members and to buy weapons, but really wanted to go to Pakistan for military training. He journeyed to Kosovo the ancestral family home, bought weapons there, and was arrested by officials on suspicion of terrorist activities and turned over to U.S. authorities.

Patterns emerge about these American suspects. First, they move to small towns but near the symbolic buildings they plan to destroy—federal buildings or military installations, or skyscrapers with hundreds of workers. They try to fit in to the local communities where they live, drinking beer, dancing, helping neighbors, while also practicing prayer, fasting and rituals privately. To confederates or confidantes they express their anger with American customs and their willingness to kill as many people as possible to dispel or fulfill their hatred. Neighbors or even family members are always shocked when they hear the news of "nice young men" arrested in such horrific schemes.

John Walker Lindh and David Hicks were Muslim converts who traveled to Afghanistan to fight for the Taliban and were captured in 2001. Lindh was tried in a federal court and sentenced to 20 years in prison. The Australian Hicks was classified as an enemy combatant and the military court sentenced him to seven years in prison. He is now free in Australia. From 2001 to 2008 the Administration obtained 309 convictions in terrorism cases in federal courts, with an average of 16 years in sentences. The Americans Jose Padilla, the shoe bomber, and Ali Saleh al-Marri, an al-Qaeda sleeper agent, were apprehended under military law but transferred to federal courts and are serving sentences in federal prisons.

The federal courts have been more effective in convictions than military tribunals and are more appropriate, giving out more convictions and longer sentences, for terrorists who plot terrorism against Americans in America. Military tribunals are more appropriate for those caught on the battlefield.

Yet despite Islamic governments and educational programs that foster nothing but Muslim ideology, even those Muslims who have lived in the West can be induced to engage in terrorist activities such as those in London, Holland, Germany, Russia, Spain or the U.S. For example, four British men of Pakistani descent bombed the London subway and a bus on July 7, 2005 killing 56 and wounding at least 700, the worst terrorist attack in British history.

On December 22, 2008, a federal jury convicted five Muslims (three brothers, Shain, Eljvir, and Dritan Duka, and Mohamad Shnewer and Serdar Tatar) in their mid-twenties of conspiring in 2007 to kill American soldiers at Fort Dix in New Jersey. They were all Muslim immigrants who lived in south Jersey near Philadelphia and had armed and trained themselves in weapons to attack the base and military personnel there. [4] They had illegally purchased several machine guns for $1,400. The three Duka brothers, who were ethnic Albanians, were in the U.S. illegally. One defendant had videos on his computer that showed clips of dead U.S. soldiers and victims about to be beheaded. Recordings of them showed them regularly talking about al-Qaeda inspired videos and practicing shooting assault weapons.

American citizen Ehsanul Islam Sadequee, 23, was convicted on August 12, 2009, of aiding terrorist groups by sending videotapes of American landmarks overseas and plotting *jihad*. He was born in the U.S. a son of Bangladeshi parents. He drove from Georgia to Washington DC in 2005 to film the Pentagon and other potential terrorist targets, mailed videotapes, and then discussed his terrorist plans with other militants in Toronto and Sarajevo who have since been convicted of terrorist activities. His conviction is a good example of international cooperation that resulted in arrests in Copenhagen, London and Toledo.

Others like disaffected American Colleen R. LaRose, 46, a.k.a. "Jihad Jane," apparently acquire militant views online. Unknown to her neighbors this unemployed Pennsylvania woman, who had converted to Islam but revealed no outward signs of her acquired faith, became a terrorist sympathizer and martyrdom volunteer. She traveled to Sweden intending to kill a Swedish artist, Lars Vilks, who had depicted Mohammad's head on top of the body of a dog. She had multiple contacts on *jihad* websites, made no attempt to hide her identity, and solicited funds for her activities. She was arrested in October 2009.

What Islamic recruits have in common is to join a common international identity that transcends nationalism, a passion for a cause that could result in their death, and a consummate belief in violence as a means of defending Islam. It is the same motivation any soldier has except that the compelling incentive is usually nationalism. Unlike conspiracies and groups plotting suicide or death squads, many Islamic extremists are lone-wolf individualists who take it upon themselves to defend Islam and kill infidels. It is not always clear when and if single terrorists may or not be a part of a cell or larger group.

There have been at last two notorious cases of American Muslim soldiers who have committed atrocities against their own fellow soldiers. In 2003 Sgt. Hasan Akbar, 31, of the 101st Airborne Division was convicted of killing two of his fellow soldiers at a camp in Kuwait and wounding 14 others by throwing grenades into his commanding officer's tent and then opening fire on the occupants. The year 2009 was especially troubling as news about terrorists in the U.S. expanded.

I am going to do God's work. (Maj. Nidal Malik Hasan to a neighbor)

Major Nidal Malik Hasan, 39, the premeditated mass killer at Fort Hood, Texas, was apparently a sole avenger. He killed 13 and left 30 wounded on November 5, 2009. We may never know the exact psychological motives for his actions, but his militant religious persuasion was likely the chief motive. He was definitely a loner and had no friends, not even at the mosques he frequented. Investigators found new business cards in his Spartan apartment after the shootings describing himself without his military rank and as "SoA," which was interpreted as meaning "Soldier or Servant of Allah."

Physicians at Walter Reed Hospital in Washington DC supervising his work had problems with his behavior, especially with his aggressive proselytizing of his Muslim faith to patients. His supervisor gave him such a poor evaluation as would have prevented him from working in the private sector as a psychiatrist. He also failed to meet physical fitness requirements. Supervisors explicitly recommended transfer to Ft. Hood where there were wider choices for mental health services.

Hasan received praise from a former imam of his in Falls Church, Virginia after the shootings. Imam Anwar al-Awlaki was an American citizen of Yemeni descent born in New Mexico. He received a Master's degree in Educational Leadership from San Diego State University and served as an imam in San Diego and Virginia. Surveillance officials knew about Hasan's Email communications with al–Awlaki but did not follow-up because no terrorism activities had been discussed. However, al-Awlaki had previously been in contact with other known and arrested Islamic terrorists in the U.S. and knew and counseled three of the 9/11 Muslim hijackers.

Contact with al–Awlaki by anyone should have been enough to initiate a serious inquiry. Hasan was a self-recruited Islamic warrior and, by his actions, a traitor in an American soldier's uniform. Al-Awlaki left the U.S. in 2002 and went to Yemen, his ancestral home. The Obama Administration placed on its capture or kill list in 2010 and he was killed in a drone strike in 2011.

Here is what al–Awlaki said on his blog about Maj. Hasan's killing spree:

> Nidal Hassan [sic] is a hero. He is a man of conscience who could not bear the contradiction of being a Muslim and fighting against his own people. No scholar with a grain of Islamic knowledge can deny the clear-cut proofs that Muslims today have the right—rather the duty—to fight against American tyranny.

Within days, al-Awlaki's website went blank, he went to ground in Yemen and off everyone's radar. He has released videos saying that suicide bombers do not have to distinguish between military and civilian targets.

The army had all the troubled signs of a bureaucratic breakdown. Nidal's erratic behavior, questionable temperament, poor academic record, weak service record, fascination with Islamic militancy, preaching about Islam, and criticism against the war were noted in his file. Nevertheless he was rewarded with satisfactory reviews, promoted, kicked up the career ladder and forwarded to another post to become someone else's problem. Without knowing the motives of his military supervisors we can safely assume that even outside fields of combat the army cannot seem to detect a potential enemy in its midst, and hide incompetence even of its officer corps under the cover of political correctness and departmental denial.

A similar self-recruited intended suicide bomber was Umar Farouk Abdul-Mutallab, 23, son of a prominent Nigerian banker and engineering graduate of University College in London, one of the top five universities in the world, who attempted to detonate an explosive device on a flight destined for Detroit on Christmas Day, 2009. He flew from Ghana to Lagos, Nigeria, then to Amsterdam and on to Detroit. The highly explosive material, pentaerythritol (PETN) was taped to his thigh and he was to ignite it with a syringe filled with the detonating liquid. PETN is the same material Richard Reid used to try to ignite his shoe. Umar's father had reported him missing and alerted authorities to his extremist views, and he was added to the 550,000 on the Terrorist Identities Datamart Environment (TIDE), but not to the 400,000 on the Terrorist Screening Data Base (TSDB), or the 14,000 selectees for mandatory secondary screening, or to the 4,000 on the no-fly list. The protective layers for airline flight failed in Umar's case.

Like Umar, Abdulhakim Mujahid Muhammad, 25, (a.k.a. Carlos Bledsoe) disappointed his father when he turned to radical Islam. Abdulkakim fired a semiautomatic rifle on an Army/Navy Career Center in Little Rock, Arkansas in May 2009 killing one soldier and wounding another. Like other American youth he grew up as a normal, happy kid playing basketball and was raised as a Baptist.

Abdulhakim became religiously observant as a student at Tennessee State College, journeyed to Yemen to learn Arabic, married a Yemeni woman, taught English in the port city of Aden, and was imprisoned in Yemen in 2008 for overstaying his visa. Yemeni police found in his possession fake Somali identification papers. FBI agents interrogated him but did not think him a threat. Yemen deported him in January 2009. In May 2009 he shot soldiers less than three miles from where he lived.

Here are more examples of terrorists in the U.S. A federal judge convicted Syed Ahmed, 24, a former student at Georgia Tech, on June 10, 2009 of conspiracy to provide material support to terrorists. He was born in Pakistan but raised as a U.S. citizen near Atlanta. He took photos of landmarks in Washington DC, including fuel tanks, that he forwarded to terrorist recruiters in Iraq and Pakistan. He traveled to Pakistan in July 2005 as part of a plan to train with *Lashkar-e-Taiba*, a known terrorist group.

Mir Aimal Kansi, a Pakistani immigrant to the U.S. who on January 25, 1993 shot several CIA employees in their cars on their way to work at CIA headquarters in Langley, Virginia while they waiting at a stoplight. Kansi fired an AK-47 at these CIA commuters. He killed Lansing Bennett, 66, an intelligence analyst and physician, and Frank Darling, 28, a communications officer in the operations branch. Three others were wounded. Several hours later Kansi went to Mohammad Yousaf's grocery store in Herndon, Virginia, where he often shopped, and asked for a plane ticket to Pakistan, probably through the Hawala money transfer system. The following evening Kansi was a flight to Pakistan about the time authorities were distributing sketches of his features drawn from eyewitness accounts.

In the weeks preceding this attack Kansi had purchased ammunition, an assault rifle, handguns and a bulletproof vest. He had originally wanted to attack the Israeli Embassy in Washington DC but it was risky for a single attacker and he didn't know how to manufacture a bomb.

Kansi's father, Malik Abdullah Jan Kansi, was a Pastun tribal leader in Baluchistan and a relatively wealthy man who, besides Kansi, had four sons and three daughters. The family had a home in Quetta where Kansi grew up. It was widely rumored that Kansi's father and possibly Kansi himself and some of his siblings were involved in running guns for the CIA during the Soviet occupation of Afghanistan. Kansi attended St. Francis grammar school in Quetta, earned a bachelor's degree from a college in Quetta, and a Master's in English Literature from the University of Baluchistan. He enjoyed Shakespeare and Milton, according to Jessica Stern who interviewed him while in prison, and as recorded in her book *Terror in the Name of God.*

Kansi had met with militant groups in Afghanistan and Pakistan but never joined them. Friends and colleagues in Virginia, where he lived and worked in the Pakistani immigrant community, reported that he was socially inept. Kansi hid out in Afghanistan for four years, was on the FBI's ten most wanted list, and had a $3 million bounty on his head. He was lured to Pakistan where he was captured and immediately extradited to the U.S., contrary to Pakistani law. A large bribe was paid to a lower level ISI official to reveal where he was hiding and then he was followed.

Kansi's revenge and retaliation was personal. His motive may have been a kind of tribal revenge, a common impulse among the Pashtuns. More likely it was vengeance for American wrongs done to Muslims. Kansi was executed by lethal injection in a Virginia state prison on November 14, 2002.

Although some terrorists do not operate individually, many plot their nefarious activities in small groups. Tarek Mehanna, 27, an American citizen and pharmacist, was arrested in Boston with two other co-conspirators in October 2009 for plotting to kill politicians and U.S. soldiers and randomly kill people in a mall. He and his associates had traveled to Iraq, Pakistan and Syria seeking training in terrorist camps, but for unknown reasons they were turned down. (Ahmad Abousamra, one of his co-conspirators, escaped to Syria in 2006).

That same week, three Ohio men were convicted of plotting to recruit and train other terrorists to kill American soldiers in Iraq. Mohammad Amaawi, 29, received a 20-year sentence; Marwan El-Hindi, 46, the apparent leader, received a 12-year sentence; and Wassim Mazloum, 27, was sentenced to 8 years in federal prison.

Luqman Ameen Abdullah, 53, an imam, was sought and killed in a raid by federal officers who tried to arrest him at a Detroit warehouse in October 2009. He was to be charged with conspiracy to sell stolen goods and the illegal possession and sale of firearms along with ten others. He advocated violent acts against the U.S. and secession to establish an independent Islamic state.

David Headley, a.k.a. Daood Gilani, 49, was born in Washington DC of a Pakistani diplomat father and American mother but was raised as a devout Muslim in Pakistan until he was 17. Unusually, he had one blue eye and one brown eye. He lived a double life in Philadelphia with his mother where he enjoyed life as a U.S. citizen and helped his mother in the bar she owned known as the Khyber Pass. He failed to manage it properly and she was forced to sell. Ultimately, he gravitated toward an extremist Islamic cause. He flew regularly to Pakistan and in 2002 spent three weeks in basic jihad training with *Lashkar-e-Taibi* a known terrorist group, a proxy terrorist organization of Pakistan's military intelligence service, the ISI.

He was a conspirator in a plot to bomb the Danish newspaper offices of

*Jyllands-Posten* that originally published the satirical cartoons of Mohammad in 2005. Headley had hoped to enter a synagogue in Denmark to learn about and get close the Danish cartoonist, Kurt Westergaard, he thought was a Jew.

In 1988 he was arrested for smuggling heroin into the U.S. and because of his cooperation was given only two years in prison and was sent undercover in Pakistan to work for the Drug Enforcement Administration. His lack of business acumen and his unstable social life, combined with his criminal activity and devotion to Islam combined to attract him to terrorism. He was subsequently indicted for conspiring to aid in the bomb plot in Mumbai in 2008. He was arrested in Chicago airport in October 2009 as he was about to leave for Pakistan.

He was captured with two items: a book with the improbable title of "How to Pray Like a Jew," and a yellow notepad. Even terrorists need to take notes lest they forget something in their plots. The code words he used for his activities included "Magic eyes" for surveillance cameras. "Mixed fruit dish" meant whether an attack would include bombs and gunfire. "Making investments" stood for planning an attack. "Gotten married" meant a terrorist was killed.

In court testimony in New York he spoke in haltering English for days about his terrorist exploits in a trial of Tahawwur Hussain Rana, his businessman accomplice from Chicago accused in supporting the Mumbai attacks that killed 166 in 2008.

The diversity of planned attacks could be a measure of al-Qaeda's strategy of smaller scale attacks, less likely of detection, rather than larger ones that involve too many co-conspirators that might be more easily disrupted. Although estimates vary, according to a Pew survey in 2007 there were 2.35 million Muslim Americans of whom about 35% were African American. Islam attracts many African Americans who say they are attracted to its tenets of equality, discipline and family values.

Individuals with special talents are either selected or volunteer for al-Qaeda. A federal judge denied bail to Sabirhan Hasanoff, a combined American and Australian citizen, in Manhattan in May 2010 and a fellow co-conspirator, Wesam El-Hanafi. Both were arrested in Dubai and deported to the U.S. for trial. Hasanoff, who has an accounting degree from Baruch College in New York, had sworn an allegiance to al-Qaeda and conspired to provide money for the organization and special software for encryptions over the Internet.

Finally, Faisal Shahzad became a terrorist notoriety in May 2010 when he left a car running laden with explosives in Times Square in New York City. Faisal became a U.S. citizen in 2009, at a time when he swore to uphold and defend the Constitution and laws of the United States. He attended the University of Bridgeport in Connecticut, had an M.B.A degree, a respectable accounting job at Elizabeth Arden, a suburban home, an American wife, Huma Mian, and two small children. But the attributes we commonly associate with good citizenship do not apply to radicalized Muslims whose single new mission in life is to become a good Muslim and eliminate non-believers. He went to Waziristan in Pakistan in late 2009 to receive bomb training. Muslim Men go to Pakistan for two reasons: to obtain a wife or receive terrorist training.

But the question remains of how to identity potential terrorists, some of whom may be naturalized American citizens. The obvious factors of owning a home, being married and having children, having advanced degrees, holding good jobs and other characteristics do not necessarily apply. The one outstanding and common factor is that they are Muslim. The violence within Islam is the only reason they seek to kill non-Muslim infidels and to cherish that religious role.

Islamic Calligraphy

# CHAPTER FIVE
# THE PSYCHOLOGY
# OF SUICIDE BOMBERS

Japanese samurai warriors who died for honor achieved the ultimate revenge over enemies. Samurai evolved around the 8th century and lasted until the collapse of the Japanese empire beginning in 1868. A samurai's fighting spirit and death brought heightened family honor. Its discipline was based on regal and clan loyalty, as ritual suicide avoided humiliation. Failure brought shame, unlike the mercenary ninjas who were just common assassins.

During World War II Japanese samurai warriors, mostly pilots in the Imperial Navy, dedicated themselves to suicide missions by flying their aircraft directly into American ships when they ran out of artillery or were short on fuel. Their hara-kiri motivation was monarchical nationalism, unwavering commitment to the Showa Emperor, Hirohito (1901–1989), or the "Heavenly Sovereign," Japan's longest reigning emperor.

By the late 1930 militarists had seized control of Japan's government and Hirohito was unwilling or unable to stop or confront invasions into Manchuria or China, fearing a coup or another assassination attempt on his life. The general consensus is that he did nothing to stop the attacks in Asia or on the United States, though he did urge restraint that the military systematically ignored. Only the dropping of atomic bombs on Hiroshima and Nagasaki in August 1945 brought the emperor and the Japanese to concede defeat. General Douglas MacArthur forced him to renounce his divine status in 1946.

So strong was American antipathy toward the world's death merchants and dictators that I remember vividly my grade school art projects consisted mostly of drawing caricatures of Hitler, Mussolini and Hirohito and having U.S war planes bomb them. But during the war in Asia from 1941-45 Japanese suicide dive bombers and soldiers willingly gave their lives for an emperor who represented a divinity on earth and a just national military cause, a blend of Shinto fatalism and Japanese national identity.

There is an eerie similarity between this ancient Japanese warrior death wish with their collective cult of *seppuku*, and Muslim suicide bombers. The willingness to die for a believable militant cause in this generation is now an integral part of Islam's identity. Yet willingly giving up one's life in suicide missions is neither a Japanese or Arab stigma. It is an exhibition of high devotion in a human tragedy.

In this chapter I explore the psychological dimension of this death wish belief system and its implications for Muslim extremists. Sometimes it involves the very young who have been impressionably induced into killing themselves.

Rania, a fifteen-year old girl with chubby cheeks and the baby fat of a young girl, was arrested in August 2008 in Baqouba, Iraq, as she was about to detonate herself. She had a vest around her chest packed with explosives. An alert policeman found her suspicious. He chained her to the bars of a window, stripped off her dress, and deactivated the bomb. Under interrogation the following day Rania seemed dazed and she spoke about those who had forced her to wear the vest and had apparently drugged her, principally her husband whom police believe was a member of al-Qaeda, and her mother. She said she didn't believe the wired vest was a bomb.

Rania was in the same prison cell with Baida, one of sixteen would-be female suicide bombers who were arrested by police in Diyala province in northern Iraq. About the same number of female suicide bombers had already blown themselves to pieces. Baida knew she was on a suicide mission; Rania said she didn't know. Rania was sentenced to seven and a half years in prison. She said to a *New York Times* reporter who interviewed her, " As a foreigner, it is halal (good) to kill you." [1]

Female terrorists do not differ significantly from their male counterparts. They are motivated by trauma, revenge, nationalism, community outrage and negative feelings. [2] Of the forty Chechen Muslim terrorists who took over the Dubrovka Theater in Moscow in October 2002, nineteen were women who had bombs strapped to their bellies. They were said to be motivated to act in revenge for the death of husbands, brothers, fathers and sons.

Like Rania and Baida, Hanadi Jaradat, 29, from Jenin in Palestine's West Bank, the oldest of nine children, was perfectly calm as she arrived on October 4, 2003 at Maxim's, a cosmopolitan Haifa restaurant at the end of a jetty facing the Mediterranean. Her taxi driver, a young Israeli Arab who spoke fluent English, had driven her to Maxim's, owned in partnership by an Arab and a Jew, a cooperation that expresses the deep level of business partnership between many secular Arabs and Jews in Israel. Many Arabs were a part of Maxim's staff.

Hanadi came from a respected Palestinian family and had studied law in Jerash in Jordan. But like most Palestinian women she was stuck in her enclosed environment in a society where she was not accepted as equal to men. Her brother and fiancé had been members of *Islamic Jihad* both of whom the Israelis had shot on June 12, 2003 in a targeted killing aimed at eradicating extremists.

When the taxi driver excused himself to leave, Hanadi walked over to two Jewish families, three generations, eating Shabbat dinner and pulled the pin on her suicide vest killing herself and twenty-one people, including several children, and wounding about fifty others. The Palestinian Authority's Ministry of Culture released a "Book of the Month" poetry collection on August 22, 2005 glorifying Hanadi's suicide terrorist death in a special edition of its publication *Al-Ayyam*. Here is one example:

> Oh Hanadi! Shake the earth under the feet of the enemies! Blow it up! It is
> the wedding of Hanadi the day when death as a Martyr for Allah becomes
> the highest goal that liberates my land.
> (http://www.pmw.org.il/murder.htm.)

In January 2004, in a courtyard art exhibition in Stockholm's Museum of National Antiquities called *Snow White and the Madness of Truth* displayed a toy sailboat floating in a pool of blood. On the boat's sail was the smiling portrait of the Palestinian suicide bomber Hanadi Jaradat who had killed 21 people in Haifa just months earlier, but whom the exhibit's sponsors labeled a freedom fighter. The art exhibition was part of a conference on genocide.

Then, in early 2009 Samira Ahmed Jassim al-Azzawi, 51, mother of five, code name: "The Mother of Believers," was arrested in Iraq for recruiting 80 female suicide bombers, although she confessed to only recruiting 28. Once she had convinced them to become suicide bombers she led them to a farm where they were trained for their targets, often police stations. Her arrest was a peek into the wave of female suicide bombing that occurred throughout Iraq. Insurgents preyed on disturbed and fragile women, according to al-Azzawi, to help in the cause, many suffering from severe emotional or psychological problems or abuse. She did not discuss what led her to become a recruiter.

On April 23, 2009 a crowd of women and children had gathered in Baghdad's central Karada district to receive emergency food aid. Most of the crowd had been displaced by the war. A woman wearing a black *abaya* and holding the hand of a small girl about five years old, tugging her along, began to nudge her way to the center of the crowd waiting to receive bags of flour, bottles of cooking oil and other food staples. When she reached the center of the crowd she set off her explosive device instantly killing twenty-eight people and twelve police officers, and it was unclear how many were children. Fifty more were wounded.

By the end of July 2009, a least 60 women had carried out suicide bombings in Iraq. The rationale that women become suicide bombers because of mental illness, frustration with their status in Islam, or other psychological factors is speculative. Some were old, some young, some believers, some just criminals.

Moreover, most female suicide bombers are not necessarily Muslim. Many were nurtured in Hindu or Christian families. More than 85% of female suicide bombers since 1981 committed their acts on behalf of secular and not religious organizations. From 1980 to 2003, 76 of 315 global suicide attacks were carried out by the Tamil Tigers in Sri Lanka. Hamas committed 54 and *Islamic Jihad* 27.

These individuals, unlike terrorists who attack hotels or hijack planes, are typically not trained for their actions. They are peripheral figures who join the suicide ranks on an *ad hoc* basis from an identifiable social community like a soccer club. Scholars have studied the nature of suicide attacks of Palestinians in Israel and looked, not at the hierarchical structure of an organization that sponsored and supported attackers, but at horizontal relationships. [3] They examined social networks, tribal affiliations and family groupings and found that suicide bombers came largely from smaller, community groups rather than from groups like Hamas or al-Qaeda. Social networks that are leaderless but have social hubs are more responsible for suicide attacks than are large Islamic organizations. The only real skill needed to be an Islamic suicide bomber is zeal. These women have led oppositional lives based on the hatred of others, including and especially Jews, and their subjugation to men, and so they need a big event like a suicide pact to give meaning to their fragile lives.

Unquestionably, the path to violence can take many routes. Some may be idealists who seek a more meaningful life even if it comes with death.

Others may respond to the camaraderie of bonding with other lost souls and fellow revolutionaries, adventurers, converts, or desperate men.

Websites of *jihad* have various slogans and code words that identify the recruitment and military intent. Here are a few.

> Mujahideen of Islamic Emirate of Afghanistan military operations against the kafirs, munafiqs and the worshippers of Idols.

> Martyrdom Operation kills 15 American invader terrorists in Khost Monday afternoon 08-09-2008, a courageous Mujahideen of the Islamic Emirate of Afghanistan, Abdullah said "Allahu Akbar" and open fire with R.P.G rockets on American invaders . . . in which two tanks were destroyed and fifteen invader terrorists were killed and few were wounded. We ask Allah to accept our brother among martyrs in Eelleyeen (high rank in the paradise). [4]

But whatever benefits potential suicide bombers obtain from the Internet, the Koran provides the ultimate, and most alluring prize: the promise of Islamic paradise. Although we may never know the exact motivation for every suicide bomber it is clear that admittance into Islamic paradise is one of the most powerful incentives because many potential bombers have said so. According to clinical psychologists interviewed for this study, some, like Americans Jamie Paulin-Ramirez and Colleen R. LaRose, both of whom tried to kill Lars Vilks a Danish cartoonist, are prompted by borderline personality disorders.

## The Allure of Paradise

> Why was I born if it wasn't going to be forever?
> (Eugene Ionesco, *Exit the King*)

To understand the motives that propel Islamic suicide bombers we have to turn again to the Koran before we investigate psychological theories. There are scores of passages in the Koran that describe paradise, most of them repetitious and all of them sensual and bodily. There is no sense of a spiritual, non-bodily entity in the Muslim paradise. Rather it is of a world of enticements and pleasures such as can be found in this life. The paradise is an oasis, filled with difficult-to-obtain fruit, beverages including wine, and lots of fine jewelry: gold, silver and pearls. It is instructive to review so many of these passages because they reveal what ultimately motivates Islamic suicide bombers.

> Say: Shall I give you glad tidings of things far better than those? For the righteous are Gardens in nearness to their Lord, with rivers flowing beneath: therein is their eternal home with Companions pure (and holy); and the good pleasure of Allah. (*Sura* 3:15; repeated in 3:136, 4:57, 5:85, 5:119, 20:76, 22:14)

> For them (the Righteous) will be Gardens of Eternity; beneath them rivers will flow; they will be adorned with bracelets of gold, and they will wear

green garments of fine silk and heavy brocade; they will recline therein on raised thrones. How good the recompense! How beautiful a couch to recline on! (*Sura* 18:31, repeated in 76:21)

But for those who believe and work deeds of righteousness—to them We shall give a Home in Heaven—lofty mansions beneath which flow rivers––to dwell therein for ever—an excellent reward for those who do (good). (Sura 29:58)

Verily the Companions of the Garden shall that day have joy in all that they do; they and their associates will be in groves of (cool) shade, reclining on Thrones (of dignity); (Every) fruit (enjoyment) will be there for them; they shall have whatever they call for. (*Sura* 36: 55-57)

You enter the Garden, you and your wives, in (beauty and) rejoicing. To them will be passed around, dishes and goblets of gold: there will be there all that the souls could desire, all that the eyes could delight in: and you shall abide therein (for ever). Such is the Garden of which you are made heirs for your (good) deeds (in life). (*Sura* 43: 70-73)

Mohammad's paradise is presumably real and not an imaginary garden to Muslim believers, like the story of Adam and Eve in *Genesis*, and not a place of transcendental spirituality. There is an abundance of fruit not described, and companions who have big, lustrous eyes. Why just these special companions are offered and no others with different characteristics is not explained. This is not the Philosopher King's spiritual home or residential environment of intense intellectual ferment, or the locale where companions meet to discuss issues about the meaning of life and death and activities to do in the afterlife. It is a fantasy world where objects denied in life are mystically created for life hereafter.

In innumerable passages in the Koran the garden is described as having rivers beneath it, which, if taken literally, would erode the earthly foundations of a real garden. In deserts water is the lifeblood, and rivers are a rarity, so water becomes magically abundant in a transcendental heaven. Nobody will age in an Islamic paradise. Everyone sits on cushions and wears garments of green silk and brocade. (Satin at the time of the composition of the Koran had not been invented nor linen processed). The power of this repeated images, of pleasures many would not find nor could afford in their lives, is the primary motivation for Islamic suicide bombers.

The Underworld, Valhalla, Heaven, Purgatory, Paradise and other examples of the afterlife have been used throughout history to rule minds and kingdoms. Saints and Sufis have had transcendental, spiritual experiences they associated with an appearance before the Deity. As a comparison, ancient Egyptians lined their burial tombs with goods needed for transport to the afterlife. In addition to the canopic chest that contained the innards of General Antef in 2,050 BCE, preparers filled his tomb with a fillet of beef, a bird, loaves of bread, the head and shank of a gazelle, leeks, a fig, cuts of meat, a heart, endives, an ox head, lotus, a table covering with reeds, and a libation water vase. Since all these commodities were found still with him 4,000 years later, either he never had need of them, or his journey had not yet begun.

92

Islamic suicide bombing in Europe, America and the Middle East has become a new occupation for Muslim youth. Its causes do not lie merely in depression, anxiety and guilt but in Islamic religious persuasion. This does not mean that feelings of humiliation and anger are not present. But the overall belief among Muslims is the arrogance of the West's culture toward Islam and its rejection of western values, according to Farhad Khosrokhavar in *Suicide Bombers, Allah's New Martyrs*. Professor Khosrokhavar drew on interviews with jailed Islamic militants in France who came from various Islamic countries. [4] He found that whether the militants originated from the developing world or a middle class family living in France that rejection of the West came from personal feelings of racism and discrimination, of living as marginalized exiles in an impersonal metropolis. What appealed to them was the stateless *umma*, the community of believers who don't need a country to have a sense of belonging. Such expatriates living in the midst of western values feel like marginalized foreign exiles.

They categorize the West as the ultimate Evil, the Great Satan as Iranian officials note, and as an Evil Empire as former President George Bush once labeled Iran. The simple stereotyping of the West as Evil allows for no ambiguities of interpretation of any one national culture, much less an entire civilization. Evil as a personal or cultural label, whether enunciated by a President or ordinary terrorist, reveals a lack of thoughtful nuances in the complexity of human social and cultural groupings, and is usually a projection of a religious persuasion that trumps reason. Life becomes less complicated with such an easy, antagonistic term that defines the enemy as satanic. In such a simplistic view, there are no personalized individuals, just diabolical and despised entities.

Ironically, the idea of a good and an evil God originated in Persia with Zoroaster and became influential with the Canaanites and subsequently with biblical scribes. Satan, Lucifer, and devils are ancient, anthropomorphic ideas of competing deities. But the idea of divine dualism or twin competing gods was resurrected in Baghdad, then a part of Persia, by the post-Christian prophet Mani (216–276 CE), whose followers were known as Manichees, or as Albigensians or Cathars in southern France for whom the Roman Catholic Church declared the first Inquisition and Crusade (1209–1229). Mani said he was the prophet of the last divine revelation, as did Mohammad. Religious ideas are much older than psychology, and might still tend to appear in sermons, if not among therapists, as desirable or undesirable psychological traits.

Islamic suicide bombers satisfy many of the genetic, psychological and social characteristics of Westerners who commit to die or be killed for causes they believe in. Since experimental data, or even extensive interviews are nearly impossible to obtain about the psychology of Islamic suicide bombers, let two current examples serve as illustrations that open a discussion into probable causes of this death-wish phenomenon.

In 2006 U.S. intelligence agencies captured piles of documents from terrorist groups that revealed the bureaucracy of recruitment, infiltration and implementation of terrorist activities for al-Qaeda in Iraq. Abdallah Awlad al-Tumi was a 36-year–old who was recruited from a large mosque in Dublin. Ireland may seem like a placid holiday location. But the allure of

Islam is global. Al-Tumi flew from Turkey to Syria before entering Iraq where he turned himself over to recruiters. His previous occupation had been massage specialist, but his new job was listed as "martyr." Like any recruit into a system, he first had to fill out forms for his handlers.

Shirwa Ahmed was the first known suicide bomber who was an American citizen. He blew himself up with other suicide bombers while driving a vehicle laden with explosives in October 2008 in northern Somalia that killed as many as thirty people. Shirwa came to the U.S. with his family, settled in Minneapolis in 1996 and graduated from Roosevelt High School. He returned to Somalia after recruitment by *Shabab*, an Islamic militant group suspected of having links to al-Qaeda. Since his identification, nearly two dozen of his young male associates have disappeared, leading to the suspicion that he may have been part of a Muslim cell. The disturbing case of Shirwa Ahmed, radicalized into militant Islam, perverts the typical immigrant story of making good in the U.S. after a life of hardship elsewhere.

The suicide attacks are not just against westerns but included many foreigners. In southern Yemen, a suicide bomber attacked a group of South Korean tourists as they posed for a photograph near the ancient fortress of Shibam, a UNESCO World Heritage site. Al-Qaeda militants have a strong presence in Yemen and were believed to be responsible for similar suicide attacks in July 2007 when they killed eight Spaniards and two Yemenis, and in January 2008 when they killed two Belgians and a Yemeni driver.

On April 3, 2008, British prosecutors laid out the case for eight British Muslim men living in London accused of planning suicide attacks on trans-Atlantic planes flying from London to the U.S. and Canada. These terrorist plotters in August 2006 had identified seven American and Canadian planes leaving within a couple of hours of each other. They planned to smuggle bombs onto the flights with explosive hidden in soft drink bottles. The drinks were to be liquid explosives. A mixture of hydrogen peroxide and tang was to be detonated with a substance known as HMTD hidden in AA batteries that could have been ignited with metal wires or a flash from a disposable camera. Since these men have been arrested, everyone who now flies has been inconvenienced, unable to take bottled beverages on board. These intended flights would all have been vulnerable because once detonations began during flights no one could have prevented the other flights from deadly on-board explosions. Six of these conspirators were found guilty of a terrorist plot in British courts.

It is hard to believe the ingenuity of the attack, the planning, and the willful death of the attackers for taking the lives of so many others. These suicide terrorists were like French Foreign Legion soldiers, but are now the mercenaries of Allah, attacking the infidels who have invaded Arab lands and are, they believe, corrupting Islam with heretical values.

For an Islamic radical there is no delicate art of coexistence with the infidels. For the confirmed terrorist, viscera have taken over and have abandoned reason. Loyalty to the Islamic cause has captivated the identity of the radicalized psyche and now rules over all emotions. The sense of dedication bonds the militant with like-minded confederates, perhaps in a mutual suicidal embrace, hoping to join companions in the hereafter.

Aggression and physical retribution are human tendencies, and not peculiar to religious zealots. Still, select psychological theories may help partially explain Islamic death wishes. Most people have a tendency to label unpleasant behavior with odious designations like "crazy," maniacal," "demonic," or sadistic." Thus labeled, these individuals, and those who perform similar acts, become socially isolated. Westerners, and particularly Americans, have stereotyped Muslims with prejudices, and have not uniformly regarded Islamic suicide bombers as misguided, or as mental health patients.

The principal reason for Muslim suicides is religious motivation, the strongest and most compelling of all human incentives. Nevertheless, to be inclusive I identify the major psychological theories and evidence that may also add to understanding this unique behavior.

## Major Psychological Theories

The four major psychological theories are the cognitive, behavioral, psychoanalytic and the evolutionary. Whether one believes in one of these theories exclusively, or some combination, it's possible that not one accepted theory accounts for all human behavior, and certainly not one that takes into account religion and the ultimate willingness to die for a religious cause. The neuro-scientific is my preference as it is based on evolutionary psychology, [5] which in turn is based on Darwin's theory of natural selection. [6] Darwin in *The Descent of Man* (1871) was one of the first natural experimenters to propose that the most dramatic of all human struggles is warfare. Men, he said, used warfare as a means of capturing women and the necessary reproductively relevant resources needed to sustain them such as food, tools and more territory. Among Muslim men prone to suicide in the cause of Islam, the evolution of warfare to obtain resources can also be linked to the protection and preservation of the most treasured resource—religious belief.

The psychoanalytic theory popularized by Freud but expanded on by Carl Jung and Alfred Adler among others has much to say about Muslim radicals who exhibit psychodynamic tendencies like hate and anger, shame, envy, guilt, dependency, aggression, paranoia, and victimization. Many of these symptoms can be treated through therapy and with drugs. But all of these symptoms are biological and originate in the brain. It is astonishing to see how many of them share many of these traits, states and characteristics as clinical borderline personalities. Westerners generally see themselves as able to control some of their own destiny, whereas Muslims tend to see their world as shaped by external forces.

Let me briefly describe four psychological issues based on the evolutionary theory I believe are relevant to how young Muslim men and a few women become radicalized and willing suicide bombers. The popular psychological topics are:

    1) Developmental issues
    2) Territorial instincts
    3) Herding instincts
    4) Social bonding

These can all be linked directly to evolutionary psychology—though others may claim they can also be a part of other psychological theories like behaviorism, cognition, or psychoanalytic theory. Evolution, natural selection and evolutionary psychology provide the indispensable substratum for the neurosciences and the theory that all organic and human life is driven by genetically inherited characteristics that, combined with environmental conditions, compel our actions. I offer this examination of psychological principles—some of it in my text *Advanced Psychology for Teachers*—as a means of understanding the complexities of human behavioral patterns, especially when a particular behavior, like suicide is on the rise among Islamic extremists.

## Evolutionary Psychology

We are hard-wired, to borrow a topical technological metaphor, to conform to selective socialized behaviors. Scientists reveal how natural diversity arises from changes in DNA and constitute complex cultural modes. Darwin's original idea of natural selection as a way of explaining organic diversity has produced abundant research evidence validating his theory, the most fruitful in the natural sciences. Research in gene theory, memory, mind, and consciousness reveal the place locations in the brain and the relationship between brain activity and human behavior. [7]

Once we become socialized to what is accepted in a society or cultural group, we crystallize our behaviors to conform to socially standardized expectations.[8] Genetic propensities encoded in the brain become environmentally informed and habituated through behavioral encoding. In most Muslim societies, the idea of martyrdom, of sacrificing one's life for the cause of a nation or a religion, has been legitimized in the culture, authenticated by the clergy, and sanctified by the Koran, all of which make suicidal motivation highly reinforced. Scriptural permissions give suicide divine legality. In a behavioral sense, a potential suicide attacker is emboldened and reinforced because others have preceded the bomber using this method of self-destruction. [9]

We know from brain studies that the amygdala is the region that controls aggressive tendencies and is associated with pain and discomfort. [10] Moreover, testosterone is higher in more violent, criminal offenders. We also know that more highly frustrated individuals tend to be more aggressive. [11] In other words, there is reliable and abundant evidence for the genetic and neuro-scientific conditions that leads to suicidal actions, including Muslim suicide bombers. [12]

## Developmental Stages

The evolutionary theory implies developmental stages of life in all organic life. Erik Erikson's theory of adult stages of life development begins with the young adult's experience of the conflict between intimacy and isolation. [13] The young adult must adapt to intimate relationships, which may or may not include marriage as a life choice. The young adult may begin to experience a sense of independence from parents, and devotion to a particular cause. The maturing sense of intimacy will come from working in a collegial environment where interpersonal relationships and team play are essential for satisfactory proficiency in a job. Each psychological phase of Erikson's eight life stages is systematically related to all the others, and depends on proper development sequentially. Moreover, each stage exists in some form prior to normal development, that is, in a previous stage. Erikson proposed that each organic phase of the developing organism was tied to psychological stages.

Erikson, in a dialogue conducted in the 1960s, believed that identity formation was a "restructuring of all previous identifications in the light of an anticipated future . . . Identity develops through all earlier stages . . . but the adolescent has to go through many stages until the adolescent identity crisis. Mixed in with all the positive identity, there is a negative identity composed of what he has been shamed of, punished for, and what he feels guilty about. Identity means an integration of all previous identifications and self-images, including the negative ones. Much of this goes on in the unconscious." [14]

Applied to the potential Muslim suicide bomber, Erikson's sense of guilt is that he or she is not a good enough practitioner of the Muslim faith and that he or she can only find redemption and salvation in martyrdom.

Besides stage theories of human development, cognitive and genetic theories of developmental can help explain suicidal behavior. [15] The average age of suicide bombers falls within the ages of 18–35, an age range when young adult men are still coping with discovering personal identity and masculinity, and are imbued with idealism and a powerful sense of commitment and purpose within a group. This age group is susceptible to demagogues, firebrand religious preachers, and anyone who can sway them to a cause they can believe in, or to whom they can attach themselves as followers. They may not yet at such a life stage have developed a healthy skepticism that would allow them to filter out information that will let them discriminate between true believers from false prophets.

As a comparable analogy, how else can we explain the followers of the misguided aberrations of Marshall Herff Applewhite, leader of the Heaven's Gate movement, whose followers sought to follow the spaceship they believed was trailing behind the Hale-Bopp comet? All thirty-eight members of this group committed suicide together in an attempt to join the aliens in 1997.

Jim Jones in Jonestown, Guyana led his more than 900 followers in a mass suicide in 1978. The cultist David Goresh and his Waco, Texas religious cult followers had similar visions of a paradise. Eric Harris and Dylan Klebold of Columbine High School in Littleton, Colorado both sought vengeance on their schoolmates for harassing them by murdering them ruthlessly and then committing suicide. There are multiple examples of religious believers bent on self-destructive death-wish tendencies in America not related to Islamic terrorists. [16]

However, Muslim terrorist recruiters also prey on the disabled. A British court sentenced Nicky Reilly, 22, to a minimum of 18 years in jail in January 2009 for launching a failed suicide attack at a restaurant in Devonshire. Reilly, 22, mentally handicapped and suffering from Asperger's Syndrome—a mild form of autism whose victims have difficulty making friends and engaging in normal social relationships—converted to Islam in 2002 or 2003 and had contacts with recruiters in Pakistan. Reilly, after changing his name to Mohammad Rashid Saeed Alim, had prepared three bombs with glass bottles with about 500 nails mixed with caustic soda and kerosene. One exploded in his hands and he suffered sever facial injuries. The other two did not explode where he planted them in a toilet of Giraffe's Restaurant in Exeter. No one was injured except Reilly as patrons had safely fled the restaurant.

That fanatical Muslims would even attempt to exploit the mentally ill and socially handicapped and use them for cowardly actions speaks volumes about their depravity. Recruiters may use the developmentally challenged for simple suicide missions but prefer better educated Islamic devotees for missions that require precision planning and execution.

## Defending Territory

We can compare Muslim suicide bombers to Americans willing to go to war, as they did in droves during World War II, to protect Europe from totalitarianism and to punish Japan for military aggression. We can also compare Muslim suicide bombers to Americans in nearly every American war, from the Revolutionary War to protect the homeland from foreign occupiers, through the Civil War to protect the tenuous unity of the country, to Vietnam to protect the world from what Americans thought were the advances of communism, and to Afghanistan to fight militants who were trained to murder Westerners. None of this is meant to absolve Muslim suicide bombers or to excuse warrior behavior grounded in religion. It is only to help explain, by means of militant comparisons, why some individuals exhibit warlike courage. Many men and a few women are willing to die to uphold values they believe in strongly reinforced by behavior they see conducted by others. [17]

Humans, like all other mammals, are genetically disposed to protect territories, the home turf. The current confrontation between the Israelis and Palestinians is as much about ancient territorial claims as it is about religion. Whether the argument is that we as a people have been here forever, or that God gave this land to us, is only a rationale for the fact that we are settled here and we don't like outsiders and newcomers settling on the land where we, the ethnic group, have lived on for centuries.

Additionally, there is a strong propensity toward Arab land once ruled for centuries by Ottoman Turks who were Muslim. Israel is viewed as such a political aberration and the Jews as perpetual enemies. Foreign troops, unless they were British soldiers helping Arabs to overthrow the Ottomans at the turn of the 20th century, are also aliens. Marine barracks were bombed in Lebanon and Saudi Arabia because most Muslims felt they did not belong on Muslim territory. Muslims are recruited for insurgent activities based on the territorial premise that foreigners ought not to occupy Muslim lands.

# The Herding Instinct

Together with the compulsion to defend territory is the herding instinct. Many aspire to lead, but more are destined to follow. The two instincts of leading and following may compete with each other, but when a leader is chosen, the instinct to follow the leader is compelling, whether it is a real or metaphorical shepherd, a tribal chieftain, a chief cleric or a President or Supreme Leader. Young men especially have a strong impulse for structure and direction. What that means psychologically is that such individuals instinctively need a leader to direct them so they can model themselves after examples and mimic behaviors. Once the leader or leaders demonstrate the correct behaviors, the followers adopt that behavior as their own, even if it means killing themselves to preserve the territory, the culture, the religion or the acknowledged set of values. [18]

Muslims have internalized their belief system and are continuously reinforced in their religious values by a closed society, even immigrant families living abroad, that rigidly enforces conformity to beliefs and established rituals. They are not encouraged to lean about our religions or cultures. The same is true of certain communal religious groups, like the Fundamentalist sect of the Church of Jesus Christ of Latter-Day Saints (LDS) who live in small communities like Hillsdale, Utah, Colorado City, Arizona, or The Yearning for Zion ranch in El Dorado, Texas. But when these religious beliefs conflict with civil laws, like the marriages to older men to underage girls, then authorities intervene. Conformity to group pressure is enhanced when the leader seeks a commitment. Commitments can be increased until suicide is accepted as the norm.

Conformity is extremely high and reinforced by a defined social hierarchy. The power status of the male population is enhanced, as is the herding instinct of the females and the children. Everyone obeys the leader. The patriarch, leader or cleric becomes the model for exemplary behavior and everyone emulates and adopts those values. In closed societies where social conformity is deeply entrenched there is little leeway for nonconformist activities or individualistic behaviors. The influence of others in unclear social situations determines your actions. You observe and follow the herd leader or Alpha male.

Leon Festinger proposed a theory of cognitive dissonance in 1957, a state of mental tension whereby a person holds simultaneously two opposing ideas, beliefs, attitudes, or opinions. [19] Ego defensive behavior or denial reduces the tension and lets the individual keep a positive image of the Self. Whether there is denial of cognitive dissonance, or, in the case of Muslim suicide bombers, an external justification for suicide acts (do heavenly virgins have bodies and normal desires?) there are beliefs in either internal or external rewards. For internal satisfaction, you can deny you have made a mistake. Or, for external satisfaction, you can demonize the adversary. The anticipated horrible form of death, like being blown apart by explosives, is offset by the expectation of delights in a heavenly, transcendentally perceived reality, an idea first introduced into western culture by the Egyptians, later more explicitly by Plato, and then by Christianity which made it a central tenet of its belief.

# Social Bonding

From my personal experiences, social bonding among Muslim men is as strong a social tie as any in the human family. Muslim men, as least in the Arab world, share the same religion that has been in their family for centuries, and often the same ethnicity, clan, or tribal affiliation. It is rare to live in the Arab world unless you are a Muslim, and occasionally dangerous if you are not. Neither an ethnic mix nor the Arabic language has been diluted for centuries. Even if the leadership of al-Qaeda were eliminated, there would still be Muslim youth willing to serve as recruits in the terrorist camps and on suicide bombing missions because of well-established social networks. Men and women bond tightly, or seek to bond tightly with their respective age and identity group, tribe, clan or social network, while also reaching out to find new friends.

The social bonding may also be across human cultural and racial divides. A Pew Research Center poll in 2007 found that 63 percent of foreign-born Muslims had a "very unfavorable" view of al-Qaeda compared to only 36 percent of African-American Muslims. [20] Why twice as many American Muslims would be disposed to view al-Qaeda more favorably than other Muslims is unknown but troubling.

Young, radicalized U.S. Muslims fit a growing pattern of men who joined militant groups in 2010. They are bonding less for religious rhetoric and more with personal bonds of loyalty, kinship ties, and a sense of obligation with the *umma*, the community of global Muslim believers. A push toward terrorist acts, and not just sympathy for *jihad*, can be accelerated by a sense of frustration with a western lifestyle, even if they are married with children, or an event like a drone strike, the killing of civilians, or storming a mosque that galvanizes their frustration and attachment to *jihad*.

The new converts of actual and potential suicide bombers are informal groups of bonded, socially cohesive young Muslim males and a few females, who together undergo the process of becoming radicalized in their religion. The leadership of al-Qaeda is irrelevant as an organizational entity to inspire these disaffected youth. The release of the National Intelligence Estimate in 2007, [21] and the statements of Britain's Home Secretary, warned that counter-terrorism officials were following hundreds of networks, over 2,000 individuals and over 30 active plots. [22]

One case in Britain involved minimal damage but could have been much more destructive except for the clumsiness of the terrorists. A British physician, Bilal Abdulla, 29, of Iraqi origin, was convicted in London in December 2008 of a bungled car bombing in London and his Jeep Cherokee ramming the entrance to the Glasgow airport in June 2007. Khafeel Ahmed, 28, died a few days after the incident from extensive and severe burns when the car ignited. Abdulla was a medical doctor and Ahmed a doctoral student in engineering. The educational attainment level for Muslim men does not constitute an obstacle for recruitment as a terrorist. [23]

Abdulla and Ahmed had driven to London's trendy West End the previous day before the Glasgow airport incident in two Mercedes-Benz cars that were primed with bombs and gasoline canisters and propane cylinders and 2,000 nails. They parked their cars outside a nightclub near a busy bus stop. The cars failed to explode though the terrorists repeatedly used mobile phones to trigger the bombs. They had learned to construct such bombs from Islamic extremist websites. Either the website was imperfect in details or the would-be assassins in execution.

Abdullah was trained as a physician in Iraq and had been in contact with Sunni extremists. As a medical student in the late 1990s, according to statements he made to interrogators, he became embittered when the Western-imposed economic sanctions on Iraq curtailed his hospital conditions and training. He became angrier at the indiscriminate bombings when the U.S. invasion. Because he believed that allied troops did not distinguish between soldiers and civilians he thought he had a right to kill civilians too.

The lack of toleration among Muslims is not the case in the Western world where multiculturalism, and its corresponding value of multi-ethnic acceptance, has been actively promoted. The American national identity, and to some degree identities in most of the European nations, have been fashioned over the past century to be accepting of a variety of ethnic, religious and cultural backgrounds brought about primarily because of immigration policies and the importing of foreign workers. No such politically correct tolerance exists in the Arab world and would be repulsed were it to be introduced.

Until recently, and accompanying the discovery of oil, no immigration existed in the Arab world because no one sought to live or work there. The only tourists to the Arab world were pilgrims to Mecca. All the latest immigrants are guest workers and would, under no circumstances, be admitted as citizens in any Arab country. Even if they were devout Muslims, they might not be eligible to become a citizen. [24]

What I have omitted psychologically may also be as significant as what I have delineated. Radicalizing behavior is too primal, instinctual, and too visceral to have us believe that such behavior has been arrived at after considering alternative cognitive routes. Suicidal behavior does not come from long-term memories of the consequences of aberrant behavior. Rather, for the largely young male adult, killing oneself for a cause is an attempt to gain acceptance in the group, notoriety within the nuclear family—perhaps even cash payments to the family from donors—and entrance into a transcendental reality. The young men who commit terrorist acts may not be illiterate but they are nevertheless uninformed and lacking real-life experiences in a mature adult world. In a behaviorist sense, they are closer to conditioned behavior where the conditioning has systematized their actions and the accompanying responses to select stimuli. In a neuro-scientific sense, they have developed neuronal pathways that have encoded behavioral traits. [25]

So what can we conclude psychologically from those who have chosen to kill Westerners that might help us understand their psychological composition? Absent the prejudice and stereotyping, we can conclude that they are more like us than we are prepared to admit. S. P. Rosen has made the compelling case in *War and Human Nature* (2005) for war as the result of human biology based on brain studies, emotions and the endocrine system. If we study human behavior long enough we know that the dark side, like the Id, has a lurking preponderance that is often controlled by the Ego or Superego, to use Freudian terms. But that once released the Id can subsume control that seeks vengeance, retaliation, revenge and any form of aggression against real or perceived enemies. Now try applying the idea of a runaway Islamic Id, with religiously permissible sanctions from clerics, and wrecking havoc on ordained enemies—as soldiers are so trained in any war—and see how it is that western psychological ideas might be able partially to explain what we think of as bizarre or irrational behavior inspired by an intense religious devotion.

Lastly, the ultimate social bonding is based on belief in the hereafter and the joining of like-minded martyrs in heaven after they have fulfilled their suicide or death missions. Mormons have a similar belief whereby spouses joined together in life will remain joined together in heaven. The idea of Islamic martyrs meeting again with brothers, relatives, clan or tribal members or friends is a powerful method of cultivating social bonding. It implies that even after the stress of normal living that the young will join with religious brothers in paradise is alluring and makes the bonding stronger and ordinary life more tolerable.

Moreover, the sexual bonding promised to young martyrs is very explicit. Young martyrs entering paradise are promised to enjoy the company of female virgins. The number of seventy-two virgins is apocryphal and comes from a medieval legend, but is believed as if it were in the Koran, where it is only implied. But whether fully believed or not, the enticement of one of the most fundamental human drives of sexual satisfaction is, according to the accumulated evidence from evolutionary psychology, a powerful social bond of unlimited fantasy sex enjoyed in the Islamic paradise. In this scenario, the Muslim suicide bomber does not have to compete with other males in the survival game for the choicest females. In his religiously approved thinking, he just has to kill himself in the campaign against Islamic enemies.

Murals of Paradise in a Muslim Elementary School

# CHAPTER SIX
# MUSLIM INTEGRATION
# INTO EUROPEAN SOCIETY

Muslims have been unable to adapt to the world in its new form, and have found themselves obliged, both at home and in their own countries and as immigrants abroad, to adopt to a new way of life incompatible with their religious laws and beliefs. (Wafa Sultan, *A God Who Hates*, 2009, p. 222)

Islam has made a claim on Europe but Europe has not accepted Islam. My former neighbors cooking curried dishes in East London, my *halal* butchers and grocers in Copenhagen, and my Muslim friends in the U.S. are not a part of a vast Islamic conspiracy. They have adapted to civil society and brought spicy diversity to their adopted countries. Many Muslims have accepted European norms and values, but many have not. Islamic believers are preoccupied neither with their ethnic or national origin as much as their Muslim belief. However, a younger generation of second, third, and an approaching fourth generation of European Muslims, has given radical Islam new allegiances. From 2001 to 2008 there were over 1,400 arrests in Europe connected to Islamic terrorism.

Islamic militancy arrived in America on 9/11 and Europeans were generally sympathetic to America's losses, but still accused America of unilateral imperialistic ways and were often more sympathetic to the Arab world, almost as if America were the enemy. Shortly after 9/11 there was dancing throughout Arab streets everywhere, in Gaza, and by Moroccan immigrants in the Dutch town of Ede.

Strong strands of anti-Americanism and anti-Semitic sentiments run throughout European society. Meanwhile Europe is in denial about the challenge of its unemployed, belligerent, young Muslim men—one and a half million in the Paris suburbs—who will never adopt their resident country or its culture, and who soak up Europe's generous welfare payments. It took a few jots of Islamic terrorism to awaken Europe that there really isn't any Muslim integration.

The death of Dutch activist Pim Fortuyn on May 6, 2002 was viewed as an attack by a crazed assassin on someone who dared point out the threat of Islam to Dutch democracy. Fortuyn was rounded demonized by the Dutch establishment for his supposedly eccentric views they characterized as racist. His death upset their belief that Europe could accommodate all peoples peacefully. Then, Theo van Gogh was assassinated on November 2, 2004 for making a documentary film, *Submission*, that revealed the atrocities of Islam toward women. The two assassins rattled the imperturbability of the Holland, a country like Sweden and Norway that had been more concerned with not offending Islamic sensitivities, even while imams were openly preaching against gays, women and democracy in European mosques.

Earlier in 2004, on September 1st, about thirty armed terrorists seized Middle School Number One in the town of Beslan in Russia, and held 1,300 hostages, most of them children. The terrorists denied the children food, water and medicine. When Russian police stormed the school, terrorists shot fleeing children. Over 331 civilians and 11 soldiers died. The terrorists had come from all over the Islamic world. Suddenly, Europeans had to cope with the fact that Islamic militancy was more than a multicultural initiative and misunderstanding.

None were more sensitive to Muslims to the British, nor none more somnolent about the dangers of radicalized Islam. Born and bred British Muslims became four suicide bombers on July 7, 2005. Their bombs tore through three underground railways (the tube system) and a double-decker bus in Tavistock Square killing 56 people and injuring over 400. The succession of these murders and bombings in English backyards brought about a mini-mindset in European society. The terrorist perpetrators were not visitors or immigrants but local young men, reared in Leeds, two of them married with young children, beneficiaries of British social largesse, health care and education. It was clear from their statements and videos that they saw themselves as self-appointed soldiers of Islam out of avenge the foreign policies of western nations.

The year following these tragic events, as if to demonstrate where Britain really stood on preventing terrorism on its soil, Parliament passed the *Racial and Religious Hatred Bill* in 2006 which made it a crime to incite hatred against a person because of religion, in effect for criticizing Muslim radicals for taking the lives of British subjects. Meantime, hundreds of thousands of Muslims had marched in English streets protesting the wars in Iraq and Afghanistan, but none marched protesting the killing of British civilians by Muslim radicals. On July 23, 2005, just two weeks after the London bombings, Anthony King reported in the *Telegraph*—"One in Four Muslims Sympathize with Motives of Terrorists"—that a quarter of Muslims either fully supported or were in sympathy with the London attacks. Only 6% said that bombings were fully justified, but that amounts to about 100,000 British Muslims. And 18% of those surveyed said they had little or no loyalty to Britain at all.

The cosmetic issues that are challenging European political leaders and society include: Muslim dress, notably a woman's *hijab*, in public or in workplaces, religious holiday schedules, public accommodation for Muslim prayers, building permits for mosques, animal rights and slaughtering of animals in public, burial rights in public cemeteries, teaching religion in schools, and divorce laws. The deeper issue is that most Muslims will never adopt Europe's culture, and their sheer demographics will one day slowly overwhelm selective countries.

It wasn't until the morning of March 11, 2004, when Muslim terrorists bombed set off several bombs at Madrid train stations killing 191 and wounding nearly 2,000 that European realized that the hatred of al-Qaeda's *jihad* was against the West and not just America, a concept that was predictable to anyone familiar with Islamic ideology. Spain's long slumber and delusion about its Muslim militants came to an end, but not Europe, which continued to blame poverty, colonialism Israel for the globe's ills and not acknowledge that it had a determined enemy that it had coddled all these years within its borders. Spain's socialist party won in the election two days following, and agreed to pull Spanish troops out of Iraq. Terrorists had succeeded in making democracy work for them.

Based on my living experiences and research in Europe, I have found that many Muslims do enjoy the shared values of European democracies and want to live without social prejudice in Europe without sacrificing their primary beliefs. But they are shadowed by a small fraction of dedicated Muslim radicals who take the Koran literally and seek to kill non-Muslims. The young radicals have dominated the discussion and brought fear into Europeans, and indeed into all western nations. After all, the penalty for renouncing Islam is death. Muslims cannot just walk away from their religion without penalty. The life stories of those who have abandoned Islam are compelling. Being a moderate Muslim means that you reject or ignore the passages in the Koran advocating violence to infidels, and live a life that is nominally Muslim without its radicalized tendencies.

Jyette Klaussen, born in Denmark and a professor of comparative politics at Brandeis University, says that Muslim terrorism is incidental to the conflicts over the accommodation of Muslim religious practices in Europe. Many Europeans disagree. The growth of right-wing political party members testifies to an opposing stance. Bruce Bawer's 2006 book *While Europe Slept* documents how Europe's cultural sense of toleration has overshadowed the new radical Islamic challenge. European governments want to assist in integration but a growing political faction seeks to restrict that option. Klaussen interviewed over 300 European Muslims and found that most seek a liberal democratic partnership that views them as equal to other religious groups.

Europe initially welcomed Islamic immigrants who came as guest workers to satisfy labor shortages and received generous welfare benefits and political asylum. Besides riots against Denmark for its satirical cartoon of Mohammad in 2005, polygamy was accepted in Sweden, and radical mosques and preachers tolerated in Britain. Bombings in Spain and England, assassinations in Holland, honor killings, and restrictions on minarets in Switzerland and public Muslim female dress in France were the beginning of restrictions on Muslim acceptability. Since 2001, for example, France had expelled 129 radical Muslims, 29 imams, including Ali Ibrahim el-Soufany to Egypt for calling for a fight against the West and spurning western values.

What passes for satire in the western world could be blasphemy in the Islamic, and possibly with the Vatican. On December 11, 2010, Stockholm and its peaceful and tolerant Swedes were rocked by two explosions in the heart of the shopping district. Two people were injured but the only death happened to the suicide bomber, Taimour al-Abdaly, 28, whose family moved from Baghdad to Sweden in 1992. He initially moved to Britain to attend a British university. He had carried pipe bombs and a backpack filled with nails. Lars Vilks, 64, a newspaper cartoonist, like his Danish counterpart, had drawn cartoons of Mohammad. This supposed illustration sacrilege, and Sweden's 500-member NATO troop concentration in Afghanistan, apparently were enough to invite Islamic retribution. Sweden's immigrant Muslim population is only 5% of 9.3 million.

If the tensions popping up in several countries are an indication, Europe is right to worry about repercussions from the more radical side of Islam.

Muslim immigration and population increase appears to Europeans to endanger national cultures and to destabilize precarious economies. Many Muslims do not want to become European citizens, or to accept the rights and obligations of the national identity in the country where they live, though they willingly accept the generous worker, health, and education welfare benefits.

The confrontation between secular Europe and devout Muslims is often expressed in women's garments. The *burqa* is the full-length outer garment and the *nijab* the facial veil. [1] Muslim women fled the impertinences of the veil in Egypt, Iran and Turkey decades ago. Now their granddaughters insist on wearing it in Europe, and sometimes the head-to-toe Muslim swimsuit known as the *burquini* that the French have officially banned in public swimming pools for hygienic reasons. The social and political debate in Europe about Muslim dress is over the suppression of women—that required clothing is a sign of Muslim servitude—the rights of minority religions to express themselves freely, and the maintenance of secularism that does not permit religious forms of expression in sponsored public spaces. France decreed the covering of women's faces illegal in 2011, illuminating one crucial distinction between secularism, the equality between men and women in the state.

Europe has a higher percentage of immigrant workers than does the United States, and a per capita higher percentage of a Muslim population. In the middle of the 20th century there were virtually no Muslims in Europe. According to a Gallup poll in 2009 there were approximately five million Muslims in France (8% of the population), four million in Germany (4% of the population), 2.5 million in England (3% of the population), and one million in London alone. The total Muslim European population in 2009 was 20 million. The U.S. Intelligence Council estimates that Europe will have 40 million Muslims by 2025.

The demographic shift in population presents unique challenges to European countries that believe their national identities are under siege. Clearly, the nature of European citizenship in a world of migrant communities, when many do not wish to integrate and whose religion poses a governance threat to established law, has agitated citizens and lawmakers. Meanwhile, American Homeland Security officials worry about radicalized Muslim European nationals coming to the U.S. with acceptable passports and visas. It has usually been assumed that over time immigrant workers and their families would integrate into civil society to become responsible citizens and, to a lesser degree, assimilate culturally. But recent evidence indicates that that this not true among many Muslims.

The emergence of large numbers of Muslims in Europe has raised the ugly hackles of xenophobia, but has also underscored the rise of Muslim radicalization. So the question of postmodern critiques of diversity of the religious experience, or of ethnic identities and their multicultural influence on European societies, does not adequately describe the profound effect Islamic terrorism has had on Europeans.

Let me describe research from interviews and surveys conducted in Europe since 2005 with colleagues in six European countries on teacher attitudes toward the integration of Muslim students into civil society. [2] My colleagues and I gathered evidence about how civic integration and cultural assimilation was proceeding among Muslim European immigrants and their descendants. Results yield some information about how a sample of European teachers views the integration of students into society.

## Muslim Immigrants in Europe

There is a tension between secular and nationalistic values favoring the individual and strong views about religious identity that disfavor individual freedoms. Many in the political mainstream believe that Islam cannot be reconciled with European values. According to a Pew Global Attitudes survey in 2006, 42% of French Muslims consider themselves French first, but 47% say they are Muslim first. In Britain, the numbers are only 7% British first, while 81% say they are Muslim first. These are not healthy ratios for civic integration.

A similar survey conducted for the Institute for the Study of Labor in England in 2007 discovered that even if Muslims were well–educated, well-paid and living and working among non-Muslims that they persisted in maintaining a Muslim identity. The usual methods of integration, such as decline in segregated neighborhoods, a rise in the level of education and income, simply do not apply to Muslim immigrants. [3] On the other hand, a Gallup poll in 2008 of 30,000 in 27 countries indicated that joblessness and poverty were a higher source of European Muslim tension than Muslim identity, and that non-Muslims have misunderstandings of the Muslim/non-Muslim relationship.

A survey by the Indonesian Survey Institute in 2011 found a similar trend among Muslim youth aged 15-25 in Indonesia. Nearly 48% said that they were Muslim first and Indonesian second. A similar survey in Malaysia found that about 80% said they were Muslim first. The emphasis on Islamic values and not national values is a progressive trend among Muslims living in either Islamic countries or European countries. Here are a few examples of the emphasis on Islamic values in Indonesia.

| | |
|---|---|
| Disapproval of premarital sex | 96% |
| Reject drinking alcohol | 89% |
| Drinkers should be caned | 69% |
| Wrong to be gay | 99% |
| Reject pornography | 96% |
| | |
| (Source: Saragih, *The Jakarta Post* 2011) | |

A new Gallup report on Muslims in August 2011 in America revealed that Muslim Americans are more likely than members of other faith groups to reject attacks on civilians by either the military or individuals.

More disturbing is that 57% of Irish Muslims want Ireland to become an Islamic state, and 15% of British Muslims believe suicide missions to kill British military are legitimate. About 85% of Muslim students describe their religious beliefs as "very important," as compared to 35% of non-Muslim students. In Germany, 81% of Turks come from a religious background compared to 23% of Germans. These percentages, that appear to be representative, do not bode well for future integration of Muslims into European democratic societies where western law and traditions of multicultural acceptance precede individual religious persuasion.

| LEVELS OF MUSLIM INTEGRATION IN BRITAIN, FRANCE AND GERMANY | | | |
|---|---|---|---|
| | Isolated | Integrated | Tolerant |
| British Muslims | 10% | 60% | 30% |
| French Muslims | 46% | 31% | 23% |
| German Muslims | 35% | 43% | 22% |
| | | Source: Gallup Poll, 2009 | |

Germans are requiring immigrants to sign an "integration contract," that includes accepting German values. Europeans are tiring of parallel societies that do not seek to become assimilated into the culture of the countries they inhabit. Britain and Holland have introduced citizenship tests to ease the integration process. Moreover, there is often denial of the radical Islamic threat in Europe, or appeasement according to Bruce Bawer. His 2009 book *Surrender, Appeasing Islam, Sacrificing Freedom*, provides multiple examples of European kowtowing to Islamic threats, and special treatment for religious purposes and sensibilities.

The Swiss approved on November 30, 2009 by a plurality of 57.5% a referendum to halt the construction of additional minarets with new mosques. Existing minarets can remain. The majority of Swiss felt that new minarets—un-necessary for the call to prayer as all are now recordings and are officially banned—were a symbol of political Muslim power disproportionate to its minority status. The Swiss constitution guarantees freedom of religion, but a rightist political party organized a campaign on behalf of the cessation of new minarets. The vote plays on similar fears among other European countries about the spread of Islamic values and influence. [4]

Muslims clerics called the referendum vote racist. In Egypt, where sentiment runs high against minority Coptic Christians building new churches, and where churches of any kind are banned in Saudi Arabia, Muslim clerics said the Swiss vote was an assault on religious freedom. Others would say it was an expression of democracy. Switzerland has 300,000 Muslims in a country of seven million.

As an example of the terrorist threat in Europe, in the spring of 2009 a trial opened in Dusseldorf of four Islamic militants charged with plotting a series of high-profile bombings throughout Germany, including the Frankfurt airport and Ramstein Air Force Base. It was the biggest terrorist trial since the Red Army faction trials in the 1970s. The terrorists were said to be in advanced stages of bombings. The suspects were found with 26 military detonators and 12 drums of hydrogen peroxide, similar to the main ingredient in explosives used in the London bombings in 2006. Mixed with other chemicals the explosion would have been enough to equal that of 1,200 pounds of TNT. All the suspects had visited terrorist training camps in Pakistan. They were convicted on March 4, 2010. Three additional suspects were arrested in April 2011 in the Dusseldorf area planning a similar attack.

In many countries in northern Europe the educational and economic progress of Muslim immigrants has been limited and cultural alienation more pronounced. How much of this alienation is caused by discrimination, or the ethnic and religious identification of immigrants and their families, or by government policies is difficult to determine. But the creation of ethnic islands has hindered the assimilation of Muslim immigrants into the larger cultural milieu and national economy.

In the past few years Europeans in general have turned against Muslim migrations. Over 80% of the Dutch are in favor of stronger measures to get Muslims to integrate. More Europeans fear the results of Muslim youth becoming radicalized and engaging or supporting terrorist attacks. Stricter tests for Muslims entering Europe have been instigated, and the once-lauded concept of multiculturalism has been largely ignored or dispensed with. [5]

The debate over individual rights vs. collective rights has mingled uneasily in Dutch society. Muslim extremists began to take advantage of Holland's tolerance for unorthodox individual beliefs. The rights of women clashed with the lenient national policy and culture towards immigrants. The religious issues became social and legal. There were multiple social issues that applied only to Muslims:

- Some men were taking multiple wives
- Many Muslim women underwent genital mutilation
- Clinics specializing in repairing broken hymens were covered by National Health insurance
- Employers would not hire women wearing headscarves
- There were honor killings for violating female virginity

The Dutch were discovering that its tolerant approach by forming alliances between disparate groups in Dutch society did not dovetail with Muslim beliefs. One indication of signs of integration is marriage statistics. Denmark's *Aliens Act* legislated stricter marriage requirements. Danes who married non-EU spouses could no longer reside in the country. Finding spouses in Pakistan, Europeans argued, is not a way to assimilate into the host country.

Over the next few decades there will be a growing number of European Muslim enclaves especially around urban areas, complicating efforts to assimilate and integrate, and creating more tense and unstable social situations. Slower economic development will make it difficult for Europeans to increase job opportunities even at the lower end of the economic scale. Coupled with job discrimination and educational disadvantages, Muslims will be confined to low-wage jobs that deepen their anxieties and sense of alienation, further separating them from the common civic and cultural life.

## Teacher Attitudes Toward Muslim Students

There is general agreement that formal schooling is the primary institution for nurturing social and civic integration. Teachers are seen as the societal linchpins for inculcating necessary values for civic integration and cultural assimilation. What do European teachers believe about the acceptance of traditional democratic values and the integration of Muslim students into communities and schools?

Survey results come from six European countries (Denmark, Norway, Finland, Belarus, Austria, Belgium) that face the same absorptive workforce and cultural dilemmas accepting Muslim workers and immigrants as other European countries. My European colleagues and I provide evidence of teacher attitudes toward educational and cultural values, including immigration policies, religious preferences, and civic and social integration that can expand the public discourse and perhaps lead to new policy initiatives about immigrant integration into national and communal European societies.

Conclusions indicate that teachers but do not believe that Muslim students will integrate successfully nor renounce violence. This is not a healthy sign for future integration of the Muslim communities when radicalization among Muslim youth might be stronger. [6]

Danish society was traumatized in 2006 by global Muslim outrage over the publication of satirical cartoons about Mohammad in September 2005 drawn by Kurt Westergaard for the Danish newspaper *Jyllands-Posten*. (A Somali man was arrested in January 2010 for forcibly entering Westergaard's home in Aarhus with a knife and axe to kill him). Blasphemy is recognized, religious offense easily taken, and death to the offender religiously sanctioned. Muslim immigrants commit 75% of all violence in Denmark, and 75% of the victims are ethnic Danes.

With my colleague at Aarhus University I interviewed Ahmad Abu Laban (since deceased), the chief Imam in Copenhagen on July 4, 2006. He was the Muslim cleric who broke the news about the Danish cartoon controversy to clerics in Lebanon and Egypt, but claimed when I questioned him that the cartoon scandal was a "misunderstanding." "Muslims were seeking help," he said, "not wanting to incite violence." He lied.

The violent attacks that followed on Danish embassies in Syria, Iran, Libya, Pakistan and Indonesia, and to Nordic individuals throughout the Islamic world and the boycott of Danish commercial goods, shattered the tranquility of Scandinavian insouciance and exposed the hypocrisy of the peaceful explanations for *jihad*. Apparently, Abu Laban either did not know his religious culture well enough to realize the kind of violence that could be unleashed when the Prophet Mohammad is blasphemed satirically, or else he was speaking out of another side of his mouth. Abu Laban insisted when I pressed him that *jihad* is restricted to self-defense and that Muslims reject harm to others. But scriptures in the Koran contradict him. As a knowledgeable cleric he would be well aware that he was deceitful, as lying is permitted in the Koran in defense of Islam. [7]

The Danish cartoon crisis revealed that Europeans tacitly assumed there was an understanding that Muslims would respect free speech and the dignity of personal, religious expressions. On the contrary, Muslims made it clear that their religious freedom superseded freedom of speech. Muslims had no tolerance or respect for the religions of others or the hard-won personal freedoms of the West. Rather than stand up to Islamic religious discrimination and their disrespect from secular values, such as the equality of the sexes, Europeans tended to submit to Islamic intimidation and concede to Muslim intolerance, a dangerous precedent.

Denmark has the most robust economy in Europe, with a potent agricultural system and strong industries in transportation, oil and energy. It enjoys comfortable living standards, a generous welfare system and a stable and reliable currency. Denmark joined the European Union, but did not convert to the Euro in order to maintain the strength of its currency. Until recent decades it has been an ethnically homogeneous society with a strong secular and liberal democratic core.

The population of Denmark was 5.4 million, of which one million, two hundred thousand lived in the greater Copenhagen area. And 83% of Danes are nominally members of the Lutheran church. There are more than a quarter million Muslims, an expanding population group compared to the native Danish population. In 1982 there were 35,000 Muslims living in Denmark. By 2010 there were 220,000, a six-fold increase in 27 years. Muslims constitute 40% of the welfare spending, and commit a disproportionate number of the crimes like rapes on non-Muslim women, foment anti-Semitism and promote *sharia* law. [8]

Denmark has passed laws in an effort to speed Muslim immigrant integration into Danish society by limiting the practice of second-generation Muslim Danes returning to ancestral countries to find husbands and wives. Most recently, Muslim immigrant population birth rates have declined nearly matching lower European birth rates. This pattern of Muslim immigrant population increase has been duplicated in Spain, Italy, France, Germany, and Austria.

There are strong religious values among immigrant families and a rising trend in recent years among Muslim immigrants towards more religious values than there are similar trends among native Danes who tend to be more secular. It has been reliably reported that only about 13% of Danish Muslim immigrants actively attend Friday mosque ceremonies. This does not always reveal irreligious sentiments, however, as Islamic websites provide abundant sources of literature, news and information from the Islamic world, devotional content, and even radical recruitment for *jihad* movements. There is also a pronounced increase in religious values in second-generation immigrant families. Although Danes have a high tolerance for all religions, the increase in Islamic religious values has disturbed the tranquility of Danish social homogeneity.

The typical environment for assimilation in western societies is the school system, which is why my colleagues and I chose educators to glean attitudes about these social imperatives. Denmark, for example, has both public and private Muslim schools. Both native Danish and third and second generation Muslim Danes teach in both kinds of school. Norway has a scattering of Muslim immigrant families throughout the country. Belarus has a new surge of Muslim immigrants seeking entry into the European

Union and an older resident Muslim community who are integrated and are descendants of the Cossacks. Austria has a strong Catholic tradition and has an uncomfortable relationship with Muslim immigrants. Belgium has both public and private schools, Catholic in the south among the Flemish but Protestant in the north.

Providing opportunities for undertaking service learning activities, following current events, discussing problems in the community, and engaging students in dialogue about controversial issues can lead to further civic and community commitment. [9] Yet, according to our interviews with teachers, who are instructors of Muslim students, there is an unwillingness to participate in such activities or even to learn the content of most school subjects, including math.

Although the initial prompting of this study was the cartoon crisis that engulfed Denmark and the world, we interviewed selected candidates to design a survey instrument with topical content. Initial interviews were conducted in July 2006 in Copenhagen and Aarhus, two cities in Denmark with large concentrations of Muslims, and included an imam, headmasters at both public and independent Muslim schools, professors and teachers. Sample interview questions:

- Do Muslims denounce radical Islamic *jihad* and violence?
- Can Muslims integrate successfully into a western, secular society and still preserve their religious identity?
- Do Muslims understand the secular nature of western societies, which is to preserve religious plurality in the nation?
- Can (name of country) grow to accept and respect Muslim immigrants while preserving other religious persuasions?
- Should schools give any special privileges to Muslim students?
- Should more tolerance for all faiths be taught in schools?

Based on responses, we designed a survey instrument, pilot-tested it with selected individuals, and administered it to Danish teachers. The survey was translated into Norwegian and administered in the Trondheim region of Norway, into Finnish, into Russian and administered in Minsk in Belarus, into German for administration in the Vienna region, and Dutch for administration in Belgium.

Although 55% of Danish respondents indicated they were Protestant, primarily Lutheran, 29% admitted to having no religious belief. The third largest religious group was Muslim, at a higher percentage than all other religious groups combined. [10]

There was consistent agreement among the respondents about the main values selected: for tolerance, equality, freedoms, and against violence. These values, not the commodities or products of the developed world, are the bright, shining attractions of American and European governments, often lacking in under-developed nations and many Muslim states. What was clear was that there appeared to be a high degree of teacher professionalism and unanimity across countries and national borders that revealed the necessity for teaching the core democratic values.

# Jihad and Violence Among Muslim Students

Muslim and non-Muslim Teachers generally agreed with the statement "Some Muslim students look favorably on *jihad*." For whatever reason, teachers believe that they are confronting a value among Muslim students toward violence that may not only may impede social integration, but is clearly adverse to acceptable democratic values.

Most pronounced is the difference on whether or not Muslim students will integrate successfully into society. Muslim teachers have a relatively high level of agreement that Muslim students will integrate, whereas non-Muslim teachers are only barely in agreement. When asked to respond on the statement, "Muslim students reject jihad and violence," teachers do not agree. Teachers do not want to believe that Muslim students look favorably on *jihad*, but neither do they think that Muslim students actually reject it.

The set of values of a nation or community has is its own uniqueness, not just its language, developed over centuries in historical isolation when transportation was more arduous and communication more remote. Our analysis indicated that teacher respondents highly agreed on the need for students to learn commonly accepted values in a democratic society, for learning tolerance for all religions, on the rejection of violence, on the necessity of treating everyone without prejudice and with equality, and respecting democratic political and intellectual freedoms. This conclusion validated our preliminary findings from interviews. In general, respondents were less in agreement that teachers in their schools actually teach these values.

Teachers universally did not believe that there should be an increase in Muslim immigrants to satisfy the labor shortage, although from other economic sources it is evident that for the European economy to expand immigrant workers will be required. Northern European countries are now drawing immigrant laborers largely from eastern European countries and less from Islamic countries.

Teachers agreed on the key values inherent in democratic societies, but had less agreement about the value of Muslim student integration. On the one hand, accommodating the immigrant worker with the same social acceptance level as a native born citizen exists in all industrialized countries. It is unclear whether terrorist attacks in several European countries—certainly Spain, England and Holland—may have biased the population against Muslims in general and particularly those living in one's own country or community. The probable fear of a terrorist attack may appear to outweigh the need for foreign laborers to assume needed jobs in the manufacturing or service sectors.

Whatever values teachers seek to inculcate in students, student acceptance of the violence of the *jihad* movement among Muslim youth is universally conclusive, at least among teachers whose particular job it is to forge civic integration in a society. The *jihad* movement among Muslim youth is likely formed by influences outside the school, commonly believed to come from websites but not from the mosques or sermons.

The convergence of Islam and national and cultural identity in Europe, exacerbated by external events like a murder, assassination, riot, embassy bombing, or even a satirical cartoon, has the potential for disrupting civic order and eroding movements towards cultural assimilation and national integration. Revealing the sources of cultural dissonance between Islamic faith and national identity can have a profound influence on how societies prepare for Muslim immigrant problems throughout Europe and America.

## The Muslim Brotherhood

We should have no illusions about the Muslim Brotherhood, who they are and what they want. (Bernard Lewis, quoted in B. Weiss, "The Tyrannies are Doomed." *The Wall Street Journal*, April 2-3, 2011, A13.

Hasan al-Banna, an Egyptian elementary school teacher, founded the Muslim Brotherhood in 1928, an Islamic revivalist movement known as *ikhwan* in the Arab world. It is based on Wahhabism and the installation of *sharia* law that seeks a return of the Caliphate. It was a return to purity in Islamic thinking and a turning away from secular, western ways, except that al-Banna used political means and western propaganda to convey his message. Al-Banna blamed the Arabs for not following the "straight path," the pure way of the Koran. Included in his program was training in cells and through sports for *jihad*, an idea that appealed strongly to a young Osama bin Laden who attended King Abdul Aziz University in Jeddah then staffed with Brotherhood instructors. One of Osama's instructors was the brother of Sayyid Qutb, a notable exponent of Brotherhood principles. A Muslim Brotherhood member assassinated the Prime Minister of Egypt in December 1948, and four members assassinated Anwar Sadat President of Egypt in 1981. Al-Banna was himself killed by Egyptian government agents in February 1949. Its activist members usually work underground.

The message of the Brotherhood is the adoption of a social order that is destructive of individual freedoms. To paraphrase the rallying call: God is the objective; God's messenger Mohammad is the guide; the Koran is the constitution; *jihad* is the path; and death the ultimate desire. There is no rule by the people, no allowances for non-Muslims, and no maneuverability for compromise. No member will accept any government not based on Islamic principles. All Muslims need to be liberated and re-united under the banner of Islam. All means are permitted to bring this about including *taqiyya*, deliberate lying or cheating to protect the faith. [11] This is considered not a moral matter but one of honor, protecting status and avoiding shame.

When a Muslim Brotherhood member attempted to assassinate President Nasser in 1954, hundreds were arrested and more fled to neighboring Arab countries where they spread the movement's goals and practices. Nasser sought to gain their support by releasing those arrested, but some still attempted to assassinate him. The Muslim Brotherhood under Mubarak was officially banned but thrived as an underground movement with financial support and an active *jihad* group worrisome to the Egyptian government. The Hamas organization in Gaza is a militant cousin of the Muslim Brotherhood.

By the time of the Arab spring and the ouster of Mubarak in 2011, the Muslim Brotherhood emerged as the leading political party in parliamentary elections as power shifted away from Egypt's military towards a more democratic governance. The U.S. initiated a new diplomatic policy that sought improved relations and active dialogue with the group. [12] Whether dialogue will advance or retard democracy in Egypt or elsewhere is an open question.

Here are the six principles of the organization that have not changed.

1. Build the Muslim individual
2. Foster practicing Muslim families
3. Create an Islamic society
4. Build an Islamic state
5. Create a Caliphate
6. Mastering the world with Islam

Note that the creation of strong principles in the individual, family and society are legitimate virtues easily identified with any religion. But the last two principles, of creating a unity of nations around Islam, a Caliphate, and "mastering the world with Islam," are territorial and globally ambitious. Islam has ultimate political objectives that go far beyond just satisfying the meditative or spiritual needs of its devotees. The Brotherhood at its home base in Egypt will likely use its new political power to advance its principles instead of employing a strategy of open opposition to the government as it did under Mubarak.

As an example of a contrasting set of philosophical principles to the Brotherhood, see the list by Ibn 'Arabi (1165–1240), the greatest Islamic Sufi mystic and philosopher.

1) Service to the needy
2) Purity of heart
3) Good will to the believers
4) Thinking well of everyone and everything [13]

Ibn 'Arabi's list needs little explanation, as it is for individuals and is not an Islamic political statement, but serves in stark contrast to the global political and religious expansion aims of the Muslim Brotherhood. Ibn 'Arabi says that whoever possesses these attributes will be saved.

The current chief exponent of the principles of the Muslim Brotherhood is the grandson of the founder. Tariq Ramadan (b. 1962), grandson of the Muslim Brotherhood's founder, Hassan al-Banna, is a preacher and political propagandist in the Islamic tradition, as was his father, Said Ramadan, who was responsible for propagating the Muslim Brotherhood form of Islam throughout Europe. Tariq's father established the Islamic Center of Geneva, still used as the family home. This center, administered by Hani Ramadan, Tariq's brother, spreads the message of the Muslim Brotherhood throughout Europe. Tariq's mother was the favorite daughter of the founder Hassan al-Banna. His name, Tariq, echoes the name of Tariq Ibn Zyad, the first Muslim conqueror of Spain. Gibraltar means "rock of Tariq". [14]

Tariq is thoroughly imbued with the philosophy of the Brotherhood. Though currently on the faculty of theology at Oxford University, he has no training in theology. The Faculty of Arts of the University of Geneva approved his doctoral thesis reluctantly and without honors. He has not published it. It is not a scholarly research treatise but an encomium in praise of Hassan al-Banna, his grandfather and founder of the Muslim Brotherhood.

He was denied entry into France for fomenting hatred and incitement to violence, and the U.S. Department of Homeland Security revoked his visa in July 2004 but reinstated it in 2010. He has been banned in Tunisia, Saudi Arabia, Syria, Algeria, and Libya. England, on the other hand, is eager to honor articulate Islamic preachers in its conciliatory quest to find peace in our time.

Tariq was fired from his position as integration advisor for the city of Rotterdam in The Netherlands. He had been touted and carefully cultivated his stance as a Muslim moderate when in fact he was a stealthy radical. He had spoken about the rule of law and democracy but only if it does not contradict Islamic principles. He journeyed to Iran and was paid fees for multiple appearances on Iranian TV. The Dutch government had been sponsoring his government positions and his lectureship at Erasmus University. He is a good example of the attempt at Islamic spokespersons to enter the intellectual debates about Islam who are eventually exposed because they cannot conceal the militancy embedded in Islam.

His method of teaching is theologically medieval—to use a passage from the Koran or *Hadith*, explain the meaning, and then interpret it in a contemporary context. He describes this in his 2010 book, *What I Believe*, a misnomer of a title. [15] The book is not a reliable description of what he believes but rather his opinions about what the West needs to do to accommodate Muslims. He calls his approach "reformist," but it is a scholastic argumentative method Duns Scotus and Thomas Aquinas would approve. But unless one is keen to read only devotional literature, his method is irrelevant in a scientific age in which new knowledge is gained through experimentation and testing of hypotheses.

His lack of rigorous scholarship and scientific research is not necessarily an impediment to academic standing. But his non-reliance on scholarly methods, even historical or social science data, reinforces his preaching and propagandistic style. His message criticizes westerners for not welcoming Muslims, but he systematically avoids writing about the violence embedded in Islamic scripture and in radicalized young men. Thus, he is not objective. He cites his own books but no authors, no literature, includes no references, nor does he quote social science scholarship. He doesn't even structurally interview other Muslims. His books are essentially an argument for total Islamic acceptance, an apologia. He defends Islam without equivocation, which in itself should make everyone suspicious. He gives unsubstantiated opinions without acknowledging Muslim extremism, the very essence of the challenge with the West. Nor does he respond to why Muslims appear to want to integrate yet seek their own *sharia* law in local communities.

He carps on Europe's historical attitude for absorbing immigrants and attempting to integrate them for preaching Muslim identity. He does not respond to the natural question of why Muslims do not want to return to their homelands. Muslims want Europe's freedoms from tyranny and economic deprivations, but many do not want to integrate into European national cultures. Ramadan writes about the psychological trauma to European Muslims but not about the trauma to Europeans of Muslim terrorist attacks that are not, for example, committed uniformly by, let's say, Presbyterians. No other specific religious group, nor atheists or agnostics, are responsible for targeted assassinations (Pim Fortuyn, Theo Van Gogh), state-sponsored attempted assassinations (Salman Rushdie), attempted assassinations (Ayaan Hirsi Ali, Kurt Westergaard, Lars Vilks), and indiscriminate bombings meant to kill innocent civilians in western countries. He does not understand, or cares not to acknowledge, that a nation's first impulse is to protect its citizens, and not just the exercise pluralistic social values, and that only Muslims have been known recently to engage consistently in terrorist attacks.

Tariq writes as if Muslims were the victims of overwhelming psychological and environmental conditions. He stresses how Muslims must confront multiple western identities, the impact of globalization—which he equates with westernization—"economic exile," and, my personal favorite, "fear of dispossession," as if these were somehow the unique defining characteristics of Muslims and not all immigrants. Preserving a Muslim identity for Ramadan means not assimilating into western culture except on Islamic terms. This implies resisting the state for not letting girls wear headscarves, for forcing them to play sports, and for teaching evolution in biology classes. He wants freedom of choice for women to wear headscarves but not freedom of choice for European non-Muslims to act freely.

He does not explain why Islam advocates death for those who renounce their faith, why Islam supports polygamy but not mixed marriages, nor why corporal punishment (stoning and whipping) for certain offenses is still condoned. Would Sikhism, Judaism, Christianity or Mormonism be welcomed in most circles for tolerating these beliefs? He does not condemn Islamic extremism.

In the final analysis, Ramadan's world (he calls it his "universe") is defined by his Muslim faith that overrides everything, including any nation's laws that contradict Islamic principles, and to globalize the Islamic message. An Appeals Court in Lyon, France on May 22, 2003, in a libel suit brought by Ramadan against the publication *Lyon Mag*, declared that preachers like Ramadan "can influence young Muslims and can serve as a factor inciting them to join up against those engaged in violent acts."

In the developed world civil law prevails, not any one religion. Tariq Ramadan is a product of the Muslim Brotherhood and its most articulate and dangerous spokesperson. His widespread admiration is misdirected and his agenda is sinister. He equivocates on all substantive issues about Islam, but especially about violence and terrorism. He is essentially a preacher and, although he projects himself in the forefront of intellectual life, he is an affront to that station, and only is respected by the Left because no other articulate Islamic spokespersons are available.

# American Muslims

Muslim terrorists and their supporters and sympathizers are a minority faction of Muslims. Muslims themselves admire Islamic fanaticism and violent extremism least, according to the Gallup Poll that has conducted the most impressive worldwide surveys of Muslims. [16]

Researchers interviewed Muslim teenagers in four public schools in the American Midwest. Using a variety of theories, such as "critical spiritual theory," these researchers attempted to explain the identity of selected Muslim students through expressed spiritual frames of reference. One girl who wears the *hijab* avoids becoming "Americanized," and was referred to as "soldiering," or not wanting to assimilate. "Americanized" is an odd category that does not distinguish between nationality, good citizenship, or cultural assimilation. "Soldiering" may express boldness in choice but also conveys a militant posture. Another boy was described as having "compliant withdrawal," or not wanting to assimilate at all but, because he was adopted, and not wanting to dishonor his adopted parents. It wasn't clear from these researchers if these social behaviors were indicative of typical adolescent development factors or were specific to Muslim identity.[17] Such contemporary researchers do not use traditional theories of sociology, psychology or cultural anthropology that explain or predict behavior, even religious behavior, and rely instead on coined words or phrases that do not really possess theoretical support. a

For example, honor killings were one of the more perverse cultural codes but they can occur anywhere. Faleh Al-Maleki, 49, admitted to killing his daughter, Noor, 20, because she had become too westernized. Noor had reputedly married a man in Iraq but returned to live with a boyfriend in Arizona. Kaleh used his Jeep Cherokee to run down his daughter and another woman, the mother of her boyfriend, on October 20, 2009 in Glendale, Arizona in suburban Phoenix. He pleaded not guilty to the charges because he believes in his tribal culture he must atone for his daughter's shameful behavior to the family by killing her. He was convicted in 2011 and sentenced to 34 years in prison.

The root cause of Islamic extremism generally does not include manipulation of the poor and uneducated. Evidence indicates that Islamic political radicals are more educated, tend to be more affluent, are more frustrated, and are more religious. However, almost universally they are also more likely to be threatened by the dominance of the West and they don't believe that better relations with the West will resolve anything.

Nevertheless, from 2001 to 2008 there were 527 terrorism charges in the U.S. (about a third the number in Europe) resulting in 319 convictions, with additional trials pending. The per-capita Muslim arrest rate in the U.S. is 2.5 times as high as it is in Europe. This does not speak well that improved socio-economic conditions or better cultural relations will solve the problem. Terrorism is un-related to economics. [18]

American Muslims have a more satisfied sense of their lives than do most Muslims in other Islamic countries. In fact, American Muslims by and large approximate the levels of life satisfaction of all Americans. If we further sub-divide American Muslims into convenient ethnic groups, the poll found that Asian American Muslims, for example, are better educated, more affluent and have a higher sense of life satisfaction that Muslims whose country of origin is, for example, Pakistan or Indonesia. American Muslims, like any other demographic group, are not homogeneous. Like other Americans, Muslim Americans view a religious life as essential to their wellbeing.

Kareem Rashed Sultan Khan, 20, a graduate of Southern Regional High School in Manahawkin, New Jersey, died an American soldier in Iraq in 2008. He had been eager to enlist in the army since 9/11 when he was fourteen years old. On the other hand, an Arab-American, Sirhan Sirhan, born in Palestine, murdered Robert Kennedy in 1968 because of his grievance over the Kennedy Administration's posture toward Israel.

Take the case of Syed, an American Muslim living in a large metropolitan area and an acquaintance of mine. He is in his mid-fifties and works for a car dealership. He has two adult children who have been well schooled and work successfully in professional careers. Syed works part-time also as a caterer offering a wide variety of typical Pakistani and Indian dishes—Tikka, Biryani, Korma, Nihari, curried dishes, and Seekh Kabobs—for home and businesses. He sells all his food preparations and specialties at the local mosque after Friday prayers.

Syed was born in Karachi, Pakistan and came to the U.S. with his family when he was a teenager. His father had been a customs inspector and his grandfather was an artist and a part of the staff of Mohammed Ali Jinnah, the father of Pakistan and friend of Gandhi before the partition of Pakistan from India in 1947. At the time Karachi was the capitol of Pakistan until it was moved to Islamabad. Though not born in the U.S., Syed is a Pakistani American whose native language is Urdu but who is thoroughly Americanized, and who has been American educated with children born in the U.S. His career and those of his children are the typical immigrant story of arriving in the U.S. with little or no money who have successfully navigated through American schooling and several business opportunities to provide for their families and live the American dream.

Immigrants everywhere seek what everyone seeks—improved living standards for themselves and their families. Immigrants crowd into ethnic and immigrant ghettoes where they associate largely with their own linguistic, ethnic or national kin. Because of the nature of large urban apartment housing complexes, many immigrants do not assimilate well, if at all, in a single generation. The lack of high-paying jobs because of a general lack of further education restricts them to unskilled labor, and cottage industry or small business jobs. Moreover, all available evidence about European and American Muslims points to the fact that they universally retain Islam as a religious preference, and that a small number of its young males among this minority population unfortunately become enchanted with the *jihad* message of Islam.

After flirting with the fundamentalist side of Islam, like the Salafi movement, they are reinforced in the lifestyle ideology of *jihad*—sometimes emboldened in videos with jihadist rap songs—and become consumed with Islamic justice. They are now radicalized to fight and die defending their religion. Once radicalized, a young Muslim male can go fight for the Islamic cause in a foreign country like Yemen or Somalia, and possibly return to act in or promote terrorism in the West.

Omar Hammadi was also one of those homegrown American boys. He grew up in Daphne, Alabama, the son of a Christian mother and Muslim Syrian father, a bright, curious boy who was a favorite of jocks and nerds alike in high school. Because of his high grades and ACT score that placed him in the 93rd percentile, he skipped his senior year in high school and enrolled in the University of South Alabama where he joined the student Muslim group and became a spokesperson for the Salafi movement whose members week a strict return to the fundamentals of Islam. He was indicted for terrorism and is at large fighting for the *Shabab* militia in Somalia. [19]

Another radicalized group that included six Miami men, said to be affiliated with *Islamic Jihad*, were convicted in a Miami court on May 12, 2009 of plotting to blow up the Sears Tower in Chicago. Two mistrials preceded their conviction as prosecutors failed to convince jurors that the poor young men, mostly of Haitian descent and dubbed the Liberty City Seven (two had already been acquitted), were gang members and not dedicated terrorists. [20]

The same day in 2009, a federal jury in New York convicted a Lebanese-born Swede, Oussama Kassir, 41, born in Beirut but living in Stockholm, of attempting to establish a weapons training post in Bly, Oregon in 1999. This rural location was to be used to train European Islamic militants in the U.S. He also was convicted of distributing terrorist manuals over the Internet as he had created at least three different websites, according to U.S. Department of Justice records. [21] He fought in the Lebanese civil war and had had weapons training and, according to his own account, was a follower of Osama bin Laden and *jihad*. Czech authorities arrested Kassir in 2005 on a stopover as he was traveling from Stockholm to Beirut. He had previously been convicted in Sweden of possession of illegal firearms, assault of a policeman, and drug-related offenses. He was extradited from the Czech Republic to New York in 2007.

Radicalized Muslims who live in America have a condescending view of the West but live with western individual freedoms where they can speak freely, including hate speech, without fear of retribution, as they could not in their home countries. [22] The new Muslim assault is an attempt to eviscerate western culture by imposing its own cultural norms, starting with dress codes and religious distinctions. This is a prelude to attaining political strength through numbers and using the democratic plebiscite to vote themselves privileges.

For example, The Fiqh Council of North America, a group of Islamic scholars, issued a *fatwa* in February 2010 that forbids Muslims to undergo body scanners at airports because it violates teachings about nakedness. An option is for Muslims to undergo pat-downs. But the real issue is whether or not Islamic law, where it conflicts with civil law anywhere in a democracy, can ever supersede secular law applicable to all.

Europe and America for the foreseeable future will need imported labor to maintain sustainable economies. But there is no easy solution for how to integrate an immigrant people successfully into civic society. The more immediate concern is for democratic societies to be vigilant about radicalized Muslim youth and the inculcation of a Muslim culture that does not recognize civil or personal liberties of non-Muslims.

The vigilance includes Canada. A group of 18 Islamic extremists were arrested in 2006 in Toronto. One radical leader, Zakaria Amara, 24, was sentenced to life in prison in 2010 for a conspiracy that involved a one-ton truck bombing of the Toronto stock exchange. Amara learned to make a fertilizer bomb on the Internet. The rest of the plot included storming the Parliament building in Ottawa and beheading the Prime Minister.

But the most significant difference between the fundamentalist Muslim world and the West is the distinct values of the rule of law. *Sharia* law is religious law and Muslims make no distinction between it and any other law code. It's as if the West had to follow exclusively the *Code of Canon Law*, the religious law of the Catholic Church. Civil law in the West means that all civilians are obligated to follow the adopted law, even if they may not agree with it because that is what unites a democratic people—the unity of adherence to the law.

Americans are perennially adjudicating between two constitutional principles, like free speech and a national security law that restricts free speech. In June 2010 the U.S. Supreme Court by a vote of 6-3 decided in *Holder v. Humanitarian Law* that a law making it a crime to provide "material support" to a terrorist organization is upheld. In other words, the national security concerns of not providing tangible evidence to terrorist group does not violate the 1st Amendment's protection of free speech. Any kind of support to an identified terrorist organization is criminal.

A civil rights lawyer, who had sought to provide legal advice to a Kurdish workers' group in Turkey, had challenged the law. Other litigants had wanted to aid only non-violent activities of terrorist groups like the Tamil Tigers in Sri Lanka. The Supreme Court made it clear that any aid— legal advice, training, advice or service—is tantamount to furthering the terrorist activities of the group and lends validation to the group's cause. Now, because of the court's ruling in favor of national security, certain limits have been placed on free speech, one of the most cherished of democratic freedoms.

Muslims have arrived in the West but they all have not made a social compact. They have largely not accepted Western values and considered them corrupt, and therefore incapable of allegiance. They prefer that Europe give them free rein and unrestricted willingness to let Muslims behave in any way they choose in the name of religious freedom, and regardless of whether or not their practices violate democratic values of free speech, tolerance for other beliefs, or gender equality. Islamic immigrants want western economic values but don't value western individual values. [23]

Religion must not determine what happens in the public sphere in Europe or the West. If visitors to a mosque must remove shoes, females should remove veils before entering schools. If Muslims want even uneasy accommodation with western societies they must collectively and publically renounce the violence embedded in Islam.

Europe in its complacency is often behaving toward radical Muslims like an irritant mother-in-law upset with her grandchildren. A few Islamists want to terrorize westerners through brazen suicide attacks. The rest appear to be simply colonizing the nations in which they live and hoping to subdue Europeans over time with gradual advances of their religious prerogatives while denigrating and feeling contempt for the languages, cultures and people in countries where they reside.

The Danish Cartoon that Sparked Riots in 2006

# PART II

# COUNTRY PERPSECTIVES IN THE ROILING MIDDLE EAST

In these concluding chapters I review the global Islamic militancy movement in other continents and countries to show both the diversity of its reach and the perceived unity of its confrontation with western ideals. A billion people who claim one faith are finding difficulty seeing where modernity and secularism can, or cannot, easily merge with a fundamentalist religion. For the few alienated and misguided, this can only mean a turn to violence to stamp out the infidel.

I had originally written a descriptive chapter on how the Bush Administration had mistaken invaded Iraq and how that error contributed to a debilitated American image in the Islamic world and made worse a chaotic situation in the Middle East. I abandoned the Iraq chapter because in the interim Saddam had been captured and executed and American troops had left. The invasion of Iraq was a gift to al-Qaeda and other militant organizations because, with the loss of Taliban-controlled Afghanistan by November 2002, it gave members new experiences in a new fighting ground to kill Americans. Internal Iraqi threats from the deep-seated sectarian divisions, that I predicted in 2003 would result in civil war at the time of invasion, began to fracture the fragile country. Iraq's experiment with democracy even during the occupation has not yet resulted in national unity or civil order but in political and governmental dysfunction. Besides the U.S. invasion blunder, the greatest misstep was in continuing to recognize Iraq as one country, a mistake the British made after World War II. The Kurds should have been given their own homeland in the North.

America typically tallies the cost of its wars in body counts and money spent. From the perspective of the Islamic world, the body count in Muslim lives lost because of America's invasion of Afghanistan and Iraq was about 150,000 in Iraq and 35,000 in Afghanistan. There is no way to gauge the anger, resentment and potential revenge to be extracted from this loss of life but the consequences are surely the possibility of many more recruits for Islamic militancy from brothers, sisters, uncles and relatives.

The Arab spring in 2010 inaugurated a glimmer of hope for democratic reform initially in Tunisia, then in Egypt, and with riots in Bahrain and Syria. The Arab youth, tuned in to social networks, were conscious of how under-developed were the countries they lived in compared to Europe and America and rallied to express their rising discontent with dictatorships. Militancy groups did not disband, however, and saw opportunities for gaining power through participation in a political process and not just through armed rebellion. It is unknown if this change in strategy will cause them to forego violence as a means to achieving the goals of Islamic governance.

Pakistan's nuclear weapons and fear of India, Iran's belligerency toward America and the West—a signal trait of fundamentalist Islam—and quest for nuclear armaments, the civil chaos in Iraq and Syria, the stalemate between Israel and the Palestinians, the growing military strength of Hezbollah, the fragility of Lebanon, the conflict in Syria—none of these predicaments bode well for successful transformation to democratic rule in any one country or peaceful coexistence between neighboring states.

# CHAPTER SEVEN
# ISRAEL AND PALESTINIANS

We imbibed with our mother's milk hatred for the Jews and for anyone who supported their cause. We justified this hatred by devising a conspiracy theory, and we called upon anyone who disagreed with us a Zionist agent. This conspiracy theory helped keep Muslims inside the straightjacket in which Islam had imprisoned their minds. (Wafa Sultan, *A Good Who Hates*, 2009, p. 188.) [1]

On November 30, 1947, the United Nations voted to partition British-ruled Palestine into a Jewish and Arab state. The next morning a band of Arab fighters shot up a bus east of Tel Aviv killing five Jews. The armed conflict between Jews and Arabs began within hours and did not end until March 10, 1949 when Jewish forces defeated the Arab irregulars, and then Egypt, Jordan, Syria and Iraq. Over 700,000 Arab refugees fled the chaos of war never to return, a number that has since nearly tripled and strained refugee camps in Lebanon and Jordan and diplomatic initiatives to allow them to return to their original homes. In 2009 I interviewed a few of these second generation immigrants in Lebanon whose parents were driven from Israel.

Neither party is willing to make territorial concessions. The possibility for reconciliation between Israel and the Palestinians is as bleak as it has ever been. Partitioned land is at the center of the antagonism. Israeli unwillingness to give back land earned in war, and Islamic militancy to retake it, contribute equally to the stalemate. Arabs have never accepted either a bi-national state or a partition. Arabs view the conflict with Jews as a religious struggle against infidel usurpers. Israelis fear that even with a recognized state next to its borders that terrorism against it would not diminish. This implacable stance has not changed since the meeting of the Third Palestine Arab Congress in 1920. The electoral legitimacy in Gaza of Hamas, a group that sanctifies a cult of murder/suicide and espouses the death of non-believers, has no maneuverability for compromise. Hamas Islamized the political problem of the Palestinians and made it a religious mission. If the land belonged to Allah, Jews could never live there.

Palestine is a state of mind. Originally a part of the Ottoman Empire until 1918, what Arabs regard as Palestine has no recognized territorial sovereignty. It was never founded as a separate country, has no defined borders, no separate currency, and is not recognized as a country by any other country. On the other hand, though the United Nations recognizes Israel as a separate nation, Arab countries have not accepted military defeat in the 1967 and 1973 wars, and hence do not accept Israel as a nation, and they have an implacable hatred of Jews. Diplomatic talks start, stall and then stop from time to time. But the hostile situation does not change.

Moreover, that Jews, whom all Arabs hold in contempt, were able to defeat Arabs in battle on former Arab land in 1948 was a humiliating revelation that continues to simmer. Subsequent defeats of Arab armies in 1967 and 1973 have only deepened the resentment. Arab self-esteem and militant soldierly pride was wounded when Israel was established as a separate state. Israel does not appear in any Arab maps of the region, nor in reference books or newspapers. No one who has an Israeli stamp in a passport will be able to enter an Arab country. All this is another denial of reality, and repetitive slogans and boasts that are attempts to retain some sense of honor that no amount of negotiation can regain. The clash of Israel with the Palestinians and the Arab world may offer a peek into a future clash of the West with Islam.

Khaled Meshal, one of the leaders of Hamas, born in 1956 in Ramallah, is heavily guarded while living in Damascus. He says Hamas seeks only those areas lost to Israel in the 1967 war for a Palestinian state. Hamas does not recognize Israel and never will. He wants everyone to ignore the Hamas Charter that calls for the obliteration of Israel through *jihad*. He won't revoke the Charter but wants all to believe him when he calls for peace through an unconditional Palestinian state to be carved out of existing land controlled by Israel. The U.S. position is not to speak to Hamas unless it renounces violence and recognizes Israel. The Hamas Charter is quite explicit in its aims:

> The Islamic Resistance Movement believes that the land of Palestine is an Islamic *Waqf* [endowment] consecrated for future Muslim generations until Judgment Day. It, or any part of it, should not be squandered: it, or any part of it, should not be given up. [2]

One of the best examples of how the Islamic militancy movement has expanded in this millennium is the overthrow of the Palestinian Fatah organization by Hamas within Gaza. Hamas stands for "Islamic Resistance Movement" and means "zeal" in Arabic. Fatah was founded at the beginning of the first *intifada* by the religious leader Sheikh Ahmed Yassin who was assassinated by Israel in 2004. The rise of Hamas, a proxy militia funded largely by Iran, exposed the civil war between the secular and moderate Palestinians and the alliance with other violent Islamist groups like *Islamic Jihad*, al-Aqsa Martyrs Brigade and Hezbollah. Al-Aqsa Martyr's Brigade was actually a militant front organization operated by Yasser Arafat.

I have taught Palestinian graduate students, and it is difficult to imagine how anyone of them could not be resentful. I have seen the bitterness on their faces and the spite in their eyes. Thus, recruitment of soldiers for the fight against Israel or the West in general would make any young man who sought peace, or was stoic in the face of such adversity, a rare exception. In such an environment, stone-throwers, rocket-launchers and suicide bombers find their warrior Muslim identity and achieve a forged Arab manhood and militant status. The Arab young are educated in a cult of malevolence toward all enemies. It would be nearly impossible to isolate those who are withdrawn or non-committal to the cause of Islam, not just the rescue of Palestinians from Israeli oppression.

As a contrast, Israel's $100 billion economy is larger than all of its immediate neighbors combined, and has the highest average living standards in the Middle East. The per capita income in Israel exceeds that of the UK. Israel leads the world in the number of scientists and technicians in the workforce, with 145 per 10,000, as opposed to 85 in the U. S., 70 in Japan, and less than 60 in Germany. It produces more scientific papers per capita than any other nation by a large margin—109 per 10,000 people—as well as one of the highest per capita rates of patents filed. Israel's ranks third in the industrialized world holding college degrees, after the United States and Holland, and 12% hold advanced degrees. The combined Arab world has no equivalent.

Israel with a population of about seven million is an economically developed country whose per capita income is 29$^{th}$ in the world, higher than Portugal, South Korea or Taiwan, and higher than any country in Latin America or Africa. Israel has more venture capital and than country in the region and leads the world in per-capita spending in research and development. Tel Aviv rivals Silicon Valley for high tech start-ups. Israel has registered more patents in the past thirty years than Egypt or Saudi Arabia by a factor of over a hundred.

## Arabs and Jews

There is no solution for the Palestinian question except through *Jihad*. Initiatives, proposals and international conferences are all a waste of time and vain endeavors. [3]

Shortly after noon on June 5, 1968, Sirhan Sirhan, a Palestinian born in Jerusalem in 1944 stood in the kitchen of the Ambassador Hotel in Los Angeles and shot Robert F. Kennedy three times with a 22 caliber revolver. Kennedy was a presidential candidate, and had just finished giving a speech in a campaign for the California primary. He died the following day just five years after his president brother had been assassinated.

Sirhan, who had emigrated to the U.S. in 1956, was an aggrieved, angry Arab assassin. His mother said he killed Kennedy because of Sirhan's Arab nationalism and Kennedy's support for Israel in the 1967 war. Sirhan's employment at the time was as a stable hand at the Santa Anita racetrack. He was convicted and sentenced to death that was subsequently commuted to life in prison. He is incarcerated in the California State prison at Corcoran and has been denied parole thirteen times. Reports at the time tried to label Sirhan as a man of diminished capacity. He is not irrational, only acting out his beliefs as a confirmed assassin, the same as any lone terrorist, dedicated to murder to avenge purported grievances.

The anti-Semitic propaganda Sirhan Sirhan learned from his hateful parents, who thought of themselves as Arab nationals and not assimilated Americans. His Jordanian schooling in East Jerusalem was rife with violence and invective. Such ethnic enmity toward Jews is still perpetrated by Palestinian parents, politicians and teachers and is no less vitriolic or malicious.

The main figures in the Palestinian and Israeli drama are like walk-on characters in an Anton Chekhov play—alone and locked into their own religious ethnicities, clans and cultures, but somehow wanting to connect with each other even marginally. At the moment social isolation for fundamentalists on either side defines them more than inter-cultural urge for social linkage. They are cantankerous neighbors living cheek to jowl with a dividing, un-neighborly fence between them without an acceptable, just mediator to resolve long-running and acrimonious disputes.

> The hatred of Israel and our obligation to pursue jihad was somehow
> worked into every subject we discussed in school. In fact, clearly, the main
> goal of our education was to instill a commitment to destroy Israel. Peace
> was never discussed as an option . . . (Nonie Darwish, *Now They Call me
> Infidel*, p. 9).

The militancy and extremism among Muslims runs too deep to think that a Palestinian state will be any more responsive to peace than it was during the so-called occupation of the territories. After all, Egypt, Jordan and Syria all attacked Israel in the 20th century, so the creation of another Arab state is no guarantee that peace will come because state status is achieved for Palestinians. The battle is over land and honor and Israel's right to create its own nation out of the territory Palestinians believe is historically theirs. But it is more than that. It is also an excuse for Islamic militias and extremists to unleash their violence on Jews whom they have historically hated. [4]

Israel receives billions annually from the U.S. in grants and loans, and is granted access to some of the best military equipment including fighter jets and the latest weaponry. Israel's military is one of the best trained with some of the most sophisticated military technology. [5]

Palestinian society is equally complex and fragmented into political, religious and ideological factions. [6] Both Israel and the Palestinians are skeptical about proposed support from the international community, profoundly distrust each other, and lean on few friends. Israel is threatened by calls for the destruction of Israel by Iran's President, by armed militias of Hezbollah in Lebanon, by Hamas militants in Gaza, and by Israel's own Palestinian Arabs whose loyalties lie more with their people than with their state, a condition similar to many Muslims in Europe. In 1967 at the first Arab/Israeli war there were two million Jews in Israel. In 2009 there were 5.5 million that included 1.3 million Arab Israeli citizens who have since become more radicalized, openly avowing a Palestinian identity. The birth rates for Israeli Arabs—among the highest in the world—are roughly twice that of Israeli Jews. [7]

Regardless of what compromise Israel offers the Palestinians, it will never be enough. The Palestinian negotiating offer is to get back everything they lost in war, unconditionally and without concessions. The typical response to a proposal they reject is violence, usually in the form of rocket attacks but also suicide bombings. [8] At present, Palestinians are themselves divided, as Israelis have always been, between those few who want some kind of settlement, and those like Hamas who seek the abolition of Israel, even after an uneasy agreement between Fatah and Hamas in May 2011. The Holocaust defines Israeli Jews; lost land and the displacement of Palestinians in Israel's War of Independence (or the *nakba* or "catastrophe" in Arabic) defines the Palestinians.

An Arab Peace Initiative, adopted by 57 Arab and Muslim countries by the 14th Arab Summit in Beirut in March 2002, called for full diplomatic and normal relations with Israel in return for a comprehensive peace agreement ending the occupation. [9] The Arab League agreement was to be ratified when Israel withdrew fully from all Arab territories occupied since June 1967, including the Golan Heights, and that Israel must accept an independent Palestinian state with East Jerusalem as its capitol. All Muslim countries endorsed the plan. It was unrealistic and had no complementary provisions or concessions from Palestinians. Israel will never accept any Islamic control over Jerusalem.

Israel has relentlessly continued to build housing settlements in disputed territory and in East Jerusalem contrary to its signed agreements to United Nations Resolution 242 and 338. UN Resolution 242 unanimously adopted by the Security Council November 22, 1967 called for the withdrawal of Israeli forces from occupied territories. UN Resolution 338 signed on October 23, 1973 called for implementation of 242 and for negotiations to begin to establish a just and durable pace. Additionally, these agreements were upheld again in the 1993 Oslo Peace Accords, during the Bush Administration's 2003 "road map," and the 2007 Annapolis Understandings. Palestinians have asked only that these accords be honored and that Israel return territory it seized illegally subsequently in order to construct new housing for Jews and to uphold its own agreed-to treaty obligations. [10]

In the view of most Arab states the U.S. is an arm of Israeli influence. The world acknowledges that Hezbollah and Hamas are proxy militias for Iran. But the Arab world sees Israel as a proxy state for America, or at least a partner in constraining Arab interests. The impasse will not abate soon no matter how many documents are signed or handshakes extended. Continuing U.S. support of Israel means that the West will have a front line ally militarily and economically to confront perpetual Muslim militant aggression, especially coming now from Iran.

But what if the Arab world was perceived as a complicit ally of the Nazis and its hatred of the Jews and holocaust? In fact, the Grand Mufti of Jerusalem, Amin al-Husseini (1893–1974), met with Adolph Hitler in Berlin on November 28, 1941, and the following is what he said as recorded in the minutes of German Foreign Policy documents.

> The Arabs were Germany's natural friends because they had the same enemies as had Germany, namely the English, the Jews, and the Communists. Therefore they were prepared to cooperate with Germany with all their hearts and stood ready to participate in the war, not only negatively by the commission of acts of sabotage and the instigation of revolutions, but also positively by the formation of an Arab Legion. [11]

The chief religious figure of the Arab world, who served as a soldier in the Ottoman army, admitted to the most hated figure of the 20th century, Hitler, that Arabs and Nazis both had Jews as enemies and was willing to offer the whole Arab world as Nazi participants. Arab and Muslim identification with Nazism was influenced in part by Arab hostility toward French and English colonialism, but clearly by hatred of Jews.

Hitler, with the support of Amin al-Husseini, formed a group of Nazi Muslims known as the Hanzar SS Division—whose members wore a fez with the logo of a skull with crossed bones and an SS eagle—who were responsible for the deaths of Bosnian Jews. At the time of course, Jews had no state, no political identity and were a minority everywhere. The general attitude of Muslims toward Jews, despite the existence of Israel since 1948, has not changed over the centuries. The Palestinian Authority distributed copies of Hitler's *Mein Kampf* in 2003.

## A Holy Land, A Scarred Land

The Sykes-Picot agreement of 1916 between France and Britain defined the territories for the British in Palestine and Iraq, and for the French in Syria and Lebanon. At the end of the war the League of Nations awarded these territories to Britain and France but as mandates, not colonies, a diplomatic equivocation not understood by anyone then or since.

The Balfour Declaration of November 2, 1917 was one facet of British diplomacy that appeared to recognize a Jewish homeland in return for the favor of responsiveness to British interests. It was written by the British Foreign Secretary Arthur James, Lord Balfour, to Lord Rothschild, the international banker and financier, in order the obtain Jewish support for the allies in World War I (1914–1918).

A Zionist movement had been circulating since the late nineteenth century instigated by Theodore Herzl (1860–1904) whereby Jews would find a homeland where they could live in peace and practice their religion unencumbered. Palestine seemed to fit that geography. Chaim Weizmann, a Russian chemist who developed acetone used in explosives, revived the Zionist movement during World War I. He became acquainted with the British Foreign Minister, Arthur James, Lord Balfour, in 1904, and argued for a Jewish national home state specifically in Palestine.

The agreement with the Arabs was that not all of Palestine would be recognized as a Jewish state, nor that the rights of the Arabs would be diminished. (Later, Weizmann became the first President under the British Mandate in 1920 after the war and the collapse of the Ottoman Empire). Here is The Balfour Declaration in the form of a letter.

Foreign Office, November 2nd, 1917

Dear Lord Rothschild,

I have much pleasure in conveying to you on behalf of His Majesty's Government the following declaration of sympathy with Jewish Zionist aspirations, which has been submitted to and approved by the Cabinet:

His Majesty's Government view with favour the establishment in Palestine of a national home for the Jewish people, and will use their best endeavours to facilitate the achievement of this object, it being clearly understood that nothing shall be done which may prejudice the civil and religious rights of existing non-Jewish communities in Palestine or the rights and political status enjoyed by Jews in any other country.

I should be grateful if you would bring this Declaration to the knowledge of the Zionist Federation.

Yours sincerely, Arthur James Balfour [12]

Some influential Jews in Europe protested, saying ironically that the proposed declaration was anti-Semitic because it would divide the loyalties of Jews between their current national identity and a new state. The richest Jews in Britain, France and America were opposed to the idea. Nevertheless, it was adopted by the League of Nations.

It is an extraordinary document because it promised to a religious and ethnic group a country of their own that at the time only existed in the realm of another empire, the Ottoman. In other words, one imperial government, England, promised to a group of people, Jews, the creation of a new country, Israel, but in another empire. Apart from the diplomatic niceties and backroom negotiations between European powers, it is imperative to see this from the Arab viewpoint. Arabs saw through the support for Jewish influence as merely a way in which colonial powers would be carving up Arab lands for settlers that didn't belong there.

In 1947 the United Nations approved the partition of Palestine into two states, one Jewish and one Arab. Jews accepted, Arabs refused, and the war began. The war has been ongoing since the British left the region at the end of World War II, and the Palestinians fought to regain a lost land. Both Jews living in Palestine and those fleeing persecution in Europe moved in to begin a new state.

My Syrian friends have told me that they do not have bad feelings against those Jews and their families who have always lived in the region known as Palestine. But they are antagonistic to Jews who emigrated from Europe to live in Israel because it is a Zionist state. Most Muslims think such Jewish immigrants do not belong in a region that has been Muslim for centuries. On the other hand, Jews believe that because they are descendants of Hebrews, whom God reputedly gave the land to, they have a special right to live and occupy Israel, the land God gave to Abraham.

When the British withdrew from Palestine on May 14, 1947, Israel declared itself an independent state on the same year the next year, May 14, 1948. It was recognized by the United States during the Truman Administration within hours. The Palestinians took up arms to drive out the Jews. Other Islamic nations—Jordan, Syria, and Egypt—assisted Palestinians in their cause during the 1967 and 1973 wars, but were defeated by Israeli superior military technology. Egypt nationalized the Suez Canal in 1956 and forbade Israel from using the shipping lanes. In the Six Day War in 1967 Israel simultaneously made air attacks against Egyptian, Jordanian and Syrian air bases and totally defeated the combined Arab forces. Israel then acquired the Golan Heights, the Sinai Peninsula, the West Bank of the Jordan River, and the old city of Jerusalem.

Border skirmishes, suicide bombings, hijackings of planes and ships, rocket launches have all been used from time to time against Israel. These attacks have been met with retaliatory strikes in Gaza, the West Bank, and raids into Tunisia and Lebanon where Yasser Arafat once had headquarters of the Palestinian Liberation Organization.

The 1973 war between Israel, Egypt and Syria was a lesson for all three countries of the misunderstandings of wartime intelligence, excessive trust in military technology, and the fragilities of life. Arabs were unforgiving to those who had emigrated from Europe after World War II and had established residence in what Arabs believed to be their ancestral homeland.

There had always been a lingering resentment against these Jewish carpetbaggers and illegal settlers. The Arab world saw no need for the establishment of a Zionist state in what they believed was their land. Besides, after 1967 the humiliation of the disastrous defeat that only lasted six days, the Arabs were still simmering for revenge.

The Arab/Israeli conflict has had a series of on-again, off-again diplomatic trials and reluctant peace agreements. The land on the West Bank of the Jordan River, and the Gaza strip are still contested land, technically not a part of any country. Israel has peace agreements with Jordan and Egypt, but no other Arab nation. The future of Jordan was at stake too. Unless the Palestinians can establish their own independent state somewhere on the West Bank, they could de-stabilize Jordan, itself a buffer state between Saudi Arabia, Syria, Iraq and Israel.

In 1988 in response to international pressure, Arafat vowed to recognize Israel and renounce terror as a tactic. He lied. When he attacked beaches near Tel Aviv trying to raid embassies and U.S. hotels, President George H. W. Bush suspended dialogue with Arafat and attempted to undercut his authority with Palestinians. The collapse of the Soviet Union removed one of the strongest of Arafat's financial supporters. Rivals emerged from his weakened position as more radicalized Palestinians challenged him, and several uprisings, or *intifadas*, failed. Arafat was always conciliatory when speaking English but defiant when addressing crowds in Arabic.

The Middle East peace process, always about Israel and the Palestinians, is like a yo-yo. For every good spin in the desired diplomatic direction there is retrenchment to a previous position. Yitzhak Rabin (1922–1995) and Yasser Arafat (1929–2004) had a famous handshake on the lawn of the White House on September 13, 1993 after concluding a *Declaration of Principles* for a proposed interim government for the Palestinians. Both Rabin and Arafat, together with Israeli Foreign Minister Shimon Peres, received the Nobel Peace Prize in 1994.

The Palestinian Liberation Organization (PLO), based from the late 1960s in Jordan, continued this terrorist armed struggle against Israel. Not surprisingly, Jordan never granted the Palestinians a separate state but gave the refugees Jordanian citizenship. Nearly two million Palestinians still live in Jordan, nearly a half million in refugee camps.

The PLO, essentially a mercenary army, was admitted into the United Nations in an observer status, enhancing a terrorist organization as a legitimate political presence in the global body. It declared itself to be a national liberation movement. With logic that beggars reason, this of course meant the elimination of another nation-state, Israel. Western countries, including the Vatican, embraced PLO ideology and conferred diplomatic recognition on it, though if its aims had been met the result would have been the elimination of Israel. In actuality, the PLO's chief tactic was assassination of its opponents, the hijacking of aircraft, and the taking of hostages. With the death of Arafat the militancy movement among Muslims became emboldened as Hamas and Hezbollah emerged as armies and not merely as political organizations.

## Mahmoud Abbas, Fatah Leader

For forty years Abbas was a devoted follower of the failed policies of Arafat. When Arafat died in November 2004, Abbas became the new leader, a man who supposedly renounced terrorism and favored an agreement with Israel. His repudiation by Hamas and the humiliating defeat of his policies and police force in Gaza not only fractured the Palestinians into radical extremists and moderates but disintegrated any hope for Israel's agreement with a unified Palestinian authority.

Abbas received his doctorate from the Oriental University in Moscow in the early 1980s. [13] The title of his dissertation was *The Secret Relationship Between Zionism and Nazism.* This peculiar research denied the Holocaust and preposterously asserted that Zionists provoked the Nazis into killing Jews so that a few could immigrate to Palestine. His thesis blamed the Jews for all the world's problems. It is an old, discriminatory, false rumor that still resounds in conversations throughout the Middle East. I have heard it repeated by businessmen in the Persian Gulf. Muslims also unbelievably blamed the 2001 attacks on New York and the Pentagon on Jews so America would attack Muslim countries. Abbas wrote: "The Zionist movement led a broad campaign of incitement against the Jews under Nazi rule in order to arouse the government's hatred of them, to fuel vengeance against them, and to expand the mass extermination." [14] Abbas cited no sources for his wild, unsubstantiated allegations.

As the heir apparent and leader of Fatah it is hard to see how this brand of hate ideology passes for legitimate scholarship, even in Russia. The acceptance of this sort of absurdity as scholarship shows how vacuous and spurious was the Soviet Union's sponsorship of Third World candidates who would write such ludicrous tracts under the auspices of legitimate research. The Soviets could just as easily given him a degree for poetic imagination or inbred cynicism and anti-Semitic prejudice.

Hamas won an election in Gaza in 2006 by defeating Fatah, the organization founded by Arafat. Hamas then proceeded to harass and then kill Fatah police to consolidate its power in Gaza. There were now two distinct Palestinian governing authorities: Hamas in Gaza and Abbas' Fatah in the West Bank. Israel soon realized that if Abbas and his organization fell part or relented in favor of Hamas, that Hamas would immediately take over the West Bank and resume war against Israel rendering any peace accord meaningless.

## King Hussein of Jordan

Ronald Reagan, in private correspondence with King Hussein of Jordan, wondered what kind of fish were in the Dead Sea and whether he could send some California fish to invigorate its waters. The King's response was polite but he assured Reagan that the Dead Sea really was dead of marine life. This polite trivia passes for American diplomacy, but often reveals the ignorance and lack of understanding even American presidents have of the world they purportedly lead.

Hussein's life (Hussein bin Talal 1935–1999) spanned the conflicts of the Middle East and the multiple assassination attempts on his life—from machine-gunning of his motorcade, to mutinous army officers, to domestic poisonings—show his survival instincts and fortitude. Hussein was personally charismatic. Educated at Harrow and Sandhurst military academy in England he always favored the British in diplomacy. Hussein engaged in peace talks, most often clandestinely with Israeli over many years. I knew a deceased high Israeli official who secretly snuck across the border at night with Dr. Yaacov Herzog, the high Israeli government leader of these peace initiatives, to conduct secret meetings with Hussein.

The Emirate of Jordan was created out of the ruins of the old Ottoman Empire at the end of World War I in 1918. Its borders make no geographic sense unless one considers British strategy at the time. This is the era when Sharif Hussein of Arabia, the guardian of Arabia's Islamic holy sites of Mecca and Medina, inaugurated a revolt against the Ottoman Turks that the British army officer, T. E. Lawrence, the legendary Lawrence of Arabia, wrote about in *Seven Pillars of Wisdom*.

During the war of Jews against the British forces who had taken control of Egypt, Iraq, the Gulf emirates, and Palestine, Palestinian refugees from 1948-49 and again in 1967 flooded into the area then known as Transjordan, or the land across the Jordan River. Abdullah received the makeshift territory from the British at the end of the Paris Peace Conference in 1919. Abdullah was the grandfather, mentor and model for the young King Hussein.

When the Arab/Israel War broke out in 1948 Abdullah moved his Arab legions into Palestine and captured East Jerusalem. This move aborted the Palestinians from obtaining their own state and homeland, a crucial action rarely acknowledged in negotiations about past grievances, and one not precipitated by Israel. Abdullah was assassinated in 1951 by a gunshot to the head, fittingly it was said, by a Palestinian nationalist, in the al-Aqsa mosque on the Temple Mount. I have seen the bullet markings on the pillar inside the mosque near where he fell. His grandson, later King Hussein, witnessed this assassination. Hussein's mentally ill father abdicated the throne a year later and Hussein the teenager—only seventeen at the time—became King of the Hashemite Kingdom, so called because the rulers trace their ancestry back to the tribe of the Prophet himself. Hussein found himself in a country half of whose population were Palestinian refugees.

Jordan lost the West Bank to Israel in the Arab war with Israel in June 1967, and received another 200,000 Palestinians for his efforts. The 1967 war was a vainglorious and misguided attempt initiated by Egypt to regain Israel through military means, a war which neither Egypt, Syria or Jordan were prepared for, completely under-estimating and miscalculating Israel's military strength. As a result, Jordan lost Jerusalem and much of the West Bank.

When Arafat's Palestinian terrorists in 1970 flew three hijacked planes to Jordan and blew them up, King Hussein expelled Arafat, and he and his army fled to Lebanon under Syrian protection. Then in September 1972, an offshoot of Arafat's terror group, Black September, murdered eleven Israeli athletes at the Munich Olympic games. Later, a member of Mossad, Israel's intelligence agency, tracked down the Black September attackers and killed all but one of them.

Jordan had no real power, either militarily or economically because it had a fragile economy and no oil, its influence in foreign affairs disproportionate to its status, especially with Americans who once had Hussein on a CIA payroll. Hussein always had to do a delicate dance between the western powers, principally Britain and the U.S., with his Arab neighbors like Egypt, Syria, Iraq and Saudi Arabia, and with factions among the Palestinians.

Negotiations between the Americans, Israelis and Arabs including Palestinians, always involve promises, some indifference, a lot of ignorance and certainly deviousness. King Hussein experienced all of these during his attempts to arrive at compromises, both those conducted secretly and openly with President Sadat of Egypt and with American presidents Reagan, George H. W. Bush, Carter and Clinton. None of the principals in any Middle East negotiations, regardless of the degree of their optimism, could control the deep divisions.

King Hussein died in a hospital bed in Amman in 1999, only sixty-three, with his fourth wife, the Lebanese American Queen Noor, beside him.

## Eyeless in Gaza: Hamas Terrorism

Promise was that I
Should Israel from Philistian yoke deliver;
Ask for this great Deliverer now, and find him
Eyeless in Gaza at the Mill with slaves,
Himself in bonds under Philistian yoke.
(John Milton, *Samson Agonistes*, 1671)

Hamas is the stepchild of the militancy embedded in the Muslim Brotherhood and has sworn never to recognize Israel as a Jewish state. When Hamas sent scores of rockets daily into Israel in late December 2008, believing as many Muslims claimed, that Israel was a rhetorical paper tiger and pulling its tail was going to be annoying to its enemy and satisfying to Hamas. The more sophisticated rockets were landing more than 30 miles north of Gaza, farther than they had before. Israel responded in late December 2008 with devastating multiple air attacks on the Gaza strip, with a population of one and one-half million, and on Gaza City, on Hamas' living compounds, mosques where weapons were stored, the Al-Aqsa television station, the Islamic University, the headquarters of leading Hamas militants, and by bombing hidden tunnels where supplies were secretly transported from Egypt. Over a period of three weeks until the U.S. presidential inauguration on January 20, 2009, Israeli jets and tank artillery pounded buildings while Israeli soldiers roamed streets and alleyways to destroy militants. There was an enormous humanitarian outcry over the thousands killed, homes and infrastructure destroyed.

Israel's blunt military campaign against Hamas signaled its patience had expired. Israel was purging itself of the criticism it received from the partially successful destruction of Hezbollah resources with raids into Lebanon in 2006. The war against militant Islam had taken a more forceful and ugly turn. Israel's disproportionate military response to Hamas was intended to demonstrate the brutality matching Islamic militancy to what Hamas called armed resistance.

Hamas was preparing for new elections and wanted to gain support for its militant strategy toward Israel. It assumed that Israel was weakened by the 2006 invasion of Lebanon to destroy Hezbollah. Neither Hezbollah nor Israel could claim a victory. But Hezbollah did emerge stronger militarily. But Hamas thought it could prick Israel with a few rocket attacks, win the support of its people and hope that Israel would not risk a Gaza invasion. It miscalculated Israel's resolve and patience and its own impending domestic elections that relied on defending citizens from blatant attacks on its civilian population.

Predictably, Sheik Hassan Nasrallah, leader of the Hezbollah movement in Lebanon, indicted his strong support for Hamas and called for demonstrations in the streets. Hezbollah called the political shots in Lebanon because it wears the pants in that country. Iran's supreme leader Ayatollah Ali Khamenei decried the silence of other Arab governments. [15] There was no general outcry, however, about the Hamas rocket attacks or of Hamas abandoning the cease-fire agreement. The one-sided expression of Arab and Muslim outrage is never about killing but about any military response against any Muslims for Muslim attacks. The United Nations, toothless to intervene in any conflict because of its charter, called for an end to hostilities.

The Palestinian Authority in the West Bank, long at odds with Hamas and its electoral victory in Gaza, had an ambivalent response. It was clearly amused that Israel was destroying the leadership and militant policies of Hamas, but could not but react sympathetically to the deaths of so many Palestinians in Gaza. Israel did not want Hamas' belligerence to overshadow a possible agreement with the Palestinian Authority in the West Bank. Arab leadership in general was reluctant to see a Hamas victory because it knew that Iran sponsored the Hamas weapons program. If Hamas can destabilize Israel it could destabilize any state in the Middle East, potentially countries like Egypt, Lebanon, Jordan and Persian Gulf states. Publicly, Arab states seek to defend Muslim colleagues and brothers but privately they wish Israel to destroy Hamas so that Iran cannot gain influence with its proxy militant armies.

The goal of Israel was to completely destroy the leadership and infrastructure of Hamas, perhaps to bring it to the negotiating table and cease firing rockets into Israel, but more likely to wipe out the organization totally. The danger is that anarchy would result if all law and order were eradicated and that neither Israel nor the Palestinian authority would be able to stop Hamas' armed resistance to Israel.

By the time relief agencies began the laborious process of redistributing food, medical and other necessary supplies to Palestinian refugees in early 2009, Hamas police seized the aid material at gunpoint from the United Nations Relief and Works Agency workers. Hamas confiscated about 3,500 blankets and more than 400 parcels of food from a warehouse at the Gaza City Beach Camp meant to serve families in the area. According to the UN agency it was the first time such supplies had ever been seized by force.

During the incursion into Gaza, Israeli intelligence had intercepted reports that Iranian supplies including weapons were being smuggled into

Gaza through Sudan. Iran's Revolutionary Guards had traveled to Sudan to coordinate the operation. So in January 2009, Israel bombed a convoy of trucks in a remote region of eastern Sudan near Port Sudan on the Red Sea that were believed to be carrying arms to Gaza.

The UN Human Rights Council's report on the Gaza incursion blamed the Israeli military for targeting the people of Gaza as a whole, and not just as a response to rocket attacks. Israelis tended to view civilian casualties during the incursion as collateral damage and as an attempt to destroy the infrastructure of the Hamas leadership. Without absolving wrongs committed on either side, it is difficult in times of war, especially with an irregular army, to avoid recklessness while dodging bullets, and to have regard for innocent life in a combat zone.

Most want the violence to cease and for peace to reign in the region, the biblical land of Eretz Israel, the Jewish homeland Yahweh supposedly gave to the twelve tribes of Israel, the Holy Land for Christians, and the site of Mohammad's ascension for Muslims. But given the fierce resentment Palestinians feel about their displacement and other legitimate grievances, together with the historical penchant of Muslims for violence, and the equally determined Israeli conviction never to be displaced again or persecuted because of their religion or ethnicity, the only solution is for one group to utterly defeat the other militarily.

The Hamas government in Gaza faces a herculean problem of governance, building an economy, maintaining a semblance of peace, all the while resisting an agreement with Israel while radicals clamor for revenge. It seeks to balance its enormous pressing daily needs with its avowed preaching of its militant ideology. According to UN figures, the level of GNP in Israel in 2009 was $27,450. In Gaza it was $2–3 dollars a day, or less than a $1,000 a year. Its focus on a continuing armed struggle with Israel means that the necessary provision of services to its citizens, and its options for maintaining stability in the population will always be limited.

Palestinian children are fed doses of Islamic propaganda of terrorist activities, hatred for Israel and Jews and fantasy images of virgins waiting for suicide bombers in the afterlife. There are reports on disturbing new inflammatory videos promoted by the Palestinian Authority, not just the more militant Hamas. Elementary school children are taught that suicide martyrdom is the highest honor for a Muslim male. They are taught to praise terrorists like Dalal Mughrabi, 19, who killed thirteen Israeli children and thirty-eight adults in a 1978 bus hijacking, and "to finish her journey." They regularly chant, "I have let my land drink my blood, and I have loved the way of the *shahada* (martyrdom for Allah)." [16] The murderer as martyr is now a role model for Palestinians.

All the psychological elements and theories come together in the Palestinian Authority's educational indoctrination of Arab children into a cult of hate, suicide and death wishes for their young. Offering prepubescent children sexual fantasies is an unworthy enough educational message. But the whole program is reinforcement of cultural indoctrination of the worst of Islam's heritage and its malignant message against anyone not Muslim.

## Militancy Prohibits Middle East Peace

The Middle East is littered with the debris of false initiatives, hollow and shallow diplomatic pronouncements, failed peace accords, two-tongued language agreements, broken promises and the bones of combatants. And there is no sanguine optimism for the future that Israel will conclude any substantive accord with the Palestinians for a separate political state. Calling for summits, often poorly timed, as was the 2000 Camp David summit, and shuttling between capitols like Cairo, Damascus and Jerusalem as Henry Kissinger did to conclude initiatives, and as Condoleezza Rice and George Mitchell futilely imitated, did not work. The roiling protests in the streets of most Arab cities and towns, oscillating between anarchy and dictatorship, threatens the instability in the region and causes sleepless nights in Jerusalem.

Israel is a nation that Palestinians and Arabs will never accept. America's well-intentioned diplomatic involvement in Israel, fueled by Jewish money and influence in America, has become a negotiating minefield where America's diplomats have been bewildered and usually out-maneuvered. Even the most respected and admitted experts in Middle East affairs admit to how disastrous most administration policies have been in the past few decades. [17]

The ground has shifted since the beginning of the third millennium and the landscape of Israeli/Palestinian ethos is no longer recognizable. It is not that the actors have changed—the death of Arafat, the incapacity of Ariel Sharon, the belligerency of Binyamin Netanyahu—but also the rise of Hamas and its electoral victory, the new boldness of Hezbollah in Lebanon, and the diminution of Fatah have revealed political chasms unlikely to be overcome. For example, the proposal of a two-state solution is improbable when Palestinians themselves cannot agree on a single state. Diplomatic fatigue has set in, and only *intifadas* or Israeli raids into Gaza enliven interest in a settlement neither side really wants.

The calls for permanent *jihad* and terrorism against the so-called enemies of Islam is as alive today as it was the followers of Mohammed moved out of Arabia to conquer non-Arab tribes and countries in the year 634. The Palestinian suicide bombers, like Islamic suicide bombers everywhere, come from this same ethos and code.

But Hezbollah and Hamas are not the only terrorist groups against Israel. The Palestine Liberation Organization (PLO) targeted Israelis everywhere in the world, including the U.S. Khalid Dunham Al-Jawary, a.k.a. Abu Walid al-Iraqi, a high-ranking member of the PLO entered the U.S. in 1973 and planted three powerful bombs near Israeli targets in New York City—two Israeli banks and the El Al cargo terminal at Kennedy airport. The unexploded bombs were discovered in rental cars. Why they did not explode is unknown. The cars were filled with gasoline, blasting caps, batteries, plastic explosives (Semtex), and propane tanks. Clearly, Jawary had been trained in explosive devices but perhaps not well enough. Jawary, who was only 18 years old at the time—the age of a senior in high school. He fled the U.S. and was not captured until 1991 when he was convicted of terrorism in Brooklyn and sentenced to 30 years in a federal penitentiary.

Unlike suicide bombers, Jawary had been involved in terrorism all his life. Investigators believe he had a role in the bombing of TWA flight 841 that had crashed in the Ionian Sea, September 8, 1974, killing 17 Americans. He was stopped at a routine border patrol as he attempted to cross from Germany into Austria. Police found 88 pounds of explosives, timing devices and detonators in the trunk. He was released before the FBI could be informed that it wanted him. In 1990 Jawary was working as a cultural attaché for the PLO in Cyprus but escaped to Iraq. When he left Iraq for Tunisia to attend the funeral of Abu Iyad, a deputy to Arafat, and head of Black September, the terrorist group responsible for the Israeli athletes during the 1972 Munich Olympics, he was detained while he was in Rome on the way to Tunis. In April 1993 he was sentenced to 30 years in prison. He was scheduled to be deported to an unknown country when he was released in 2009.

The current state of relations with the Islamic Middle East is tainted with a history of bloodshed, anger, frustration, colonialism and humiliation. I would not presume to know how peace can ever be resolved—let alone the status of Jerusalem—in a region so contentious about land, honor and religious differences. But I can envisage lingering hostility from Islamic radicals who harbor deep bitterness, resentments and malevolence toward anyone not of their persuasion. As *Al Jazeera* reports, "Israel is succeeding in doing little more than creating another generation of Palestinians with hearts filled with rage and a need for revenge." [18] My understanding is that rage and revenge have always been attitudes among Arabs for Jews whether Isreal exists or not.

Additionally, Palestinians send dual and opposing messages to the public. One message is broadcasted usually in English to the international media according to Media Watch, a group established in 1996 to monitor messages from the PLO that accuses Israel of violations of its rights and its moves toward peace. Another set of messages is in Arabic for domestic consumption and pronounces on the non-recognition of Israel, demonization of Israel and Jews and the promotion of violence to achieve their rights. [19] The distinctly different domestic messages are an accurate reflection of true Palestinian beliefs, and also reveal the hypocrisy of its propaganda machine.

Unquestionably, the events of 9/11 2001 changed America's response to the Muslim world if not the sympathies toward America and the West. I listened in 2002 in Dubai to an Egyptian businessman point out how the attacks on America were a Jewish plot to defame the Muslim world. Such blustery nonsense and persistent rumors are rife throughout the Arab world. Crowds in Cairo buses and in the streets of Gaza cheered when they heard the news of the collapse of the Twin Towers. So why would they be jubilant at the success of a Jewish scheme? Anti-Western xenophobia and anti-Semite sentiments are so ingrained that any rumor about the purported evils Jews do is automatically accepted as fact.

How can Israel conclude a peace with Palestinians, all stateless citizens, who themselves are divided into territorial sectors and into extreme political divisions, and who have divergent methods of engagement with Israel? What role can the search for peace play in this process of historical and military rivalries and antagonisms? There is little diplomatic optimism unless there is a total military victory. Palestinians have never actually had a nation state of their own, so becoming one is a diplomatic solution of resolving past grievances and the fracturing of the ethnic polity. A five state solution might be feasible if there could be consensus. The parties would include Israel and some form of combined political entity of the Palestinians, Jordan, Egypt, the U.S. and possibly Syria. There is no guarantee that the existence of a Palestinian state would function any differently toward Israel than the present conditions of a stateless entity.

In the end, a two state solution might not benefit the parties because even if the Palestinians have a state of their own, would they view Israel as simply a benign neighbor? They have never before in their history seen Israel except as an enemy. Indeed, Arafat turned down flat the 2000 concessions Israel's Ehud Barak made at Camp David with President Clinton. Nor can Israel conclude a peace with people still at war among themselves. Hamas has vowed never to agree to anything proposed by Israel and would likely reject and spoil any agreement Israel had with Fatah. [20]

This intractable conflict is a Kabuki dance without the elaborate costumes. The longstanding Israeli/Palestinian stalemate is an example of a blister of growing Islamic violence in the world and the danger it poses between nations and non-state players like Hezbollah, Hamas and al-Qaeda.

# CHAPTER EIGHT
# LEBANON, HEZBOLLAH AND SYRIA

Lebanon is a cobbled together national patchwork of fractured ethnic and religious factions. It is country of about four million at the eastern end of the Mediterranean, the crossroads of ancient civilizations, and the ancestral home of the Phoenicians who established Carthage, Rome's old enemy in northern Africa. This is the land that gave the Bible its name—from the town of Byblos (*Jbeil* in Arabic), about 25 miles north of Beirut—and where the phonetic (after Phoenician) alphabet script was created about 800 BCE. The word was literally born here.

This was also the land of the Canaanites from whom the Hebrews derived much literature and culture, where the ancient Babylonians crossed, the Persians conquered, the Egyptians fought battles, the Hebrews raided villages, the Greeks under Alexander conquered, Romans acquired under Pompey, and the Crusaders occupied until driven out by the Turks in the 13th century. Lebanon was created in 1920 for Christians, and was given independence from the French in 1943. A protracted civil war from 1975 to 1990 ruined the country.

Lebanon is about 40% Christian and 60% Muslim. The Christian community is composed of several Catholic sects—Maronite, Greek Orthodox, Melkite, Armenian and Roman Catholics. The government recognizes seventeen different religious sects. It is a mosaic of ethnic and religious villages, camps and neighborhoods that include Christians who live from Beirut to Tripoli along the coast, the Shiite *Amal* (Arabic for Hope), the Shiite group Hezbollah (The Party of God), Alawites, an offshoot of Shiite Muslim identity, pre-Christian beliefs and Christianity, and the Druze community.

The Druze faith arose in Egypt about a thousand years ago and includes monotheistic beliefs, prayer and fasting, but not daily rituals or pilgrimages, and combines elements of all religions. The Druze consider themselves Muslims but Muslims do not recognize them. There are about 300,000 in Lebanon and Syria and many live in scattered villages in northern Israel. They do not allow outsiders to join their religion and never try to recruit members.

*Amal* was a Shia organization founded in 1975 by a cleric Imam Mussa Al-Sadr and became Lebanon's primary Muslim militia. It expanded greatly with support from Syria. *Amal* subsequently folded into Hezbollah under Iranian influence that first emerged in 1983 with a series of car bombings and attacks on the U.S. Embassy in Beirut.

But as is true elsewhere in the Islamic world, there is a wide and deep Muslim awakening in Lebanon in which, according to Muslim preachers, there is a perpetual struggle against the whole non-Muslim world. Since 1967 there have been several Palestinian refugee camps, stateless individuals with a homeland but not a nationality, in Jordan and Lebanon. Three educational institutes for Palestinian refugees have captured the Sunni learning market in Lebanon: Dar al-Fatwa College, Imam al-Awazai Institute, and Islamic Preaching College, also known as al-Dawa College, founded in 1989 and funded by Libya. All insist on the rule of *jihad* and the liberation of Palestine as a moral imperative. There are about 400,000 Palestinian refugees in Lebanon, most living in twelve refugee camps.

According to a report in 2008 from Norway's Institute for Applied International Studies, one third of the population 15 years and older in the Palestinian refugee camps in Lebanon has not completed elementary education. The ratio is 70% for those 45 years and older. Only 18% of young men have finished high school. These refugees have a lower educational level than the national Lebanese population. About half have left school by the age of 16 years of age. But the educational programs for Palestinian refugees foster a political goal—to obliterate Lebanon that France created for the Christians and return it to Islamic rule. [1] The camps have morphed in a couple of generations from being just refugees to centers of global Islamic militancy. Their identity is now less with Palestine than with the worldwide movement of militant Islam.

The titles of theses and dissertations from students at these institutes confirm the strictly religious value of the educational program, and reveal that the theme of study is the decline of religion in the life of Muslims, and a call to return to when Islam was in a purer state. The writings promote the vanity and uselessness of the values of non-Muslims and opposition to Western influences or any accommodation with Western ideas. Rarely have instructors in these colleges attended accredited secular institutions and only have credentials from similar religious colleges.

The curricula are ideological and dogmatic, programs of indoctrination and not explorations in learning, or an open dialogue for forming new ideas or meanings. Since they do not teach even vocational skills, they do not contribute to productive economic development. These programs reject the present political order and a Lebanese identity to focus solely on a Muslim identity. It is only a short step to find militancy attractive as an activity or substitute for a fulltime job, and to journey to Chechnya, Pakistan or Afghanistan to fight as an Islamic mercenary.

Basim al-Kanj is an example of a militant who fought in Bosnia and Afghanistan and returned to Lebanon to establish Islamic rule. He was able to recruit over 200 jihadists in 1999 and with them took over a radio station. In the ensuing battle, fifteen militants were killed along with eleven Lebanese soldiers. Al-Kanj's goal was to establish an Islamic state in Lebanon with the Koran as the constitution. It is the ultimate goal of all Islamic militants after driving out the occupiers, like Israelis, or usurpers, or any government not in conformity with their unyielding and severe prescriptions.

But these colleges are kindergartens compared to the foreign jihadists that occupied the twelve Palestinian refugee camps like that of Narh al-Barid and who fought the Lebanese army in northern Lebanon in the summer of 2007. That confrontation lasted three months and left dead 163 Lebanese soldiers, 42 civilians and upwards of 222 militants. The Lebanese army had in the process destroyed a refugee camp that housed 40,000 people. [2]

Palestinian refugee camps were a political football between Lebanon, Israel and Syria. The Lebanese didn't want anything to do with them and allowed refugees to operate the camps with international relief assistance.

Israel wanted Palestinians to remain permanently in the host countries so they would not return to the occupied territories. Syria did not want permanent settlement, and did not want Palestinians integrated into Lebanese society, because it would deprive Syria of a powerful bargaining chip with Israel that questioned the validity of Jewish settlement in Palestine. In the new mindset, geography and the possession of old national lands is less important than the coming conflict with the West and keeps refugees from integrating into any national unity. Establishing God's law on earth is now the goal—a total Islamic victory only achieved through *jihad*.

Lebanon repeatedly has bombings, assassinations and tit-for-tat skirmishes between the regular Lebanese forces, Sunni and Shia factions, the intervention of Syria into conflicts where it has an interest, and jihadists against everyone not an extremist believer. Every man has a weapon, though not always properly trained in its use, and are roused to violence in the streets in their controlled neighborhoods at the least provocation or irritation. The alienation and disenfranchisement of unemployed young men, many conditioned by experiences fighting in Bosnia, Kosovo, Chechnya Iraq or Afghanistan, makes the social milieu flammable.

Hezbollah in Lebanon is a state within a state, militarily and politically controlling southern Lebanon, the Bekaa valley and southern Beirut. UN Resolution 1559 calls for the complete disarmament of all militias in Lebanon, a noble but unrealistic objective, similar to asking all Americans to give up their firearms. Hezbollah emerged as a potent social and political force in Lebanon in the mid-1980s when, together with a cabal of militias, it began kidnapping Westerners for terrorist-of-the-month recognition. In began in 1982 when David Dodge, President of the American University of Beirut, was kidnapped for a year. The year 1983 was the bombing of the U.S. Embassy in Beirut and marine barracks that killed 246. The journalist Terry Anderson was held for seven years. TWA flight 847 was hijacked in 1985. Lebanon was one of the most dangerous places in the world for foreigners in the 1980s when 30 were kidnapped, and some killed or held for ransom for other reasons, like the release of prisoners in Israel. The U.S. Department of State labeled Hezbollah a terrorist organization in 1997.

Hezbollah's first leader was Musa al-Sadr whose disappearance in 1978—probably with Libyan complicity—has never been resolved. Other Hezbollah leaders were Abbas al-Musawi, who was assassinated by Israel in 1982. Within months of al-Musawi's killing, Hezbollah terrorists bombed the Israeli Embassy in Buenos Aires, Argentina, killing twenty-nine. In 1994 terrorists bombed a Jewish community center also in Buenos Aires. Argentinean authorities indicted Imad Mughniyah, Deputy General of Hezbollah, who was also responsible for the U.S. Embassy and Marine barracks bombing in 1983 and the TWA hijacking in 1985. The FBI offered a $5 million reward for his capture. At 45 years of age, Imad died in a car bombing on February 12, 2008 in Damascus where he apparently thought he was safe. Syria blamed Israel for his death. Syria protected a known international wanted criminal for years.

Hezbollah's leader since 1992 is Hasan Nasrallah, who grew up in the village of Bazuriya near Tyre along the southern coast. He is despised among Israelis and Americans but highly admired in the Muslim world.

Hezbollah is a mercenary army arm of Iran but its 1980 terrorist activities exposed for the world the militancy inherent in Islamic ideology directed against the West in general and Americans, Jews and Israelis in particular.

The Lebanese government lacks the political and military will to curtail Hezbollah, and its weak army is ineffective against Hezbollah's resources and organization. Hezbollah's parallel government is a mix of social services provided to supporters. But its major objective is the elimination of Israel and the installation of an Islamic state everywhere in the Middle East. It offers the hand of welfare to its faithful believers, who might otherwise be impoverished, and the sword of retribution and enmity to everyone else.

Hezbollah promotes terrorist martyrs. Mastermind Imad Mugniyah is enshrined in the village of Nabatiye in Lebanon where children are indoctrinated into his terrorist propaganda with visuals of bombs, artillery, rockets and other armaments. Hezbollah has cells in several countries. Syria is a conduit for its weapon shipments into Lebanon. It is an unacknowledged Shiite proxy army of Iran dedicated to the eradication of Israel. Here is what Iran's Supreme Leader, Ayatollah Khamenei, said in October 2000 to Iran's National Security Council. "Lebanon is Iran's greatest foreign policy success. We repeat it across *Dar al-Islam* until all of Islam is liberated." [3]

The continuation of ethnic and religious conflicts means that in the not too distant future Hezbollah, will take control of Lebanon, persecute the minority Christians, and plague Israel with rockets and artillery prompting the inevitable responses.

In December 2008, the Lebanese Youssef Mohammed el-Hajdib, 24, was convicted in a German court with a life sentence for planting suitcase bombs on two German passenger trains in Cologne. He had been arrested in August 2006 in Kiel, Germany and discovered with two suitcases filled with explosives. The bombs had failed to detonate because of a technical glitch. He had first come to Germany to study. Surveillance cameras caught him placing the bombs. His accomplice, Jihad Hamad, 22, was arrested after fleeing Germany and tried and convicted in Lebanon. He was sentenced to twelve years in jail.

El-Hajdib was connected to an Imam in Odense, Denmark named Abu Bashar, one of the imams who had spread the word in the Middle East about the satirical Danish cartoons. I've read the profiles of these two young, disillusioned men. They wanted to be accepted in the West, but they lacked the discipline and endurance to succeed in their challenging studies. The more they studied engineering, the more they fell behind and then retreated into devout religion as a refuge. Religious fanatics convicted of crimes are the hardest to attempt to re-socialize into a civic community. Their passion and commitment to religion overwhelms all other reasonable alternatives, especially Islamic adherents that permits them to murder infidels without guilt, and then offer redemption and salvation as a reward for murderous behavior.

For Hezbollah the keeping of arms is akin to the second amendment in the U.S. Constitution giving citizens the right to bear arms, but with a keen difference. Hezbollah is not the National Rifle Association but a separate army supposedly threatening Israel but intimidating Lebanon. Disarming Hezbollah is a non-starter, and the issue is not negotiable. It is an unofficial army but stronger militarily than the Lebanese forces. Hezbollah defends its military autonomy because its real objective is the liberation of Palestine from Israel and the rescue of Jerusalem and not the defense of Lebanon. By repeatedly announcing its unique military posture it renounces Lebanese sovereignty. From its political stance it is clear Hezbollah is attempting to impose its priorities on Lebanon, and its defense of everything Syria does, and its insistence of maintaining its weapons is transparent for what it is—a proxy army of Iran using Lebanon as a base from which to challenge Israel.

Mona is a secular Lebanese woman I met in Beirut who favors the presence of Hezbollah because she believes its military will better protect Lebanon from Israeli incursions. She told me its members are Shiite but devoted Lebanese who want to preserve the country. Her views are consistent with many Lebanese I spoke with who are more religious. Hezbollah is not strictly a religious issue. The singular trait among Lebanese is their tolerance for all who reside in the country.

Although Lebanese are protective of their national interests, and therefore optimistic about the future of Lebanon, it's difficult to see how the presence of a militia, financed by a foreign government and militarily stronger than the national army, can be a calming influence. Like others in the Middle East the more vocal pundits want the U.S. out of the region, but then complain that the U.S. is not doing enough to solve the Israeli/Palestinian process.

The Lebanese cabinet democratically includes representatives of all minorities in the fractious country that also reveals its deep divisions. The convoluted nature of the demographics and the country's political balancing acts, and the influence of foreign powers like Syria and Iran could bring about this engaging country's demise. Hezbollah has the militia, the boldness and the financial and weapons backing of Iran. Saudi influence is strong and has its own financial backing as a way of countering Iranian influence. Minority leaders like the Druze want Syria involved, though Syria is in league with Iran. Alliances shift as minority groups jostle for power. Al-Qaeda's brand of militancy has found a home in Lebanon and seeks to expand its regional hegemony. Lebanon is ripe for political disintegration if not military domination by Hezbollah, or another invasion by Israel to thwart Hezbollah and its Iranian supporters.

All Middle Eastern countries, including Lebanon, want the U.S. out of the region. The U.S. wants to quit the region, but leaving means the loss of influence, access to markets, and isolation in a global, interconnected world. Staying means getting the national ego bruised. Many Middle East residents like Lebanese and Iranians personally like Americans, though their governments think otherwise. Even friendly nations are like petulant family adolescents you can't disown. The emergence of Hezbollah, the U.S. backing of Shiites in Iraq, and the blustering of Iran, will create a more potent Shia presence in the Middle East that is already challenging Sunni influence in the region. This could lead to inter-religious rivalries as belligerent as any against the West.

# Hezbollah's Educational Program

In a camp called Tyr Fil Say near the village of Jibchit in southern Lebanon and close to the Litani River and Israel's northern border, is the site where many Mahdi Scouts train to become Islamic soldiers. [4] This camp is one of a network of camps operated by Hezbollah that provides religious instruction from clerics involving diatribes against Israel. The organization strives to educate Lebanese youth in what is known as *Hala Islamiyya*, an Islamic atmosphere. Hezbollah fighters toting AK-47s discuss how to fight Israel. The camp has about 850 youth aged 9-15.

When these youth, estimated at 60,000, are on display they wear uniforms identifying their allegiance—grey sleeve-length shirts with red and black kerchiefs that droop nearly to the waist. They salute with three fingers while at attention. During the day while at camp they wear Arabic headbands or berets, outside-the-shirt ties, khakis pants and boots. They are about six times as large as any regular scout group and are definitely not affiliated with the Boy Scouts.

They carry an image of Ayatollah Ruhollah Khomeini. This one gesture alone is indicative of the pan-Arabic goal of the Islamic movement, as these youth do not celebrate a hero of Lebanon, but a dead cleric in Iran. Iran supports Hezbollah with logistical support and money, and Hezbollah supports the Mahdi Scouts. This aim exposes the purely religious and political nature of an educational program embedded in Islam and not in nationality.

Their scout-like appearance is subtly deceptive and seemingly innocuous. But the goal is to prepare a new generation for military operations against Israel. Hezbollah offers a complete program for its youth that runs from primary school to college level operations. Yet none of the educational program is dedicated to learning skills needed in a global economy. There are no books on science, the environment, math, social studies, humanities or any of sciences. The curriculum is filled with hate literature. Yet even students at West Point know that poetry, among other subjects, confronts cadets with new ideas that challenge worldviews.

The older boys in this secretive society go into the resistance movement and advanced military training. The competition for these young men are the flesh pots of southern Beirut, known as the *Dahiya* district, where discos, lingerie shops, DVD stores, Internet cafes and even Chinese restaurants thrive and where young women walk in tight jeans, their heads uncovered.

Syria relinquished its hegemony and army control but not its influence in Lebanon. Israel is poised to confront any incursion or extension of the influence of Hezbollah. The U.S. strives to maintain a relationship with Lebanon through Lebanese Christians who want to hold on to a semi Pro-Western state. All Muslims, through the activities of Hezbollah, its elected legislators and active and emboldened militia, seek to create an independent, Muslim-ruled, pro-Arab state. [5]

# The 2006 War with Israel

Sarah heard the bombs exploding from her comfortable home in northern Beirut in 2006. The explosions frightened her more than her parents and brothers who survived the bombings in 1982 when Israel invaded to oust the Palestinians before she was born. Sarah is a Lebanese American college student I interviewed. The confusion and anxiety in the Larnaca, Cyprus airport that night was nothing, she said, to the terror and hysteria in Lebanon as thousands fled the devastation in Beirut. Over a half million people had escaped Israel's bombardment of southern Lebanon, Beirut and the Bekaa Valley in 2006.

Prime Minister Rafik al-Hariri, a popular, rich, controversial political figure, was assassinated by a car bomb that contained nearly two tons of explosives on February 14, 2005. Twenty-two others were also killed in the blast. His guarded memorial grave is in the center of downtown Beirut, covered daily with fresh flowers and a major tourist attraction. The following month after his death two massive demonstrations of over a million and a half occurred on Lebanese streets. One group suspected Syrian implication in the assassination, and another group of demonstrators praised Syria for its involvement in Lebanon. Under intense international pressure, Syrian troops withdrew totally from Lebanon where they had been since 1976.

A UN Commission (UN Resolution #1644) began investigating the murder of Hariri, while a political majority hostile to Syria came to power in Lebanon. On April 26, President Bush signed an Executive Order (#13338) that blocked property of persons in Syria and Lebanon connection with the assassination. The implication was clear that Syria was deeply complicit if not directly involved. The commission discovered a large network of conspirators but few actual names.

Subsequently deaths and misadventures during the commission's investigation added to suspicions. A man questioned about the sale of phone chips used by those allegedly involved in Rafik's murder was found dead on a mountain road in mid-November 2005. Ghazi Kenaan, a Syrian Interior Minister who literally ran Lebanon for two decades, died about a month after being questioned by the commission. Syrian officials said it was suicide. Mohammad Zuhair Siddiq a barber, but known as a Syrian intelligence operative with a criminal record, was arrested in France for lying to the commission. Several journalists and anti-Syrian politicians were also murdered during the investigation.

Israel knew in 2006 that Hezbollah was conveniently close to toppling the weak Lebanese government, and it would then have been faced with a terrorist nation to its north committed to its annihilation. This conflict had been brewing for years and was predictable. Hezbollah militants invaded northern Israel in 2006 to capture two Israeli soldiers. Kidnapping was a preferred tactic in a bid to have Israel release captured Hezbollah fighters. This time the plan backfired. Israel unleashed an aerial bombing campaign that devastated Hezbollah buildings and housing facilities in southern Beirut. But in a counter-attack that startled everyone, Hezbollah attacked Israel for a month with long-range missiles that struck Haifa, raining over a hundred missiles a day into northern Israel. Hezbollah had elaborate bunkers and underground tunnels that hid men and materiel and anti-tank weapons

148

that stopped Israeli tanks and soldiers from advancing. It even sunk an Israeli ship, the INS *Hanit* that killed four Israeli sailors, with a guided missile.

Israel intended to destroy most of Lebanon to eradicate as much as it could of Hezbollah's military capability in the south. It would occupy southern Lebanon until the international community could decide whether, and with what composition, to place a more permanent UN peacekeeping force in the region. [6] Lebanon would suffer heavy civilian casualties, infrastructure damage and general economic calamity, but since both Hezbollah and Israel under-estimated the other, the 2006 war resulted in a tie with lingering misgivings and animosity.

On November 21, 2006 Pierre Gemayel, 33, Minister of Industry, the son of Amin Gemayel a former President, and grandson of Pierre Gemayel, founder of the Phalange Christian militia in 1936, was assassinated for his anti-Syrian sentiments. His uncle, Bashir Gemayel, was assassinated on September 14, 1982. The following month, December 12, 2007, General Francois al-Hajj, a Maronite Christian who had led the raid on the Palestinian refugee camp Nahr al-Bared earlier in 2007, was assassinated in a car bombing. All homicides are unresolved.

Hassan Nasrallah, the head of Hezbollah, emerged as the iconic hero of the Arab world after the 2006 war with Israel. He had challenged Israel and fought it to a military stalemate. But in unveiling its vastly improved military arsenal supplied by Iran Hezbollah tipped its hand, revealing more firepower, longer range missiles, and bolder guerilla tactics learned from U.S. military manuals and lessons from the Vietnam War. In the West Bank residents have forgotten Yasser Arafat, not only because he is dead but because a new leader that fights Israel will always be lionized.

Palestinians and Arabs could care less that Hassan Nasballah is a Shia and not a Sunni, or that he is sponsored by Iran. Taking up arms against Israel is the key to Arab notoriety. Nevertheless, Sunni Lebanese groups have only contempt for Hezbollah and often clash violently with its militants. Hezbollah's invasion of Israel to capture of Israeli soldiers was an Iranian ploy to reduce UN pressure for its refusal to yield to international pressure to quit or re-direct its nuclear weapons program. [7]

The roots of this conflict are in the Islamic world's denial of Israel's right to exist and persistent dedication to its destruction, together with the U.S.'s misguided and inerrant foreign policy in the Middle East. Oil money fuels this Islamic hatred and arms adherents to its cause. No amount of "winning the hearts and minds" strategy will soften this challenge. Only a new generation of Muslims, who could rein in despotic governments and fundamentalist religious fanatics, will military adventurism and terrorist strategies dissipate, and the western and Islamic worlds possibly find some uneasy accommodations.

## Bombing the U.S. Presence

Sunday morning, October 23, 1983 was pleasant and sunny. It was quiet and there was a light breeze blowing in Beirut. At about 6:20 AM in the Operations Center a staff sergeant, Randy Gaddo, heard shots from an M-15 rifle, but before he had time to consider where they were coming from and why, a hot flash blew across his face and he was blown off his feet. His helmet and flak jacket saved him from serious injury. He looked in the direction of the marine barracks several yards away and saw a mushroom cloud rising hundreds of feet in the air. Three soldiers, 18 sailors and 220 marines died. [8] The marine barracks had a two-foot thick reinforced concrete walls and had withstood artillery fire and naval gunfire.

In Washington DC the newly appointed National Security Advisor to President Reagan received the message that the marine barracks in Beirut had been destroyed. American intelligence confirmed that Hezbollah had planned and executed the attack from a training camp base in the Bekaa valley in northern Lebanon. Most Administration's officials wanted to act decisively, but Secretary of Defense Caspar Weinberger disagreed. He felt that our central Middle Eastern policy had to do with oil and that we ought not to rattle Muslim goodwill in the region. [9]

What happened then—and subsequently in all terrorist attacks on Americans until 9/11—was indecision and a lack of recognition of the danger of this militancy movement. The U.S. had not done anything against the central organization of the terrorists after the attacks on the World Trade Center in 1993, or the Air Force troops at the Khobar Towers in Saudi Arabia in 1996, or the bombings of the U.S. embassies in Kenya and Tanzania in 1998—although President Clinton sent cruise missiles into Sudan and Afghanistan—nor on the destroyer Cole in Yemen in 2000. The 9/11 attacks radically changed America's mood, but the attacks had been coming for years and had been predicted. After attacking Afghanistan where al-Qaeda established its camps, America failed to send enough troops or equipment to totally rout the Taliban and instead diverted the resources to Iraq, a country that had a psychotic dictator but was not a terrorist base.

Birgitte Gabriel, a Lebanese Christian, former TV personality in Jerusalem and later an American journalist, wrote a passionate account of her childhood experiences in Lebanon after Hezbollah succeeded in destroying her village, Marjayoun, in southern Lebanon, bombed her father's restaurant, and forced her and her mother and father to live constantly in a bomb shelter. [10] Hezbollah tried to eliminate the Christians in southern Lebanon. She believes Islamic terror is poised to challenge the West with a similar fate. Her book, *Because They Hate*, is an intense plea and warning to America of how real the presumed threat is from militant Islam, and how *jihad* is not just practiced by a few deluded extremists, like the former Bader Meinhof terrorist group in Germany, but is the fundamental belief of all Muslims. Her recording of the shelling and rocket attacks on her village in the 1980s, the destruction of her father's business, and the serious wounding of her mother, who was cared for in an Israeli hospital, is a riveting account of brazen and murderous attacks. She was a young eyewitness to the hatred of sponsored militants toward all non-Muslims. Her message is not subdued: Islamic terror is not idle threats, that its reach is global, and that its pronounced hatred is sanctioned by the Koran.

> After the Iranian revolution Muslims throughout the world began to see themselves only as Muslims, with a religious duty to wage holy war, a jihad, to make Islam supreme over the entire world. [11]

The difference between the two cultures has noting to do with money and everything to do with values. It is truly a clash of civilizations in its rawest form. [12]

## The Baathist Party

Michel Aflaq (1910-1989), a middle class Greek Orthodox Christian, was the ideological founder of Baathism (rebirth, similar to the Greek word for baptism), a form of secular Arab nationalism whose party ruled both Syria under Hafez al-Assad and Iraq under Saddam Hussein. Educated in French schools in Syria under the French at the end of World War II, Aflaq entered the Sorbonne in Paris for collegiate studies under a scholarship where he developed his ideas of Pan-Arab unity and socialism that he believed would offer a political alternative to western colonialism. He returned to Syria as a secondary school teacher and, with a colleague, Salah al-din al-Bitar, a Sunni Muslim, expanded the socialist and nationalist ideas in 1940 that formed the basis of a political party. [13]

Both Aflaq and al-Bitar were influenced by the rise of Nazi socialism in Germany and Bolshevik socialism under Lenin in Russia. At the time these movements served as useful political options to colonialism for intellectuals. Later, both Germany and Russia succumbed to raw dictatorships, as did eventually Baathism in Syria and Iraq. Some of the party's key ideas of Pan-Arabism appealed to the pubic as they did to dictators who used the slogans to hold power but without acknowledging the Baathist ideological and democratic underpinnings of ideas like free speech. The political propaganda machines in Syria and Iraq used the Arab unity ideas of Baathism when it was advantageous to strengthen despotic rules, and to denounce America and the West, and dispensed with it when it was not.

It might seem odd today that ideas of Nazi supremacy and Marxism might become the basis for a political movement in the Middle East. But in the early years of the twentieth century any constructive views that moved before the disaster of World War I and the subsequent global depression were regarded with modest admiration. It was only after the dictatorships of Hitler, Lenin and Stalin were revealed as the brutal grasps for power they always intended that the political movement fell from favor.

In 1949 Aflaq served briefly as Syria's education minister. After persecutions from political forces in Syria, he fled first to Lebanon in 1952 then to Brazil for a couple of years, then moved to Iraq in 1968 where the Baathist Party had come to power under Saddam Hussein. Aflaq's ideas of democracy and free speech were not popular with the dictators Hafez al-Assad in Syria and Saddam Hussein in Iraq where he was tolerated for his contributions but otherwise ignored by both regimes. Aflaq died in Baghdad in 1989.

Except for a few intellectuals, none of these social or political ideas appealed to the vast majority in the Arab world, and certainly not to Muslim extremists whose only ideological anchor is Islam. The Iraqi Parliament in 2010, dominated by Shiites, banned 511 former and present members of the party from running for political office because members were too closely associated with Saddam Hussein's former regime.

# Syria Crushing Revolts

Hafez al-Assad (1930-2000) was born poor in the village of Kurdaha near Latakia in northern Syria on October 6, 1930, the seventh of eleven children and the first to attend formal schooling. His villagers were members of the Alawites, a group associated with Shia Islam, though many Muslims consider Alawites heretics. [14] The minority Alawites claim that their name derives from Ali, the Prophet Mohammad's cousin and the fourth caliph. They constitute between 15–20% of the Syrian population.

As a student he joined the Baath Arab Socialist Party and, in 1952, the military air force. It was a time of new enthusiasm for nationalism among Arabs the Baath Party provided, a new sense of national and not just tribal or clan identity. He went to the Soviet Union in 1958 to improve his flying skills and thereafter he aligned Syria closely with the Soviet Union throughout the Cold War.

By 1963 he was commander of the air force, then Minister of Defense, and in 1969 Syrian de facto head of state. He became Chairman of the Baath Party and in 1971 was elected President of the Syrian Arab Republic in a referendum. With his central foreign policy doctrine of curbing Israel's power, he led Syria in the 1973 war with Israel with disastrous consequences for Syria and Egypt. He backed terrorist acts against Israel, and harbored known terrorists in Damascus. Backed by UN resolutions for returning occupied land to the original occupants he claimed the return of land taken by Israel, but then, following self-interest and reality politics and not logic, sent Syrian troops to occupy parts of Lebanon.[15]

In 1980 the Muslim Brotherhood began guerilla tactics in major cities against the military, government officials and Syrian infrastructure and an assassination attempt on Assad himself. These guerilla tactics included targeted assassinations and car bombings. Assad instituted a law that made membership in the Brotherhood a capital offense. Assad ordered the execution of several hundred Brotherhood prisoners in their cells. A general insurrection ensued in the fundamentalist town of Hama about a hundred miles north of Damascus in 1982.

An army patrol had been ambushed in Hama in the early morning hours of February 3, 1982 when snipers killed several patrolling soldiers. When army reinforcements were called in, the Brotherhood guerilla commander Abu Bakr called for a general uprising. Hundreds of Muslim fighters came from hiding and attempted to seize power in the city by killing officials and raiding armories. It was to be an historic moment for the Assad regime challenged as never before by Muslim militancy. Civil war was in the making and was as much about unseating him as Syria's leader as it was about establishing a puritanical Islamic national presence.

Assad's retaliatory methods were swift and ruthless. There was no diplomacy and no attempt to win over hearts and minds. The Syrian military of 12,000 troops, after urging civilians to leave immediately, sealed off the town, and bombed the city center to make it easier for tanks to enter. In the first four days, tanks demolished buildings wherever the military encountered fierce resistance. Then the army backed off and having ringed the city of 350,000, shelled it repeatedly for three weeks. Entering the city, the army tortured and executed suspected Brotherhood members, killing, it was reliably reported, over 20,000. That was the end of the Muslim Brotherhood insurrection. The city was quickly cleaned and rebuilt. Assad's son, Bashir, is performing was similar cleansing experiment of dissenters in Homs, a nearby city, in 2012.

Assad's former archenemy, Saddam Hussein, had funded the insurgents—more than 15,000 machine guns had been captured—and trained many of them in military tactics in Iraq. Hafez's son and the succeeding leader of Syria, Bashir al-Assad, believed that the Hama incident is an example of how to fight terrorism.

Hafez Al-Assad built a strong army that controlled the country and maintained order among rival factions. Because he relied excessively on socialist principles favoring the Soviet Union, like heavy subsidies for agriculture, Syria never did achieve sufficient economic progress. Much of what defined his presidency came from Muslim extremism within Syria. His personality was shaped by his nationalistic tendencies to preserve Syria as a separate power in the Middle East, and by his personal history of exploitation in the region. Though he was inspired by the idea of revolution to achieve political objectives, he mercilessly crushed religious revolt in his own country while supporting it abroad.

Hafez Assad was unable to keep Jordan and Egypt from reaching agreements with the U.S. and Israel further isolating Syria. His diplomatic inscrutability was actually quite single-minded—to sustain a counterbalance to Israel's influence and a hold on Arab identity. To that end he fomented terrorism against western and Israeli interests while turning against his fundamentalist Muslim brothers who turned their vengeance against him.

More than 5.000 civilians have been killed by government troops suppressing the protests by late 2011. [16] The government has used tanks and heavy weapons to attack residential areas in cities like Homs. The power of the Internet and the instant communication of social networks had enlightened the Arab world to the blessings of democracy and the consumer societies they have created. Arabs want a taste of that but have never experienced democracy in their home countries nor do they have the institutions that will support it if ever implemented. The Arab League expelled Syria in November 2011 and Jordan's King Abdullah was the first Arab leader to tell Assad to quit. [17]

Still, this chapter has been another example of how Muslim militancy has permeated the ideological atmosphere of Islam and imbued its youth with messages of violence as a way of gaining personal and national self-respect and a religious bonding identity. The creation of militia groups like Amal and Hezbollah are methods of channeling this propensity for violence into useful defensive and offensive coordination against western interests and Israel. The backing of such groups by Iran and Syria is an illustration of Islamic cynicism in backing away from claiming official sponsorship of terrorism while secretly supporting it.

# CHAPTER NINE
# SAUDI AND OSAMA

> Saudi Arabia may be wealthy, but it is probably the least cultivated country in the rich and multifaceted Arab world, with the most simplistic and brutal conception of social relationships. Families are headed by patriarchs and obedience to patriarchs is absolute. The only values that count in Saudi Arabia are loyalty and submission—first to Islam and then to the clan. [1]

The desert has surprisingly stark beauty: yellow and white sand, some as fine as water droplets, a still or whispering wind, and, during the spring flowers that bloom in bright and luminous colors under a cruel and unremitting sun. I know about deserts because I live in one. Only imported water and power make the Sonoran desert livable. Temperatures in Phoenix have been as high as 126 degrees Fahrenheit in July—extinguishing the weak, elderly, homeless, and those without air conditioning. Temperatures routinely reach 110 degrees in the summer months. The air is saturated with heat and the sandy soil fit only for scorpions, tarantulas, lizards and diamondback rattlesnakes. A half-day in the desert heat will bring anyone to exhaustion, certainly dehydration, and possibly embalmment. The desert has no mercy for lost travelers and the glare from igneous rocks has no gentleness.

Still, each desert is unique and the hot sands of Saudi Arabia yield little that is negotiable beyond the ancient natural gifts of frankincense and myrrh and the petroleum that keeps the wheels of global industry and transportation humming. Its moonscape and rock hills, especially in the volcanic south, have no brooding Scandinavian or Canadian skies, just the shimmering heat waves that dull all sensibilities, make the mind promise the body no strenuous actions, and make wanderers seek the shelter of anyone's tent.

I have wandered the sand dunes and desert mountains of the Persian Gulf and squatted with Bedouin shepherds in their tents in the Jordanian desert. We sipped tea and talked about our children and grandchildren. I soaked in their hospitality as we lounged on cushions with the tent floor laden with well-worn carpets. I watched the women sit quietly removed at a far corner. Docile children looked at us with bright, black eyes from just outside the tent flaps, itching to enter and join us. The desert provides its own grainy and forbidding landscape, but the Arab has always invited the stranger into his tent to find respite from the inhospitable terrain and searing heat.

Saudi Arabia is a country undergoing a social and economic transformation, a country in reform more in tune with the modern world, beginning to liberate its women and educate its youth in knowledge and skills needed in a contemporary global society. King Abdullah University of Science and Technology (KAUST), the intended Arabian higher education graduate research equivalent of MIT, about 50 miles north of Jeddah opened in the fall 2009, and allows men and women to take classes together, and women do not have to wear the traditional *abayas* nor veil their faces. It took a royal decree from the King to challenge the austere clerical stranglehold. The king ordered Aramco, the Saudi national oil company, to build the university, already endowed with over $25 billion and powered with solar energy.

Saudi may be the seat of the holy sites but it is only representative of the autocratic beliefs of global Muslims and the exclusion and incessant war with non-Muslims.

> If Mohammad was a true prophet then (it must be known that) he declared Christians unbelievers, commanded jihad against them, and declared himself quit of them and their religion. [2]

Ibn Taymiyyah (1263–1328), quoted above whose ideas found acceptance in the most fundamental of Islamic beliefs, makes *jihad* one of his main themes. This Syrian theologian lived through the tumultuous period of the Mongol invasion, the sacking of Baghdad, the collapse of the caliphate, and the beginning of the Crusades and its perils, the epitome of a Christian *jihad.*

He stood for a very conservative view of Sunni theology and a pure Muslim faith. He not only prodded Muslims into fighting a holy war against the Mongols but engaged in battle against Shiites. He was on several occasions accused of anthropomorphism and spared imprisonment after a debate in 1306 in Damascus but was arrested in Cairo one month later. Undaunted, he wrote a treatise in which he demanded that all measures of the sultans be consistent with *sharia.* He criticized the cult of gravesites saying that only the Prophet had the right to intercede on behalf of believers. He died in 1328 while still in custody.

One of the most significant admirers who heard Taymiyyah's siren song of fundamentalism was Mohamed Ibn Abd al-Wahhab (1703-1792), the founder of Wahhabism, the puritanical movement that lies at the heart of Saudi Arabia's religious culture. It would be a stretch to classify Wahhabi as a Muslim thinker. He is a copyist not a creative or insightful creator. His purity for the faith is noble, but his insistence on the most rigorous practices has made his brand of Muslim identity the most fundamental of Muslim movements. Because of its militancy, and the obligation of all Muslims to use arms to enforce its strict codes, it has become the most flourishing Islamic movement. Charles Allen describes Wahhab and his followers in *God's Terrorists, The Wahhabi Cult and the Hidden Roots of Modern Jihad.* (2007, pp. 43-68).

The Wahhabi sect of Islam is comparable to Massachusetts Puritans in the 1660s, devoted to absolute subservience to clerics who combined civil rule with religious fanaticism and a fierce intolerance for opposing religious views, like peace loving Quakers. And like early American puritans Wahhabi Islam denies freedom of conscience, and the dignity, respect and good will everyone should show all humans. Instead, it promotes hate, subservience, humiliation and death. Wahhabis think everyone who does not accept their religious vision is going to hell. Everyone who understands their vision thinks they already live in hell.

Wahhabism cannot improve its condition except by renouncing its hostile code. It is incapable of social or political progress, as its views are inimical to an increase in knowledge, innovation, technology, the arts and literature, as all are considered organs or instruments of the devil. Its fanaticism looks backward fourteen hundred years. Wahhabis have borrowed nothing from anyone, certainly not any Western ideas, and have cultivated only a venomous hatred toward those not of their persuasion. Superstition and ignorance have been allowed to dictate an anti-intellectual and nihilistic code. The mind narrows and atrophies, never rising above simple literacy, or the repetition of simple slogans, and impassioned but hateful rhetoric. It is the same spirit that galvanized the lumbering and incompetent crusaders.

The Wahhabi *Ulema* in Saudi Arabia in 1920 protested the introduction of the car and the telephone because there was no precedent for them in the Koran or *Hadith*, as if scripture is supposed to forestall technological progress. Sheikh Abdul Aziz bin Abdullah bin Baz, once Chancellor of the Islamic University of Medina, and former Grand Mufti of Saudi Arabia, and formerly the most active proponent of Wahhabism, who died in Mecca in 1999, once issued a *fatwa* denouncing all who held that the earth was round. His belief is in the Koran, in sura *al-kahf, ayat* (18:86) where the story about Zu-Alqarnain reached near the setting and rising sun he found people there suffering from the intense heat because they were closer to the sun. To the literalist, this means the earth is flat. He was forced to recant only after a Saudi prince orbited the earth in a U.S. space shuttle.

Wahhabis believe that Allah uses them as his instruments, and that if they serve him well no one can stop them. In reality, they encourage self-righteousness and intolerance in men ignorant of any knowledge except their brand of religion and what the Koran provides.

Here are some examples taken from Saudi school textbooks of what social venom is taught to Saudi children. Such statements begin in the first year of schooling and continue through high school.

> Every religion other than Islam is false.
> The apes are Jews . . . while the swine are the Christians.
> Jihad in the path of God . . . is the summit of Islam. [3]

Saudi Arabia is the embodiment of the fuel that feeds terrorist sentiments and the world's struggle with Islamic fanaticism. About a third of all instruction in Saudi schools is religious, which does not qualify graduates for many job opportunities except as clerics. Unlike other subjects, a student cannot pass to the next grade if he or she flunks a religion class. Student essays by the eighth grade are typically written on the danger of imitating infidels. But this ethnic and religious venom exists throughout the Arab world.

Saudi officials like Prince Turki al-Faisal, the Ambassador to the U.S. in 2006, trumpeted the idea that after 9/11 on a speaking tour of several U.S. cities that the Saudis had reformed and revised school texts. He lied. There had been no changes. School texts that were smuggled and independently translated revealed the same intolerant and repugnant messages. Moreover, Saudi officials funded the expansion of mosques and *madrassas* throughout the Islamic world, and loaned books free of charge, thereby exporting this brand of Islamic extremism. It's as if the Puritans of 1660 in Massachusetts were running the executive, legislative and judicial branches of the U.S. government.

As the birthplace of Islam, we should expect Saudi Arabia to hold true to the ideals of its religious base. But the world has moved beyond the intolerance and exclusivity of Islam to embrace science, the multicultural acceptance of all peoples and religions in a political union, and the avoidance of religious hatred. Regrettably, Saudi Arabia is solidly locked into Islam, and Islam is locked into the 7th century where tribal and clan rivalries prevailed and illiteracy was the hallmark of the age. The gulf between the West and Islam will continue to widen as more and more Muslims trumpet their dogmatic and discriminatory religious beliefs in the teeth of Western ideals of political, personal and social freedoms hard won over centuries, and in the rule of law and not in religious dogmas.

But the Saudis were not content just to indoctrinate their own children: they exported Wahhabi philosophy and revolts of Muslims throughout Asia. The International Islamic Relief Organization funded in 1978 is totally funded by the Saudis and the most active, richest relief group in the world. It purchases Korans for mosques throughout South Asia. But it also has financed revolts of Muslims in Kyrgyzstan, Uzbekistan and the separatist movement in Chechnya. We buy oil from Saudi, but a percentage of that money finances Muslim terrorism throughout the world. America winks and nods because, though behind every contract, a Saudi prince—and there are more than 30,000 + official members of the House of Saud—takes a commission, known in most circles as a bribe.

There continues to be a stream of financial resources flowing into terrorist groups under the guise of contributions to private charities. Donors in Saudi Arabia constitute the most significant sources of funding, but persuading the Saudis to curtail and crack down on this practice is discouraging. Kuwait and Qatar are equally involved in financial transactions and serve as transit points for funds that benefit terrorist groups like al-Qaeda.

The huge aircraft and armament purchases create jobs in several U.S. states that have large votes for incumbent politicians. The federal government gets tax revenues from suppliers, and everyone is smilingly happy until the topic of the sponsorship of Muslim radicalism comes up. Then Osama bin Laden and al-Qaeda regale Saudi for crimes against Islam and bombings occur somewhere that hurt Saudi interests.

Al-Qaeda in targeting the West and Jews seems to have alienated most Muslims because it has been responsible for the deaths of fellow Muslims, taboo under Islamic law. What is monstrous in this sentiment is that it is only Muslim deaths that are bemoaned, not all civilian deaths. The deaths of non-Muslims seem somehow to be less ignominious. Though al-Qaeda's recruiting of terrorists may have less attraction than in its early days, its reach is still global.

Saudi Arabia is rife with corruption, ostentation, domestic dysfunction and excess among the Saudi royal family and its surrogates. Revenues from oil go directly into special accounts bypassing the Saudi Treasury. A UN Security Council reported in 2003 that Saudi Arabia had transferred about $500 million to al-Qaeda since the beginning of the millennium. Saudi's cash reserves dwindled from a high of $120 billion in the early 1980s to about \$20 billion in 2003. Meanwhile its multiplying citizens have a dwindling welfare resource base. Per capita income from 1981 to 2001 fell about 75%, and the birth rate has soared—more than twice what it is in the U.S.

Big Oil and former American government officials try to capitalize as much as they can on Saudi contracts and jobs before the filmy bubble pops. One day, maybe even before the oil runs out, an assassination, riot, depletion of the treasury, or terrorist attack in Saudi will set loose the extremists on the world like a biblical plague of insects, and the special relationship with America will come unglued. If something happens to Saudi Arabia, and the oil gets turned off, the industrial heart of America, and not just its cars and SUVs, will free-fall in milliseconds.

Saudi's population growth rate and its long-term failure to invest in alternative essential infrastructure services until recently, its deteriorating education system, its strangulation of intelligent and creative voices, its failure to diversify its economy, its corrupt royal family have all contributed to economic stagnation. There is no obligation to educate girls in Saudi Arabia, and many fathers do not send their daughters to school. Saudi children cannot attend schools for foreigners. Saudi's Gross National Product is one-half that of Israel. Its economy is ranked 70th in the world after Slovakia.

## Religious Intolerance Abroad, Discrimination at Home

The hottest product of Saudi has not been oil but Islam. Its preachers have discovered impiety where none thought it existed. Islam's imagination was fired with practices that allowed men to indulge in a number of women, but did not permit women to have a voice beyond the kitchen, and no feminine image beyond the domicile. The puritanical Wahhabi imposed a harsh piety that make the desert even more uncomfortable that the heat from the sun, unrelieved from the shade of a palm tree or water from an oasis.

Saudi Arabia employs a special police force, the Society for the Promotion of Virtue and the Prevention of Vice, that ensures the Muslims pray the required five times a day, that couples are not seen holding hands or appearing to be too close in contact in public, and that women are appropriately veiled.

The Muslim Brotherhood known as the *Ikhwan* was based on Wahhabism. The Brotherhood in 1928 turned against the then ruling Saudi chieftain, Abd-al-Aziz because of his move to modernization, but he defeated them in 1930. In 1932 he unified all the tribes and the Kingdom of Saudi Arabia was born. The Wahhabi would thereafter control the civil sector and enforce the strictest of Islamic regulations, while the dynastic House of Saud would control the economy and foreign affairs. The pact created a tension in Saudi that cannot be undone. Saudi Arabia seeks to promote pluralism and anti-discrimination abroad in order to improve its image, but is compelled to maintain religious discrimination at home because of its favoritism of those who control religious and social policy.

Saudi Arabia sponsors interfaith dialogues and conferences in Europe and elsewhere to sow its respect for tolerance of all peoples. Meanwhile, it bars its own citizens, including tens of thousands of Christians, from any public worship. Islam is the only approved religion and has the only approved religious practices. Additionally, the more than two million Saudi Shiite communities are discriminated against in their religious practices, in employment opportunities and education. The present King Abdullah portrays himself as a reformer, but he is hampered by the steely political grip of the Wahhabi who complain about him reaching out to "infidels."

Saudi Arabia was terrified when hundreds of militants took over the holiest of all shrines in Islam, the Kaaba in Mecca in November 1979 after Ayatollah Khomeini assumed power in Iran and boasted that Islam does not need kings, especially ones responsible for guarding the holy cities. A Saudi extremist named Juhayman seized the Grand Mosque with hundreds of followers convinced the Saudi royals were bad Muslims and therefore should be overthrown. French Special Forces, the GIGN, was called upon to assist the Saudi National Guard in recapturing the Grand Mosque. Hundreds were killed and the leaders executed.

Saudis were alarmed when Saddam Hussein invaded Iran in 1980 because it was a horrible battle between two Muslim countries and literally in the Arabian backyard. Saddam invaded Kuwait in 1991 and that prompted the U.S. with European support to retake Kuwait. Saddam bombarded Saudi Arabia with SCUD missiles when America, at the Saudi invitation, placed troops and military supplies on Saudi soil (since removed) to arrest Iraq's potential attempt to invade the Saudi oilfields.

Osama bin Laden had earlier united Muslim feelings by playing on the fact that foreign troops were stationed in Saudi Arabia, on the sacred soil and home of the Prophet and residence of the two holiest shrines of Mecca and Medina. Osama, a Saudi by citizenship, gained notoriety and followers by this clever and strategic ploy against the ruling Saudi government, which then expelled him for his subversive activities.

The retaliations began shortly thereafter. In February 2006 guards at an oil facility opened fire on a truck full of explosives as it tried to enter a plant and it exploded without harming the plant. By mid 2008, Saudi authorities arrested 520 people suspected of belonging to al-Qaeda. The Muslim suspects, who were from Africa and Asia, were accused of planting bombs at oil installations and were found with money, arms and other munitions, some of which had been buried in remote areas. They had been organized into cells operating outside the country.

By December 2008 the Saudi government had placed 991 men on trial for participating in terrorist attacks inside the Kingdom from 2003–2006. In June 2004 terrorist plotters attacked a petrochemical plant that killed five foreigners, and another attack at a compound in Khobar that killed twenty-two. That same month there were three attacks in Riyadh when two Americans and a BBC cameraman were killed. An American engineer was kidnapped and beheaded, his video causing consternation in America.

In December 2005 five staff and four attackers were killed after an attack on the U.S. Consulate in Jeddah. Two car bombs exploded in Riyadh and security forces shot to death seven suspects in a raid on their hideout. In June 2006 police in Riyadh killed six men linked to al-Qaeda in a shootout.

Four French are murdered in a terrorist attack in the tourist ruins of Madain Saleh. In December 2007 security forces arrested a group of men planning to attack the holy sites during the pilgrimage of the *haji*.

Thousands more lingering in the black holes of the Saudi prison system had sought to go to Iraq or Pakistan and fight for the Taliban or al-Qaeda. Those who were on trial were caught planning or conducting terrorist activities inside the Kingdom. In fact, Saudis had detained thousands more and eliminated the top two or more tiers of the al-Qaeda leadership. Saudi had brought terrorists to trial to demonstrate to Saudi citizens that their actions were not consistent with Islam. But the real reason was that these militants challenged the royal family's leadership. King Fahd had declared in 2001 for the eradication of terrorism saying that Islam prohibited it. He equivocated because state actions encouraged violence against non-believers and in no way argued for its prohibition.

More terrorists have been killed and captured in Saudi Arabia than any other country not at war with militants. Fifteen of the eighteen hijackers on 9/11, and most of the foreign fighters captured in Iraq and Afghanistan, have come from Saudi Arabia. The radical militants would love to overthrow the Kingdom's royalty and replace it with clerical rule and the *sharia*. The U.S. forged its own devil's pact and special relationship with the royal family to preserve the approximately quarter of all oil sent from Saudi to fuel the American economy, and to purchase U.S. Treasury notes. The Saudis also funded the secret wars under President Reagan against the Contra rebels in Nicaragua and the presidential libraries of both Clinton and Bush.

Saudi will never repudiate its Islamic roots, since it has known no other religious experience in its history, and will never renounce its absolute reliance on *sharia* as the only form of justice. Saudi society is essentially intolerant, aristocratic and corrupt, closed to the outside world except to those few Saudi privileged and wealthy allowed to work with it.

## How to Deprogram a Jihadi

When asked why they do *jihad*, "students" in a prison class typically mouth memorized phrases like, "We do *jihad* to defeat God's enemies," or "to help strengthen Muslims," or "to kill when commanded." These young men have become radicalized with the vision of their comrades who fought as *mujahideen* in Afghanistan in the1980s. Many have never actually read the Koran. But Saudi Arabia has made a determined effort to de-radicalize Islamic extremists and as of 2010 more than 4,000 militants have gone through rehabilitations programs and have been reintegrated more successfully than ordinary criminals, according to Jessica Stern, a security expert at Harvard. Here is a quote from the manual of one of the Saudi 9/11 hijackers and terrorists that illustrates the extremist mindset that has to be rewired in programs aimed at rehabilitation.

> Make an oath to die and renew your intentions . . . All of their equipment
> and gates of technology will not prevent nor harm except by God's will.
> The believers do not fear such things. The only ones who fear are the allies
> of Satan, who are the brothers of the devil . . . When the confrontation

160

begins, strike like champions who do not want to go back to this world . . .
Know that the gardens of paradise are waiting for you. [4]

*Jihad* is so central to Islam that it can never deprogram itself to change
its ideology, even when the idea is used to overturn existing governments.
The Saudi government cannot address the root problem of *jihad* because it is
an Islamic religious dictate and therefore unalterable. A few prominent
Saudi clerics, including the Saudi mufti, the chief cleric, have taken public
stands against waging *jihad* against foreigners, as al-Qaeda does and have
issued *fatwas* against any Saudi youth who leave the country to do so. Many
young men recruited to actual fighting are not necessarily drawn because of
religious reasons but by the excitement of foreign travel, a dedicated sense
of purpose in life, and bonding with men of similar tastes.

It is much of the same reason young men and women from small town
America enter military service. Many feel unwanted and unappreciated,
some may be in an unhappy marriage or depressed, so they choose the
assignment of warrior they think will be an easy way to gain recognition and
notoriety. The majority of foreign fighters in any terrorist campaign in the
world are Saudis. But at least the Saudi government has provided centers
where former fighters are held as inmates in compounds where they attend
sessions aimed at ridding them of extremist tendencies. The inmates are
helped with material things, like a new watch, computer games, their
favorite foods, new clothes, all commodities to make them feel comfortable.
Upon release they may be given a car, help with finding a wife, perhaps a
new job. They must sign a pledge not to engage in any further extremist
activities.

Still, a few have varying degrees of recidivism. Said Ali al-Shihri was
released from Guantanamo in 2007 (his Guantanamo number was 372) and
returned to Saudi Arabia where he was placed in a rehabilitation program
for former jihadists. After completing the program he resurfaced in Yemen
where he emerged as the deputy leader of Yemeni's Al-Qaeda branch. He is
believed to have been involved in the terrorist attacks on the U.S. Embassy
in Sana, Yemen on September 16, 2008. By 2009 the Saudi government
announced that eleven Saudis who had been released from Guantanamo Bay
prison, and who had undergone the Saudi rehabilitation program, had fled
the country and were believed to be in Yemen having rejoined a terrorist
group.

Othman al-Ghamdi is a Saudi national and one of the leaders of al-
Qaeda in the Arabian Peninsula, and a former detainee at Guantanamo Bay.
He has been identified as an operational commander for al-Qaeda. Al-
Ghamdi served in the Saudi army until he deserted in 2000. He considered
fighting in Chechnya with Muslims against Russian rule. But instead he
went to Afghanistan and fought against the anti-Taliban Northern Alliance
before going to Tora Bora. Captured soon thereafter he was sent to
Guantanamo Bay, but in 2006 was released into a "rehabilitation program"
in Saudi Arabia. After the completion of his program he slipped into Yemen
in 2009 and became a ranking member of al-Qaeda.

Radicalization in deprogamming, besides Saudi Arabia, existed in
Kuwait, The United Arab Emirates, Singapore and Yemen, though it lasted
only three years in Yemen. So is it possible to change the mindset of a

terrorist? Are all de-radicalization programs equally effective, since they do not offer all the same incentives? Should programs focus on religious re-education or social behavior modification, or even on vocational life skills? The jury is out on all answers as recidivism rates are highly suspect even if some anecdotal evidence of limited personal successes.

## Sayyid Qutb (1906–1966)

One of the writers Osama bin Laden most admired was Sayyid Qutb who trained as a teacher and was an Egyptian member of the Muslim Brotherhood. Although he is Egyptian I include him here because his ideas about Islam influenced the most radical of Muslim believers, including Osama and the Saudi terrorists of 9/11.

Qutb lived in the United States from 1948–1951. He was deeply troubled by the racism and commingling between the sexes he experienced while he received a Master's degree in education from Northern Colorado State University. Muhammad Qutb, Sayyid's brother, became a professor and was one of Osama bin Laden's mentors. Sayyid Qutb's principles form the contemporary vision of radicalized Muslim militants.

Qutb was imprisoned for ten years, tortured and finally executed in 1966 in Egypt. His most influential book is *Milestones* in which he consistently claimed that every way of life and society not based on absolute submission to Allah was false. No nation, no group of people and no individual can have authority over anyone, an idea that did not sit well with Egyptian authorities. For Qutb there is no secular authority, no King or Queen, Pope, Oligarchy, President, collection of people (a democracy), or even personal conscience, that can supersede God's authority. There is no nation or church in Islam. Islam is the only true civilization.

> No political system or material power should put hindrances in the way of preaching Islam. It should leave every individual free to accept or reject it, and if someone wants to accept it, it should not prevent him or fight against him. If someone does not do this, then it is the duty of Islam to fight him until ether he is killed or until he declares his submission. [5]

His message that so influenced Osama bin Laden and his militant and ideological followers because it was devout, dogmatic and uncompromising with the West. This is not revolutionary. It is a correct reading of Muslim history and tradition and is completely in line with passages in the Koran. The Prophet's revelation is actually not just a new religion; it is a new world order that seeks to eradicate all other governance systems. Not until the mid-twentieth century had anybody articulated the doctrinal concepts so forcefully. The word was out that Islam now sought the destruction of Western civilization and all it represents and that thousands of young recruits have swallowed this message with all that it entails.

# Osama bin Laden: Militant Recruiter

Bin Laden was not a Muslim leader; he was a mass murderer of Muslims
(President Barak Obama, May 1, 2011)

Osama bin Laden's (a.k.a. USB) death on May 1, 2011 caused jubilation in the western world, consternation among Islamic radicals, malice from Hamas, and silence among most Islamic states that issued bland statements about his passing. Osama had declared war on the United States in 1996. He was incited by a federal court on June 10, 1998 for conspiracy to attack U.S. defense installations. Thus, killing him in resisting arrest was legal. The war against al-Qaeda is not just about Iraq, Afghanistan or any geography or country.

His death at age 54 at his expensive and well-fortified compound in Abbottabad, about 60 miles north of Islamabad at the foot of the mountains, and about 750 yards from a Pakistani military base, was immediately confirmed by digital face recognition software, DNA samples previously taken from family members, and a daughter's testimony. It took American intelligence agencies and special forces nearly a decade to track, locate and execute him. But he lived for several years so close to a key Pakistani military base that the kitchen staff could have walked over with pizzas. Osama was buried at sea in the same waters, the Arabian Sea, that he conspired with others to attack the *U.S.S. Cole* in the port of Aden, Yemen, that killed 17 sailors in 2000.

Based on Osama's cell phone found in his compound after his death, investigators discovered that he used the militant group *Harakat-ul-Mujahedeen* as his support network and its leader, Maulana Fazul Rehman Khalil, both of whom are protected by Pakistan's spy agency The Directorate of Inter-Services Intelligence, or ISI.

Abbottabad was also where Umar Patek, an Indonesian responsible for the bombing on Bali in 2002, hid, and where Abu Faraj al-Libbi, a senior lieutenant in al-Qaeda after Tora Bora, lived for a time prior to capture in 2005. Why did so many known Al-Qaeda members choose to reside in a rural town surrounded by Pakistani active and retired military unless they knew it was safe?

The 79-man team (and one trained dog) that flew in from Afghanistan, entered the compound and killed Osama and two brothers and Osama's son (three women and nine children were unharmed), leaving egg on the face of Gen. Ashfaq Parvez Karzani, Chief of the Pakistani Army, and Lt. Gen. Ahmed Shuja Pasha, Chief of the Pakistani Intelligence Services both of whom had claimed that Osama could not be found. The Pakistanis then blamed the U.S. for entering their sovereign air space without permission. The common consensus was that elements inside the army or the Inter-Services Intelligence Directorate (ISI) were sympathetic to al-Qaeda and were informing Osama about possible moves to capture or kill him and his commanders.

The mission absconded with a trove of computer files and equipment that indicated that Osama was not just a passive inspiration but still strategically active in plots to kill Americans, including a possible attack on U.S. railroads on the 10th anniversary of 9/11. Osama's computer files has led to the whereabouts of other Al Qaeda operatives and the proposed plots against identifiable targets.

The Navy Seal team #6 that conducted the operation is so special that members cannot apply to join it. Instead, they are recruited from the pool of existing Navy Seal teams, which is what makes them the best of the elite. They are a part of the Joint Special Operations Command (JSOC) that oversees the army's Delta Force, and eight of them usually form a team. They typically carry a SIG Sauer pistol, and either an M4 or M16 on missions.

Osama's demise brings the partial funding leadership of al-Qaeda to an end. Though members may view him as a martyr, he was in fact the embodiment of a psychopath who happened to have abundant finances. No one will ever assume his stature in the organization that may be temporarily filled with figureheads, if they dare expose themselves and their whereabouts. His legacy will live on, and perhaps his veneration among like-minded terrorists. But the message against infidels he fostered is still found in the Koran where his followers can discover scriptural imperatives for murderous designs against infidels. American prosecutors dropped 1998 indictments against him for conspiracy to attack U.S. defense installations. A part of that indictment charged Osama and his operatives with crimes against 18 American soldiers killed in an ambush in Mogadishu, Somalia in 1993, and conspiracy against the bombing of the U.S. embassies in Kenya and Tanzania in 1998.

Ironically, his prolonged organized terror plots against the West kept in power the very tyrannical despots he sought to overthrow. A younger Arab population is seeking greater freedoms in their countries and not revenge against western powers. The old turban-headed Osama bin Laden may have temporarily made Islam feel that it had damaged the western image, but in the end he was ineffective in delivering anything positive, as hatred was his sole message.

Osama was born in Yemen March 10, 1957 to a Saudi developer, Mohammad bin Laden. He migrated to Jeddah in Saudi Arabia and organized a construction business in the 1930s and 1940s building houses, roads, offices, hotels, and cultivated the Saudi royal family. Relations with the Saudi royal family and its thousands of princes, of whom about 200 wield the most influence, remains a family mix of deal-making, where power and money are exchanged over mobile phones, or with handshakes and kisses through social networks. Nothing is ever written; no contracts signed.

Mohammad, Osama's father, took multiple young wives. His seventeenth son, of 54 children, born of a Syrian wife in 1957, was Osama. Mohammad died in a plane crash in 1967. Unlike his siblings who cavorted in Geneva and London, Osama attended King Abdul Aziz University in Jeddah, prestigious by Saudi standards. Like his brothers and sisters he subsisted on about a one million dollar annual allowance. One of his college instructors was Abdullah Azzam, a Palestinian who would become the spiritual leader of Hamas. Another instructor was Mohammed Qutb, the brother of Sayyid Qutb. Here Osama learned the lessons of *jihad*. He graduated in 1981 in economics and public administration. [6]

Osama spent his early years in Saudi Arabia bivouacking in the desert, toughening his life with a Spartan existence with water and little else, sleeping on the sand. He became much more religious and, beginning in 1979, fell under the influence of Abdullah Azzam, a Palestinian cleric who became his mentor. That mentorship was to last nearly a decade and only declined when Osama turned to violence as a way of showing his Islamic religiosity. [7] The war in Afghanistan against the Soviets changed everything for Osama who raised an all-Arab army to battle them.

Many young Arab men have lost their heritage of life in the desert. In earlier generations they moved from oasis to oasis on camels living sparsely off simple foods and water. They have forgotten how to ride, to be self-reliant, to become hardened to the elements, and not to use their native intelligence and vigor to confront adversity. Arab youth, like youth in the developed world, had become soft and indulgent. This desert, Spartan life preceded Islam and taught the young to live in a hostile environment. Osama resurrected that ancient lifestyle by his personal example and it changed the motivation of his al-Qaeda recruits to live as he did without superfluities and extravagance, even though he had sufficient money to live a life of ease and luxury. He was the embodiment of a leader willing to sacrifice everything for his cause and expects no less from his followers.

After he was expelled from Saudi Arabia in 1994, Osama fled first to Sudan. He moved to Afghanistan in the 1996 where the Taliban under Mullah Omar greeted him as a kin brother in war against all infidels. There he built al-Qaeda and training camps that fed the global insurgency and planned the terrorist attacks of 2001. Between 1996 and 2001 it has been reliably estimated that al-Qaeda trained 30,000 Islamic militants from around the world. Even the Taliban at this time consisted of about a third non-Afghans. At least a dozen Uighurs, Muslims from western China captured later in Afghanistan by Americans, were held in Guantanamo. Others hid out in the Pakistani tribal areas.

Shortly after 1986 Osama had fallen in with Ayman Al-Zawahiri, an Egyptian physician, who would help him plan his attacks with improved logistics, and convince him to wage war against the real aggressors and colonialists—the Americans. With the assistance of another cleric, a blind Egyptian living in New Jersey, Sheik Omar Rahman, Osama raised the ideological level of his war with a religious edict. Sheik Omar was later tried, convicted and imprisoned for his role in the bombing of the Twin Towers in 1993. From Sheik Rahman Osama extracted a *fatwa*, the religious order he needed to declare war on the United States.

On February 23, 1998, Osama sent a message over a satellite phone to a London-based Arabic language newspaper in which he unleashed his rage against Jews and Crusaders. His manifesto outlined his grievances against the American military, those who supported Israel, the House of Saud, and his own undying militancy and raised his international stature among like-minded Muslims throughout the world. His charisma and boldness in attacking Western forces appealed broadly to recruits and sponsors eager to help him fight a real *jihad* against America and the West. There had never been such a direct frontal challenge like this before. Osama was capitalizing on his wealth, his exiled and privileged status, his sense of victimization, and his global acclaim to proclaim a holy war.

His new plan was to kill Americans everywhere. Few took him seriously until 1998 when he was responsible for the bombing, just minutes apart, of two American embassies in Kenya and Tanzania that killed over 200 and injured over 4,000, many of them Muslims. [8] By 1998 when al-Qaeda bombed U.S. embassies in Kenya and Tanzania European nations and America knew the danger was real and began an intensive campaign of police infiltration and intelligence to capture cells of al-Qaeda that had long lived under cover in western cities.

As early as January 1996 the CIA's Counterterrorism Center opened an office specifically to track Osama bin Laden. The office was staffed with about twelve people. Code-named "Alec Station" it was housed in rented space in a suburban Virginia office park and operated like a foreign-based CIA station. Michael Scheuer ran this office. Richard Clarke ran a similar operation for the National Security Council out of the White House in the Clinton Administration. Based on President Clinton's *Presidential Decision Directive–39* a new urgency was given to intelligence gathering on anyone who had, or was planning to obtain, access to weapons of mass destruction, and this included Osama. Richard Clarke made a proposal to capture Osama while he was in Khartoum, Sudan. But before anyone could even plan a *sub rosa* collection of him, Osama had slipped into Jalalabad, Afghanistan. [9] Within a year, the Taliban were solidly in power in Afghanistan and Osama was an honored guest in Kandahar behind a walled compound. His presence drew young, restless Muslim recruits from all over the Islamic world. His safety, and American disinterest in him as an extravagant self-proclaimed sheik, would all soon change. He was by now on the radar of American intelligence agencies.

On Friday, August 7, 1998 two teams of suicide bombers rolled into action in Nairobi, Kenya and Dar es Salaam, Tanzania and attacked the U.S. embassies just minutes apart. They drove trucks loaded with homemade explosives prepared by Osama operatives who had flown in from Pakistan and had fashioned the bombs in rental houses in each city. In Nairobi 213 died, among them 12 Americans, and 32 Kenyan embassy workers. Over 4,000 were wounded. In Dar es Salaam 11 Africans were killed and 85 wounded. The war with al-Qaeda had begun in earnest. Suddenly, Afghanistan, a backwater country that even the Soviets were forced to withdraw from, and in which the U.S. had no strategic interests, but which Osama was hiding in, suddenly rose to the top of the diplomatic, political and military foreign policy heap.

Later in 1998 counter-terrorism officials together with the CIA had plans to capture Osama at Tarnak Farm where he often stayed with one of his wives outside Kandahar. Top intelligence officials worried that too many civilians would be killed in the raid and the idea was scrapped. Two missile launching submarines were stationed in the Arabian Sea to fire missiles if Osama was found to be stationary long enough for a lethal strike. The policy debate among the intelligence community was between those who wanted to take more deliberate steps and those who wanted immediate action. President Clinton had signed several Memorandums of Notification, one that ordered Osama to be captured and brought to the U.S. for trial, and another ordering his death if necessary.

In October 1999 the United Nations passed Resolution 1267 demanding that the Taliban regime hand over Osama bin Laden and cease proving sanctuary to terrorists. The Taliban refused.

On October 7, 2000 when suicide bombers blew up their boat next to the *USS Cole* anchored in the waters in the Bay in Yemen, killing seventeen sailors, everyone knew the terrorist threats were serious. By September 11, 2001, the war of terrorism achieved the global status Osama wanted among Muslims. No one knew then how many sleeper cells there were, where they were, or when they would attack again.

Lyman Faris (a.k.a. Mohammad Rauf), a naturalized U.S. citizen living in Columbus, Ohio, worked as a truck driver with a license to carry hazardous cargo. He was in fact a one-man sleeper cell for al-Qaeda. He had immigrated from Pakistan in 1994 and had traveled to Afghanistan and Pakistan in 2000 and met Osama bin Laden and his top lieutenants, including Khalid Sheikh Mohammad, the mastermind of the 9/11 attacks. When he returned to the U.S. in 2002, Faris was intent on harming the U.S. and its citizens. His aim was to disable the Brooklyn Bridge and to derail a passenger train in the Washington DC area. He is said to have arranged for 2,000 sleeping bags to be sent to al-Qaeda in Afghanistan.

The National Security Agency had uncovered his plot through its wiretaps-without-warrants intercepts and had heard "Brooklyn Bridge" mentioned repeatedly. This caused the agency to pass the information to the New York City Police Department that then began massive bridge surveillance. A commissioned study revealed that indeed a single blowtorch could disable the old cables and send the bridge collapsing, as the plotter had recognized. In June 2003, Faris pled guilty to being a member of al-Qaeda and to felony charges for planning terrorist plots.

At the time no one could trace the conspiracy to Osama or find any evidence of his complicity in criminal terrorist acts. But by 1999, with the blessing of CIA Director George Tenet who, with the counter-terrorism team was pursuing Osama assiduously, a network of Afghani covert operatives were attempting to track his movements. However, Osama practiced intense operational security, and his inner circle was composed only of trusted Arabs, not Afghanis or Pakistanis. The CIA had satellite images, tracking teams and paid scouts on the ground as they followed Osama around Afghanistan in 2000. The goal was to capture and not just kill him. Everyone remembered what happened to a Delta Force unit, Desert One, known as Operation Eagle Claw that self-destructed in a sandstorm in the Iranian desert on April 24, 1980 attempting to rescue 52 Iranian hostages. The American military did not want a repeat of that rescue disaster. President Clinton was concerned but never gave a firm directive to the counter-terrorism team, the CIA or Pentagon as to whether he wanted Osama killed, captured, immobilized or just contained. Even worse, Clinton had refused to declare that the Taliban as the enemy, making it more difficult to attack any of targets inside Afghanistan that might be harboring Osama.

Immediately after 9/11 officials in all relevant American agencies were plotting how to kill Osama. Confronting terrorist attacks, and knowing that Osama had declared war on the U.S. and that it was imperative to find him was supposed to be the top government priority. Yet even after 9/11

Secretary of Defense Donald Rumsfeld was incredibly unaware that special operations forces like Delta Force existed. [10] Delta Force's mission, commissioned by a presidential order signed by Bush, was to kill Osama. President Bush, against the advice of the CIA, denied the request to position 800 Special Forces in Pakistan to prevent Osama's escape to the east from the Tora Bora mountain range. The official Administration rationale was that too many Americans would be killed in the exercise. Instead the directive was to rely on Pakistani forces, the very forces that were guaranteed to protect Osama bin Laden. Rumsfeld said in his memoir: "To my mind, the justification from our military operations in Afghanistan was not the capture or killing of one person." [11] The world's most infamous terrorist was allowed to escape again because of official bungling and a misdirected and obtuse mission.

In a press forum on March 13, 2002 President George Bush said that the U.S. had marginalized Osama because he didn't have access to his training camps anymore. To even consider marginalizing one of the greatest terrorists in the history of the world seems folly. This is clearly one reason why no concerted effort was made to locate him until President Obama renewed the search intensively in 2008 by asking then CIA Director Panetta to make it his top priority.

Even such a logical request as that of Delta Force to have aircraft drop mines (CBU–89 GATOR mines), that would greatly restrict vehicular and foot traffic for al-Qaeda escapees into Pakistan, was denied. As Delta Force special operation teams were scheduled to walk into the mountains in 2002 and kill Osama, al-Qaeda and remnants of the Taliban, Afghan *mujahideen*, who refused to fight at night, were unbelievably substituted to the team operation for Army Rangers. Secretary of Defense Rumsfeld had insisted on a coalition effort. This was like inviting a troop of boy scouts to fight alongside the most sophisticated soldiers in the world. The Afghans prefer to fight just in the afternoon, or after midday prayers, but their fighting leaves room for tea, looting and evening rest, and then they retreat to a former position. It is a fighting strategy that hasn't changed for centuries. When they did kill Taliban or al-Qaeda they typically looted the bodies and then retreated and failed to hold the high mountain terrain.

The Afghan Alliance was poorly equipped, poorly motivated, imperfectly organized around a militarily timid tribal elder, and unprofessional.

Eventually, B-52 bombers were called in to rattle al-Qaeda and the Taliban in their cave redoubts when no one seemed to agree on a boots-on-the-ground strategy that had to include cautious Afghans. Except for nuclear warfare, the world's most lethal modern military technology, B-52 cluster bombs known as Daisy Cutters, were unleashed beginning on December 9, 2001 against adherents of the world's most primitive militant theology.

After the death of Osama—codenamed Geronimo in the operation to kill him—a rival Arab youth group was attempting to re-arrange the political landscape of the Middle East and posing an alternative to Osama's calls for *jihad*. Youth has no long-term memory, and Osama for them was an aberration or a lost cause that did not satisfy their bold search for improvements in the quality of their lives by rallying against dictators in Tunisia, Egypt, Yemen, Bahrain and Syria. The long lasting result of these political disturbances is at present unknown, but the fact that they occurred at all is a testament to the rising of Arab political consciousness and a rejection of the policies of Osama. Arabs recognize that the West is not responsible for Arab economic deficiencies.

## The Continuing Al-Qaeda Threat

The terrorism of al-Qaeda is stateless and not directed against a specific state or country. It is indiscriminant, unpredictable, and directed against the West. The death of Osama bin Laden colors the future of this sick, radical, loose organization whose members have declared war on the West.

Al-Qaeda began as a military organization in Afghanistan during the Soviet invasion from 1980–1988 and has remained military in nature. Its structure is not a pyramidal hierarchy but rather a webbed network of loose alliances whereby many cells operate independently. It has recruited several kinds of participants. The inner circle around Osama consisted of radicals from Egypt, Yemen and the Arabia. Another group of veterans who fought in the Afghan war against the Soviets returned home to wage home-grown *jihad* in South Central Asia. Still another group lives in the West, predominantly Europe, and have become indoctrinated and radicalized there. Others will have been educated in the West have become converts to Islam and then radicalized, or, if already Muslim, radicalized into a *jihad* mentality.

Osama's al-Qaeda organization pledged to cause America severe pain so that it would withdraw troops from Arab countries. The evidence for the threat was sequential and unremittingly clear and had been perpetrated by similar groups before al-Qaeda was formed. There was first of all the bombings in Lebanon in 1983-84 and the hijacking of TWA flight 847 in 1985. Under al-Qaeda there was the Twin Towers attack in New York City in 1993, the intercepted planned bombing of planes over the Pacific in 1995 under Ramzi Yousef, the bombing of the Khobar barracks in Saudi Arabia in 1996, and the bombing attacks on embassies in Kenya and Tanzania in 1998. All had preceded the 9/11 attacks and all the latter had been planned, financed and executed by al-Qaeda.

Sandy Berger, Clinton's Chair of the National Security Council, and the White House counter-terrorism task force under Richard Clarke and the CIA tracking unit, had followed the Osama and al-Qaeda threat daily and with growing alarm. When the Bush transition team in 2000 was ready to assume control of the White House and Administration, Berger had each NSC director prepare briefing papers on terrorism and they were quick to emphasize that this particular terror threat would be the Administration's number one priority. But the principal players—Vice President Dick Cheney, NSC director Condoleezza Rice and her deputy Stephen Hadley, Secretary of Defense Donald Rumsfeld, and to a lesser degree Paul Wolfowitz and Richard Armitage—had other ideas about foreign affairs that included missile defense, military reform, China and Iraq. Terrorism was not on the Bush Administration's radar. But George Tenet, still Director of the CIA, had terrorism at the top of his list.

Throughout the whole of the Bush Administration, from 2000–2008, there was a *dance macabre* done with Pakistan, a lot of rationalization and dodging over the collusion of the ISI with the Taliban, and general obfuscation of the need to capture Osama. The U.S. gave the Pakistani military money that was supposed to be used to purchase weapons. Somehow, the weapons found their way into the hands of the Taliban. Bush was repeatedly conned by Pervez Musharraf who hoodwinked him into believing he was cooperating in the war on terror when all the time he was protecting his military, sponsoring militias, and coddling his unsettled Muslim population, happy to have the Taliban thumb its nose at Americans and its ability to hide the most wanted criminal of all time.

Al-Qaeda intended to overthrow modern governments in majority Muslim countries like Algeria, Egypt or Morocco, and to use them as sanctuaries for terrorists and to govern with *sharia* law. That objective did not die with Osama who was planning attacks on Algeria, Tunisia and Egypt while he was in Sudan. Al-Qaeda would like to topple the House of Saud in Saudi Arabia and install a Taliban-like government. Such a government would eliminate human rights, establish brutal regimes like the Taliban had in Afghanistan, and create a modern caliphate like that of imperial Arabs over a thousand years ago, and the empire of the Ottoman Turks.

A few years ago al-Qaeda operated with impunity in the web-world where the terrorist messages were available to anyone. But in the YouTube or FaceBook world, the arena of totally open access, they are pilloried. Unfortunately, in those countries that don't permit Internet access or place it under surveillance, not everyone enjoys the same freedoms to condemn al-Qaeda's blunt messages. The world has advanced in open access and this creates a problem for the terrorist networks who haven't yet understood how widespread is the availability and access of all users to get ahead of the slow learning curve of al-Qaeda.

Moreover, a citizen of the European Union can enter the U.S. without a visa and without prior notice. Let's say that knowledgeable terrorists are aware of places in security systems that would allow them to be watched, detained and/or questioned by security officials. He knows that flying from Britain or the U.S. to and from Pakistan means he will be scrutinized. So a hypothetical British citizen of Pakistani descent travels to Istanbul or Dubai for a vacation. While there he purchases another round trip ticket to Pakistan where he attends an al-Qaeda training camp. He returns to Istanbul or Dubai, goes to the British Consulate Office and claims that his passport has been stolen. As a British citizen he is issued a new passport that does not contain the evidence that he ever visited Pakistan. He then enters the U.S. freely, meets with confederates and easily purchases the necessary and easily obtainable bomb-making equipment for a planned attack. (According to Richard Minter's sources, al-Qaeda has a store of radioactive hospital waste, enough for a dirty bomb, but difficult to transport without detection. Miniter, 2011, p. 148). Or he meets with the bomb device already smuggled into the country.

Another scenario has terrorists reconstructing homemade drones—a transferable technology—with bombs or missiles attached and set up near to targeted locations. Such devices do not require pilots as suicide bombers and could be disposed of once they fly into a target.

One method by which our hypothetical terrorist receives money to conduct his operation(s) is described next.

## Hawala Money System

*Halawa* is an alternative or parallel transfer of money system instead of regular banking. It is commonly used throughout Asia and the Middle East and originated in South Asia. It is often used today to launder money but the system itself is not illegal. It is built on absolute trust. [12]

If Abdul, for example, a hypothetical taxi driver in Detroit, wants to send $5,000 to his mother in Islamabad, he goes to Fatima who works in a carpet store and gives her the $5,000. Once Fatima has received the money, she contacts her contact, Mohammed in Islamabad, who runs an Internet café or a travel service. Fatima tells Mohammed to pay, or to have delivered, to Abdul's mother $5,000 or its Pakistani rupee equivalent. Fatima makes a note of how much she owes Mohammed, but not necessarily what the money is for. There is no receipt for this exchange and its frequently is conducted via Email or FAX. There are, however, ledger accounts kept of all transactions.

Fatima and Mohammed may be tribal and clan members, but they are always business partners. Fatima may send Mohammed travel business, or Mohammed may send Fatima rugs for sale in her store. Either way, they probably also exchange goods and services. So the next time there is a business transaction—let's say Mohammed sends Fatima rugs—Fatima pays Mohammed $5,000 more than he is owed and the business partners are even in the *halawa* exchange with Abdul, although there may have been other transactions in either directions.

Abdul benefits from this because there is usually no transaction fee and no paper trail, and it happens quickly across continents. It is very efficient. Abdul's mother can telephone him as soon as she gets the money, usually within a day or two, faster than the week or so for normal bank transfers. Most of the expatriate community in Dubai uses *hawala* to send money home to families and relatives.

For money launders, drug dealers, tax evaders or terrorists, the absence of a paper trail, as there would be with a bank or other money wire transfer, is crucial and the reason why the system is so practical. Whether the money is legitimate or not, the system is not illegal in most of the world, though it is in some U.S. jurisdictions and for international transactions. In Pakistan or India it has to be licensed. For police to implicate illegal drug money, for example, it would have to obtain any ledgers kept showing the money transfer. In South Asia this parallel economy may be as high as 30-50 percent of the whole economy.

For Islamic terrorists *halawa* is the preferred method of transferring money to pay for logistical expenses or recruits. A legitimate business—a pizza parlor, a Internet café, a travel or foreign exchange business, used car business, a rug store, an Arabic or ethnic newspaper (like in Urdu)—may also have a side business of *hawala*. Unless terrorist use cell or mobile phones to make their transactions, it is extremely difficult to track these money exchanges.

Richard Clarke, former counterterrorism chief in the Clinton and Bush Administrations wrote: "The CIA was not alone in its ignorance of this widespread phenomenon; even though there were hawallahs [sic] in New York City, the FBI did not know what the word meant either." [13] The

Interpol police in Europe had written an extensive essay about the practice in 2000.

Ubiquitous radical Islamic movements refuse to modernize and hate to confront the modern world on any terms but their own. Islamic extremists demand that everyone embrace their version of faith and target anyone who disputes it. Japanese businessmen wear suits, not their traditional dress of *yakatas*, because the Japanese have made adaptations to modernity in politics, economics and culture. The Arab world has made no such modifications—none in politics, only a little in economics, and none in society, culture or dress.

The Arab Spring that erupted in early 2011 on the streets of Tunis, Cairo, Tripoli, Sana in Yemen, and Daara and other cities in Syria revealed a new impetus for reform in the political system of Arab dictatorships. The outcome of these uprisings is uncertain, but the universal movement is symbolic of a new mood among Arabs to join the developed world in some form of democracy. But most of them will still carry the militancy embedded in their religion with them.

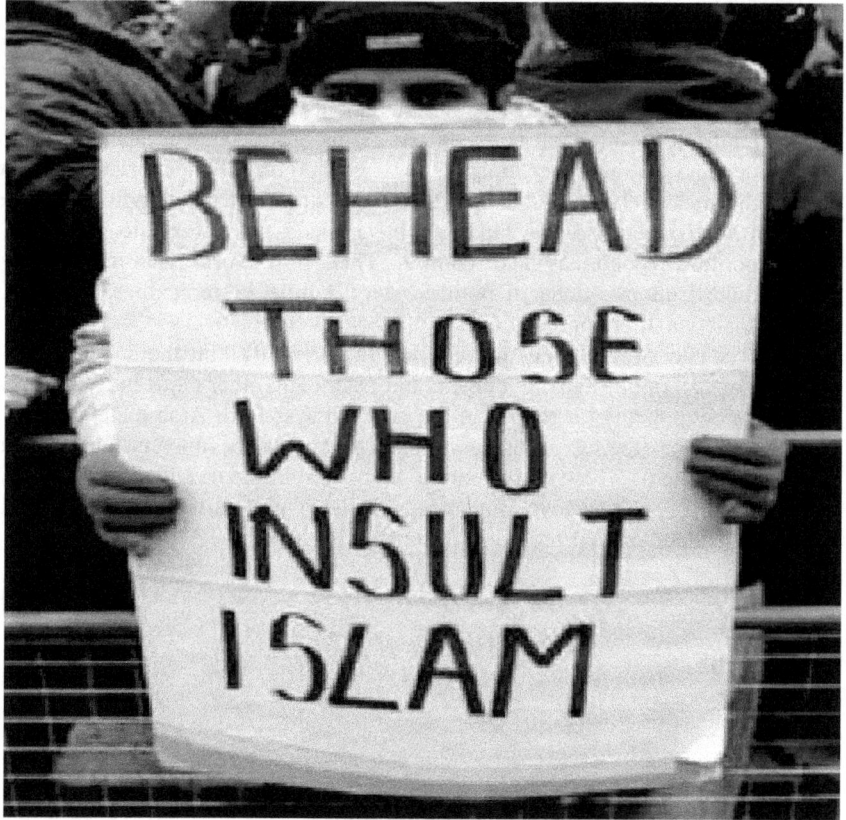

# CHAPTER TEN
# PAKISTAN:
# THE SIMMERING MILITANT POT

Pakistan today is the most dangerous place in the world. [1] (Benazir Bhutto)

The U.S. relationship with Pakistan is tenuous in the best of times, relatively robust with the military but fragile with intelligence services that seemed incapable of locating Osama bin Laden when he lived in the midst of the military elite. A fatal airstrike that killed 26 Pakistani soldiers in December 2011 showed the hesitancy, suspicion, and lack of communication between NATO forces and the Pakistani military. The debacle led to a serious downgraded change in relations.

The long term U.S. strategy was to keep Pakistan from becoming another Afghanistan, a radical Islamic state that harbors terrorists like Mexico harbors drug cartels. It is time, many assert, to treat Pakistan for the devious state it is—for harboring the Taliban enemy to defeat NATO forces in Afghanistan so it can have influence there; for animosity toward India; and for a state that has intensified, not diminished, its nuclear arsenal. We should forget about engaging Pakistan as a friend and instead contain it through trade and not military aid.

Pakistan the country is like my Pakistani colleagues. They are polite but not necessarily conciliatory. They are enigmatic but friendly, serving you tea but not knowledge or insights. They fear both India, which they have always seen as an enemy, and Afghanistan for its fragile democracy and fractious and armed tribal groups. Pakistanis have had to try to serve America's goals in the war against the Soviets in Afghanistan from 1980-89, and against the Taliban whom they created to thwart their enemies, and simultaneously to protect their national interests against enemies that surround them and they believe will threaten them once Americans leave the region.

After its formation in 1947, and until 1977, Pakistan's subsequent combination of civilian and military leaders managed a secular state. But General Zia ul-Haq's rule introduced a more fundamentalist rule and Islamic law. The Soviet invasion of Afghanistan in 1979 changed the regional dynamics and the U.S. aligned with Pakistan who created the Taliban to fight the Russians. When the Russians left in 1989 Pakistan had over three million Afghanis within its borders and a generation nurtured on *jihad*.

Now Pakistan has a fragile civilian leadership, an emboldened army, a vast network of spies and informants, paranoia about threats from India, a rattled and often militant Islamic population including elements of al-Qaeda, rising and strident anti-Americanism, and nuclear weapons.

Domestic politics, not military objectives, define U.S. war strategies. Personalities of the heads of cooperating states, the money allocated to humanitarian aid and related social imperatives, alliances with neighboring states, secrets no one in this generation will know about, and unintended consequences collude to impede military victory and create exasperation among citizens who must support the lingering battles. The cost of the war in Afghanistan, according to the Congressional Research Service, was $336 billion in 2010.

America's war in Afghanistan was to defeat al-Qaeda and to prevent the Taliban from returning to power and using that country as a terrorist base. Nation-building in Afghanistan—not a country so much as a conglomeration of tribal affiliations—is a hopeless military diversion, amid a cemetery of admirable causes, no matter how many additional troops are added. Counter-insurgency tactics, and drone strikes against terrorist leadership, will help win in Afghanistan and Pakistan, not altruistic reconciliation techniques.

Based on evidence obtained from the files found among Osama bin Laden's computers, the drone strikes in Pakistan have been very effective, killing about 20 of the top 30 al-Qaeda leaders and disrupting the plans and operations of organization.

The war in Afghanistan is unwinnable because factors for a satisfactory victory against the Taliban don't exist. Periodical military reports offer rosy portraits of progress that usually only include specific geographic locations where NATO troops have been active.

There are multiple obstacles. Psychological warfare techniques don't impact influentially on a barely literate society. The terrain is one of the most inhospitable in the world. The people are exhausted from war and resistance to foreign troops is strong. Radical Islamic ideology is more appealing as militancy has always been a part of the Afghani culture. The Taliban may be hated but do provide security from criminals. Civilians are more supportive of the Taliban guerillas either through fear, intimidation, or a motivation to end military activities.

Afghan tribal leaders are notoriously unreliable and corrupt. Fickle tribal politics is the governance norm not an aberration. Hence, once a military unit supposedly clears out an area of the Taliban, local government does not automatically step in to replace it, even if it has been trained to do so. Since the country is so poor local officials take money offered as an inducement to reduce Taliban influence as a personal favor. Over the years, the U.S. military and NATO forces have relied on western humanitarian values, like spreading money between tribal leaders, to support the armed conflict. However, trying to find elderly friends in a conflict zone is playing roulette with inter-tribal politics. So unless you rely on psychics and regularly have paranormal visions, all of these variables militate against significant U.S. and NATO military victory and signal a resurgence of radical Islamic fervor and a potential Taliban return to government.

> If I had to choose sides today, I'd choose the Taliban.
> (Hamid Karzai, December 15, 2010)

Imagine a country that has rampant drugs, an arsenal of nuclear weapons, terrorists within its borders and neighboring it, endemic poverty (reliably estimated at a third of the population), a dysfunctional educational system, corrupt ministers, and a hostile attitude toward the world. Such is

Pakistan founded as a secular, democratic state by Mohammad Ali Jinnah in 1947 after it separated from India. Successive leaders have turned it into a military Islamic state.

Balochistan is rich in minerals, which is why, following the traditional Islamic way of simply conquering other regions and states for the Muslim cause, Pakistan annexed its eastern side in 1947. Until then, Balochistan was an independent state. Now, it and its capitol Quetta seek to be independent again from its Islamic state overlord.

Balochs who have challenged the authority of Pakistan have, according to the common manner of autocratic military or police states everywhere, have been rounded up, usually tortured and often slain. In the past ten years, over 14,000 have thus disappeared. In 2011 mutilated corpses have been found in bunches. Pakistan is engaging in a form of ethnic cleansing.

Pakistan, like former Muslim leaders in history, from the militant Arabs through the Ottoman sultans, and the enraged members of al-Qaeda, seek to turn the world into an Islamic enclave. It is a militant pattern that is historically linear and has no compromises or deviations.

Young men from America and Europe gravitate to Pakistan for two reasons: potential wives and *jihad* training. Pakistan is where *jihad* training camps and Islamic extremist individuals and parties thrive. Most of the radicalized Muslim men, including U.S. citizens like Faisal Shahzad, the potential Times Square bomber, either came from Pakistan, journeyed there to obtain contacts with the Taliban or al-Qaeda, became enamored of jihadist propaganda, underwent militia training, or found financial or logistical support for potential terrorist attacks. All of Pakistan has been slowly transformed into a fundamentalist Islamic state, the source of most of the military training and recruitment for global Islamic terrorists.

Pakistan is still a feudal country with peasants working the fields of the vast landholdings, like those of the Bhutto family in Sind, while the cities bulge with poor slum dwellers. The seething resentment of the peasantry and urban poor against the West that supports the government and military has fueled the Taliban. The government's failure to build robust businesses and functioning democratic institutions has weakened support from the severely deprived underclass and left the exploding youth population little recourse except to turn to militant methods the Taliban readily supplies.

A good example of the extremism is symbolized in the case of Malik Mumtaz Qadri who assassinated Salman Taseer, a secular politician in Janaury 2011 because he reputedly committed blasphemy, a criminal offense in Pakistan. Qadri shot Taseer multiple times and when arrested and appeared in court was showered with rose petals and garlands by, among other attendees, lawyers. Thus does the murder of a politician rank higher in the minds and hearts of many Pakistanis then does someone who kills for religious purposes.

1979 was a turning point in Pakistan as it was in Iran. Zulfikar Ali Bhutto, Benazir Bhutto's father, was hanged in April 1979. The Pakistani army installed General Zia ul-Haq as President in 1977. He immediately imposed Islamic justice. Thus began the "Talibanization" of Pakistan and the reign of fundamentalist Islam. Zia ul-Haq appeased Islamic radicals, started the Taliban with the army's blessing to use insurgents to confront the Soviet Union, and to keep alive the battle against India in Kashmir. Benazir

Bhutto, who was twice Prime Minister (1988–1990 and 1993–1996), also turned a blind eye to the fundamentalists who increased their strength under her administration because she feared the same army coup that overthrew her father and had him hanged.

A second military coup in Pakistan occurred on October 12, 1999 when Pervez Musharraf seized power. Musharraf promised to restore democracy through elections and economic development. But then came the events of September 11, 2001 and the United States demanded Pakistani cooperation in the fight against terrorists. Musharraf agreed, but only reluctantly. Money flowed into Pakistan for cooperating and foreign debt was canceled. Flush with money for the military and the businesses supporting it, Musharraf then amended the Constitution to increase his own presidential powers in advance of parliamentary elections.

Benazir Bhutto returned from exile to enthusiastic campaign rallies and potential democratic election, and her assassination. It was widely believed at the time that she was assassinated by the Taliban, in cooperation with al-Qaeda, and with the aid of Taliban sympathizers in the Pakistani military and police. Bhutto was prophetic in noting the root of the terrorist threat:

> Pakistan under military dictatorship had become the epicenter of an international terrorist movement . . . First, the extremists' aim to reconstitute the concept of the caliphate . . . and second, the militants' aim to provoke a clash of civilizations between the West and an interpretation of Islam that rejects pluralism and democracy. [2]

Benazir Bhutto was assassinated in Rawalpindi, Pakistan on December 27, 2007. Pakistan by then had become a storm center for Islamic militants living in the western mountainous provinces where remnants of the Taliban and al-Qaeda resided in the tribal areas of the Swat valley and in North and South Waziristan. A UN inquiry into her assassination found that Pakistani authorities did not properly investigate her killing and in fact severely hampered local authorities by destroying evidence at the scene and preventing an autopsy. The report left the impression that the bungling of the investigation was purposeful. A Pakistani court indicted seven individuals in her assassination in November 2011, one of whom was the former police chief of Rawalpindi where she was murdered.

Elements of one or the other of these groups and their leaders were suspected of ordering her assassination. Musharraf actually signed a peace treaty with the Taliban in 2008, the Waziristan Accords, making a mockery of Pakistan's commitment to the war on Islamic terror groups and of the attempt to find her killers. Predictably, the Taliban never honored the treaty, which is why negotiations with Pakistan's leadership are always futile.

Benazir's widower, Asif Ali Zadari, Chairman of the Pakistan Peoples Party, convicted of graft, corruption and bank fraud, who spent more than eleven years in prison, assumed the presidency of Pakistan in late 2008. He was also accused in England in 1990 of attempted murder to obtain money from a businessman. He was arrested and charged with the murder of Bhutto's brother in 1996. Two hours after Zadari's gave his address to Parliament in 2009 the Taliban bombed the Marriott Hotel in Islamabad.

Zardari concluded talks with the Taliban that had overtaken control of the Swat district. The Taliban had killed police officers, held off 12,000 Pakistani army troops seeking to contain them, and punished residents who resisted them. They kidnapped diplomats and killed foreigners and journalists, and imposed *sharia* law. They destroyed over 200 schools for girls and forced women to wear the *burqa*. They coerced children as young as primary school ages to help service the militants by carrying guns and making bullets. [3]

Within weeks of this agreement seven well-armed Pakistan militants attacked a police academy near Lahore, caught hundreds of new unarmed police recruits literally off guard, killed eight and wounded more than a hundred. Four militants died and three were captured. While recruitment of hard-core militia extremists was accelerating, the terrorist tactics aimed at the Pakistani police slowed recruitment of regular police officials.

The present war in Afghanistan has its roots in Pakistan because al–Qaeda has migrated there and the Taliban resides in both countries. Americans cannot win in Afghanistan unless they distinguish the Taliban from the forces of al–Qaeda, defeat al–Qaeda, America's chief enemy, and exit leaving the Taliban, the indigenous people of the region, to be defeated by Afghan and Pakistani troops, conceivably an impossible task. Members of al–Qaeda are mostly foreigners and adherents of Osama bin Laden. So who are the Taliban?

## Birth of the Taliban

Photos of the Taliban look as if members could pass for a rock band without the makeup. Instead of guitars and drums they carry AK-47s. School was not their strong suit. They live in too many cold, airless rooms in winter where prayer is a necessity to keep faith. Men inured to staying alive in freezing mountains do not take kindly to unwanted invaders, and will make war on each other if life gets too boring.

The Pakistani intelligence services, known as the ISI (Inter-Services Intelligence Directorate), a branch of the army, created the Taliban as hired guns in the early 1980s as a counter-balancing force against the Soviets who invaded Afghanistan on December 25, 1979. Pakistan's long-standing dispute with India over the rule of Kashmir was a place where the Taliban could train in real military confrontations. The Taliban are ethnic Pashtun tribesmen who live in southern Pakistan and Afghanistan.

The Afghani Taliban was founded in 1994 and its leader is Mullah Mohammad Omar who is in hiding, probably in Quetta. The Afghani Taliban hosted Osama bin Laden from 1988 to 2002. Its goal is to oust foreign invaders and restore the Taliban government. After 2001 the Taliban relocated from Afghanistan and established a mini-state in the province of Waziristan.

After American and NATO forces invaded Afghanistan in 2002, the Taliban and al-Qaeda retreated into the western mountains of Pakistan, fleeing the mountain outposts of Tora Bora where they were sheltered by both the Pakistani military and intelligence services to the chagrin of western forces seeking to eliminate them. In 2009 the Taliban and al-Qaeda controlled large areas and established military-style depots of weapons and supplies under the cover of *madrassas*. Mullah Abdul Ghani Baradar ruled in the Taliban in Quetta in the name of Mullah Omar, who had a $10 million bounty on his head, and commanded money, narcotics, ransoms, and donations from Saudi Arabia. Combined U.S. and Pakistani forces captured him in February 2010.

By early 2009 the Taliban had essentially taken control of the Swat Valley, a corridor that runs north and south—about hundred miles from three of Pakistan's most important cities—and whose northern border extends into the Tribal Areas. The local Taliban leader, Shah Doran, read the order of the day on Taliban radio and the prescriptions always included banned activities. Prohibited as "Un-Islamic" were: listening to music, selling DVDs, watching cable television, dancing and singing, shaving beards, or allowing girls to attend school. During the broadcasts Shah Doran listed the names of those who have been killed for violating these rules and those who are about to be killed. The Swat Valley and most of the Tribal Areas have for all purposes seceded from Pakistan and established their own religious government.

The region is flush with weaponry and there is a nexus of groups well coordinated with indoctrinated youth willing to participate into guerilla activities. The new Taliban organization is more fluid than it was in Afghanistan in 2001 and independent commanders have assumed local autonomy. When the need arises, the Taliban quickly dispatches reinforcements from one area to another. New groups merge from time to time, like the Haqqani network in North Waziristan, that eventually form under an umbrella link with the Taliban or al-Qaeda. Several members of the tribe have been killed with drone missile strikes. [4]

Jalaluddin Haqqani is the patriarch of the Haqqani clan in North Waziristan, sanctuary of al-Qaeda militants. Allied forces know his mansion is in Khost, that he built a new blue-tiled mosque for the city's devotees, and that he commands about 3,000 battle-hardened fighters. His activities include smuggling and extortion, though he controls legitimate businesses in trucking and warehousing. He is reputed to be in ill health. The extensive tribal organization is managed by his son Sirajuddin Haqqani. This extensive network is wholly supported by the ISI, Pakistan's military intelligence.

The Haqqani network was importing Arab and Chechen fighters to perform opposition to the Afghan government. Fundamentalists want all foreigners out of their country, but are willing to accept foreigners as fighters. The majority of Taliban recruits are foreigners. It is an interesting twist of logic to report that Muslim fighters want to kill foreign soldiers on so-called Muslim soil when they recruit Arabs, Uzbeks, Tajiks and Afghans to fight.

The Taliban have accepted only the role of the *ulema*, the local Islamic governing council, and have purged secular rule. Their guiding principle is that the people owe allegiance first to Islam and not any country, and that their only obligation is to defend Islam. The consequences of this unacknowledged pariah state is that it has never been absorbed into any national domain nor recognized secular authority. Not much has changed since the British tried to crush the religious revolt in 1857.

Because the U.S. had withdrawn from military engagement in Iraq, the Obama Administration had a timetable for withdrawal too from Afghanistan and was prepared to participate with the Afghans in talks with the Taliban to end the conflict. The Taliban had opened an office in Doha, Qatar to facilitate that dialogue. The fear is that Pakistan will use talks as a means to gain some control over its future position in Afghanistan through the Taliban, an organization it initially organized to fight the Russians and still partially controls.

## The Nuclear Dilemma

The most disturbing aspect of Pakistan's fragile government and the presence of an active militancy within its borders is that it possesses nuclear weapons. The danger is that they could one day fall into the hands of terrorist groups either through connivance, thievery, or in collaboration with sympathetic Muslim handlers.

Pakistan's race for an atomic bomb began in 1982 when China sold it the complete design of a 25-kiloton nuclear bomb and enough weapons-grade plutonium for two bombs. Then in 1993 North Korea sold missile technology to Pakistan. In 1996 China sold it industrial furnaces for a reactor. Both India and Pakistan tested their nuclear devices in 1998 and the international community immediately imposed sanctions. [5]

Both Britain's MI6 and the CIA learned that Mahmood and Abdul Majid, retired nuclear scientists with Abdul Qadeer Kahn, the father of Pakistan's nuclear bomb, had met with Osama bin Laden and Ayman al-Zawahiri several times, the last just a few weeks prior to 9/11. [6] The fear that somehow, someday, a Pakistani nuclear weapon might become the property of Islamic terrorists haunts Western officials.

The whole complex of nuclear facilities was established through Dr. Abdul Qadeer Khan who in turn sold the technology to Iran, Libya, Syria and North Korea. His approval and financing came from the Pakistani military. He was placed under house arrest on U.S. insistence in 2001 when his network was uncovered. Neither American intelligence officials nor international nuclear inspectors were ever allowed to question him. A court ordered his released from house arrest in February 2009 and he was allowed to move around the country.

A. Q. Khan was born in Bhopal, India in 1936 and moved with his family after partition to Pakistan. After undergraduate school he pursued graduate studies in Europe and took his Ph.D. at the Catholic University in Leuven, Belgium in metallurgy. He was put in charge of a program using centrifuges to enrich uranium. He returned to Europe where he stole essential parts and the design for centrifuge technology. Once Pakistan acquired the centrifuge enrichment process, Khan began offering it to China, Iran, North Korea, clearly with the collusion of Pakistani authorities, in exchange for sophisticated nuclear weapons technology.

Pakistan has been chastened by its support of Afghanistan under the Taliban that it helped create, by its continuing support of Muslim extremist groups, by its failure to absorb tribal groups like the Pashtun into manageable governance, by its support of the renegade nuclear physicist A. Q. Khan, by its failure to seek and find a solution to the Kashmir dispute, and, finally, by its lingering distrust of India. [7]

## Mad for Madrassas

*They teach us how to memorize the Koran.*
*(Pakistani madrassa teenager)*

Education is not mandatory in Pakistan. According to World Bank estimates about 60% of Pakistanis are illiterate, with a larger percentage for females. The proportion is far below the ratio for countries with similar per capita income. The Pakistani government support for elementary education languishes. Among the Taliban-controlled areas education is non-existent.

Education in Pakistan is roiling with misguided religiosity, indicative of what the Muslim world is experiencing. A primary and secondary school curriculum has been deliberately designed to encourage the forces of hate, violence and extremism. A primary and secondary school environment is consciously designed to nurture terror, promote prejudice and breed extremism. Irrational fear, perceived external threats, India-centric paranoia and vested economic interests—all team up to produce a government prescribed curriculum that preaches hatred.

The continuing threat in Pakistan is from religious schools that have become military training camps for extremists. Youth receive free food and housing, a huge incentive to poor families with many children. Instructors in these Islamic seminaries teach military principles and tactics, brainwashing children into becoming soldiers of Allah against the West. They do not teach tolerance or goodwill, science or mathematics, humanities or the social sciences. They have become a second form of government delivering social services to the poor and special treatment to the children they recruit. Reliable estimates are that upwards of 30,000 Islamic militants have been trained in Pakistani *madrassas*. [8]

In southern Punjab province, according to local resident Daniyal Mueenuddin, a half Pakistani, half American who lives there, they have grown more powerful and their Friday sermons and in talks are largely anti-Shiite and against the Pakistani government. [9] New Islamic recruits are educated in training camps that masquerade as schools, regardless of which group they may eventually join. *Madrassas* in the Northwest Provinces and Baluchistan promote *jihad* to the detriment of all other Islamic teachings. After 9/11 some *madrassas* continued to be funded by Wahhabi groups in the Arabian Gulf. [10]

Young boys who would otherwise remain illiterate receive a religious education that instructs them in nothing about the modern world. Even within Britain 16 of 22 of these Muslim seminaries are Deobandi in nature, or the most extreme form of Wahhabi teachings. Although many do not actively promote violence they do encourage segregation from other people and culture. On the other hand, the top leaders of al-Qaeda are primarily trained in western colleges. Most are Egyptians, like Ayman al_Zawahiri, and most were married. [11] Endlessly chanting phrases from the Koran presumably inculcates a strict Islamic personality in young boys and an intense Muslim perspective. What it really does is deaden the mind to curiosity, imagination, and intellectual agility.

The *madrassa* accepts boys as young as five and keeps them until adulthood. The young men learn the code of honor and respect for clerical leaders. Taliban in the Swat Valley announced in all local mosques that every family would have to contribute one young man to their ranks, a tactic similar to that used by the Ottoman Empire to create its elite corps of janissaries from conquered Christian families. This corruption of a basic Islamic theological understanding and the espousal of extremist ideologies occur because there is no credentialing of Pakistani teachers, or governmental oversight, or testing of necessary knowledge for teachers to instruct the young.

The *madrassas* serve as a kind of orphanage where the boys learn to practice rote learning of the Koran—in Arabic, a language they do not understand—and selective military skills. (The main language of Pakistan is Pashtun in the south and Urdu in the north). The impressionable recruits quickly and forever bond with their classmates. Boys are young as eleven are induced and trained to become suicide bombers.

Asal and associates conducted a survey of 141 militant families in Pakistan who had consented to have their sons join a *jihad*. [12] They tried to determine exactly what factors contributed to a young male's decision to join a *jihad*, and what factors a family used in deciding to allow him (and in a few cases a young woman) to join. One factor was the financial benefits that accrued from the death of a *shaheed*, a martyr. A young male, who may have been unemployed, can receive wages as a fighter just like other soldiers. A large family may decide to allow a son to join a *jihad* group because they have enough children. Moreover, joining a *jihad* often means a higher social and religious status in the community for the family. Sons educated in a *madrassa* are more likely to accept the call to *jihad*. The socio-economic status of the family does not appear to be a significant factor. Those who join the militants are more likely to be better educated but also more likely to be unemployed. The stated educational purpose was to overthrow secular governments and replace them with Islamic republics.

A website of the Pakistan Teachers Organization based in Lahore promotes Islam. Begun in 1969, it has thousands of members who teach in regular schools, not *madrassas*. The goal is to replace more than two hundred years of "colonial education" with Islamic education. All theory and practice is to be brought into harmony with the teaching of Islam. The group known as *Tanzeem-e-Asatiza* has these stated objectives:

- To bring the present education system in harmony with the needs and trends of Islam
- To eliminate the impact of secular thoughts and attitudes from the minds of students and teachers
- To bring about the "Islamization" of the curriculum

Despite the presence of so many religious indoctrination schools, Muslim militants often receive foreign education in order to establish credentials from abroad that give them cache for travel and legitimacy. Even more disturbing is the number of American Muslims who have traveled to Pakistan to join *jihad* movements. Five American Muslim men disappeared from their families in Alexandria, Virginia in November 2009, traveled to Sargodha, in the Punjab province of Pakistan and joined a militant group. A Pakistani police raid captured them the following month. A Pakistani court sentenced them each to ten years in prison.

## Federally Administered Tribal Areas

The Pakistani government has created, supported and trained Islamic jihadists for decades. [13] Al-Qaeda and the Taliban established a rival state-within-a-state in the Federally Administered Tribal Areas (FATA), a mountainous region in the northwest corner of Pakistan bordering Afghanistan, the principal haven for insurgents waging war against NATO forces in Afghanistan. These mountain areas are a destabilizing geographic part of Pakistan as they operate autonomously with their own security forces. They conduct raids across the border into Afghanistan. The hill villages are nearly inaccessible, with steep mountain ranges, shale rocks, and impassible roads, which is what the cloistered inhabitants prefer.

The Tribal Areas have no controlling government, only the rule of the local chieftain, the Taliban and its Vice and Virtue Brigade. Political parties do not exist, nor can citizens claim protection of Pakistan's judicial system or its Constitution. About US$20 billion in aid during the Bush Administration went to Pakistan annually to counter this threat but much of it wound up in the hands of the Taliban. The Pakistani army used to be a secular institution. By the turn of the twenty-first century it had become riddled at senior officer levels with Islamic fundamentalist ideologies. [14]

FATA has some of the worst economic and social conditions anywhere on earth. Less than twenty percent of the inhabitants can read or write. The female literacy rate is generously reckoned at three percent. Literacy is a little higher in Baluchistan in the southern mountains, reckoned at fifteen percent. There are poor sanitary conditions and a poor water supply. A variety of aid packages, including $60 million from the Agency for International Development for infrastructure support in education, health and social services, and $200 million from the U.S. Department of Defense were intended to secure the border and train Pakistani military to cope with the growing militancy that flows into the area. Large amounts of funds found their way into the pockets of the Pakistan military and then to the coffers of insurgents. There never has been effective government, except for the landlords who were either killed or fled when the Pakistani army invaded in the summer of 2009. Tribal fighters have been supported as surrogates for a potential war with India, or to keep Afghanistan from falling into Indian or American orbits of influence. [15]

Parents in Western Pakistan hope for two things: as many sons as possible and an unlimited supply of guns. The mountainous areas of western and northwestern Pakistan may be the most industrious gun-making region in the world. Every kind of gun is made, often by hand, and repeatedly tested. Children forge and package the bullets. Test firing is done from rooftops into the adjoining hills. Admitted guests (foreign journalists are barred) can purchase a 9-millimeter Mauser pistol for about $50, and a Karakov rifle, similar to a Kalashnikov, for about $250. [16]

Beginning in 2005 the Taliban gained control of these tribal areas by simply killing off tribal chieftains. In South Waziristan, where the notorious Baitullah Mehsud resided and held sway, commanding an estimated 20,000 fighters—he is said to have been responsible for the assassination of Benazir Bhutto—the Taliban killed more than 150 local tribal chiefs. (Mehsud was killed in a drone airstrike in late summer 2009).

One associate of Baitullah Mehsud was Abdullah Mahsud, born in 1974, a college graduate who lost a leg fighting the Northern Alliance in Afghanistan. He was captured in Afghanistan in 2001 by Americans and boarded in Guantanamo where he feigned mental retardation and was released in 2004. He quickly rejoined the Taliban in North Waziristan and was placed in command of 5,000 troops. During a Pakistani raid on his house on July 24, 2007 he blew himself up by detonating a hand grenade.

Murdering tribal chieftains opposed to their status and operations is just one form of Taliban intimidation. Al-Qaeda sponsored cross border raids into Afghanistan, killing NATO forces, Afghani soldiers and police creating political and social chaos. Additionally, they sponsored the growing, production of opium and distribution of heroin, useful for funding their military operations. Villagers were forced to allow the Taliban to use their houses as protective cover. Those who refused were killed, usually by beheading.

The most successful method American forces favor in killing top leaders of the Taliban and al-Qaeda is the silent killer of drone airplanes, the Predator and the heavier and more powerful MQ-9 Reaper. [17] The Predator has advanced radar systems with high-powered zoom photography capabilities that show images day or night in real time. It flies at 275 miles per hour at heights of 50,000 feet. Its powerful cameras have electro-optical and infrared capabilities that transmit high-resolution color videos to ground commanders. Each has as many as fourteen Hellfire missiles fired to deadly effect, usually on car convoys or at homes where insurgent leaders live or gather. In 2009 alone there were 53 Predator attacks inside Pakistan under President Obama, more than occurred in all of the Bush Administration. The use of the Predator drone more than doubled in 2010.

Some drones are as small as bugs, masquerading as insects. Military researchers design drones near Wright-Patterson Air Force Base near where the Wright brothers began building the first airplanes. The much-used Predators are about the size of a small airplane. In 2000 there are about 50 drones. A decade later there were 7,000. The RQ170 Sentinel stealth drone was used to spy on Osama bin Laden's compound. The Reaper's turboprop engine is nearly eight times as powerful as the Predator. It carries fifteen times the weapons load, travels three times faster, and has a wingspan about the same as a Boeing 737 passenger-jet. It costs about $8 million and can stay airborne for 34 hours. As pilot fatigue is not an issue, shifts of operators can be used to sustain this length of time in the air. It carries a range of weapons on a par with a conventional strike aircraft, including Hellfire air-to-ground missiles, Paveway laser-guided bombs or GBU-38 Joint Direct Attack Munitions (JDAMs). A balloon tethered at 15,000 above the surface can scan the earth for 20 miles around and watch where insurgents plant bombs. By 2012 drones had killed about 2,000 terrorists.

But regardless of the number of Taliban or al-Qaeda killed in Afghanistan and Pakistan, the aggressive web sites al-Qaeda uses continues to recruit new fighters from Saudi Arabia, Yemen, Somalia and Uzbekistan. They enter first often through Iran, then Pakistan through Baluchistan and move into Waziristan for training. The tactics now are to forgo training camps and to focus instead on mobile training teams that, for example, assemble bombs in houses.

Most actual and potential terrorists in the West were trained in the tribal areas of Pakistan and are of Pakistani origin. Yeshi Girma, 31, is the wife of Hussain Osman, one of four men observed on closed-circuit TV who was trying to detonate bombs in backpacks on the London underground and on buses in July 2005. The bombs never exploded. They were copycat suicide attacks from the July 7, 2005 attacks on London's subway that killed 52 and injured over 700. Hussain was sentenced to life in prison in 2007 for his role, as were three other men. But his wife, and her sister and brother were convicted in June 2008 after a four-month trial for their role in not alerting the police about the potential crime and not disclosing information about terrorist attacks. She was convicted because she had prior knowledge of the attacks and did nothing. She also helped her husband to escape from authorities. Her brother received a ten-year sentence and her sister a fifteen-year sentence.

Pakistan claims that it is a sovereign country. This means that its borders are defined and that it has an autonomous right to rule within its boundaries. But the so-called lawless region has never been under any government control, not even when the British occupied this part of the world when it ruled India. Additionally, the intelligence services of Pakistan have used militants as surrogates to fight as Taliban in Afghanistan. Pakistan recognized Afghanistan when governed by the Taliban. The region is a non-state area. Its male population have largely been trained as mercenaries in neighboring wars—Afghanistan, Kashmir, India, Iraq, and Chechnya among them.

The mistake was often made at the highest levels of government that the U.S. had no adverse policy against Islam as a religion. The policy that Americans favored was that no religion could actually seek to kill any who did not believe in its tenets. No one wanted to believe that as attacks continued that terrorists were not devout Muslims but perverts of the religion, not distorting Islamic doctrines, but reviving them. That misguided foreign policy is slowly changing as information about the radical nature of true Islam seeps into Western consciousness.

If you think that radical training camps are only in Pakistan, you might want to reconsider. What do the following small towns in America have in common? Hancock, New York, Deposit, New York, Hyattsville, Maryland, Red House, Virginia, York, South Carolina, Dover, Tennessee, Buena Vista, Colorado, Talinhina, Oklahoma, Tulane County, CA, Commerce, California, and Onalaska, Washington? These American compounds are complete with armed guards in traditional Middle Eastern dress, and exist for the training of young Muslims, many new converts to Islam. [18] Islamic radicals use the same traditional methods everywhere in the world.

## The Mumbai Massacre

The carnage in Mumbai (formerly Bombay) India in the last days of November 2008 was a monstrous example of barbarity, not just for the number of dead—179 and over 300 wounded—but because of the scope and brazenness of the attack. It was a carefully planned, high profile execution similarly to the attack on the Israeli delegation at the Olympic games in Munich in 1972. It was also an example of "swarming," a terrorist technique of attacking several targets simultaneously, as happened on 9/11, thereby overwhelming response services and creating more fear among the population that more attacks were imminent.

The scout and reconnaissance front man for this military attack on civilians was American, David Coleman Headley, formerly known as born of an American mother and Pakistani father, and reared as a youth in Lahore. (profiled in Chapter Four). Ten terrorists, one of whom, Azam Amir Kasab, 21, convicted in a Mumbai court in 2010, survived. The terrorists strode into hotel lobbies, restaurants, banquet halls, a train station, a Jewish cultural center and hotel rooms and shot everyone in sight. Places of hospitality were turned into morgues.

Condolences from the western world were quick and a gesture of humanitarian solidarity. Condemnations from the Arabic world were non-existent. Had there been satirical cartoons published in European or American newspapers, we would have seen riots in Arab streets. The death of infidels got no whimpers of regret or solace from Arab governments or individuals. The message of silence is that either the death of infidels is permissible, or that individuals are cowered into silence for fear of retaliation.

The ten terrorists trained for more than a year in Pakistan under the auspices of a group known as *Lashkar-e-Taiba* (meaning "army of the pure"), and its leader Mohammad Hafeez Saeed, 63, who was held under house arrest in September 2009. The terrorist group has a long history of a relationship with the ISI, but was supposedly banned in 2002 after American insistence, though it maintained government ties. According to reliable sources, *Lashkar-e-Taiba* has about 150,000 members and operates under the umbrella of a charity (*Jamaat ud-Dawa*). It can quickly and reliably train willing young men, or, as has been suggested, use former military men to conduct operations, as was suspected in the Mumbai attack. Their aim has always been against India. But whatever they the organization is called, and whatever its operating procedures, its doctrinal goal is the same as al-Qaeda.

Saeed operated a 75-acre campus about 15 miles north of Lahore. Terrorists called the organizer of the attacks in at his headquarters in Lahore, Pakistan. They had GPS navigational handset systems in piloting their hijacked boat from Karachi to Mumbai for several days beginning on November 23, 2008, and were shown Google Earth maps of their targets. Each terrorist carried one AK-47 rifle, a 9-millimeter handgun with two 18-round clips, 100 rounds of loose ammunition, grenades, and 5,400 rupees, about $110 dollars. They used Email messages with Urdu language voice-recognition software so investigators could not identify their ethnic or regional language use. They used satellite phones with voice-over Internet protocol numbers to talk to their leaders while traveling, making their transmissions more difficult to trace. Once in the hotels, they grabbed the cell phones of the guests to talk to each other so police could not trace their calls during the attacks.

The weapons used in the attacks were traced to a factory in Punjab Province in Pakistan under contract with the Pakistani military. The same factory makes grenades that were used in other terrorist attacks in India and in a bombing of the Indian Embassy in Kabul, Afghanistan in July 2008. A German company had licensed the factory in the Punjab to manufacture weapons for the Pakistani military. [19]

The true names of the terrorists may not be known as the practice is for them to change their names periodically so they cannot easily be traced or linked to any other sponsoring terrorist organization. The bodies of the nine terrorists killed remained in an Indian morgue because not even leaders of the Muslim community, the second largest Muslim population in the world after Indonesia, who called the terrorists by their rightful designations, "murderers," and not their self-designations, "martyrs," have been unwilling to bury them in the Muslim cemetery. The attack, they say, was an insult to both India and Muslims in India.

Indian authorities were woefully unprepared and under-equipped to manage such an attack. [20] There were fundamental flaws in Indian intelligence. Intelligence signs of an impending attack from the sea were ignored. The Mumbai police had no local SWAT team. The terrorist response team had to arrive from Delhi, hours and hundreds of miles away. The police had no high-powered weapons to match those of the terrorists. Indian police had no sniper guns or telescopes to distinguish civilian hotel guests from terrorists. A clutch of police in the train station huddled and watched as gunmen killed 25 people. Eventually most of the police simply ran away.

It is too traumatic to describe the horrific sequence of this one bloody rampage. But at 9:40 PM two gunmen standing outside on the street began shooting into the Leopold Café for at least one-minute killing six patrons—three of them foreigners—and two waiters. The murdered waiters were both Indian Muslims. The gunmen then strode via a back alley to the rear entrance of the nearby Taj Mahal Hotel where they killed and terrorized guests for two days. A Turkish couple was spared because they were Muslim, an action that exposes the true nature of the massacre.

It is enough to re-emphasize that this is another expose of the depth of Islamic extremism and its corps of dedicated killers, the instructors who train them, the so-called preachers who extol the virtues of killing infidels and westerners, the team of collaborators who provide the suicide death squads with observational details and logistical support, and the financiers who underwrite the whole effort. If the brutality of the Mumbai attack is not enough to rouse inert populations to the dangers of extremist Islam it is impossible to imagine what would agitate a somnolent and apathetic global public to defend its citizens against indiscriminate and planned slaughter.

There have been successes in thwarting terror attacks. In July 2004 Naeem Noor Khan, 25, the son of the executive of Pakistan airlines was arrested in Lahore. He had studied in London and was the communications chief for al-Qaeda in Pakistan transferring Email messages to terrorist cohorts. He had computer files that showed surveillance photos of the World Bank, International Monetary Fund, New York Stock Exchange and Heathrow Airport in London. His arrest led to several arrests in Britain and the U.S. Twelve foreigners and fifty-one Pakistanis were also arrested in Pakistan, including Ahmed Khalfan Gailani, a Tanzanian who participated in the 1998 bombings of U.S. embassies in Africa. [21] By 2008 Pakistan had captured 689 al-Qaeda operatives and turned over 369 to American officials.

## Quetta and Karachi: Taliban Havens

The *Jamiat Ulema-e-Islam* is a fundamentalist religious political party in Pakistan that insists on strict enforcement of *sharia*. It helped establish thousands of *madrassas* in Pakistan, more than any other religious movement, and originally helped establish the Taliban. Maulana Abu Ala Maudidi, who proposed a Marxist revolutionary approach to Islam in his book, *Jihad in Islam,* founded the group in 1941. The organization blossomed after it gained political favor in 1977 under General Mohammad Zia ul-Haq who sought to establish "a general Islamic order" in Pakistan. The unanticipated international Islamic propellant of the Iranian revolution in 1979 further revived fundamentalist organizations. Wahhabi money from Saudi Arabia began to flow into their Pakistani coffers.

The group handed over a suburb of Quetta known as Pastunabad to the Afghan Taliban as a safe haven. Hidden and protected there is Mullah Omar, the one-eyed cleric who once ruled Afghanistan and ordered the world's largest statute of Buddha to be blown up. With its geographic proximity to Afghanistan, Quetta has a reputation for Islamic fighters like al-Qaeda and the Taliban to enjoy a place to regroup, enjoy rest and relaxation, stock up on supplies and weapons, and plan the next offensive. Thousands of longhaired, black-turbaned Taliban roam the streets in Pastunabad. They purchased or forced out of their businesses hotels, merchants, teashops and homes. They thus have a safe suburb of a major Pakistani city. Not even the police enter this area. [22]

Karachi, population about 14 million, has been a stew of ethnic identities and a festering pot of gang and drug-related violence. Radicals and the Taliban have also established safe havens and an aggressive presence there and have frequently clashed with the Pashtun nationals. Though the financial hub of Pakistan, Karachi is among the most illiterate cities of Pakistan and is dominated by two ethnicities: Urdu speaking Mohajirs and Pashto speaking Pashtuns, both Sunni Muslims. It is usual for sectarian violence to appear in Karachi. A huge remote-controlled bomb tore apart a bus carrying Shiites to a religious procession on February 5, 2010 that killed 25 and wounded more than a 100. A second bomb blast planted on a motorbike occurred at a hospital where the wounded were carried from the first bomb.

Addressing a large Karachi gathering via telephone in early November 2008, the *Quaid* (supreme leader), Altaf Hussain, warned the "Sufi-loving people of Sindh" and "peaceful people of Karachi" that a systematic campaign was underway to "Talibanize Karachi." Taliban leaders were sending people to Karachi and many cable operators, CD shop owners and girl schools were asked to shut down operations because they are un-Islamic. Altaf alleged that Taliban elements "collected nearly 2 billion rupees" in ransom over the past two years and there were nearly "5 million small arms in the city." He urged his activists to "be ready to defend themselves and get training in self defense and get arms' licenses."

Pakistan controlled the Taliban but never acknowledged active support. The ISI provided safe houses in Quetta in southern Pakistan, gave logistical support like fake passports so al-Qaeda leaders could escape to Persian Gulf states, built hospitals for the Taliban wounded near the Afghanistan border, and provided artillery cover for those returning from skirmishes with American and NATO forces in Afghanistan. With Pakistani support, the radicals were able not only to have safe houses but safe cities in Quetta and Karachi.

News finally emerged in 2011 that Pakistani soldiers were linked to an ambush on May 14, 2007 attack on Americans meeting at a Afghan village called Teri Mangal near the border with Pakistan. They were there to sort out differences about an outpost's positioning. Pakistani soldiers retaliated for past grievances at the end of the meeting by firing automatic weapons at the departing Americans and Afghanis. Duplicitous Pakistani soldiers continued to fire from the open windows of the classrooms, where the meeting had just been held, onto departing troops riddling the cars and occupants with bullets. One Pakistani attacker was killed. [23]

Pakistan is on the brink of a governmental meltdown. It has an insurgency in its western provinces that constitute an Islamic rival government, and potential anarchy. The feckless government and military demonstrate a chronic failure of leadership, and allowed a bad insurgency situation to get worse by failing to carry out a counterinsurgency program. Western provincial institutions are paralyzed to act. *Sharia* law replaced Pakistani law. It is estimated that about 12% of Pakistan is in control of the Taliban that seeks to overthrow the Pakistani government. By the middle of 2009 over 180 kidnappings for ransom had occurred just in Peshawar. [24] The mean age of suicide bombers is sixteen. Over 20 million of Pakistani youth under 17 are not in school. Except for Somalia, already an anarchic state, it's hard to imagine a more depressing future for a nuclear-armed country.

The war in Afghanistan is to prevent the Taliban from taking over the country again, and from denying a base for al-Qaeda. Afghanistan is not a country, but regions and provinces controlled by tribal elders and the Taliban. The war with Islamic extremists is in Pakistan where the goal is totally to defeat al-Qaeda and destroy its leadership, financing, infrastructure and motivation. National boundaries are irrelevant. Unlike Vietnam, there can never again be nearby country sanctuaries for the enemy. Pakistan has a semi-feudal system of government bent on preserving its class interests and cannot seem to confront modern challenges. The army and wealthy landowners essentially control the country. Add to this mix the rise of Islamic jihadists, a nuclear arsenal and you have fuel for a national conflagration and perpetual conflict with Taliban extremists.

Pakistan continues to support the Taliban because it needs that organization because of its profound distrust of India, an attitude reaching paranoia. It believes that when American forces leave Afghanistan that India may seek to control it, and the Taliban is Pakistan's assurance that it will not. According to leaked diplomatic correspondence, Pakistan's public face is in league with NATO to defeat the terrorists. Its private face supports the very organization it says it seeks to eradicate. [25]

American Rangers in Afghanistan

# CHAPTER ELEVEN
# IRAN AND REVOLUTION

Iran will be the biggest foreign policy challenge facing the West in the coming decades because it seeks a global Islamic caliphate. It has a paranoid governmental hatred toward America. It vociferously protests any foreign policy U.S. action in the Middle East, but remains silent about the treatment of Uighurs in China and Muslims in Chechnya because it needs China and Russia as trade partners. It supports the proxy militias of Hamas and Hezbollah because of its visceral hatred of Israel and Saudi Arabia.

If Iran is the principal foreign policy thorn in the side of American policy officials, imagine what similar Islamic theocracies could do if all of them were acquiring nuclear weaponry? That is the worst case scenario of militant Islam controlling the apparatus of a nation and imbued with hatred of the West.

Iran's clumsy bungling of an attempted plot in October 2011 to assassinate the Saudi Ambassador to the U.S., Adel Al-Jubeir, a close friend of the royal family, in Washington DC, exposed the Islamic nation as willing to carry out terrorist attacks not just on Americans but in America. Hiring the dual American/Iranian citizen, Mansour J. Arbabsiar, 56, a used car salesman from Corpus Christi, Texas as the instigator of this plot shows how desperate and brazen the Quds force of the Revolutionary Guards (see below) has become. Mansour attempted to hire an assassin from among a member of the Zetas drug cartels in Mexico who luckily turned out to be an FBI informant.

Iran is the powder keg of the Middle East, seeking to build atomic weapons, the destruction of Israel, the fall of the Saudi royal family, and to dominate the Middle East and all Persian Gulf states as a stepping stone to establishing a global Islamic caliphate. Its terrorism strategy is an age-old tradition of Islamic militancy.

Iran portrays itself as the living embodiment of Ancient Persia that sees itself as a victim of past invasions, most recently by Iraq in 1980, and the self-righteous, enigmatic image of the modern Islamic state. Blind to its own past, it does not see itself as a victim of the Arab invasion in 642 that ended the Persian Empire. [1]

The National Commission investigating the 9/11 2001 bombings raised the issue of whether or not there was an Iranian connection. The report indicated that there was "strong evidence" of Iranian support. According to a court ruling filed in May 2011, two defectors from the Iranian intelligence services (whose identities were sealed by the court) testified that officials had foreknowledge of the attacks. A federal lawsuit seeking damages was filed in New York because of Iran's "direct support for, and sponsorship of" the worst terrorist attack in American history. The lawsuit contends that both Iran and Hezbollah helped al-Qaeda plan the attacks with training and travel logistics.

At about the size of Alaska, Iran is a study in contrasts. The Imam mosque in Esfahan, one of the largest in the world, has posters that read "Death to

Israel." Soldiers stand guard among the worshippers during Friday prayers. Iran is a managed police state with no guaranteed personal freedoms, where religion and politics intertwine, and the glorification of martyrs and the activities of Hezbollah, Hamas and hatred of America and Israel control the government's propaganda machine.

This view differs considerably from the view of indigenous and expatriate Iranians who are sympathetic to western ideas, especially since the election of President Barack Obama and what most believed was a fraudulent Iranian presidential election in the summer of 2009. The protests about the legitimacy of the presidential election revealed deep chasms in Iranian society between the elderly clerical keepers of the revolution flame, and its more youthful citizens who want democratic freedoms. Arrested demonstrators went on trial charged with "waging war against God," an indictment that could only occur in a theocracy.

The death on June 20, 2009 of a young woman protestor, Neda Agha-Soltan, was an image seen by millions on YouTube that outraged the world. Neda was killed by Iran's special security forces, the Bassidji. (see below) Her brother was imprisoned. Her fiancé fled to his native Turkey as did her sister. The physician, an eyewitness, who tried to save her while she lie dying in the streets of Tehran, fled to England. Authorities tried to convince her mother she was a victim of protestors and would give her a martyr's pension. She refused. Neda's video image became a symbol of the Iranian protest movement, and the exposure of the barbarity of the imperious regime cloaking itself in religious garb for sacrosanct legitimacy.

According to my interviews, many Iranians, and several high-ranking clerics believe that Iran has lost moral integrity because of the cruelty of the regime toward politically peaceful demonstrations that resulted in the imprisonment and deaths of political opponents. The Iranian opposition is younger, more technologically sophisticated, and certainly more cynical about government propaganda that routinely blames all troubles on foreigners.

Iran is a sphere of influence in the Gulf and has oil. Iran seeks to carry the banner of Islam to gain wider recognition among the global Muslim community. But returning every reform movement into a return to Islam—including Islamic dress codes, curtailment of press and speech, puritanical gender relations, a reliance on trusted religious devotees instead of those with managerial expertise—does not provide for political, social or monetary improvement. Iran's ambition is the same for all devout Muslims, which is why its machinations abroad, posturing and persistent militancy, present such a huge test for western endurance.

Iran has a weak economy that features high unemployment, double-digit inflation, and an inefficient state sector. It is starved of foreign investment, has a heavy reliance on exported oil revenues, and a fragile grip on peoples' loyalties. It has the world's second largest reserves of oil and natural gas, but subsidizes food and energy. Entrepreneurship is sluggish. Educated and trained Iranians have fled in droves over the past two generations for employment in developed nations. Iran has political ambitions that exceed domestic capabilities. Its bureaucracy is the epitome of clerical and managerial clumsiness. According to official decrees and statements, Zionists and American devils cause Iran's failings. Iran defines itself in opposition to the Great Satan.

## Ayatollah Ruhollah Khomeini, Chief Militant

Imam Ruhullah Al-Musavi Al-Khomenini was born September 24, 1902 in Kumayn, about 75 miles south of Tehran. He was educated in the extended family by an elder brother after bandits murdered his father, the town's chief mullah. His mother and aunt died in the same year. When he was nineteen he entered religious studies in a nearby town of Arak. Within a few years he traveled to Qom where he became knowledgeable in ethics and jurisprudence. Soon he was giving twice weekly lectures in the 1930s attended by hundreds of followers. His devotional writings and lectures would form the basis for his ideas about the revolution and an Islamic state. His writings, speeches and life were a revival of fundamentalist Islamic thought and belief and led to the overthrow of the Shah, the establishment of the pure Islamic state, and the inspiration of Muslim radicals everywhere.

In 1963 Khomeini denounced the Shah's cosmetic White Revolution because it took away powers of the clergy and was therefore, according to him, a violation of the faith. By denouncing secular rule that he had tolerated for years, and reformatting religion as the principal concern of the people, he began the leadership of the Islamic Revolution sixteen years before it actually occurred. [2]

To quell the growing popular religious uprising, the Shah's police, the dreaded Savak, raided the theological centers at Qom March 22, 1963 arresting dozens of students. In the melee that ensued the police killed two students armed only with copies of the Koran. Khomeini's subsequent speeches were impassioned and a rallying cry for martyrdom and agitation. Khomeini was soon arrested, and then rioting became widespread and destructive. Khomeini had boldly opposed the Shah and exposed the tyrant for his injustices. He was released from prison in 1964 and was in exile in France. But he had stirred the raw passions of Iranians to view the Shah Palavi as the embodiment of how secular and kingly rule as a turning away from Islam, and how reliance on the West was a recipe for religious disaster. The seeds of clerical rule, the rise of Islamic militancy, and the birth of suicide bombers had their origin and spiritual leader in Khomeini. The Shah had tried to steer Iran toward the ancient cult of imperial rule. Khomeini turned Iran into a spiritual nation through religious dissent. By undermining the authority of kingship, Khomeini sought to undermine all secular authority and reinstall justice through the rule of Islam.

Khomeini, "the respectful one," then 78 years old, who had lived a regimented and ascetic life in exile in Turkey, then Iraq and finally France, returned triumphantly to Iran on February 1, 1979 and began a campaign of rabid anti-Americanism and Islamic governance. Almost immediately, black

194

chadors replaced hip-hugging jeans for women. Khomeini's militant mullahs orchestrated events to oust secular leaders, re-draft the constitution to make clerics in charge, and quickly executed all those deemed unworthy during the Shah's reign. He would change the term *mellat-e Iran*, the Iranian nation, to *ummat-e Islam*, the nation of Islam, thus transforming a national revolution into an Islamic one.

Thus began the exportation of Islamic militancy throughout the world, and the opening of military training camps for zealous Muslim men. The spread of Islamic militancy began with the attempted assassination of other Islamic monarchs in Bahrain in 1981, Kuwait in 1983, and Saudi Arabia during the *Haj* in 1986. But its militancy found a home among the 35% *Shia* population in Lebanon, especially after Israel's invasion in 1982 to destroy Arafat and the PLO. Hezbollah arrived, and its proxies kidnapped foreigners, bombed Marine barracks and embassies, and hijacked airlines.

Islam is the religion of militant individuals. (Ayatollah Khomeini) [3]

The writings of Khomeini are based on the same kind of dogmatic thinking that religious principles govern all life, even political life, and that nothing surpasses that faith. No other way of life, socially, politically or economically, must take precedence. While reading Khomeini I was reminded of how so unbendingly theological was Thomas Aquinas or Duns Scotus, medieval scholars who had complicated theological arguments, but who were unremittingly boring. Khomeini was like that: totally theological, with legendary references to Mohammad and unerringly predictable without substantive insights (if one is familiar with Islamic principles and history) and only motivational like a sermon. Khomeini was the reincarnation of an eighth century Islamic scholar because one cannot distinguish in his writings anything that could not have been written centuries earlier, except for a few references to the *Hadith* or some of his clerical forbearers.

Throughout his academic, religious and political life the thread that runs through all Khomeini's writings and speeches is that all state activity must be subordinate to Islamic goals. The essence of Christian behavior is non-violence, though not all follow its prescriptions. The heart of Islam, on the other hand, is militancy toward non-believers.

Khomeini's writings exhibit the leitmotif of all Islamic literature. He does not deviate from the theological norm. He is the norm. His argument is laden with the same militancy used today by radicals and even Iranian politicians to condemn the West as imperialistic and immoral.

His writings have no sense of authentic history, except his biased views—such as those about the "peaceful" Ottoman Empire and how the imperialists divided it—nor any other perspective than the Islamic theological. In fairness, he sees the plight of the downtrodden and oppressed in Iran and is sympathetic. However, individual opinion cannot intervene in matters of government or divine law. [4]

What I personally find disingenuous is the constant repetition in all his Islamic writings of the phrase about peace upon the Prophet and his successors.

The phrases include: "the Prophet (upon whom be peace) . . . "Our Imams (upon whom be peace)" . . . "The time of the Twelfth Imam (upon whom be peace) . . ." "The Commander of the Faithful (upon whom be peace) relates that the Most Noble Messenger (upon whom be blessings and peace) . . . " etc. The fact that peace is insisted on so often is favorable to the founders and elders. Yet the essence of Islam is militancy and this seems highly inconsistent with principles of blessing and peace on those who supported *jihads* against non-Muslims.

For the Jews there is only condemnation. Khomeini writes: "We see today that the Jews (may God curse them) . . ." that they "wish to establish Jewish domination throughout the world." [5] He is imperious enough to admit that Islam should dominate all religion and politics. This concept of global domination is not modified by the history of communism, Nazism, Fascism or any other ideology. Khomeini relies on rumor, innuendo and implication to make outlandish statements unsubstantiated by any facts, historical comparisons or evidence.

Here is an historical example of the Prophet's non-peaceful attitude towards Jews in his own lifetime. The Bani Qurayza was a Jewish tribe living in Medina at the time of Mohammad. During the Battle of the Ditch in the fifth year of Islam they collaborated with the force from Mecca that opposed Mohammad. The Most Noble Messenger killed all the Jewish men of that tribe, yet, unbelievably, still received peace and blessings for such activities from clerics. The Most Noble Messenger and his followers were not at all peaceful. Indeed, Muslim believers are urged to follow his example that included murder rationalized as the defense of Islam.

And who is it exactly who was damaging Islam while Khomeini was alive? Primarily, it was other religious centers: "The evil propaganda run by the churches, the Zionists, and the Bahai." [6] The fact that other religions sought to disseminate their beliefs is an affront to Islam, according to Khomeini. "They are destroying Islam," he writes. Is it not reasonable then to see how, after the 1979 Revolution, that non-Muslim religions were purged? This is another hypocritical example of how a tolerant religion, having established a supposedly just government, seeks to eliminate religious opposition.

For example, Dr. Sunghar Samali, a physician practicing in Paterson, New Jersey, was only five years old in 1985 but remembers the day when her father's factory was set afire, blinding him in one eye. She recalls how the family tried to escape in a smuggler's jeep and the army shot out the tires and the windshield and the family spent years in prison before finally escaping to Pakistan. She and her family were Bahai. Its members since 1979 have had a well-documented set of human rights abuses chronicled by Amnesty International, among other organizations. But after the establishment of the Islamic Republic Khomeini had the audacity to claim that his government would be impartial, as when he declared on the first day of his government, April 1, 1979: "There will be no difference between men and women, or between the religious minorities and the Muslims." [7] This was a promise never kept as Iran banned Bahais in 1983, branding the faith an apostasy.

In modern societies political legitimacy comes from popular will, however imperfect, and not from divine authority, however religious individuals may be. Can God ever be wrong? And who is to say so? Can the Pope ever err if he says he can't in matters of faith? Can Karl Marx ever be wrong for a devoted communist? The days have passed when absolute legitimacy was in the hands of divinely appointed clerics who can twitter God, or kings who thought they inherited divine wisdom, except in places like Iran where simmering resentment has surfaced against religious ideology. Infallibility has been replaced with popular choice. The tiara and the turban, along with their geriatric wearers, remain, but they have less relevance than at any time in history.

Khomeini died June 4, 1989 aged 87. On his burial day, his body, clad in a white shroud was carried on a litter in a glass-enclosed, air-conditioned capsule, in a hundred degree heat through crowds in the millions who jostled to touch him. His litter suddenly rocked and the half-naked body fell to the ground as escorts tried to prevent the crowd from touching him further. The irony was that another leader had ignominiously fallen because of a frenzied crowd. A helicopter swooped down and lifted him away.

There are parallels in Europe's history that illustrate that Islam is not alone is sponsoring the use of violence in defense of its religious imperatives. The Crusades, inspired by Pope Urban II at the Council of Clermont in 1095, was Europe's merger of militarism and religion. Urban imperiously declared to the assembled knights, priests and princes: "I, or rather the Lord, beseech you as Christ's heralds . . . To destroy that vile race (Muslims) . . . All who die by the way, whether by land or by sea, or in battle against the pagans, shall have immediate remission of sins. This I grant through the power of God with which I am invested." [8] This was a Christian military vengeance with a promise from the Pope, God's anointed Christian representative on earth, of swift passage to the hereafter.

The most ferocious examples of violence emerge when, like the rabid Jewish Zealots that Titus and his Roman legions defeated in 70 CE, religious fanatics converge with nationalistic zealots. Warriors and martyrs who seek heavenly rewards and the establishment of an amorphous caliphate are the latest example of a blend of national and religious movements that also espouse violence.

Individuals may choose or not to practice religion without governmental interference, except in those states that mandate a religious imperative, like Saudi Arabia or the Vatican. Even the Texas School Board always seeks to legislate religion in the schools. The assertion of any prevailing orthodoxy is as rigid as Catholic dogmatism, or the *ulema*, the Muslim clerical authority, prescribes. Islam attempts to make the religion of individuals the religion of the state wherever it can, and Saudi Arabia, the birthplace of Islam, and Iran are the most conspicuous examples. Earthly rule and heavenly guidance are thought in theocracies to be synonymous. [9]

## Bassidji: The Quds Force

Shortly after the establishment of the regime under Ayatollah Khomeini, the new government formed a counter-revolutionary, paramilitary force known as the *bassidji* ("mobilization"). This was a so-called "people's army" distinct from the regular army. According to official figures, there are about 10 million members, youth like the Boy Scouts but with police powers. The creation of new militia with state authority, whether under the control of the head of state, like Hitler's Waffen SS storm troopers, Stalin's cadres, Mao's Red Guards, or Iran's Hezbollah or Hamas, function as an extra-legal military arm to impose ideology or crush opponents. The *Bassidji* encompasses both these activities of advancing what it considers puritanical virtue, and suppressing vice—like listening to music—and ridding the state of dissidents who oppose state (read Islamic) activities. Its adherents have assimilated the martyrdom ideology of Islam and married it with the fervor of nationalism to embrace the cult of the clergy and devotion to the Ayatollah. Members of the *Bassidji* are like sanctioned members of a state gang who would always have an enemy—the infidel. [10]

The continuation of the Iranian revolution was in doubt when Iraq under Saddam Hussein sensing Iran's weakness attacked Iran in 1980 in a war that lasted eight years with hundreds of thousands killed on both sides. Democratic movements in Iran ceased in the face of the invasion threat. The *Bassidji* took the lead in repulsing the Iraqi army and against political opposition inside Iran, what became known as counter-revolutionary tendencies. The organization recruited boys as young as fourteen to serve as soldiers, and martyrs for the cause of Khomeini.

Schools were the logical choice for the recruitment of these boy soldiers. *Bassidji* leaders created a hierarchy independent of the school establishment that reported directly to the Ministry of National Education. Joining meant they received academic recognition many did not deserve. Boys between the ages of 12–17 were accorded an adult status in the militia community their maturity level did not readily accommodate. During the Iraq/Iran war, in order to earn their so-called manhood and stripes in the organization, they engaged in such manly activities as learning to handle mines.

The Iraq/Iran war created new graveyards for young men. But the real cemetery is Islamic ideology devoid of compassion, mercy and kindness. It promotes and sanctifies a religious death cult among its youth by sermons from its mullahs. While these youth were consumed with Shiite apocalyptic visions and a morbid religiosity, many male youths in the West were absorbed with egocentric addictions. It's unclear who was more poorly served, as everyone was seeking utopia either in the present or in a transcendent afterlife.

Despite the press reports of Iranian posturing against Israel and the U.S., there remains a tension in Iran between theocratic rule and its democratic tendencies. Reformers under Ayatollah Khatami in the late 1990s were unable to muster enough support for their cause and this led to Ahmadinejad's conservative victory. There is an odd sort of analogy in all this posturing between the U.S. and Iran.

I recall discussing such issues with my exiled Iranian students in the early 1980s. They saw their country then descending to a clerical rule from a dictatorial Shah that they thought would weaken its one proud stature in the world and distance itself from the Western world. Later, I interviewed several professional and managerial Iranians in Alberta in 2007. They were relieved when I told them that cooler heads would prevail and that America would not bomb Iran with nuclear weapons. I found that by and large Iranians love America, and that like many Americans, Iranians do not always agree with their government policies.

One American policy objective would be to cooperate with Iran on security measures in Iraq and Afghanistan. Iran has influence among Shiites is southern Iraq but not necessarily malevolent intentions in Iraq as a whole. Iran could help with the clerical Shiite leadership in Iraq in preventing a civil war between Iraqi Shiites and Sunni. On the other hand, opening a dialogue with Iran is not on anyone's policy agenda because, like North Korea, it has been so ambivalent, equivocating and deceitful in past discussions. The one issue that unites the West against it is its attempt to acquire nuclear weapons.

## Iran and Nuclear Weapons

The International Atomic Energy Agency (IAEA) released a report in November 2011 indicating that from the data it had collected Iran was working to develop an atomic bomb. [11] Iran has 15 known nuclear facilities and other locations like hospitals where nuclear materials are also stored. It has not suspended its nuclear enrichment activities of U-235, but continued to work to improve the centrifuges that enrich uranium to weapon grade. It was supposed to suspend these activities and the production of heavy water. The IAEA is unsure whether or not Iran has hidden nuclear facilities in underground bunkers for possible military uses.

Muslim militancy, one of the more deplorable religious traits, is now extended into the potential acquisition of the most destructive human killing devices. The developed world seeks to prevent this, and expressly for America and Israel, at the cost of military intrusion.

Espionage plays a role in slowing down the advance of a nuclear weapon. A huge explosion at Bid Kaneh, a major missile-testing site just outside of Tehran, was a major setback for Iran's long-range, advanced, solid fuel missile program. Previous setbacks have included multiple assassinations of key Iranian nuclear scientists on the streets of Tehran, and a sophisticated Internet worm known as Stuxnet that corrupted the main nuclear facilities running high-speed centrifuges for uranium enrichment. By early 2012 five top nuclear scientists had been assassinated by unknown assailants.

Earlier, on Friday morning, September 25, 2009 President Obama stood with the Prime Minister of Britain and President of France to announce that Iran had secretly built a new nuclear uranium enrichment plant within a military installation for the Revolutionary Guards and inside a mountain near Qom about 100 miles southwest of Tehran. American and western intelligence officials had known of the existence of the site for years, but announcing its presence on the eve of official talks between Iranian and U.S. officials altered the diplomatic and negotiation initiative, demanding new inspections and threatening tougher sanctions for non-compliance with international rules for Nuclear Non-Proliferation. This was the equivalent of President Kennedy announcing the existence of Soviet missiles in Cuba in 1962. Iran was clearly dancing around its nuclear development program. It lied to the International Atomic Energy Agency and to the world.

An Iranian dissident group had previously uncovered the existence of the atomic facility at Natanz, about a hundred miles southeast of Qom. But the one at Qom had never been acknowledged, indicating that cheating was a priority. Iran kept explaining that its nuclear development was for peaceful purposes. A small nuclear weapon only requires about 55 pounds of highly enriched uranium, whereas large quantities of low enriched uranium are needed to fuel power plants making electricity.

On November 30, 2009, in an act of outrageous defiance of international resolutions, Iran announced that it was planning to build ten new uranium enrichment plants to expand its nuclear program. Uranium needs to be enriched to 90% in order for it to be used for atomic weaponry. It was an inconceivable boast because Iran cannot afford it, nor secure the necessary resources or equipment. The tactic exposes the bluster and boldness of its nuclear ambitions more than its search for international cooperation. President Ahmadineijad flatly declared that Iran would enrich its own uranium to a higher level, thereby scrapping its agreement with the IAEA just days earlier. He then defiantly ruled out further talks. By 2112 the developed nations imposed stringent economic sanctions on Iran that deflated the Iranian currency, the rial, by half and made it much harder for Iran to conduct financial interests through western banks.

Iranian officials have contradicted each other, reneged on promises to international atomic energy officials and generally gamed the international community that questioned its good faith proposals. Bad faith and deceit are, and always have been, standard Islamic negotiating tactics. Iran has blustered its way into a nuclear program, using the issue as a political weapon more than a physics breakthrough, hoping to frighten its enemies and gain respect in the Muslim world. The international community is united against its atomic ambitions. Economic sanctions have a deep effect on the economy, teetering on a financial meltdown at a time when its young population is restive and resentful.

Iran has in the past obtained many electronic components used in the development of nuclear or biological weapons through intermediaries, including Iranians living in the U.S. The typical ploy has been to order equipment through legitimate U.S. companies, ship it to Dubai or Malaysia where it is transshipped to Iran. Israel will not let Iran develop nuclear weapons for potential use against its land or people.

In 2007 Iran issued a new bank note. On one side was a photo of the Supreme Leader and founder, Ayatollah Khomeini. On the other side of the 50,000 Rial note (about $5) was the nuclear symbol of electrons orbiting a nucleus.

The U.S. rejected a plan by Israel to bomb Iran's atomic energy site at Natanz in north central Iran in 2007.[12] Israel had sought America's bunkerbusing bombs that would penetrate deeper into the earth and go through hardened cement but was reputedly rebuffed in the request. Israel does not have the bomber capacity to conduct over time a long-range and long-term campaign, nor does it have adequate refueling tankers to get its planes there and back.

Iran's development of a nuclear weapon could happen eventually as its clerics seek to have a measure of global respect, perhaps the kind it enjoyed in Persia's long 2,500 year-old dynastic empire when Cyrus, Darius, Xerxes ruled most of central Asia. Persians always gave the Romans and Ottoman Turks fits when they rebelled. Reclaiming an image and prestige is one thing; developing a nuclear bomb to impress adversaries and the West is another. Fighting for an ideal in God's name gives rulers and adherents awesome justification for waging a campaign of terror. Iran's proxy armies of Hamas and Hezbollah are demonstrable examples of interference in other countries' domestic affairs, and reveal the real agenda of the dominance Iran seeks in the region and perhaps the world.[13]

Iran seeks a nuclear weapon based on its encounter with Iraq in the war from 1980–1988 when it was the recipient of poison gas from Saddam Hussein who, it is believed, would have used an atomic weapon against Iran had he had one. Of secondary importance is Iran's need to divert citizen attention from domestic problems and to bolster its international stature. Iran has played a strategically shrewd diplomatic game with the U.S. and the world, sometimes engaging in talks with scientists while buying time to slowly build atomic capabilities.

The proliferation of nuclear weapons is the greatest threat faced by the global community. Iran is a signatory to the Non-Proliferation Treaty but is nonetheless pursuing the bomb in open contempt. If Iran turns into a nuclear power, the Non-Proliferation Treaty will be meaningless. President Obama and Russian President Dmitri Medvedev signed a landmark nuclear arms agreement in Prague on April 8, 2010 that would reduce nuclear stockpiles. The U.S. at the time ruled out nuclear response to attacks from countries involving chemical, biological or conventional weapons, but not for countries that do not comply with the Nuclear Non-Proliferation Treaty. This includes Iran.

Iran wants to join the nuclear club of countries surrounding it—Russia, Pakistan, India and Israel. Its claim that it is building its nuclear capability because it needs a civilian energy program is misleading because it has only partially capitalized on its existing petroleum industry. It has limited uranium resources, no functioning nuclear reactors, but abundant petroleum resources. Even if Iran were to produce an atomic weapon it would only serve as a deterrent to others rather than as an offensive weapon toward, say Israel, despite protestations about eliminating Israel. Any nuclear offensive would invite annihilation. A sense of paranoia about the outside world, that infidels exist everywhere and need to be confronted, and that its own population does not believe anymore in the revolutionary mood, all drive the momentum to acquire a nuclear program. [14]

Iran mastered the process of nuclear enrichment, of making uranium purer for a bomb. Too many possible scenarios warrant against standing idly by. If Iran sends a missile to Israel's nuclear facility, the U.S. would have to intervene. If Israel retaliates, Hezbollah would retaliate along Israel's northern border. Iran nuclear facilities are spread over 300 sites including in large urban area like Tehran and Isfahan. The other danger is that other Arab states would not let Iran have a nuclear capability without also wanting one, spiraling the nuclear games race. [15]

Iran has systematically skirted export laws in order to obtain sophisticated technology. An Iranian businessman can contact a friendly Islamic country, for example Malaysia, and locate an importer who can fake an invoice for a nonexistent front company. So an American company ships specialized parts, like quality electronics or circuit boards, to a fake company in Malaysia, which then forwards them on to Iran. All this is conducted on the Internet or via Email. Even more alarming is a report by the Institute for Science and International Security that details the illicit military procurement of Iran for nuclear technology.[16] By February 2011 Iran told atomic inspectors that it was unloading nuclear fuel from its plant in Bushehr, an unusual but not unprecedented move. It had previously admitted that a viral computer worm known as Stuxnet had infected the nuclear plant. [17]

Moderate Islamic states, mostly autocratic, and especially Saudi Arabia, fear Iran, not because it is Islamic but because its influence would tend to obfuscate and overrule their initiatives in the region. Washington will never be able to control Iranian influence in the Middle East. [18]

Iran is a quite different country ideologically than it was after the revolution in 1979 and after the conclusion war with Iraq in 1988. It has rejected the idea of martyrdom and embraced a more pragmatic approach to its culture. The people, though not necessarily the government or clerics, no longer demonize the West and hope secretly for a rapprochement with the U.S. A generation has matured that has no personal history with the revolution or what spawned it, and are trying to move past the old clichés and clerical dominance.

The ruins of Persepolis (city of the Parsa, or Persians in Greek), set in an immense landscape remote from any village, was the ancient city founded by Cyrus the Great about 515 BCE. Its rulers included Darius the Great and his son Xerxes. It remained the capitol of the Persian Empire for over two hundred years. Alexander the Great destroyed the city in 313 BCE and it was never reconstructed. Iranians hope that similar fate does not happen to the fervor of revolution that consumes the present government. But the fate of empires, including America's, is always thus: that time, aggressive tendencies in human nature, and the rise of new world powers brings older governments to ruin. From the few remaining pillars of Persepolis, to the walls of the Islamic seminaries in Qom, the deities, whether the Zoroastrian Ahura Mazda or Allah, must snicker at the ignoble deeds of mankind.

# CHAPTER TWELVE
# GLOBAL ISLAMIC CONFLICTS

Islam is global and its fringe militancy movement, whether cultivated by states or state-sponsored organizations, has taken radical root in the hearts and minds of a growing number of youth. The meteoric rise in Islamic militancy has reverberated in Africa and threatens stability in countries like Pakistan, Kenya, Tanzania and Nigeria, Sudan, Yemen, and Somalia. The Great Rift Valley is literally forcing the horn of northern east Africa away from the continent. Somalia, a Libertarian paradise (as it has no functioning government), is sliding into Islamic fundamentalism. The militant Islamic group *Shabab* has been attempting to overthrow the government in Somalia, a country used as a base for pirates to seize ships at sea.

Today, Somalia continues to drift into anarchy and a potential Islamic takeover. Sudan murdered its western citizens in the Darfur region. Nigeria fights off extremists who attack police stations and western influences. In January 2012 the Islamic militant extremist group known as *Boko Haram*— roughly translated as western education is bad—killed nearly 150 in the northern metropolis of Kano, a city with nearly nine million. The Islamic groups attacked five police stations, two immigration offices and the headquarters of the Nigerian secret security force.

The extremist Muslim group *Shabab* from Somalia slips into Kenya and recruits young men with promises of paradise and some cash. Kenya has been attacked almost daily by heavily-armed *Shabab* fighters coming from Somalia in raids across the porous border aimed at intimidating children and closing schools. In October 2011 Kenya retaliated with cross-border raids of its own attacking elements of *Shabab* fighters. Kenyan troops crossed into Somalia in retaliation.

Uncertainty in Islamic countries that have experienced uprisings and revolutions—Tunisia, Libya, Egypt and Syria—cast a long shadow over whether militant groups can gain toeholds in former dictatorial states. The emergence of the so-called Arab Spring that compelled dictators to flee—as did Ben Ali in Tunisia—or killed—as was Muammar Qaddafi—strengthened democratic forces but also released underlying social and rival tribal tensions. The exact nature of these transformations will differ from country to country as each country will have to grapple with corruption, dysfunctional bureaucracies, nepotism, elements of extremism and at least a 30% unemployment rate among youth. Nevertheless, the active participation of citizens in a global social network system that led to widespread demonstrations illustrates the power of communication and is a source of people power in the Arab and Islamic world, the thirst for some form of democracy and the dread of tyranny.

The focus on Africa as a continent of Islamic militancy began in earnest on August 7, 1998, when hundreds were killed in simultaneous truck bombings outside the U.S. embassies in Dar es Salaam, Tanzania and Nairobi, Kenya. The perpetrators were linked to local members of Egyptian *Islamic Jihad*. Immediate focus was on Osama bin Laden whom the FBI quickly put on the list of its most wanted. His death deprived the movement of its strategic leader but not its lethal mission. Yemen was one of the countries on the Saudi peninsula that was often linked to African extremism. Yemen received renewed counter-terrorism attention after Umar Abdulmuttallab, the Christmas 2009 shoe bomber, was known to have received training there.

By 2011 Islamic insurgents allied with al-Qaeda forces from the Islamic Maghreb began systematically attacking Nigerian police with improvised explosive devices in the northern provinces in and around the town of Maiduguri near the border with Chad. Nigeria has not been a hotbed of global terrorism, but the Islamic militants are attacking a largely Muslim part of the country in a move that reveals how they are broadening terrorist attacks throughout all parts of Africa.

Let's explore briefly in this final chapter how the Islamic militancy movement has expanded into countries once considered relatively peaceful from internal violence.

## Tunisia

Who would have thought that a Tunisian street vendor, Mohamed Bouazizi, who immolated himself in December 2010 in his hometown of Sidi Bouzid because of public, face-slapping humiliation from a policeman for not having a sellers license would have started the Arab Spring of toppling dictators in Tunisia and Egypt and bred street protests throughout the Arab world? The rosy glow of faint glimpses of democracy anywhere in the Arab world is a welcome sign of the strength of people rule and the erosion of Arab totalitarianism.

Within months Tunisia had transformed itself from a dictatorship by President Zine El Abidine Ben Ali into a functional democracy. It voted in a moderate Islamist party known as Ennahda in national elections in October 2011. This was Tunisia's first free and fair election that made a peaceful transition from autocratic rule. The Ennahada party says it poses no threat to the West or western interests. It seeks a return to traditional Islamic values and promised to protect women's rights.

But remains to be seen at this writing whether or not Ennahda will adhere to Tunisia's liberal tradition, similar to that of Turkey, or revert to a more militant code. Some claim that there is nothing to fear from *Sharia* law. I believe that establishing it is a misguided and confused respect for religious values with the presumed benefits of a legal code.

*Sharia* (meaning "path") law is a religious law, derived from the Koran and the *Hadith* (teachings of Mohammad and religious leaders) and governs behaviors in most Islamic states. Its laws governing domestic issues like marriage and divorce are not as controversial as are its criminal codes that allows for legalized honor killings, requires the cutting off of limbs for theft, flogging, or blood money for murder, or prohibitions against drinking of alcohol.

No religious code, not canon law or *sharia* law, can be a substitute for, or be integrated into, most secular legal systems. For a country to rid itself of a dictator and then impose a harsh religious code as a substitute for social order may not be the best way to transition to a democratic government. The 1979 Iranian revolution deposed a dictator, Shah Pahlavi, who thought of himself as an ancient Persian emperor. But the revolution quickly turned into a clerical dictatorship with the persecution of all Iranian minorities who had lived side by side with Muslims for centuries.

This is not about respect for ethnic or religious values—as illegal displays of the 10 Commandments, debates about abortion, or prayer in school in the U.S. testifies—but an acknowledgement that secular law rules in all non-Islamic nations. The American Constitution's 1st Amendment solidifies the prohibition against the establishment of any religion, including religious laws.

## Yemen

The protests that ignited the Arab and Islamic world in 2011 brought about the delayed resignation of President Ali Abdullah Saleh of Yemen. Whatever government emerges will have to deal with that failed economic state, and not just its al-Qaeda base and separatist movements. The scattered remnants of al-Qaeda and other insurgents will be of secondary concern. It is likely that another strongman will assume the head of state, promise reform and institute soon thereafter a heavy-handed policy of force to control unstable elements in the population, and an Arab country about to run out of oil to salve its economy and water to slate its thirst. Saleh had been dictatorial but cooperative with the U.S. on terrorism. His departure could lead to anarchy, possible division of Yemen into separate states as it once was, bringing greater instability to the region and embolden hardcore al-Qaeda operatives. About 70% of Yemenis are rural and deeply religious, and most are supportive of al-Qaeda.

Osama bin Laden's father was born in Yemen. The attack on the *USS Cole* occurred in the port of Aden harbor in October 2000. Osama's contacts were in a house in Sana, Yemen that was the operational center for the 9/11 attacks. Telephone intercepts monitored by the NSA had tracked messages between handlers in that house and terrorists for years, but failed to alert other intelligence agencies in 2001. Tapping one phone line in Yemen yielded 260,000 phone numbers around the world revealing the extensiveness of the network. Armed terrorists attacked the U.S. Embassy in Sana on September 17, 2008 and several guards were killed. Yemen is the training site of the Christmas Day, 2009 bombing plot on Northwest flight 253. Released Guantanamo detainees like the Saudi national Ibrahim Suleiman al-Rubaysh, 30, have resurfaced in Yemen as so-called theological guides, but are a part of the terrorist infrastructure. Many Yemenis extremists who fought in Iraq have returned to Yemen eager to fight new battles.

A drone strike in May 2011 attempted to kill Anwar al-Awlaki, an American citizen born in New Mexico, a cleric who once resided in Fairfax County, Virginia and counseled other alleged terrorists. He fled to Yemen where he hid out until he was killed in a CIA drone attack by a Hellfire missile in September 2011. He had recruited English-speaking Islamic militants to carry out attacks overseas and broadcast radical sermons over the Web.

Indeed, Yemen has become a safe haven for a larger aggregate of al-Qaeda operatives. Ali al-Shihri, a Saudi released from Guantanamo, became deputy head of the Yemeni branch of al-Qaeda. Abdullah al-Qarawi, 35, another Saudi who escaped, has been operating from Iran since 2005 with about a hundred other operatives leads al-Qaeda operations in the Persian Gulf. Located on the southern part of the Arabian Peninsula, Yemen is the second most dangerous country in the world after Pakistan, and home to al-Qaeda in the Arabian Peninsula, a recent merger of the Saudi and Yemeni branches. Its population doubles every two decades because its rate is 3.5%, too high to sustain with meager natural resources.

Yemen is twice the size of Wyoming with a population of about twenty-four million. Water is limited. Unemployment is between 35-40%. Life expectancy is 63 years. Illiteracy is more than 70%. Half of the population exists below the poverty line. It is the poorest Arab country and relies exclusively on petroleum for 85% of national revenue. Oil will be exhausted soon and there are no plans for any financial substitution for lost revenue. Its weak government, fragmentation into clans and tribal structures, lawless regions, and intermittent rebellions make it ripe for a new Taliban-like environment for flourishing terror groups. According to reports in 2012, Iran was seeking to expand its sponsorship of supporting terrorist groups in the region by supplying arms to the rebels in Yemen. (See Eric Schmitt, 2012).

By 2011 Yemen was experiencing a national revolt against President Saleh, a reignited separatist revolt in the south, a Shiite revolt in the north among the Houthi clan, and intensified al-Qaeda activity everywhere. Its government is mostly based on *sharia* law but with approved customary local tribal law. Its most persistent problem in the future will be coping with its distressed economy whichever government is in power.

The south of Yemen, centered in the port city of Aden, became a Marxist state in 1979 under the influence of the Soviet Union but merged with its northern neighbor in 1990. The socialist experiment put an end to child marriage, made women have equal rights and championed literacy. But overt discrimination by the north against the south, the presence of a better educated population in the south, and a growing southern insurgency movement, point to continued violent conflict.

An assassination attack on the Saudi royal family originated from Yemen and occurred in late August 2009. The target in Jiddah was Mohammed bin Nayef, Saudi's Assistant Interior Minister and a Saudi prince. The prince was slightly wounded but the bomber died. The Saudi crackdown on al-Qaeda extremists caused determined adherents to relocate in Yemen, an unstable country where authorities have little control outside the capitol.

Yemen's conflict with rebels in its north, known as Houthis after their slain leader Hussain al-Houthi, enhanced Saudi that fears of the intrusion of this Shiite menace (possibly supported by Iran) and because it was invading Saudi territory. Al-Qaeda operatives used the rebel advance as a route to infiltrate operatives in Saudi Arabia. The rebels enjoyed tactical superiority, proven discipline, experience in the terrain and the use of land mines, though it lacked air support and armored vehicles.

With a 700,000-man army, Yemen has been unable to suppress this northern rebellion militarily despite repeated attempts. Saudi engaged 200,000 troops in its counterattack. However, Saudi credibility was at stake and feared the long arm of Iranian influence already present in Gaza, Lebanon and southern Iraq. The fact that Yemen is a major haven for al-Qaeda is worrisome to all who seek to reduce the influence of organized terrorism.

American-born Sharif Mobley, from an immigrant Muslim family of Somalia, traveled to Yemen ostensibly to study Arabic but became radicalized and was arrested for joining al-Qaeda. Mobley was a maintenance worker at five nuclear power plants along the east coast of the U.S. Although he had a low security clearance he was knowledgeable about perimeter security, like the number of guards, the kind of weapons used and procedures at entry gates, and about the cooling system of nuclear power plants. Pumps and water intake pipes are unprotected outside the plants. Mobley undoubtedly passed this information to al-Qaeda in Yemen.

## Militant Activity in Africa

The Islamic advance into Africa began when Arabs conquered Egypt in 639 CE. Militants quickly overran North Africa, fixing its base in Tunisia, and pushed into Visigoth Spain in 711 where they remained around Grenada until 1492. *Jihadi* groups coming from Mauritania overran most of West Africa in the 19th century, conquering local populations, converting them to Islam and ruling by *sharia* law. The process of the *Islamization* of Africa—from Egypt to Morocco, and south from Egypt into Sudan and along the east coast—was accomplished through trade, some peaceful Muslim colonization, the offering of theological alternatives to Christianity, but primarily by conquest. Islam's method of persuasion is the sword, not preaching. Today, half of Africa is Muslim. But although Europe has renounced its colonial ways, Islamic militarism has not. Yet African scholars regularly denounce the evils of colonial imperialism as if it were still the origin of all their problems.

The population demographics of most of the Muslim world illustrate how population outstrips the ability of countries to provide even reasonable social services to its people. Algeria serves as one example. In 1954 it had a population of 8.5 million. Within a quarter of a century, by 1980, it had 26.6 million, a tripling of its citizens. Although many travelled to France to work, the young outnumbered everyone, and the women, whose life expectancy rose because of improved health care, had an average of eight children. [3] By 2009, births ratios had declined and its population stabilized somewhat at thirty-four million. But by then the explosive population had eviscerated the economy in spite of a strong oil-base.

Algeria gained independence from France in 1962. Almost immediately the Islamic Salvation Front (FIS), whose membership had accelerated, challenged the government. The military intervened in 1991 and postponed elections when it appeared Muslim extremists would win an electoral victory. Between 1992-98, over a hundred thousand died in massacres of whole villages. Eventually, the military gained strength and the FIS disbanded in 2000. Yet by 2006 another *Salafist* group joined with al-Qaeda formed to conduct terrorist activities against the Algerian government and western interests.

In June 2010 federal officers arrested two New Jersey men, Mohamed Mahmood Alessa, 20, and Carlos Eduardo Almonte, 24, both U.S. citizens, bound for Somalia to fight with *Shabab* jihadists who claim to be ideologically associated with al-Qaeda. Authorities were concerned that had they fought in Somalia and survived they could have returned to the U.S. to conduct a terrorism scheme. They were both tape-recorded by an undercover officer planning to conduct *jihad* against western targets. Experts estimate that as many as 20 Americans have been recruited to fight in Somalia.

Mohamed Osman Mohamud, 19, a naturalized US citizen from Somalia, a graduate of Westview High School in Beaverton Oregon and a sophomore engineering student at Oregon State University, planned to explode a van filled with explosives in downtown Portland, Oregon at the height of a Christmas tree-lighting ceremony that approximately 10,000 attended. He had been planning this crime for months and said that he was committed to *jihad* since he was five years old. An alert Muslim friend brought his radicalized behavior to the attention of the FBI that quickly placed him under surveillance. FBI operatives engaged him as though they were sympathizers from Pakistan to help him execute the attack. He was arrested as he tried to use a cell phone to detonate what he thought was a bomb, but was a dud concocted by the FBI. [4]

Immediately after 9/11 counter-terrorism experts focused on hunting al-Qaeda suspects in Muslim countries beside Afghanistan. Potential terrorists, many thought, would be in North Africa where Osama, while living in Sudan in the 1990s, had financed revolts and demonstrations against African governments. Remote islands and jungles of The Philippines were also high on the priority list. Beginning in 2002 the U.S. Department of State began working with the governments of Mali, Chad, Nigeria and Mauritania to combat the proclaimed global war on terror. The military effort in Mali included teacher education, job and business training for young men, and radio programs.[5]

Mauritania has been especially vulnerable to the attacks of al-Qaeda in the Maghreb. Mauritania is an Islamic republic that underwent a military coup against the democratically elected president in 2008. Afterwards, the U.S. suspended aid. It is 100% Muslim but has a literacy rate of only about 50%.

One example of an African Muslim militant, a criminal who found his violent propensity suitable in radicalized Islam, is Sidi Ould Sidna, a young man from Mauritania whose unusual career makes the case for counter-terrorism more difficult and the education and recruitment of Muslim radicals unpredictable. He enjoyed stealing cars, smoking hashish, drinking wine, dancing and hanging out with older boys. In his late teens he got religion by joining a *mahadra*, an Islamic seminary the same as a *madrassa*, and was inspired by listening to *jihad* recordings of American tanks blown up and American troops killed. He began patrolling the neighborhood enforcing Islamic rules. In the spring of 2006, he entered a *jihad* training camp in northern Mali. Sidi, then 21, returned to Mauritania and with three accomplices killed four French tourists with his Kalashnikov on December 14, 2007. He was captured, escaped, and then re-captured. [6]

Muslim terrorists, some of whom previously have been just criminals, who have used conveniently used Islam as their excuse for killing, have found their niche in life. They hang suspended between being human and posing as inhuman objects posed for death, like figures in a Marc Chagall or Pablo Picasso painting.

In north central Africa, in the nation of Mali—the world's fifth poorest country but a functioning democracy—American troops trained with Mali troops to guard the borders against infiltration of Islamic militants from nearby countries. Mali, south of Algeria, is a former French colony about twice the size of Texas that includes the legendary city of Timbuktu on the Niger River. The combined troops train to combat the African Islamic fighters who have used their desert bases as staging areas for attacks, kidnappings and extortion.

In late July 2009 over several days, over 300 were killed as Islamic militants stormed police stations in northern Nigeria near the borders of Niger and Chad, attacking with fuel-laden motorcycles, bows and poison-tipped arrows. Interreligious clashes often flare in Nigeria where Muslims inhabit the northern parts of the country and Christians in the south. But this violence emanates from an obscure group known as *Boko Haram* opposed to the police whom members believe enforce western education. They are unhappy over any deviation from strict Islamic principles. Nigerian security forces raided the group's compound, where the army found the usual mixture of fighters, bombs and weapons in Maiduguri and killed its leader, Mohammad Yusuf and dozens of his followers.

In March 2010 organized Muslim youth attacked Dogo Na Hawa, a Christian village a few miles east of Jos in central Nigeria, killing hundreds in the predawn darkness. There had been similar killings of Muslim villagers by Christians in the preceding months. Christians have lived here for centuries but there has been an Islamic attempt to overthrow it almost as long.

Sub-Saharan Africa will remain unstable politically for decades because of its faulty infrastructures, government corruption, population pressures, lack of economic productivity, a high incidence of disease including HIV/AIDS, and civil conflicts. As a result of these tensions, weak countries—and none are very strong politically or economically—will experience pronounced ethnic and religious clashes for limited resources and be subject to terrorist and criminal incidents.

The al-Qaeda talent scout in Dar es Salaam thought he had found the perfect candidate, though he was hardly literate and had no known skills. But he was African, a Tanzanian from Zanzibar with knowledge of local languages like Swahili. Khalfan Khamis Mohamed, 20, attended a local mosque regularly and was agitated about the global plight of Muslims. The recruit willingly used his own money to travel to Afghanistan for training.

When he returned to Tanzania he rented a house where he and his associates manufactured bombs. Immediately after the bombings in Nairobi and Dar es Salaam 1998, using al-Qaeda cash and new identity papers, he fled to South Africa where he was arrested in 1999 working in a fast food restaurant in Cape Town.

The mastermind of these Nairobi and Dar es Salaam attacks, Ahmed Ghailani from Tanzania, was transferred in June 2009 from Guantanamo, and into the custody of the U.S. Department of Defense where he had been held since 2006, to New York City where he faced 286 criminal charges for his alleged role in the murder of 224 people in the African bombings.

A suspect in the African bombings, Fazul Abdullah Mohammed, a native of the Comoros Islands off the African coast, escaped a Kenyan police dragnet in August 2006. He trained with Osama bin Laden in Afghanistan before becoming a religious schoolteacher in northern Kenya. The police held his immediate family as accomplices because they prevented his capture. He had a $5 million reward bounty on him. He was once captured for credit card fraud in 2002 but escaped to Somalia.

## Egypt: Secular Hammer and Islamic Sword

Modern Egypt is a weak comparison with the storied past of its pharaohs. Egypt has a broken education system, high unemployment, a population clinging to the Nile, a country outrunning its limited resources, horrific traffic and eye-polluting smog in Cairo, infuriating incompetence, and a rising militancy movement among Muslims. After the revolution that began in Tahrir Square in 2011, a place I visited in the summer of 2011, Islamists attempted to seize local political control of parts of Cairo among citizens dissatisfied with liberating progress.

There was tumultuous exhilaration on February 11, 2011 when Hosni Mubarak resigned the presidency after 30 years of overseeing perpetual martial law after the assassination of Anwar Sadat he witnessed in 1981. The peaceful demonstrations of the revolution in Egypt began after a revolt in Tunisia in January 2011. The Egyptian army sidestepped the Constitution about presidential succession, assumed power, dissolved Parliament and began transitioning to democratic rule.

The votes for parliamentary seats on November 28, 2011 resulted in a 40% electoral percentage for the moderate Muslim Brotherhood with its Freedom and Justice Party. Parliament opened for the first time in 84 years in 2011 and with a formerly outlawed Muslim Brotherhood majority in the legislative chamber. The fundamentalist *Salafis* garnered about 25% of the vote and immediately challenged the Muslim Brotherhood for not supporting a full conversion of the country to *sharia* law. The Muslim Brotherhood leader, Khairat el-Shater, 62, is the Nelson Mandela of Egypt, because he will emerge as an important political figure and has been in prison for years.

The transition to a sound economy will be more difficult as Egypt's percentage of state workers was 35% compared to only 13% in Turkey. Egypt will be engaged in a major political transformation, but the repercussions will send shivers throughout the autocratic Arab world.

The loss of Nasser's secular vision of a pan-Arab coalition, and the loss of image and status in the 1967 and 1973 wars inaugurated a period of retreat into religious fundamentalism nurtured by the rise of the Muslim Brotherhood. No women in Egypt in 1970 wore a veil or the *hijab*. Today it would be considered blasphemous to even discuss the possibility of not wearing one.

Egypt, a land where 95% of the population lives on 5% of the land, had 83 million people in 2009, most bordering on abject poverty and intellectual desolation. About 25% live in absolute poverty. Its population increases by about one million every few months, more than the combined increase in the population of Jordan, Israel, Lebanon and the Palestinians. [7] Unlike other Arab countries about 10% are Coptic Christian (Copt = Egypt), the largest percentage of minorities in the Islamic world.

Nearly a half million graduates enter the job market annually. While 90% of job seekers have intermediate or higher education diplomas, 75% of new job entrants are unemployed. About 60% of college graduates are in the bloated public employment—armed forces, civil servants, teachers. The literacy rate remains at about 50% and the per capita GNP frozen at just a few hundred dollars per year. The economy lacks an industrial base and has to provide governmental subsidies for basic food necessities.

Egypt no longer produces independent thought, journalistic analyses or investigative reporting as it once did just a few years ago. Israel produces 4,000 books annually; Egypt produces less than 400 books a year. There are no astute commentaries on the political scene as there once were. Literature and the arts are barely taught.

Egypt has over 25,000 schools and over a million poorly paid teachers. It also has 70,000 popular mosques. Fundamentalist Islamic teachers have effectively seized control of the educational establishment and altered the curriculum to conform to Islamic tenets, even playing recordings of Muslim preachers in class. Ayman al-Zawahiri, an Egyptian-trained physician from a well-known and respected middle class family in Cairo, is Osama bin Laden's deputy. Egypt after Mubarak is on its way slowly to becoming a transformative political state that hopefully can marginalize and control its Islamic militants.

## Central Asian Insurgencies

I am a member of the political party, Hizbut Tahrir. The goal of this organization is the creation of an Islamic way of life, including the creation of an Islamic caliphate. [8]

What do Chechnya, Mindanao in The Philippines, Pattani in southern Thailand, Kosovo, Bosnia, Kashmir, Somalia, Baluchistan, Tartarstan, Kyrgyzstan and Kazakhstan have in common? They are home to indigenous Muslim residents who seek—or in the case of Bosnia-Herzegovina have already attained—independence from the countries where they live. This global thrust for independence is not separation from a colonial empire but to find an autonomous Islamic identity distinct from a civil state. Andrey Piontkovsky, a Russian political scientist and fellow at the Hudson Institute, writes that Russia is engaged in a war against Islamic fundamentalism in the Caucasus and is a serious threat to the Russian Federation. Islamic radicalism has spread throughout the region beyond Chechnya.

Militancy movements in South Central Asia have in common fighters who have often served in Afghanistan with the Taliban, or in Iraq honing their military skills to be used in insurgencies in their home countries. They rent a house where they live together, stockpile Kalashnikov rifles and watch martial arts on DVDs to reinforce their fighting spirit. Security forces, like those in the Fergana Valley in Kyrgyzstan just north of Afghanistan and Tajikistan, often find where they are holed up, shoot their way into the house, and kill the insurgents, unless some blow themselves up with a grenade first. These Muslim militants and their supporters believe they are upholding the spirit of Islam, often belong to *Hizb ut-Tahrir* a global radical Islamic group that seeks to re-establish the caliphate, or pan-Arabic rule throughout the region.

Tartarstan is also home to bands of religious revolutionaries who seek an independent homeland for Muslims. The members of *Hizbut ut-Tahrir*—allowed to operate in the U.S. and the European Union, but closely watched—is a political organization unabashedly fundamentalist toward Islam. Several young men have gone on trial for membership in what the authorities call a terrorist group and for fomenting plots to overthrow the government.

From a population of 140 million, the Russian Federation has between 15–20 million Muslims. Since the fall of the Soviet Union over 50 new mosques have been built and *madrassas* opened. Russia has long fought with separatist movements in the North Caucasus and Chechnya where there has been a rising movement toward independence and the formation of Islamic states. None is more notorious than Chechnya.

# Chechnya and North Caucasus States

Chechnya, with a population of slightly more than one million and with its own native language, borders Georgia to its west, and is about 50 miles west of the Caspian Sea, just north of Azerbaijan and the Caucasus Mountains. The region has had a tumultuous history with Russia and is experiencing a rise in violence. After the Bolshevik Revolution in 1917 Chechens again declared a separation that the Bolsheviks crushed. During World War II Chechens collaborated with the invading German army, so Stalin deported about half a million residents to Siberia, Kyrgyzstan and Kazakhstan.

Shortly after the collapse of the Soviet Union in 1991, Chechen separatists, who are largely Sunni Muslim, declared an independent republic. President Boris Yeltsin imposed martial law and then repealed his decree. Civil war ensued but Russian troops assembled in haste and soon encountered fierce resistance. By 1996 a tentative and uneasy peace was concluded and Chechnya was accorded some autonomy but not full independence. The Chechen resistance movement attracted Islamic militants from all over the world.

In early 1999 the new leader Aslan Mashkadov declared *sharia* law to be phased in over three years. Then in August 1999 Chechen fighters slipped into neighboring Dagestan directly to the east to support Islamic warriors where a *jihad* had been declared against Russia. Russian President Vladimir Putin quickly put down that rebellion. Within weeks bombings in Russia in which about 300 died were blamed on Chechen militants. In a second campaign, Russian troops engaged the militants in an inconclusive outcome but forced hundreds of thousands to flee while the capitol Grozny was reduced to rubble.

On September 1, 2004, about 32 Chechen separatists attacked a Russian school in Beslan in Northern Ossetia in which over 1,200 teachers, pupils and relatives were taken hostage. The school was completely destroyed two days later, and 344–394 civilians massacred, including 186 children. The sole surviving attacker was found guilty on May 26, 2006 but spared the death penalty because of Russia's moratorium on executions.

Ramzan Kadyrov, Russia's new handpicked ruler, has not stamped out the insurgency but stamps out critics and opponents. Kadyrov was sponsored by Russia's Prime Minister Vladimir Putin and installed in a rigged election. The Kremlin sought to control the Islamic insurgency using strong-armed, extra-judicial, counter-insurgency tactics. He recruited pro-Kremlin Chechens to find the local militants. Russia cleverly turned the conflict against them into an internecine war. With the backing of the Kremlin, Kadyrov killed most rebel leaders, and granted amnesty to many in exchange for loyalty to him. Through a series of human rights violations Russia and its minions have established relative calm in the troubled region. [9]

Chechnya rebels claimed responsibility for a terrorist train bombing in late November 2009 that killed 26 and wounded scores more. Chechen separatist leader Doku Umarov issued the claim saying the train bombing between

Moscow and St. Petersburg was carried out in the name of the Emir of Caucasus Emirate, meaning him. He is reported to be the chief of a network of separatist cells throughout the North Caucasus region. The group was also responsible for two Russian airline bombings and a subway attack in 2004. A police station in Ingushetia was bombed in August 2009 that killed 20.

Natalya Estemirova, a human rights activist and single mother in her 40s, was last seen in July 2009 as she was hustled off into a car as she left her home in Grozny, the Chechen capital. Her body was later found by the side of a road in Ingushetia, shot twice in the head at close range, the seventh opponent of Kadyrov to have been murdered within a year.

Chechen resistance has emphatically come under the influence of global *jihad*. Russia and the U.S. share a common international terrorist threat, and to a lesser degree China too. The spread of the idea of regional autonomous republics throughout the titular ethnic Muslim republics is a toxic blend of potential secession through violence. [10]

The political status of Russia since 1989 is returning to a more authoritarian and centralized government in which large regions now have less autonomy than under the Soviet Union. This may be a contributing resentment factor among Muslim communities. On the contrary, politics is only an attenuating issue. The primary motivation is the global rise of the Islamic militancy movement.

The Chechnya separatist movement in the 1990s resulted in the destruction of the capitol Grozny—as complete as that of Titus in Jerusalem in 70 CE—and undoubtedly hardened Chechen resistance that received aid from Saudi Arabia, funding and tactical guerilla assistance for terrorists groups abroad in this lingering struggle. After 1999 the Chechen leadership had clearly moved from mere resistance to a confirmed terrorist state based on an al-Qaeda model.

The Islamic threat in the Caucasus has parallels elsewhere. Any war brings about destabilization, accelerates fractiousness between ethnicities, destroys previous consensus agreements and invites violent retaliation—the essence of *jihad*. Islamization in the north Caucasus shortly after the demise of the Soviet Union hastened the spread of nationalistic fervor and Islamic extremist views and tactics. More serious is the possibility of Russian Muslim terrorists acquiring sufficient weapons of mass destruction—nuclear, chemical or biological—from one of hundreds of poorly secured sites throughout Russia, attach it to a SCUD missile, or an Alazon rocket with a range of about eight miles, sail it on a ship up the Chesapeake Bay and fire it on Washington DC.

## China and the Uighers

Two men aged twenty-eight and thirty-three from Kashgar in China's far western Xinjiang province ambushed a military police unit armed with explosives and knifes killing sixteen officers and wounding another sixteen in an attack in August 2008 in the first days of the Beijing Olympics. The men drove a dump truck and rammed it into soldiers on a jogging exercise killing ten. They then leapt from the truck and stabbed other soldiers, and lobbed grenades at nearby barracks but without injuring anyone. China claimed that these men were radical Muslims, members of the East Turkestan Islamic Movement that both China and the U.S. list as a terrorist organization. [11] However, photographs taken by a tourist from a nearby hotel showed that uniformed members of the police were actually involved in the machete slayings. A court in western China for Xinjiang province on December 17, 2008 sentenced to death two Uighurs, a taxi driver and a vegetable vendor, for an this attack that killed 17 paramilitary officers. Both men were Turkish-speaking Muslims and the military they killed were Han Chinese. The Chinese report of the verdict did not provide any details about evidence used in the attack.

In a Chinese government newspaper, *Procuratorial Daily*, on January 4, 2009 China reported that 1,100 people had been indicted in Xinjiang province, an unusually high number. In 2007, as a comparable example, only 742 people had been arrested on suspicion of anti-government activity. [12]

China has imposed harsh rules on Islam in its far western territory of Xinjiang province. The imam's sermon can last no more than half an hour, and prayer is forbidden outside the mosque. Muslims can only worship in their own town. No Muslim is forced to attend services. Only authorized copies of the Koran are allowed, and Arabic can only be taught in special schools.

The Chinese government is intent on limiting the spread of Islam and controlling its religious fervor in this semi-autonomous region inhabited by Uighurs, most nominally Muslim. Whether or not Uighurs are fomenting because of discriminatory practices against their ethnic group, or are acting as Muslim terrorists against authorities they believe are corrupt and too secular, is unknown.

I spoke with Uighur peoples as a guest of the Qinghai Educational Authority in Xining in 1988, and in Alma Ata in Kazakhstan in 1991 and again in 1996. They have a clear sense of their distinctive ethnic identity living along the ancient route of the Silk Road. A few have become radicalized and separatist, and several have joined militants in war zones. Among the 241 detainees at Guantanamo prison, 17 are Uighers from Xinjiang province, captured in either Pakistan or Afghanistan in 2001 and 2002. Federal courts have determined that the evidence against them is ambiguous.

The Uighur riots that occurred in the summer of 2009 in Urumqi in the far western province of Xinjiang, in which over 197 died, was one of China's nightmares. There was subsequent unrest in the Uighur city of Kashgar, a city of 3.4 million. The Xinjiang Uighur Autonomous Region is known as a Muslim crucible of resistance to China's rule, some of whose residents seek a Uighur homeland. It is a tense region, as Chinese officials tightly regulate the citizens, as many locals strive for a nationalistic and autonomous Muslim identity apart from China. [13]

# Bangladesh

Bangladesh has an ineffective government, an economy in which half the population lives below the poverty level, over-population and unemployment. Islamic militants thrive in such soft targets that create opportunities for armed insurrection, unless periodic and lethal floods don't ruin the state first and literally dampen enthusiasm for reform. Bangladesh has a number of well-organized and financed Islamic militias and a government police force that panders to them. Police have failed to capture those responsible for high-profile murders, like that of the respected academic and anti-fundamentalist proponent, Professor Mohammad Yunus.

Nor has the government solved the 2004 grenade attack on the secular, westernized political party, the Awami League, in Dhaka that killed 22, including the party's leader, Ivy Rahman, and wounded over 200. Radicals have been released from jail, investigations stalled, and arrests so infrequent that it is difficult to believe that there is not police collusion in fundamentalist activities. A moderate Muslim country like Bangladesh, with a population exceeding 160 million, does not need to have the government overthrown in a *coup d'etat* to achieve its militant objectives. It needs only to control the government, or have enough election votes to win approval and force the government to concede to its demands.

Muslim fundamentalists have placed or recruited officials already in government to their cause. One consistent propaganda strategy among these groups is to identify and vilify enemies, generally members of other ethnic or religious groups, Hindus, Buddhists, and Christians especially. Persecuted minorities tend to migrate elsewhere, if they are not killed or terrorized first. Hindu fundamentalism in India has helped the Muslim cause in Bangladesh.

Bangladesh became a new state on December 16, 1971 when it separated from Pakistan. East Bengal became East Pakistan in 1955. Pakistan failed in its attempt to absorb completely its eastern Islamic cousin in 1972 and East Pakistan seceded. Militant Islam began its insidious inroads soon thereafter. Politicians have been attempting to pacify radical Muslim demands since 1975, and have usually compromised in their favor on issues like the role of women, secular forces, social workers, outside influences, the banning of entertainment, any and all western projects, and the censoring and killing of cultural artists. [14]

The Indian Government and newspapers indicated a rise in the number of mosques and *madrassas*, over a thousand, along the Indian-Bangladesh border. While Kolkata (the former Calcutta), a city of 14 million, had 131 *madrassas* and 67 mosques, the smaller border town of Krishnanagar had 408 *madrassas* and 368 mosques. [15] Besides teaching only theology and Arabic, they are centers of potential terrorist activity, and provide the cover of a religious school serving as a training camp and storage facility for weapons. Over 70,000 *madrassas* are estimated to exist. Islamic militants, since they reside close to Indian borders, hide from Indian authorities by escaping into Bangladesh. Indian authorities have done little to curb the flow of illegal immigrants from Bangladesh into India.

The goal of the *Jamaat-e-Islami*, the fundamentalist political organization in several Muslim Asian countries, is the same as any Islamic radical group— the destruction of a country's multi-party parliamentary form of government, and the legal and constitutional basis of secular law, and the establishment of *sharia*. Such organizations never want just political change, but revolution, as occurred in Iran in 1979. The motto of *Jamaat* and similar groups is simple and ruthless in means and echoes the Muslim Brotherhood: Allah is Lord; Muhammad is the leader; the Quran is the ideal; *jihad* is the means; salvation the end. Its simplicity can appeal even to the illiterate, and certainly to the uncritical and unquestioning. All recruits need are to have memorized a few phrases in Arabic from the Koran, and the techniques of an AK-47, crude explosives, or similar weapons, and they can be suicide bombers to help populate the companionable afterlife, as long as oasis space in paradise continues to expand too.

Bangladesh is a secularized, moderate Islamic country whose population is largely disinclined to follow the bigotry of extremist groups. But it is perpetually threatened from within and funded from without by radicalized religious and extremist Islamic groups whose sole purpose is the destruction of secular government and the installation of Islam. Bangladesh is an ideal breeding ground for Islamic fundamentalism, and has already made its deadly presence felt in government inaction against criminal perpetrators, in the increased presence of fundamentalist *madrassas,* in government concessions to its radical demands, and in terrorist activities against minorities.

## Malaysia and Indonesia

Kartika Sari Dewi Shukarno, 32, a nurse, had been granted a last minute reprieve in 2009. She had been sentenced to a whipping with canes for drinking beer in a hotel lobby, an Islamic crime in Malaysia that she acknowledged. Muslims in Malaysia can be arrested and punished for snacking during daylight hours during Ramadan, the fasting month, or for being in close proximity to a member of the opposite sex not a spouse, or for drinking.

I lived in Malaysia's capitol, Kuala Lumpur, in 1976-77 as a Fulbright scholar. The country then maintained a tense but exuberant multi-cultural and multi-ethnic mix. It had a laid-back, colonial, humid informality that Somerset Maugham (1874–1965), who lived in the region and wrote short stories it, would have appreciated. Its population is about 60% Malay, 24% Chinese, 11% native Orang peoples, and 7% Indian.

I also served another Fulbright assignment in Malang, Indonesia in the summer of 2011 where I declined an offer to meet with an imprisoned terrorist because I believed he would just lie to me.

Islam is the official religion of Malaysia and the government actively promotes the spread of Islam. All ethnic Malays are Muslim, and according to

218

the Constitution would be required to surrender ethnic status if not a Muslim. [16] The Pan-Malaysian Islamic Party is a political party seeking to establish Islam, and has publicized its mission to establish *sharia*. In 2008 the party won 82 of the 222 seats in Parliament and managed to take control of the west coast state government in Kedah.

The most notorious and increasingly violent Islamic extremist group in Indonesia is *Jemaah Islamiyah*, responsible for the bombing of a nightclub in Bali, one of the most peaceful places on earth, on October 12, 2002 killing 202, mostly Australians. A suicide bomber and a white van filled with 1.12 tons of potassium chlorate and powdered aluminium, with a combination of sulphur and TNT, parked outside Paddy's Club in Kuta, Bali. It was the deadliest terrorist attack in Indonesia's history. The perpetrator Idris was convicted and executed by firing squad in 2008. [17]

*Jemaah Islamiyah's* spiritual leader, Abu Bakar Bashir, encouraged killing non-Muslims. The group was closely associated with al-Qaeda. Although initially reluctant to crack down on this group, Indonesian authorities began to infiltrate and round up operatives after a bombing at a Marriott Hotel in Jakarta in 2003 and on the Australian embassy in 2004.[18] Over 400 militants were arrested and explosive caches and weapons confiscated. Three men convicted in 2003 for that bombing were sentenced to death for the Bali bombings. Indonesians, unused to such openness in their society, realized that they had a serious domestic and not a foreign threat in their midst. Three who were convicted in 2003 were executed by firing squad, bringing an end to a tumultuous period when the government feared a backlash from their executions.

Abu Bakar Bashir was tried in an Indonesian court on July 17, 2011, convicted of conspiracy of masterminding and operating a terrorist training camp in Aceh, on northern tip of the island of Sumatra. He was implicated in the 2002 and 2005 Bali bombings. The 73-year old was sentenced to 15 years in prison where he will hopefully not be allowed to continue to communicate with militants. Indonesian prisons are notorious breeding grounds for terrorists and sympathizers. He continually preached armed fighting in the way for Allah. His disciples live everywhere in Indonesia. He did not acknowledge the legitimacy of the court ruling saying it was an infidel court with laws made by men not Allah, a typical belief of Islamic fundamentalists. [19]

Perhaps overly focused on catching operatives and not enough on preventing terrorism, Indonesia authorities, like those in Malaysia, have unintentionally allowed the militancy movements, especially among clerics, schools, and some radical publishing houses, to continue to flourish. Though officials have arrested hundreds of active militants, the culture of Islamic militancy thrives. The Council of *Ulema* illustrates the growing political power of a group of Muslim scholars that once were a minority under previous dictators but are now a major political force in Indonesian politics espousing a radical view of Islam. It advocates *sharia* and for the exclusion of minority Islamic sects like *Ahmadiya*, a group that says Mohammad was not the last prophet. Though the Council is influential, with networks throughout the island country and in the Indonesian banking community, the majority of Indonesians support a more moderate view of Islam. Indonesia does not have tough anti-terrorism laws because it prefers a more democratic approach to differing ideas and does not want to appear to be too authoritarian. [20]

Finally, there is the Abu Sayyaf group of Islamic extremists and criminal gangs operating on islands like Lamitan and Basilan in the southern Philippines that have terrorized tourists and locals alike. American soldiers have been active to root out these homegrown Muslim militants, but neither they nor Philippine soldiers have been entirely successful. These lawless criminals, using the camouflage of a Muslim identity, have repeatedly attacked Philippine soldiers and kidnapped tourists for ransom money that feeds their activities. The Abu Sayyaf group received help from al-Qaeda in the early 1990s and is believed to be hiding members wanted in Indonesia.

The militancy movement has not abated and has taken on a life of its own on all inhabited continents, but only minimally in South America and Australia. It operates on a religious code of violence, secretly in the West, and openly in countries where it prevails. It seeks to undermine civil law and democratic principles and to install an Islamic government wherever it can. If ordinary citizens living far from the actual conflicts between Islamic militants and western powers remain unaffected by this movement, they should quickly educate themselves and their children about this confrontation that will engage the West far into the future.

Dome of the Rock (Harim al-Sharif) in Jerusalem

# EPILOGUE

*Radical Islam has declared war on America and the West, and the majority of Muslims either support or make excuses for terrorism* [1]

The western outrage about Islam did not begin with the Iranian Revolution in 1979, although Americans were infuriated at Iran for kidnapping diplomatic hostages. But puzzlement turned to affront and indignation when Ayatollah Khomeini issued a *fatwa* against Salman Rushdie in 1989 for his novel, *The Satanic Verses*. The death sentence was an unequivocal rejection of any criticism, even literary, of Islam. It was an imperious intrusion into western values, an arrogant imposition of Islamic values on a western citizen, and a pronouncement of a death sentence absent internationally recognized judicial proceedings. It was a defining moment that shook the political foundations of western civilization by a Muslim cleric as official head of state. That singular event marked the beginning of the intimidation posed by Islamic extremists and authoritarian clerics across the globe.

September 11, 2001 really did change the world's worldview, not just America's. It was clear that retribution would be coming, but against whom? Modern wars had always been against nation states or empires. To attack a loose confederation of active terrorists funded by a psychopathic fanatic who had cohorts in several Islamic countries, or a religious zealot who happened to be head of state who thought he could pass judgment on a citizen of another country, seemed equally mad.

So American officials, usually clueless about messy foreign affairs, conveniently declared a "war on terror," because they didn't know where threats might exist, perhaps even in the U.S. The Bush Administration, bowing to the public's instinct for revenge, decided to attack the one country, Afghanistan, that is really not a country at all as much as it is unrelated groups of tribal entities harboring al-Qaeda militants as Islamic guests.

Then, because of arrogance and a hasty impulse to restore what they believed was America's tarnished image, the U.S. attacked Iraq in anger only to discover that America's image became even more blemished, and the invasion a colossal miscalculation built on deceit and surprising naivete about the Arab world. The Obama Administration had to exit ungracefully in late 2011 after a decade of Bush Administration blunders to preserve the minimum of a sloppy foreign invasion divorce settlement.

The Danish cartoon crisis in 2005, and the attempted assassination of cartoonist Kurt Westergaard in January 2010, highlighted again the confrontation of Islam and the West, and the clash of western values and freedoms and Islamic dogmatic assumptions about what is permissible in free societies. Since then, the silencing of critics, artists, journalists, and the liberal western public's accommodation to Islam's hard fundamentalism exacerbated tensions and fomented distrust.

If westerners were not convinced of the depth of the suicidal and deathly intentions of radicalized Muslims, the murders of Pim Fortuyn in 2002 and Theo van Gogh in 2004 in Holland, and the train bombings in Madrid in 2004 and in London in 2005, were evidence enough of how far Islam would go to in its misguided sense of religious defense and attacks on western ideals, and not just in America, by killing innocent civilians. Many in the far left thought it all a great misunderstanding to be resolved by more concessions and submissions to Muslim religious sentiments, even as Muslim proponents sought to establish an Islamic state with *sharia* law imposed wherever they lived in Europe.

Why is there such Muslim love of hatred and violence against Jews and Christians? Iraqi Shiite militants attacked Our Lady of Salvation Church in Baghdad in 2010, killing 50 worshippers and two priests. Half of Iraq's Christian population has fled the country since 2003, from a land they have occupied for centuries, because of targeted violence against them.

Why is there a tolerance for glaring social injustices among Muslims? Why do Muslims blame Israel and America for all their problems? What is the best response for confronting the most radical elements in extremist Muslim ideology?

On May 11, 2011, after a second month investigation, New York officers arrested Ahmed Ferhani, 26, originally from Algeria, and Mohamed Mamdouh, both living in Queens, for plotting to bomb a Jewish synagogue and other churches. They were not members of any known militant Islamic group but were motivated by the "cause," or *jihad*. What Ahmed had in abundance was a hatred of Jews, and a vengeance against others that Muslims everywhere were badly treated, "like dogs," he said. They were both arrested trying to purchase weapons from a police undercover team. The FBI was not involved. Hardly a month goes by that an individual Islamic terrorist or cell is not uncovered in the U.S. or Europe, and whether or not they are associated with an identifiable terrorists organization. They become radicalized from friends or through Internet web sites.

President Bush described Islam as "a great and peaceful faith that has been hijacked by a few extremists." On the contrary, Islam has scripturally authorized violent extremism. Much of the terrorism in the world—Chechnya, Bali, the southern Philippines, Sudan, Somalia, Bosnia, Indonesia, Nigeria, Thailand, Kashmir, to the streets of London and Madrid—can be directly traced to Islamic militancy.

A September 2009 report by the Pew Research Center showed a decline of support for al-Qaeda among Muslims. The report cited wide disparity among Muslim countries, with 87% in Pakistan rejecting suicide and violence against civilians, but only 17% in the Palestinian territories. The average of nine Islamic countries was 53%, not a high enough ratio to inspire sanguine optimism.

Human rights abuses top the list of inhuman practices Islam adheres to, including honor killings of women accused of sexual misconduct, trading women like chattel and subjugating them, periodic clan blood feuds, and the cutting off of limbs for selected offenses. Additionally, anti-intellectualism and rejection of all scientific and secular ideas that are not directly responsive to its sacred beliefs are forbidden. Banning television, dancing, movies, photography, kite flying and chess are the least of its prohibitions.

Religion may inform citizens about moral and ethical principles. But at least in the West, religion no longer substitutes for democratic governance. In Saudi Arabia the struggle is to sustain the kingdom and royalty, and in Iran the theocracy. And in other majority Muslim states, the struggle is to keep radical groups from turning governments into theocracies. The challenge of the 21st century is both with radicalized individuals who seek to kill and destroy individuals not Muslim, and tottering Islamic governments who seek to return to the rule of religious orthodoxy. Supreme Leaders may once have thought they had divine right to rule over peoples' lives, but they were just as tyrannical as Mao Tse Tung was in China, Josef Stalin in Russia, Adolph Hitler in Germany, Muammar Qaddafi in Libya, military juntas in Burma, or maniacal rulers in North Korea. The coming of the Arab Spring in 2011 was an Arab awakening prompted by popular recognition of the tyranny throughout the Arab world and the lack of economic satisfaction.

Death, suicides, guns, killings and coups against Islamic states in the name of religion are not winning over the Arab world. Mainstream Muslims are disgusted at the militias—and a few backward thinking clerics like Khomeini— in countries like Iran, Iraq, Afghanistan, Algeria, Gaza, and Lebanon that have dragged nations and peoples into senseless wars. Militants hearken to a hostile past that rejects modernity, and cannot imagine building a new, improved world on western ideas.

The Hindu concept of non-violence (*ahimsa*) championed by Gandhi and a hallmark of Hindu belief is in stark contrast to calls for violence by Muslim groups. Asoka (d. 232 BCE) was the Emperor of India who united all of India including what is today Afghanistan. After his bloody conquests he repented and converted to Buddhism abandoning war and violence. He adopted *ahimsa*, a virtue of peace and non-violence, and made Buddhism the state religion of India. He engraved his set of beliefs of compassion, truthfulness, non-violence, non-acquisitiveness and non-injury to animals on stone columns throughout the kingdom and founded hospitals for humans and animals. Non-violence, he believed, should be extended to all living things. Hereafter, conquest was to be by *dharma*, or the principles of right life. The Brahmin, the upper caste in Indian society, interpreted and disseminated Asoka's ideas until they became an integral part of Indian Hindu spiritual belief. The Hindu idea of non-violence is as much a component of Indian life as violence is among some Muslims.

Other mythologies try to reconcile the aggressive and gentle tendencies in human nature by locating both traits in divinities. Pele is the Hawaiian volcano goddess who simultaneously destroys everything in her path while creating new land for cultivation. Likewise, Shiva, one of the supreme gods in Hindu lore, is known as the Destroyer who wears a garland of human skulls surrounded by demons. But he is also the symbol of the ascetic, meditating in the Himalayas and, with his consort Parvati (also known as Uma), doing a cosmic dance. Islam has no mythologies, no stories reflective of human wisdom, because it is not based on literary sources but on revelation.

Clearly, it is difficult to reconcile the peaceful pronouncements of some who believe that all religions, like Buddhism, have sensible, divine aspirations for the good of humanity. Mohammed's violent statements, ascribed to God, are the controlling vision of Islamic culture and Muslim youth. At the top of the list is hatred for Jews. All Muslims are taught that loving a non-believer would make one a *kafir*, a non-believer.

Similar passages against paganism can be found in the Judaic scriptures, and date from a time when biblical prophets exhorted the Hebrew faithful to denounce the practices of their Canaanite neighbors who worshipped Baal, the bull god. But biblical passages were never interpreted as a modern equivalent of a perpetual war against those not Jewish. In the beginning of Jewish monotheism and Hebrew national identity about 2,500 years ago, and during the time of Mohammed in the sixth century CE, both religions were struggling against polytheism and so promoted the idea of only one God. [2]

Today, we are faced with Muslim believers who take select divine passages literally and not metaphorically, and wage campaigns openly or in secret, to kill non-Muslims. Their excuses are the promotion of secular ideas, the foreign policy of the United States, former colonialism, the existence of Israel, or the plight of the Palestinians. The logic of religious zealotry is not necessarily that its propositions or proponents are rational, but that the believer invests every emotion in the defense of its beliefs, and is willing to die for them. The enemy of their religion, they believe, is not only obnoxious and loathsome, but is the enemy of God and therefore can be legitimately dispensed with.

The majority of Muslims in the Arab world view the United States as the latest replacement of European colonialists, new infidels seeking to dominate the Islamic world. Yet the Middle East is confronted with appalling regional economic neglect and underdevelopment. Besides the vast wealth from oil production everyone knows will soon be depleted, the Middle East has been deprived of sensible infrastructure investments, well documented by a series of international reports. Real GNP has dramatically fallen, and population has exceeded revenues to support it. While global exports are about six percent, the region's exports, 70% of which are oil or oil-related, only grew at 1.5%.

Vali Nasr at Tuft's Fletcher School of Law and Diplomacy believes that the rise of the Muslim middle class in the Arab world will soften the voices of terrorism and tilt sentiment toward secular governments like Turkey.[3] He believes capitalism and business will triumph over religion. But he neglects to note that Turkey's revolution came about politically and militarily through Kemal Ataturk and not because of commercial interests. He ignores the fact that Iran was authoritarian and secular prior to its revolution in 1979.

According to the report, *Changing Course: A New Direction for U.S. Relations with the Muslim World*, sponsored by Search for Common Ground and the Consensus Building Institute, the cause of Muslim violence originates from frustration, non-participation in politics and lack of economic opportunities.

Only a tiny minority of Muslims is involved in violence against the U.S. and its allies. The extremists' ability to recruit, operate, and inflict harm depends on a more widespread set of active and passive supporters. In many Muslim majority countries and Muslim minority communities, that support is driven by deep-seated frustration with poor governance, constraints on political activity, and lack of economic opportunity. [4]

Lacking in this list of politically correct grievances is the intensity of religious fundamentalism, and the statement that "only a tiny minority of Muslims is involved in violence against the U.S. and its allies." I question the validity of evidence for that assertion as polls have shown a near universal hatred for the U.S. and its allies—including tiny Denmark for its satirical cartoons in the Muslim world—and the moral and logistical support for attacks against the U.S. and its allies, depending on the particular country, if not the actual engagement in terrorist activities.

Islamic terrorism will be present for decades because of the pressures of population growth in the Middle East, the lack of jobs, the consequences of increased unemployment, and the failure to accelerate economic productivity to accommodate even modest population increases. But most of all it will continue to be prevalent, if not ubiquitous because of its scriptural imperatives. According to the National Intelligence Council report, *Global Trends 2025: A Transformed World*, after Africa, the Middle East will be the most vulnerable to economic disparities, the stresses of population that place competition for energy, food and water, and political instability that terrorist networks will seek to exploit.

Americans readily admit to the strength of evangelical Christians—those who figuratively carry a gun on one hip and a Bible on the other—to set the political agenda domestically and to support messianic candidates with money and votes. Unquestionably, religion is a primary force in the recruitment of Muslim young men and a few women to die for what they believe are blasphemies and insults to their religious beliefs, and not just their economic or political conditions. I believe this is an egregious error of omission in this otherwise sensible, but often naïve, report about how to improve U.S./ Muslim relations.

Islamic extremism is a militant movement like Marxism, anarchism or nationalism each of which has arisen and diminished over the last century. Al-Qaeda has an un-achievable strategic objective—it can never defeat the West. Its ability to attract broad-based support has eroded because of the brutality of its methods. Counter-terrorism methods, even in Arab and Islamic states, has disrupted many of its activities and killed or captured many of its leaders, Osama bin Laden chief among them. Thoughtful Muslims realize that terror against the West will not cure unemployment, poverty, elevate the lack of educational standards, cure environmental degradation or dysfunctional governance among Muslim countries, which is why the Arab Spring erupted so thoroughly throughout the Arab world in 2011.

The Muslim world believes that the highest defilement is the presence of

U.S. troops on Arab sand, even troops that kept Saddam Hussein from occupying the Gulf States. In reality, the defilement of the Islamic world, with its over-arching resentment, hatred and victimization, is inside its own religion and psyche. Al-Qaeda's influence over time will be curtailed but Islamic radicalism and terrorism will linger throughout the 21st century providing opportunities for terrorists, continuing inconvenience for travelers, and headaches for counterterrorism officials.

> Unless the world community acts decisively and with great urgency, it is more likely than not that a weapon of mass destruction will be used in a terrorist attack somewhere in the world by the end of 2013. [5]

The report cited above only points out how little the U.S. has rallied to prepare itself and citizens for this war that knows no geographic limits from determined Islamic radicals. To paraphrase Winston Churchill, we need to fight them in the hills of Pakistan, in the sands of Yemen, Somalia, Sudan and Saudi Arabia, in the streets of Gaza and Quetta and Karachi, in the teeming slums of Cairo, and in the mosques where hate-filled sermons are preached until the pernicious ideology is silenced.

I vividly recall as a young boy the radio announcement that Sunday morning December 7, 1941 that the Japanese had attacked Pearl Harbor in Hawaii. The ensuing war affected every American one way or another, through the premature deaths of its young men, or the sacrifice of its citizens. The attack of September 11, 2001 was no less a day of infamy. The difference is that the present war is composed of religious zealots, even absent the inspiration and plotting of Osama bin Laden, and not country nationals. But unless everyone wants to convert to Islam, the objective is no different than other guerilla wars—find and defeat the enemy wherever they exist.

# GLOSSARY

Abaya   Clothes covering
Adhan   Call to prayer
Aib   Shame
Al–Bara Shunning outsiders (see Al-Wala)
Al–Ikhwan   Muslim Brotherhood
Allahu akbar   God is great, a slogan of joy
Al–Qaeda   *The Base*, a network founded by Osama bin Laden
Al–Wala   Loyalty to Muslims (see Al-Bara)
Ali   Son-in-law & Mohammad's adopted nephew; Shiites
Arb   Honor
Baiat   Oath of religious allegiance
Dar ul-Islam   Domain of Islam
Dar ul-Harb   Domain of Enmity
Dawah   Persuasion, reason
Dhimmi Infidel
Ekhlass Fidelity
Emir   Local leader
Eid   Festival marking end of Ramadan
Fakir   Holy man
Fatwa   Clerical order
Fedayeen   Men who sacrifice
Figh   Islamic jurisprudence according to the mullahs
Fikh (fiqh)   Islamic jurisprudence
Firdaws Paradise
Ghazi   Great fighter; champion
Hadith   Tradition; statements of Mohammad.
          (Koran + Hadith constitute *Sharia*)
Haji   Pilgrimage to Mecca, one of the five pillars of Islam
Hafiz   Having memorized the Koran
Halal   Good
Haram   Bad/forbidden
Hakim   Judge or doctor
Hegira   A holy flight or journey
Hijab   Women's covering
Huur Al-Ay   Virgins in paradise
Ibn   Son of
Ijtihad   Independent interpretation of Koran
Imam   Prayer leader
ISI   Pakistan's Inter-Services Intelligence Directorate
Islam   submission
Jahiliya Ignorance
Jamaat   Assembly or political party

Jannah   Paradise
Jihad    War against non-Muslims
Kaffiya  Head dress
Koran    Sacred book given by Allah to Mohammed (Quran)
Kufr     Heathenism
Kuffar   Heathen infidels
Madrassah   Seminary, religious school
Mahdi    Shiite Hidden Imam who will appear in the final days to return Islam
         to former glory
Masjid   Mosque
Maulana  Teacher more learned than an Imam
Mufti    Judge
Mujahedeen   Militant Islamists who undertake Jihad
Mujtahid     An interpreter of Koran
Mukawama     Perpetual war
Mullah   Someone who knows; religious teacher
Muhktar  Chief
Muslim   One who submits
Mutawihin   Religious police
Qadi     Magistrate; judge
Ramadan  Holy month of fasting
Salaam   Blessing/peace
Salafi   Religious ideology
Salat    Prayer or service
Sayyid   Descendant of Mohammad; or chief
Serah    Trial marriage by contract
Shahada  Belief
Shaheed  Martyr (also Shahid)
Sheikh   Arab leader
Sharia   *The path*, the laws of Islam
Shia     *The party*, minority sect of Islam who believe Ali is the rightful
         descendant of the Prophet
Shirk    Ascribing God's attributes to others
Sufi     Islamic mysticism
Sunna    custom or practice
Sunni    The main sect of Islam
Sura     A chapter in the Koran
Taliban  Seekers of knowledge
Takfir   Apostasy
Takfiri  A Sunni militant who divides people into believers & non-believers
Taqiyya  Lying & deception; obligation to lie to protect the faith
Tawhid   Islamic monotheism
Ulema    Learned religious men
Ulama    judges and canonists
Umma     World community of Muslims

Wahhabi   Followers of Muhammad ibi Abd al-Wahhab (1702-1792),
    fundamentalist who raised Jihad against all except the most devout Muslims
    and all infidels
Zakat    Muslim Tithe, one of the five pillars = 1/40 of all income
Zindik   Heretic or freethinker

# ENDNOTES

*Preface*

1.President Obama made the jubilant, historic and dramatic announcement of his death near midnight May 1ˢᵗ, 2011. The recognizable terrorist face and head of al-Qaeda, Osama bin Laden, the inspirational leader and mastermind of global Islamic terrorism was killed in his compound in Abbottabad, about an hour drive north of Islamabad, the capitol of Pakistan. A chapter in the long history of the fight against Al Qaeda ended with Osama's death, though al-Qaeda continues as a terrorist organization. Operational control of Al-Qaeda quickly fell to Saif al-Adel, c.50 years old, former Egyptian special forces soldier with two decades of ties to Osama. He has been implicated in the assassination of Egyptian President Anwar Sadat in 1981. The FBI already has a bounty price of $5 million for his role in the embassy bombings in Tanzania and Kenya in 1998. Bin Laden had declared war on the U.S. and western allies and been indicted in 1998 for 224 murders of the embassy bombings in Kenya and Tanzania. After 9/11 2001, President Bush said he wanted him dead or alive, signed an Executive Order to that effect, and put out a $25 million dollar bounty on his head. Islamic radicals classify him as a martyr; the rest of the world will celebrate the administration of raw justice for his murderous deeds. Al-Qaeda in the Arabian Peninsula publishes a magazine, *Inspire*, as a recruitment tool. Its producer, Samir Khan, was killed with Anwar al-Awlaki in the same vehicle in a CIA drone strike in September 2011. http://publicintelligence.net/inspire-al-qaeda-in-the-arabian-peninsula-magazine-issue-6-july-2011/

2. Ali Allawi, *The Crisis of Islamic Civilization*. (New Haven: Yale University Press, 2009). Allawi was the former Minister of Defense and Finance in the post-invasion governments.

3. Bayat, A. (May 31, 2011). Moving Towards a Muslim Democracy. *The Straits Times*, A21.

4. A. Aciman, "After Egypt's Revolution, Christians are Living in Fear. *The New York Times*, (November 20, 2011), A7.

5. C. Allen, *God's Terrorists, The Wahhabi Cult and the Hidden Roots of Modern Jihad*. (New York: Da Capo Press, 2007).

*Introduction Endnotes*

1. W. Durant, *The Age of Faith*. (New York: Simon and Schuster, 1950), pp. 175–176.

2. http://www.islamicsupremecouncil.com/iscc-fatwa-against%20terrorism.htm.

3. Stankov, L, *et. al.* (2010). "Contemporary Militant Extremism: A Linguistic Approach to Scale Development." *Psychological Assessment*, 22(2), 246–258.

4.http://www.gallup.com/consulting/worldpoll/26410/Gallup-Center-Muslim-Studies.aspx.

5. E. Stern, "Don't Fear Islamic Law in America." *The New York Times*, A15.

6. A. Jalal, (*Partisans of Allah, Jihad in South Asia*. (Cambridge, MA: Harvard University Press, 2008). See M. Bonner, *Jihad in Islamic History*. (Princeton: Princeton University Press, 2006).

7. For a perspective from critical pedagogy and against racism see Kincheloe, J. L. & S. R. Steinberg, C. D. Stonebanks. (2010). *Teaching Against Islamophobia*. (New York: Peter Lang).

8. W. Sultan, *A God Who Hates*. (New York: St. Martin's Press, 2009), p. 58. According to Mosab Hassan Yousf, son of one of the founders of Hamas, "The militants had the full force of the Qur'an to back them up." M. H. Yousef, *Son of Hamas, A Gripping Account*

*of Terror, Betrayal, Political Intrigue, and Unthinkable Choices.* (Carol Stream, IL: Salt-River, Tyndale House Publishers, 2010), p. 57.

9. S. P. Huntington, *The Clash of Civilizations and the Remaking of the World Order.* (New York: Simon and Schuster, 1996). See also *Global Trends 2025: A Transformed World.* National Intelligence Council. (Washington DC: US Government Printing Office, November 2008).

10. M. Desai, *Rethinking Islamism, The Ideology of the New Terror.* (London: I. B. Tauris, 2007).

11. N. Darwish, *Now They Call Me Infidel, Why I Renounced Jihad for America, Israel, and the War on Terror.* (New York: Sentinel, 2006), p. 149 & p. 212.

12. W. McCants, J. Brachman, & J. Felter, *Militant Ideology Atlas.* (West Point, NY: Combating Terrorism Center, 2006).

***Chapter One Endnotes***

1. J. R. Schmidt, "The Unraveling of Pakistan." *Survival*, 51(3), (June/July 2009), p. 42.

2. R. Payne, *The Holy Sword, The Story of Islam from Muhammad to the Present.* (New York: Harper & Brothers, 1959). The Quraysh were the tribesmen of Mohammad who turned against him when he proclaimed his message.

3. Vikings were polytheists and their principal gods, described poetically in *The Prose Edda*, were Odin, or Wodin, from which we have Wednesday, Odin's son Thor, the Hammer God, from which we have Thursday, and Frey and his sister goddess Freyja, from which we have Friday. Freyja controlled the Valkyries, the virgin daughter warriors of Oden who escorted Viking slain warriors to Valhalla, the eternal battle-scarred veterans resting place. See S. M. Margeson, *Eyewitness Viking.* (London: Dorling Kindersley, 2002) & Y. Cohat, *The Vikings, Lords of the Seas.* (London: Thames and Hudson, 2004).

4. In October 2008 Taliban insurgents stopped a bus in southern Afghanistan, pulled out all of its passengers and beheaded as many as thirty of them because they thought they might be soldiers without uniforms.

5. W. Durant, *The Age of Faith.* (New York: Simon and Schuster, 1950), p. 289. Masons and Shriners are the contemporary examples of these Mohammedan representatives with their red Moroccan Fez hats, secret handshakes and codes, and their Islamic shrine-inspired buildings. J. B. Glubb, *The Great Arab Conquests.* (Englewood Cliffs, NJ: Prentice-Hall, 1963) & H. U. Rahman, *A Chronology of Islamic History, 570–1000 CE.* (London: Ta–Ha Publishers, 1995) for a year-by-year chronology and descriptions of Arab conquests.

6. Hugh St. John Philby's *Harun Al Rashid.* (New York: D. Appleton-Century Co., 1934).

7. H. Kennedy, *The Early Abbasid Caliphate.* (London: Croom Helm, 1951).

8. J. J. Saunders, *A History of Medieval Islam.* (New York: Barnes & Noble, 1965). Cf. S. O'Shea, *Sea of Faith, Islam and Christianity in the Medieval Mediterranean World.* (New York: Walker and Company, 2006). E. Karsh, *Islamic Imperialism, A History.* (New Haven: Yale University Press, 2006)

9. E. Gibbon & S. Ockley, *The Saracens, Their History and the Rise and Fall of Their Empire.* (London: Rederick Warne and Co., 1873), 120–146.

10. D. Sharpes, "An Inquiry into Values of Islamic Fundamentalism." *JVI*, XXI, 1987, 309-315.

11. C. Barks, *The Essential Rumi*, (San Francisco: HarperSanFrancisco, 1995).

12. J. Wetherford, *Genghis Khan and the Making of the Modern World.* (New York: Three Rivers Press, 2004).

13. R. Payne, *The Holy Sword, The Story of Islam from Muhammad to the Present.* (New York: Harper & Brothers, 1959), p. xiv.

### Chapter Two Endnotes

1. J. Goodwin, *Lords of the Horizon, A History of the Ottoman Empire.* (New York: Henry Holt and Company, 1998). See also I. M. Lapidus, *A History of Islamic Societies* (2nd Ed.) (New York: Cambridge University Press, 2002).

2. The Ottoman name is derived from Osman.

3. By the 16th century about 20% of the Balkan population was Muslim, except in Bosnia where the percentage of Muslims was about half. Within a month of the killing of Osama bin Laden by American special forces, the ultra-nationalist Serbian General Ratko Mladic, was finally arrested in lat May 2011 after over 16 years eluding capture. He had been indicted for war crimes in 1995 for the ethnic cleansing of thousands of Bosnian Serbs in the village of Srebrenica, infamous thereafter as the site of a massacre of Bosnian Muslims. Mladic was obsessed with revenge against Muslims seeing them as descendants of Ottoman Turkish occupiers. His murderous pathology may have been fuelled by religious zealotry. He took UN peacekeepers, many Dutch, as hostages whenever they interfered with his runaway civilian casualties. He was hidden for years, often in the open by sympathizers. The Dutch had refused to permit Serbia's entrance into the European Union until Mladic was arrested. The fact that a Christian military general turned loose his army on Muslim civilians because of perceived wrongs shows the power of historical memory.

4. E. D. Sokol, *Tamerlane.* (Lawrence, Kansas: Coronado Press, 1977), pp. 32–33.

5. A. Lawler, "Iran's Hidden Jewel." *Smithsonian*, 40(1), (April 2009), p. 40.

6. B. F. Manz, *The Rise and Rule of Tamerlane.* (New York: Cambridge University Press, 1989), p. 17.

7. Sokol, *op. cit.*, 1977, p. 234.

8. J. M. Roberts, *History of the World.* (New York, Oxford University Press, 1993), p. 754. Cf. too S. Runciman, *The Fall of Constantinople 1453.* (Cambridge: The University Press, 1965).

9. N. Barbaro, *Diary of the Siege of Constantinople 1453.* (Trans. J. R. Jones). (New York: Exposition Press, 1969), p. 77. See E. Gibbon's Chapter 68 of *The Decline and Fall of the Roman Empire* on the fall of Constantinople.

10. H. Lamb, *Suleiman the Magnificent.* (Garden City, NY: International Collectors Library, 1951).

11. The Venetian walls are still intact around the ancient Famagusta fort and city that Northern Cypriot Turks call Magosa.

12. T. C. F. Hopkins, *Confrontation at Lepanto, Christendom vs. Islam.* (New York: Tom Doherty Associates, 2006). Cf. also R. Crowley, *Empires of the Sea, The Siege of Malta, The Battle of Lepanto, and the Contest for the Center of the World.* (New York: Random House, 2008).

13. J. Stoye, *The Siege of Vienna, The Last Great Trial Between Cross and Crescent.* (New York: Pegasus Books, 2007). A. Wheatcroft, *The Enemy at the Gate, Habsburgs, Ottomans and the Battle for Europe.* (New York: Basic Books, 2008).

14. T. Akcam, *From Empire to Republic, Turkish Nationalism and the Armenian Genocide.* (London: Zed Books, 2004), p. 23.

15. S. H. Astourian, "Modern Turkish Identity and the Armenian Genocide, From Prejudice to Racist Nationalism." In R. G. Hovannisian, *Remembrance and Denial, The Case of the Armenian Genocide.* (Detroit: Wayne State University Press, 1998) pp. 23–49. S. Tavernise, "Nearly a Million Genocide Victims Covered in a Cloak of Amnesia." *NYT*, (March 9, 2009), A6.

16. J. Chang & J. Halliday, *Mao, The Unknown Story.* (New York: Alfred A. Knopf, 2005).

17. A. Toynbee, *A Study of History.* (London: Oxford University Press, 1949), pp. 171-178. A. Sarafian, "The Archival Trail, Authentication of the 'The Treatment of Armenians in the Ottoman Empire, 1915–16." In R. G. Hovannisian, *Remembrance and Denial, The Case of the Armenian Genocide.* (Detroit: Wayne State University Press, 1998), pp. 23–49 For Armenian children hidden by Turks and raised as Muslim see D. Bilefsky, "Secrets Revealed in Turkey Revive Armenian Identity," *NYT* (January 10, 2010), p. A9.

18. Akcam, *op. cit.*, 2004, p. 13.

19. In 2003 a suicide group with ties to al-Qaeda drove four trucks filled with explosives into two synagogues, the British Consulate and a bank killing 60 people and wounding hundreds. Dozens were convicted in the attack. In 2008 three assailants fired on the U.S. Consulate in Istanbul killing three Turkish police officers but were themselves killed in the return fire. In mid-January 2010 more than 25 suspects were arrested on links to al-Qaeda in Ankara and Adana. Based on intelligence from those arrests, authorities arrested an additional 120 terrorist suspects of the Turkish branch of al-Qaeda the following week in 16 cities and seized explosives, arms, forged identity cards and passports and medical supplies.

### Chapter Three Endnotes

1. William Keough, since deceased, whose death was hastened, I believe, by his incarceration and daily threats on his life while in captivity.

2. B. Gabriel, *Because They Hate, A Survivor of Islamic Terror Warns America.* (New York: St. Martin's Press, 2006), p. xiii.

3. T. E. Lawrence, *Seven Pillars of Wisdom.* (London: Jonathan Cape, 1935), p. 38.

4. J. Gettleman & M. Ibrahim, "4 Teachers Are Killed in Raid By Islamists on Somali School." *NYT*, (April 15, 2008), A5.

5. http://www.thedailybeast.com/author/gerald-posner.

6. M. Crenshaw, "Explaining Suicide Terrorism: A Review Essay." *SS*, 16(2), (January-March 2007), 133–162. And see K. Ballen, *Terrorists in Love, The Real Lives of Islamic Radicals.* (New York: The Free Press, 2011).

7. See a letter indicating in the London Arabic daily, *Al-Sharq Al-Awsat* on December 21, 2001 written by Dr. Sahr Muhammed Hatem from Riyadh, "Our Culture of Demagogy Has Engendered bin Laden, Al-Zawahiri and Their Ilk."

8. Ayann Hirsi Ali quoted in an interview in *NYT*, February 4, 2007, p. wk3.

9. S. Crimp, & J. Richardson, *Why We Left Islam, Former Muslims Speak Out.* (Los Angeles: WND Books, 2008), pp. 35ff. N. Darwish, *Now They Call Me Infidel, Why I renounced Jihad for America, Israel, and the War on Terror.* (New York: Sentinel, 2006), pp. 177ff.

10. "Teaching Terrorism in Indonesian Prison." (July 2, 2011). *The Jakarta Post*, p. 3.

11. V. Asal, C.C. Fair, & S. Shellman, "Consenting to a Child's Decision to Join a Jihad: Insights from a Survey of Militant Families in Pakistan." *SCT*, 31: 973–994.

12. J. Felter, & B. Fishman, *Iranian Strategy in Iraq, Politics and 'Other Means.'* (West Point, NY: West Point Academy, October 13, 2008), p. 57.

13. *Arab Human Development Report 2009, Challenges to Human Security in the Arab Countries.* New York: UN Development Program, Regional Bureau for Arab States. Cf. E. Hanushek, "The Economic Value of Education and Cognitive Skills," in G. Sykes, *et al.*, Eds., *Handbook of Education Policy Research.* (New York: Routledge, 2009), pp. 39–56.

14. Al-Bukari living about 870, after researching Islamic traditions, established, in what he called the *Correct Book (hadith)*, 275 legendary episodes of Mohammed that emboldened the Prophet's life.
15. http://www.ibe.unesco.org/en/access-by-country/arab-states/saudi-arabia/profile-of-education.html.
16. PISA is a part of OECD, the Organization for Economic Cooperation and Development with a membership of 30 countries. And cf. http://cbuilding.org/news/u-smuslim-engagement-project.

***Chapter Four Endnotes***
1. The rise in political and social militancy in the U.S. by non-Muslim disaffected individuals and groups is also on the rise. See the magazine *Intelligence Reports* by the Southern Poverty Law Center.
2. S. Qutb, *Milestones*. (New Delhi: Islamic Book Service, 2001), pp. 118–119.
3. *Stratfor* intelligence report, June 30, 2011.
4. P. von Zielbauer & J. Hurdle, "Five are Convicted of Conspiring to Attack Fort Dix," *NYT*, (December 23, 2008), A18.

***Chapter Five Endnotes***
1. A. Rubin, "How Baida Wanted to Die." *NYTM*, (August 16, 2009), pp. 38–43. Ken Ballen interviewed Islamic militants in Saudi Arabia as reported in *Terrorists in Love, The Real Lives of Islamic Radicals*. (New York: The Free Press, 2011).
2. A. Speckhard, "The Emergence of Female Suicide Terrorists." *Studies in Conflict and Terrorism,* (November 2008), 31: 995–1023. See also L. O'Rourke, "The Woman Behind the Bomb," *IHT*, August 5, 2008, p. 6. Colleen R. LaRose and Jamie Paulin-Ramirez became radicalized Muslims because they likely both had borderline personality disorders. Other female terrorists, like Aafia Siddiqui, may be lauded as national heroines in Pakistan, but may also exhibit a bipolar disorder or similar personality defect.
3. Pedahzur, A. & A. Perlinger, *op. cit.*, M. Sageman, 2004, 137ff., F. Khosrokhavar, *Suicide Bombers, Allah's New Martyrs*. (Ann Arbor, MI: Pluto Press, 2005), & M. Crenshaw, "Explaining Suicide Terrorism: A Review Essay." *SS*, 2007, 16(2), 133–162. Jessica Stern in *Terror in the Name of God, Why Religious Militants Kill*. (New York: HarperCollins. G. Knezevic, *et al.*, "Militant Extremist Mind-Set: Proviolence, Vile World, and Divine Power." *Psychological Assessment*, (2010), 22(1), 70–86.
4. Khosrokhavar, G. (2005). *Suicide Bombers, Allah's New* Martyrs. (Trans. D. Mace) Ann Arbor, MI: Pluto Press.
5. H. Plotkin, *Evolution in Mind, An Introduction to Evolutionary Psychology*.
(Cambridge, MA: Harvard University Press, 1998); J. H. Barkow, L. Cosmides, & J. Tooby. *The Adapted Mind, Evolutionary Psychology and the Generation of Culture*.
(New York: Oxford University Press, 1992); G. M. Shepherd, *Neurobiology* (3rd Ed.)
(New York: Oxford University Press, 1994); & M. S. Gazzaniga, *Nature's Mind, the Biological Roots of Thinking Emotions, Sexuality, Language and Intelligence*. (New York: Basic Books, 1992).
6. C. Darwin, *The Origin of the Species*. (New York: Hill & Wang, 1979) & *The Descent of Man*. (London: John Murray, 1888). D. M. Buss, "The Great Struggles of Life, Darwin and the Emergence of Evolutionary Psychology. *AP*, 64(2), (February-March, 2009), 140–148. S. A. Shields & S. Bhatia, "Darwin on Race, Gender and Culture," *AP*, 64(2), (2009), 111–119. J. C. Confer, *et al.*, "Evolutionary Psychology," *AP*, February/March 2010, 110–126.
7. M. D'Esposito, "The Neural Basis of the Central Executive System of Working Memory." *NAT*, 378, 1995, 279–81; R. P. Ebstein, (1996). "Dopamine D4 Receptor (D4DR) Exon III Polymorphism Associated with the Human Personality Trait of Novelty

Seeking." *NG*, 1996, 12, 78–80; H. J. Neville, "Developmental Specificity in Neurocognitive Development in Humans." In M. S. Gazzaniga (Ed.) *The Cognitive Neurosciences.* (Cambridge, MA: The MIT Press, 1995); & R. Shadmehr, & H. H. Holcolm, "Neural Correlates of Motor Memory Consolidation." *SC*, 1997, 277, 821–825.

8. D. Ames, "Repetitive and Compulsive Behavior in Frontal Lobe Degenerations." *JNCN*, 1994, 6(2), 100–113.

9. R. J. Greenspan, "Understanding the genetic construction of behavior." *SA*, 1995, 72–78; & F. Beyotte, "Genes and behavior take center stage." *PSA*, 2003, 14.

10. P. Giancola, P, & A. Zeichner, "Neurophysological performance on tests of frontal-lobe functioning and aggressive behavior in men." *JAP*, 1994, 103(4), 832–835.

11. A. Bandura, *Aggression, A Social Learning Analysis* (Englewood Cliffs, NJ: Prentice-Hall, 1973).

12. D. M. Kingsley, "From Atoms to Traits." *SA*, (January 2009), 300(1), 52–59.

13. E. H. Erikson, *Childhood and Society*. (New York: W.W. Norton, 1950, 1963); Cf. *Identity and the Life Cycle*. (New York: W.W. Norton, 1980), & *Insight and Responsibility*. (New York: W.W. Norton, 1964).

14. R. I. Evans, *Dialogue with Erik Erikson*. (New York: Praeger, 1964, 1981), 35–36.

15. S. Jones, *The Language of the Genes, Solving the Mysteries of our Genetic Past, Present and Future*. (New York: Anchor Books, 1993), & *In the Blood: God, Genes and Destiny*. (London: HarperCollins, 1996).

16. B. Rogoff & P. Chavajay, "What's Become of Research on the Cultural Basis of Cognitive Development?" *AP*, 1995, 50(10), 859–877.

17. B. F. Skinner, *The Behavior of Organisms, An Experimental Analysis*. (New York: Appleton-Century-Crofts, 1938); *Science and Human Behavior*. (New York: Macmillan, 1953), & *Reflections on Behaviorism and Society*. (Englewood Cliffs, NJ: Prentice-Hall, 1978).

18. I. Chen, "The Social Brain." *Smithsonian*, 40(3), June 2009, 38–43. The search for the biological basis for social behavior has led researchers into examining the brains of gorillas, whales and elephants to see if there are common elements. The most striking finds in recent years have been the von Economo neurons that large mammals appear to have in common. The current working hypothesis is that large social animals have specialized wiring for empathy and social intelligence.

19. L. Festinger, *A Theory of Cognitive Dissonance*. (Stanford, CA: Stanford University Press, 1959).

20. http://people-press.org/report/?reportid=329.

21. http://www.sourcewatch.org/index.php?title=National_Intelligence_Estimate#The_2007_NIE.

22. http://press.homeoffice.gov.uk/pressreleases/counter-terror-bill-statement.

23. J. Burns, "British Doctor is Convicted in Failed Bomb Attempts." *NYT*, (December 17, 2008), A6.

24. Multiculturalism has two meanings rarely distinguished. On one hand, it refers to a society made diverse by mass immigration, and on the other to the policies governments employ to manage such diversity. The failure to distinguish between these meanings has made it easier to use attacks on multiculturalism as a means of blaming minorities for the failure of government policy. Mass immigration has been a boon to Western Europe. It has brought great economic benefits and helped create societies that are less insular, more vibrant and more cosmopolitan. Thirty years ago, Britain was a very different place than it is now. Racism was vicious, visceral and often fatal. "Paki bashing," the pastime of hunting down and beating up Britons with brown skin, became a national sport in certain circles. I remember organizing patrols on the streets of East London during the 1980s to protect South Asian families from rampaging racist thugs. Workplace discrimination was

endemic and police brutality frighteningly common. Anger at such treatment came to an explosive climax in the riots that rocked London, Liverpool, Birmingham, Bristol and other cities during the late 1970s, early 1980s and the summer of 2011. It was in response to this rage that Britain's multicultural policies emerged. The British government developed a new political framework for engaging with minority groups. Britain was now in effect divided into a number of ethnic boxes—Muslim, Sikh, Hindu, African, Caribbean and so on. The claims of minorities upon society were defined less by the social and political needs of individuals than by the box to which they belonged. Political power and financial resources were distributed by ethnicity. The new policy did not empower individuals; instead, it enhanced the authority of so-called community leaders, often the most conservative voices, who owed their positions and influence largely to their relationship with the state. In 1997, the Islamist groups that had led the campaign against Salman Rushdie's *Satanic Verses* during the 1980s helped set up the Muslim Council of Britain. Its first general secretary, Iqbal Sacranie, had once declared death "too easy" for Mr. Rushdie. Polls showed that fewer than 10 percent of British Muslims believed that the council represented their views, yet for more than a decade the British government treated it as their official representative.

25. M. J. Farrah, "The Neural Basis of Mental Imagery." In M. S. Gazzaniga (Ed.) *The Cognitive Neurosciences,* (Cambridge: The MIT Press, 1995), 963–975.

***Chapter Six Endnotes***

1. The *burqa* is the heavy full body female covering, almost always in hues of dark blue, usually worn in Afghanistan. The *hijab,* usually black and often with a grill for the eyes, is the female headscarf. The *niqab* is the full face covering.

2. Denmark, Norway, Belarus, Austria, Belgium and Finland.

3. A. Bisin, *Are Muslim Immigrants Different in Terms of Cultural Integration?* (London: Institute for the Study of Labor, 2007). A. Al-Azmeh, & E. Fokas. (Eds.) *Islam in Europe, Diversity, Identity and Influence.* (Cambridge, UK: Cambridge University Press, 2007). The mood is similar throughout Europe. See "L'Islam de France Bien Integre," *Figaro,* October, 29, 2008, & P. Hockenos, "Europe's Rising Islamophobia." *The Nation,* (May 9, 2011), pp. 22-26.

4. *L'Orient Le Jour*, November 30, 2009, p. 10.

5. F. Fukuyama, "Europe vs. Radical Islam." *Slate,* (February 27, 2006). D. Bilefsky, "Danish Antiterror Police Seize 9 Men, Mostly Young Muslims," *NYT,* (September 6, 2006), A12. My own interviews in northern Europe since 2006, and on a Fulbright research grant in 2007 to Denmark, have confirmed the rise in terrorist plots in Europe.

6. M. Bortin, "Poll Finds Discord Between Muslim and Western Worlds." *NYT,* (June 23, 2006), A3. "Teacher Attitudes Toward Muslim Student Integration into Civil Society." In D. Sharpes *et al., Handbook of International Studies in Education* (Charlotte, NC: Information Age Publishing, 2010), pp. 141-153.

7. Osman Ostroprak, Headmaster of Selam Friskole in Aarhus, Denmark, conceded that *jihad* has multiple meanings, an equivocation as the Koran is clear about its militant meaning.

8. D. Pipes, "Muslim extremism: Denmark has had enough," *The National Post* (Canada), August 27, 2002; *The Jerusalem Post* August 28, 2002; *The Jewish World Review* (27) under the title "What Denmark can teach America about dealing with Muslims—and what we ignore at our own risk," August 27, 2002.

9. J. E. Kahne & S. E. Sporte, "Developing Citizens: The Impact of Civic Learning Opportunities on Students' Commitment to Civic Participation." *AERJ,* Vol. 45(3), (September 2008), 738–766.

10. In Belarus over 60%, belong to the Russian Orthodox Church. In Norway, respondents are evenly split between those who belong to Protestantism and those who espouse no religious belief. 57% of Danish teacher respondents had Muslim students in their class.

11. http://www.islam-watch.org/Warner/Taqiyya-Islamic-Principle-Lying-for-Allah.htm. D. Pryce-Jones, *The Closed Circle, An Interpretation of the Arabs.* (Chicago: Ivan R. Dee, 2009), pp. 4 & 38.

12. The *Chicago Tribune* reported in September 19, 2004 that a Muslim Brotherhood chapter was operating in America legally but clandestinely. The Supreme Leader in Egypt of the Muslim Brotherhood, Mohammed Habib, acknowledged its existence. It remains to be seen whether or not new overtures to the Brotherhood, that has reversed a longstanding policy, will result in modifying the Brotherhood's strategy. Cf. D.D. Kirkpatrick & S. L. Myers, "Overtures to Egypt's Islamist Reverse Longtime U.S. Policy," *The New York Times*, A1ff.

13. In *Divine Governance of the Human Kingdom*, c. 1459.

14. C. Fourest, *Brother Tariq, The Doublespeak of Tariq Ramadan.* (New York: Encounter Books, 2008).

15. T. Ramadan, *What I Believe.* (Oxford: Oxford University Press, 2010).

16. http://www.gallup.com/consulting/worldpoll/26410/Gallup-Center-Muslim-Studies.aspx.

17. M. Thomas & R. Nayan. (2010). *Muslim Teenagers in Public Schools.* Paper Presented at the Annual Meeting of the American Educational Research Association, Denver, May 2, 2010.

18. D. Pipes, "Which Has More Islamist Terrorism, Europe or America? *The Jerusalem Post*, (July 3, 2008).

19. A. Elliott, "The Jihadist Next Door." *NYTM*, (January 31, 2010), pp. 26ff.

20. D. Cave & C. Gentile, "Five Convicted in Plot to Blow Up Sears Tower as Part of Islamic Jihad," *NYT*, (May 13, 2009), A19.

21. http://www.usdoj.gov/opa/pr/2007/September/07_nsd_760.html.

22. N. Darwish, *Now They Call Me Infidel, Why I Renounced Jihad for America, Israel, and the War on Terror.* (New York: Sentinel, 2006), pp. 143ff. "It is very clear that a good Muslim will never compromise on *aqidah* (basic principles of Islamic teaching) that should be obeyed without reserve. Muslims can still work together with followers of other faiths . . . but they will never work together in terms of religious beliefs." (Aries Musnandar, Lecturer at the State Islamic University in Malang, Indonesia as reported in *The Jakarta Post*, April 22, 2010. Aries was an attendee at a lecture I gave at the State Islamic University in Malang in July 2011.

23. B. Bawer, *While Europe Slept, How Radical Islam is Destroying the West from Within.* (New York: Broadway Books, 2006).

***Chapter Seven Endnotes***

1. Jumanah Imad Albahri, a Muslim student at the University of California at San Diego, publicly called for genocide of all Jews. Posted by Jamie Glazov on *FrontPage Magazine* on June 18, 2010.

2. http://www.mideastweb.org/hamas.htm.

3. *Ibid.* See also M. H. Yousef, *Son of Hamas, A Gripping Account of Terror, Betrayal, Political Intrigue, and Unthinkable Choices.* (Carol Stream, IL: Salt-River, Tyndale House Publishers, 2010). Yousef is the son of Sheikh Hassan Yousef, one of the founders of Hamas in 1986. He was a long-time collaborator with Shin Bet, the Israeli internal security forces, and became a Christian while in an Israeli prison and later moved to the U.S. in 2007.

4. Hezbollah militias are typically trained in Iran, some in Syria and in Lebanon's Bekaa Valley. Palestinian militia members cannot leave their territories in the West Bank or Gaza so they are schooled within the territories in terrorism, rocket firings, weapons and suicide bombings. F. Ajami, "The Ways of Syria, Stasis in Damascus," *FA*, 88(3), (May/June 2009), pp. 153–158.

5. J. J. Mearsheimer & S. M. Walt, *The Israel Lobby and U.S. Foreign Policy.* (New York: Farrar, Strauss and Giroux, 2007), 31–32.

6. R. M. Mead, "Change They Can Believe In, To Make Israel Safe, Give Palestinians Their Due." *FA*, 88(1), (January/February 2009), 61–63.

7. B. Morris, "Why Israel Feels Threatened." *NYT*, (December 30, 2008), A21.

8. A. Pedahzur & A. Perlinger, *op. cit.*

9. D. Sharpes, "Towards Peace and Security," *JT*, March 20, 2002.

10. H. Siegman, "A Last Chance at Middle East Peace?" *TN*, (January 12, 2009), 25–27.

11. http://www.tellthechildrenthetruth.com/gallery/index.html.

12. http://www.mideastweb.org/mebalfour.htm.

13. B. Gabriel, *Because They Hate, A Survivor of Islamic Terror Warns America.* (New York: St. Martin's Griffin, 2006), p. 178.

14. *Ibid.*,

15. www.leader.ir.

16. http://www.thedailybeast.com/author/gerald-posner. H. Evans, "Poisoning Minds in Bethlehem." *USNWR*, 2008, 145(14), 76. The Youth Division of Fatah regularly honors her. A public square in Ramallah was named in her honor in 2010.

17. H. Agha, H. & R. Malley. "How Not to Make Peace in the Middle East." *NYTRB*, (January 15, 2009), 42–45.

18. Mark LeVine on January 13, 2009 on *Al Jazeera* at: http://english.aljazeera.net/focus/war_on_gaza/2009/01/2009110112723260741.html.

19. I. Kershner, "Finding Fault in the Palestinian Messages That Aren't So Public. *The New York Times*, (December 20, 2011), A14.

20. R. M. Mead, "Change They Can Believe In, To Make Israel Safe, Give Palestinians Their Due." *FA*, 88(1), (January/February 2009), 59–76; & H Agha & R. Malley, "How Not to Make Peace in the Middle East. *NYRB*, (January 15, 2009), 42–45, and "Obama and the Middle East." *NYBR*, LVI (10), (June 11, 2009), 67–69.

***Chapter Eight Endnotes***

1. B. Rougier, *Everyday Jihad, The Rise of Militant Islam Among Palestinians in Lebanon.* (Cambridge, MA: Harvard University Press, 2007), pp. 200ff.

2. Nir Rosen at: http://bostonreview.net/BR33.1/rosen.php (January/February 2008).

3. Quoted in R. Baer, 2008, *op. cit.*, p. 55.

4. R. F. Worth, "Up North, Hothouse of Tension in Lebanon." *NYT*, (October 16, 2008), A6ff; & "To Fuel Quest, Hezbollah Harnesses Youth Piety." *NYT*, (November 21, 2008), A1ff.

5. See reports from the Combating Terrorism Center at West Point at: www.ctc.usma.edu/Iran_Iraq.asp.

6. W. Phares, "The Intelligence Services in Lebanon During the War 1975–1990," *JICI*, 7(3), 363–381. A. Kober, "The Israel Defense Forces in the Second Lebanon War: Why the Poor Performance?" *JSS*, 31(2), (February 2008), 3–40. 10. Baer, 2008, *op. cit.*, pp. 158–160.

7. J. Felter, J. & B. Fishman, *Iranian Strategy in Iraq, Politics and Other Means.* (West Point, NY: West Point Academy, 2008).

240

8. R. Gaddo, "Lebanon's Bloody Sunday." *NYT*, October 23, 2008, A27. Col. Tim Geaghty, retired Marine Commander, and one of the endorsers of this book, was the marine commander in Beirut in 1983.

9. R. C. McFarlane, "From Beirut to 9/11." *NYT*, October 23, 2008, A27.

10. B. Gabriel, *Because They Hate*. (New York: St. Martin's Griffin, 2006).

11. *Ibid.*, p. 87.

12. *Ibid.*, p. 103.

13. W. Sultan, *A God Who Hates*. (New York: St. Martin's Press, 2009), 400ff. For an extended history of the impact of Nazism in the 1930s and 1940s on the Arab world see D. Pryce-Jones, *The Closed Circle, An Interpretation of the Arabs*. (Chicago: Ivan R. Dee, 2009), pp. 184–221.

14. P. Seale, *Asad of Syria, The Struggle for the Middle East*. (Berkeley: University of California Press, 1988). Cf. D. Pipes, *Greater Syria, The History of an Ambition*. (New York: Oxford University Press, 1990).

15. A part of Assad's personal history is his knowledge of how the French ceded large swaths of what had been Syrian homesteads in the north beyond Aleppo to Turkey in 1921. Part of the land was parceled back to Damascus in 1942 prior to Syria's independence from France in 1946. This Syrian history colored his attempt to get lands returned from Israel, and even his attempt to re-acquire control over Lebanon that the French had given to Maronite Christians. Cf. Seale, *op. cit.*, pp. 322ff.

16. N. Bakri, "As Syria Hits City, U.N. Say Toll Climbs," *The New York Times*, (November, 9, 2011), A4. More than 19,000 Syrians ha fled into Turkey and were living in refugee villages.

17. N. Bakri, (November 15, 2011). King of Jordan Becomes First Arab Leader to Tell Syria's Assad to Quit. *The New York Times*, A10.

### Chapter Nine Endnotes

1. Carmen bin Laden, former sister-in-law to Osama bin Laden, in *Inside the Kingdom, My Life in Saudi Arabia*. (New York: Grand Central Publishing, 2004), p. 63. R. Baer, "The Fall of the House of Saud." *AM*, (May 2003), 53–62, & *Sleeping With the Devil, How Washington Sold Our Soul for Saudi Crude*. (New York: Three Rivers Press, 2003).

2. Ibn Taymiyya. (1984). *A Muslim Theologian's Response to Christianity*. (Ed. & Trans. T. F. Mitchell). (Delmar, NY: Caravan Books, 1984), p. 105. See *sura* 5:72-73 & *sura* 9:30-31 in the Koran.

3. N. Shea, "This is a Saudi Textbook," *The Washington Post*. (June 24, 2006), p. 13. See MacFarquar, "Anti-Western and Extremist Views Pervade Saudi Schools." *NYT*, (October 19, 2001), B1. King Abdullah in 2009 began to crackdown on Wahhabi extremism in schools and for the first time named a woman, Noura al-Fayez, as Deputy Education Minster. Cf. also C. Allen, *God's Terrorists, The Wahhabi Cult and the Hidden Roots of Modern Jihad*. (New York: Da Capo Press, 2007). The Islamic Saudi Academy, a private college prep school in Fairfax County, Virginia, has operated since 1984 funded by the Saudi government.

4. http://www.usamemorial.org/sept11036.asp.

5. Qutb, S. (2001). *Milestones*. New Delhi: Islamic Book Service, p. 57.

6. Peter Bergen, journalist, terrorism specialist and National Security Analyst, interviewed Osama in 1997. *Holy War, Inc.* (2001) and *The Osama bin Laden I Know: An Oral History of al Qaeda's Leader* (2006). It was during an interview with Bergen in 1997 in Afghanistan that Osama declared war on the United States.

7. The anti-Semite and fiery orator for jihad, Abdullah Azzam (1941-1989), ignited Muslim recruits everywhere. He was killed in a violent bomb blast in Peshawar, Pakistan in 1989 with two of his sons.

8. Osama's 1998 *fatwa* (though he is not a cleric) was short and direct. "The ruling to kill Americans and their allies—civilians and military—is an individual duty for every Muslim who can do it in any country in which it is possible to do it, in order to liberate the al-Aqsa Mosque and the holy mosque (Mecca) from their grip, and in order for the enemy to move out of the land of Islam, defeated and unable to threaten any Muslim." *Understanding Militancy & Islam Newsletter*, 7(4), July/August 2008, p. 8.

9. S. Coll, *Ghost Wars, The Secret History of the CIA, Afghanistan, and Bin Laden, From the Soviet Invasion to September 10, 2001.* (New York: Penguin Books, 2005), pp. 319–320.

10. D. Fury, *Kill Bin Laden, A Delta Force Commander's Account of the Hunt for the World's Most Wanted Man.* (New York: St. Martin's Press, 2008), pp. 68–69. Oddly, Rumsfeld's nearly 800 page memoir, *Known and Unknown, A Memoir* (New York: Sentinel, 2011) contains no reference to al-Qaeda—extremely odd for a Secretary of Defense not to mention anything about the organization led by the world's most notorious terrorist, and the sponsor of the 9/11 attack on American soil.

11. D. Rumsfeld, *Known and Unknown, A Memoir* (New York: Sentinel, 2011), p. 403.

T. Gillespie & J. A. Agnew (February 17, 2009). "Finding Osama bin Laden: An Application of Biogeographic Theories and Satellite Imagery." MIT International. Review web essay at: http://web.mit.edu/mitir/.

12. http://www.interpol.int/Public/FinancialCrime/MoneyLaundering/Hawala/default.asp.

13. R. A. Clarke, *Your Government Failed You, Breaking the Cycle of National Security Disasters.* (New York: HarperCollins, 2008), p. 134.

***Chapter Ten Endnotes***

1. B. Bhutto, *Reconciliation, Islam, Democracy, and the West.* (New York: HarperCollins, 2008), p. 210. A similar assessment is by B. Riedel, *Deadly Embrace, Pakistan, America, and the Future of the Global Jihad.* Washington, DC: (Brookings Institution Press. 2011) who offers a good summary of Pakistan's history and relations with the U.S.

2. Bhutto, *op. cit.,* p. 2. Cf. also B. Keller, "The Pakistanis Have a Point." *The New York Times Magazine*, (December 18, 2011), pp. 44ff.

3. D. Sanger, "Obama's Worst Pakistan Nightmare." *NYTM*, (January 11, 2009), p.37. S. Rahimi & C. Gall, "Pakistan Accused of Link to Kabul Suicide Bombers," *NYT*, (March 20, 2009), p. A8.

4. Zaidi, S. M. A. (October 2009). "The Taliban Organisation in Pakistan." *RUSI* 154(5), 40–47 & Center for Research and Security Studies Report, Islamabad, May 20, 2010.

5. D. Sanger, "Obama's Worst Pakistan Nightmare." *NYTM*, (January 11, 2009), 32–37. Cf. also Schmidt, J. R. (June/July 2009). "The Unraveling of Pakistan." *Survival*, 51(3), 29–54.

6. R. Suskind, *The Way of the World, A Story of Truth and Hope in an Age of Extremism.* (New York: HarperCollins, 2008).

7. C. C. Fair, "Pakistan's Relations with Central Asia: Is Past Prologue?" JSS, 31(2), (April 2008), 201–227.

8. A. Rashid, *op. cit.* & "Pakistan on the Brink." *NYRB*, June 11, 2009, LVI(10), pp. 12–16, is an update on conditions. Cf. W. Dalrymple, "Pakistan in Peril." *NYBR*, (February 12, 2009), 39–42. Reidel (2011, p. 21) reports that from 1971 and 1988 their numbers multiplied from 900 to 8,000 official religious schools and another 25,000 unregistered ones. Under Zia ul-Haq diplomas granted by the *madrassas* became the equivalent of university degrees. The *madrassa*, like cathedral schools in medieval Europe, teach only religion and adhere strictly to that mission. All *madrassas* have fundamentalist instructors.

9. S. Tavernise, "From Rural Pakistan, Tales of a Hidden World Lived and Shared." *NYT*, July 25, 2009, p. A5.

10. A. Rashid, 2008, *op. cit.*, p. 235. For a sample of jihad-inspired curricula taught in public schools see: http://www.crss.pk/rreport.php.

11. M. Burleigh, *Blood & Rage, A Cultural History of Terrorism.* (London: Harper Perennial, 2009), p. 376.

12. V. Asal, C. C. Fair, & S. Shellman, "Consenting to a Child's Decision to Join a Jihad: Insights from a Survey of Militant Families in Pakistan." *Studies in Conflict and Terrorism*, (2008), 31: 973–994.

13. F. Zakaria, "The Future of American Power, How America Can Survive the Rise of the Rest." *FA*, (87(3), (May/June 2008), 33.

14. D. Filkins, "Talibanistan, Right at the Edge." *NYTM*, (September 7, 2008) p. 57.

15. A. Rashid, 2008, *op. cit.*, p. 273, & "The Afghanistan Impasse." *NYRB*, (September 8, 2009), LVI (15), 42–45.

16. http://www.vbs.tv/full_screen.php?s=DGFE2305DC&sc=1363196

17. "The New 'Hunter-Killer." *Fortune*, (November 10, 2008), p. 128. See R. Pantucci, "Deep Impact, The Effect of Drone Attacks on British Counter-Terrorism," *The RUSI Journal*, (October 2009), Vol. 154(5), 72–75.

18. S. Crimp, S. & J. Richardson, *Why We Left Islam, Former Muslims Speak Out.* (Los Angeles: WND Books, 2008), xviii & xix.

19. J. Perlez, & R. E. Worth, "Indian Tracing Terror Attack to 2 Militants." *NYT*, (December 5, 2008), A1.

20. R. F. Worth, "Lack of Preparedness Comes Brutally to Light." NYT, (December 4, 2008), A18. Cf. "Using Tapes and a Timeline to Trace the Mumbai Massacre," NYT, November 19, 2009, p. C8.

21. A. Rashid, 2008, *op. cit.*, 237.

22. crss.pager@gmail.com.

23. C. Gall, "Pakistanis Tied to 2007 Attack on Americans," *The New York Times*, September 27, 2011, A1ff.

24. A. Rashid, "Pakistan on the Brink." *NYRB*, LVI (10), (June 11, 2009), pp. 12–16.

25. Perlez, J., D. E. Sanger, E. Schmitt. (December 1, 2010). "Wary Dance With Pakistan in Nuclear World." *The New York Times*, A1ff). Cf. also B. Alexander & A. Millar, *Tactical Nuclear Weapons, Emergent Threats in an Evolving Security Environment.* (Washington DC: Brasseys, 2003).

***Chapter Eleven Endnotes***

1. S. Mackey, *The Iranians, Persia, Islam and the Soul of a Nation.* (New York: Plume Books, 1998).

2. *Ibid.*, pp. 224ff.

3. R. Khomeini, *Islam and Revolution.* (Trans. H. Algar) (Berkeley, CA: Mizan Press, 1981), p. 28.

4. *Ibid.*, p. 57.

5. *Ibid.*, p. 127.

6. *Ibid.*, p. 128.

7. *Ibid.*, p. 266.

8. http://www.fordham.edu/halsall/source/urban2-5vers.html.

9. Meachan, J. (June 29, 2009) "Theocracies are Doomed. Thank God." *Newsweek*, p. 8.

10. See Nazila Fathi, "Iran: The Deadly Game." *NYRB*, (February 25, 2010), LVII(3), 12–14 for an eyewitness account by an Iranian and a former *New York Times* correspondent in Tehran.

11. *Implementation of the NPT Safeguards Agreement and relevant provisions of Security*

*Council resolutions in the Islamic Republic of Iran.* Vienna: International Atomic Energy Agency (November 9, 2011). "The Agency will not be in a position to provide credible assurance about the absence of undeclared nuclear material and activities in Iran unless and until Iran provides the necessary cooperation with the Agency, including by implementing its Additional Protocol." Cf. D. Sanger & W. J. Broad, "U.N Agency Says Iran Data Points to A-Bomb Work, *The New York Times*, (September 9, 2011), p. A1ff. Both the U.S. and Israel were said to have been involved in the assassination of several of Iran's nuclear scientists beginning in 2010.

12. D. Sanger, "U.S. Rejected Aid for Israeli Raid on Nuclear Site." *NYT*, (January 11, 2009), A1.

13. J. Felter, J. & B. Fishman *Iranian Strategy in Iraq, Politics and 'Other Means'* (West Point, NY: West Point Academy, October 13, 2008), p. 17.

14. C. Kane, "Nuclear Decision-Making in Iran: A Rare Glimpse," (Crown Center for Middle East Studies, Brandeis University, May 2006), No. 5. Also B. Alexander & A. Millar, 2003, *op. cit.* on tactical nuclear weapons.

15. M. Fischetti, "Nuclear Weapons in a New World," *Scientific American*, November, 2007, 74–85; F. N. von Hippel, "Rethinking Nuclear Fuel Recycling, *SA*, May 2008, 88–93; T. B. Cochran & M.G. McKinzie, "Detecting Nuclear Smuggling, *SA*, April 2008, 98–104.

16. D. Albright, P. Brannan & A. Scheel, "Iranian Entities' Illicit Military Procurement Networks, " ISIS at: http://www.isis-online.org. C. Thompson, "Is Iran Going to Build a Bomb?" *NYTM*, (August 16, 2009), pp. 22–25.

17. Stuxnet—The Trojan Horse. A Noble Weapon? *World Security Network*, February 20, 2011. newsletter@worldsecuritynetwork.com.

18. V. Nasr, & R. Takeyh, "The Costs of Containing Iran, Washington's Misguided New Middle East Policy.*" FA*, 87(1), 2008, 85–94.30. F. Leverett & H. M Leverett, "Have We Already Lost Iran?" *NYT*, May 24, 2009, wk10. B. Luers, *et al.*, "How to Deal with Iran." *NYRB*, (February 12, 2009), 45–48. The U.S. Treasury Department has sanctioned Iran's commercial banks and companies that do business with the Al-Quds force.

*Chapter Twelve Endnotes*

1. I. M. Lapidus, *A History of Islamic Societies* (2nd Ed.) (New York: Cambridge University Press, 2002), p. 416. Cf. D. Robinson, *Muslim Societies in African History.* (Cambridge, UK: Cambridge University Press, 2004).

2. See especially F. A. Tamin, "The War on Terror, Islamic Threat, Public Policy and the Phenomenon of Exclusion by Integration: The Case of Tanzania." In A.A. Oladosu, *Islam in Contemporary Africa, On Violence, Terrorism and Development.* (Newcastle, UK: Cambridge Scholars Publishing, 2007), pp. 169–184. Tamin fails to mention the 1998 terrorist attacks in his own country, but does elaborate extensively on how colonial rule is the root cause of all the country's Muslim problems. Both he and the editor Oladosu failed to respond to invitations to comment on the contents of their articles for this study.

3. M. Burleigh, *Blood & Rage, A Cultural History of Terrorism.* (London, Harper Perennial, 2008), p. 361.

4. The FBI has built a vast network of spies to prevent another terrorist attack in the U.S. See T. Aaronson, "The Informants, Terrorists for the FBI." *Mother Jones*, T. (September/October 2011), pp. 30-43.

5. E. Schmitt, "U.S. Training in West Africa Aims to Stave Off Extremists." *NYT*, (December 13, 2008). A1.

6. N. Schmidle, "The Saharan Conundrum." *NYTM*, (February 15, 2009), 34–39 & Cf. http://worlddefensereview.com/pham052908.shtml.

244

7. F. Ajami, *The Dream Palace of the Arabs, A Generation's Odyssey*. (New York: Vintage Books, 1998).

8. Almaz Khasanov quoted in M. Schwirtz, "Russia's Knotty Policies on Islam, Mirrored in a Trial." *NYT*, (June 3, 2009), A14.

9. R. Kramer, "A Rattled Chechnya is Gripped by an Epidemic of Political Kidnappings." *NYT*, (July 19, 2009), A12. C. King, C. & R. Menon. "Prisoners of the Caucasus, Russia's Invisible Civil War." *Foreign Affairs*, 89(4), (July/August 2010), 20–34.

10. G. M. Hahn, *Russia's Islamic Threat*. (New Haven: Yale University Press, 2007).

11. A. Jacobs, E. Wong, & K. Bradsher, "Attacks Add to Chinese Concerns on Security." *IHT*, (August 5, 2008), p. 1.

12. E. Wong, "China Releases Arrest Report for Pre-Olympics Crackdown." *NYT*, (January 6, 2009), A10.

13. E. Wong, "Wary of Islam, China Tightens a Vise of Rules." *The New York Times*, (October 19, 2008). A1.  A. Jacobs, "China Fears Ethnic Strife Could Agitate Uighur Oasis." *NYT*, (July 23, 2009), A6.

14. H. Karlekar, *Bangladesh, The Next Afghanistan?* (New Delhi: Sage Publications, 2005).

15. *Ibid.*, p. 80.

16. L. Thaib, *Islamic Political Representation in Malaysia*. (Kuala Lumpur, Malaysia: University of Malaya Press, 2005).

17. Minter, *op. cit.*, 2011, p. 158-59.

18. A. Kingsbury, "Defeating al-Qaeda." *USNWR*, 145(10), (2008), pp. 42-43.

19. R. A. Witular & H. Widhiarto, "Can Prison Bars Put an End to Ba'asyir's Access to Jihadists?" *The Jakarta Post*, (June 17, 2011), A1 & A3.

20. J. B. Haseman, & E. Lachia, "Getting Indonesia Right, Managing a Security Partnership with a Non-allied Country." *JFQ*, V. 54, (3rd Quarter 2009), 89–91.

### Epilogue Endnotes

1. N. Darwish, *Now They Call Me Infidel, Why I Renounced Jihad for America, Israel, and the War on Terror*. (New York: Sentinel, 2006), p. 243.

2. "You shall have no strange gods before me," and "There is no God but God."

3. V. Nasr, *Forces of Fortune, The Rise of the New Muslim Middle Class and What It Will Mean for our World*. (New York: Free Press, 2009).

4. http://cbuilding.org/news/u-s-muslim-engagement-project.

5. Commission on the Prevention of Weapons of Mass Destruction, Proliferation and Terrorism, available at: *www.preventwmd.gov*.

# REFERENCES

Aaronson, T. (September/October 2011). The Informants, Terrorists for the FBI. *Mother Jones*, pp. 30-43.

Abdo, G. (2000). *No God but God, Egypt and the Triumph of Islam*. New York: Oxford University Press.

Abdulafia, D. (1988). *Frederick II, A Medieval Emperor*. London: Allen Lane, The Penguin Press.

Abu Aabi, I. (1984). Sayyid Qutb: From Religious Realism to Radical Social Criticism. *The Islamic Quarterly*, 28.

Aciman, A. (November 20, 2011). After Egypt's Revolution, Christians are Living in Fear. *The New York Times*, A7.

Ahmad, K. (1982). *Islam, Its Meaning and Message*. (3rd Ed.). Kuala Lumpur: Dewan Pustakan Islam.

Ajami, F. August 2, 2009). Strangers in the Land. *The New York Review of Books*, 1ff.

—— (May/June 2009). The Ways of Syria, Stasis in Damascus. *Foreign Affairs*, 88(3), pp. 153–158.

—— (1998). *The Dream Palace of the Arabs, A Generation's Odyssey*. New York: Vintage Books.

Alexander, B. & A. Millar. (2003). *Tactical Nuclear Weapons, Emergent Threats in an Evolving Security Environment*. Washington DC: Brasseys.

Ali, A. Y. (2007). *The Qur'an*. Elmhurst, NY: Tahrike Tarsile Qur'an, Inc.

Allawi, A. (January 2, 2012). How Iraq Can Define Its Destiny. *The New York Times*, A19.

—— (2009). *The Crisis of Islamic Civilization*. New Haven: Yale University Press.

Allen, C. (2007). *God's Terrorists, The Wahhabi Cult and the Hidden Roots of Modern Jihad*. New York: Da Capo Press.

Akcam T. (2004). *From Empire to Republic, Turkish Nationalism and the Armenian Genocide*. London: Zed Books.

Al-Attas, M. A. (Ed.) (1979). *Aims and Objectives of Islamic Education*. London: Hodder & Stoughton.

Al-Azmeh, & E. Fokas. (Eds.) (2007). *Islam in Europe, Diversity, Identity and Influence*. Cambridge, UK: Cambridge University Press.

Al-Fakhri (1947). *Al-Fakhri on the Systems of Government and the Moslem Dynasties*. (Trans. C. E. J. Whitting). London: Luzac and Company.

Ali Khalidi, M. (2005). *Medieval Islamic Philosophical Writings*. New York: Cambridge University Press.

Allawi, A. (2007). *The Occupation of Iraq, Winning the War, Losing the Peace*. New Haven: Yale University Press.

Allen, C. (2006). *God's Terrorists, The Wahhabi Cult and the Hidden Roots of Modern Jihad*. Cambridge, MA: Da Capo Press.

Allen, R. (2000). *An Introduction to Arabic Literature*. New York: Cambridge University Press.

Amar, P. (May 23, 2011). Egypt After Mubarak. *The Nation*, pp. 11-15.

Amos, D. (2010). *Eclipse of the Sunnis, Power, Exile, and Upheaval in the Middle East*. New York: PublicAffairs.

*Appiah, K. A. (2008). How Muslims Made Europe.* The New York Review of Books, *55(17), pp. 59–62.*

Arab Human Development Report 2002, Creating Opportunities for Future Generations. *New York: United Nations.*

*Arab Human Development Report 2009, Challenges to Human Security in the Arab Countries.* New York: UN Development Programme, Regional Bureau for Arab States.

Armstrong, K. (2000). *Islam, A Short History.* New York: Modern Library.

—— (2000). *The Battle for God.* New York: Ballantine Books.

—— (1993). *The History of God.* New York: Ballantine Books.

Asal, V, C.C. Fair, & S. Shellman. (2008). Consenting to a Child's Decision to Join a Jihad: Insights from a Survey of Militant Families in Pakistan. *Studies in Conflict and Terrorism,* 31: 973–994.

Aslan, R. (2009). *How to Win a Cosmic War, God, Globalization, and the End of the War on Terror.* New York: Random House.

Astourian, S. H. (1998). Modern Turkish Identity and the Armenian Genocide, From Prejudice to Racist Nationalism. In R. G. Hovannisian, *Remembrance and Denial, The Case of the Armenian Genocide.* Detroit: Wayne State University Press, pp. 23–49.

Austen, I. (September 25, 2008). Canada Terror Trial Reveals a Group Full of Talk But Little Else. *The New York Times,* A5.

Ayoob, M. (1981). *The Politics of Islamic Reassertion.* London: Croom Helm.


Baer, R. (2008). *The Devil We Know, Dealing with the New Iranian Superpower.* New York: Crown Publishers.

—— (2003a). *Sleeping With the Devil, How Washington Sold Our Soul for Saudi Crude.* New York: Three Rivers Press.

—— (May 2003b). The Fall of the House of Saud. *The Atlantic Monthly,* 53–62.

Baker, A. (May 23, 2011). Frenemies. *Time,* pp. 37-43.

Bakhash, S. (2006). The Rise and Fall of Reform in Iran. *The Berlin Journal,* (12), 22-25.

Ballen, K. (2011). *Terrorists in Love, The Real Lives of Islamic Radicals.* New York: The Free Press.

Baran, Z. (2006). In *Varietate Concordia,* Reaching Out to Europe's Moderate Muslims. *The Berlin Journal,* 12, 12-14.

Barbaro, N. (1969). *Diary of the Siege of Constantinople 1453.* (Trans. J. R. Jones). New York: Exposition Press.

Barks, C. (1995). *The Essential Rumi,* San Francisco: HarperSanFrancisco.

Barnes S. & J. Dao, (June 2, 2009). Gunman Kills Soldier Outside Recruiting Station. *The New York Times,* A16.

Bar-Tal, D., & G. Salomon, (2006). Israeli-Jewish Narratives of the Israeli-Palestinian Conflict: Evolvement, Contents, Functions and Consequences. In R. I. Rotberg (Ed.). *Israeli and Palestinian Narratives of Conflict: History's Double Helix.* Bloomington: Indiana University Press.

Battutah, I. (2002). *The Travels of Ibn Battutah.* London: Picador.

Bawer, B. (2009). *Surrender, Appeasing Islam, Sacrificing Freedom.* New York: Doubleday.

—— (2006). *While Europe Slept, How Radical Islam is Destroying the West from Within.* New York: Broadway Books.

Bayat, A. (May 31, 2011). Moving Towards a Muslim Democracy. *The Straits Times,* A21.

Becker, J. (December 14, 2011). Lebanese Bank Was Hub of Hezbollah's Financing. *The New York Times*, A1ff.

Belasco, A. (September 2, 2010). *The Cost of Iraq, Afghanistan, and Other Global War on Terror Operations Since 9/11*. Washington, DC: Congressional Research Service.

Bell, R. (1960, 1937). *The Qur'an*. Edinburgh: T & T Clark.

Ben Z. (1990). Between Warning and Response: The Case of the Yom Kippur War. *Journal of Intelligence and CounterIntelligence, 7*(3), 363–381.

Bergen, P. (May 20, 2011). A Long Time Going. *Time*, 42-45.

Bergen, P. & K. Tiedemann. (December 2010). The Drone Wars, Killing by Remote Control in Pakistan. *The Atlantic*, pp. 50-51.

Bergen, P. & S. Pandey. (June 14, 2005). The Madrassa Myth. *The New York Times*, A19.

Berman, S. (March/April 2010). From the Sun King to Karzai, Lessons for State Building in Afghanistan. *Foreign Affairs*, 89(2), 2–9.

Berque, J. (1964). *The Arabs*. New York: Frederick A. Praeger.

Bhutto, B. (2008). *Reconciliation, Islam, Democracy, and the West*. New York: Harper Collins.

Bilefsky, D. (September 6, 2006). Danish Anti-terror Police Seize 9 Men, Mostly Young Muslims, *The New York Times*, A12.

—— (January 10, 2010). "Secrets Revealed in Turkey Revive Armenian Identity," *The New York Times*, A9.

Bin Laden, C. (2004). *Inside the Kingdom, My Life in Saudi Arabia*. New York: Grand Central Publishing.

Bisch, J. (1962). *Behind the Veil of Arabia*. (Trans. R. Spink). New York: E. P. Dutton.

Bisin, A. (2007). *Are Muslim Immigrants Different in Terms of Cultural Integration?* London: Institute for the Study of Labor.

Bonner, M. (2006). *Jihad in Islamic History*. Princeton: Princeton University Press.

Bonthous, J–M. (1994). Understanding Intelligence Across Cultures, *Journal of Intelligence and CounterIntelligence, 7*(3), 275–311.

Burleigh, M. (2009). *Blood & Rage, A Cultural History of Terrorism*. London, Harper Perennial.

Buruma, I. (May 14, 2009). Living with Islam. *The New York Review of Books*, LVI(8), pp. 11–13.

Buss, D. M. (February-March, 2009). The Great Struggles of Life, Darwin and the Emergence of Evolutionary Psychology. *American Psychologist*, 64(2), 140–148.

Braudel, F. (1993). *A History of Civilizations*. New York: Penguin.

Brettler, M. Z. (1995). *The Creation of History in Ancient Israel*. London: Routledge.

Brown, R. (1995). *Managing the Learning of History*. London: David Fulton.

Brzezinski, Z. (May/June 2009). A Tale of Two Wars, The Right War in Iraq and the Wrong One. *Foreign Affairs*, 88(3), 148–152.

Burckhardt, J. (1979). *Reflections on History*. Indianapolis: Liberty Fund.

—— (1949, 1880). *The Age of Constantine the Great*. Berkeley: University of California Press.

Burleigh, M. (2008). *Blood and Rage, A Cultural History of Terrorism*. London: Harper Perennial.

Burkitt, F. C. (1925). *The Religion of the Manichees*. New York: AMS Press.

Burns, J. (October 20, 2008). An Old Afghanistan Hand Offers Lessons of the Past. *The New York Times*, A8.

248

—— (December 17, 2008). British Doctor is Convicted in Failed Bomb Attempts. *The New York Times*, A6.

Calabrisi, M. (May 20, 2011). A Revival in Langley. *Time*, 52-57.
—— (October 24, 2011). Did Iran Plot to Kill. *Time*, 12-13.
Caldwell, C. (February 5, 2006). Islam on the Outskirts of the Welfare State. *The New York Times Magazine*, 55–59.
—— (2009). *Reflections on the Revolution in Europe, Immigration, Islam and the West*. New York: Doubleday.
Campbell, D. (2009). *Joker One, A Marine Platoon's Story of Courage, Leadership and Brotherhood*. New York: Random House.
Carter, J. (1986). *The Blood of Abraham*. Boston: Houghton Mifflin.
Chamie, J. (1981). *Religion and Fertility: Arab, Christian and Muslim Differentials*. London: Cambridge University Press.
Chang J. & J. Halliday. (2005). *Mao, The Unknown Story*. New York: Alfred A. Knopf.
Chang, K. (November 3, 2009). Creationism, Minus a Young Earth, Emerges in the Islamic World. *The New York Times*, D3.
Chen, I. (June 2009). The Social Brain. *Smithsonian*, 40(3), 38–43.
Chenoweth, E. & E. Lowham. (December 2007). On Classifying Terrorism: A Potential Contribution of Cluster Analysis for Academics and Policy-makers. *Defense and Security Analysis*, 23(4), 345–357.
Chertoff, M. (January/February 2009). The Responsibility to Contain, Protecting Sovereignty Under International Law. *Foreign Affairs*, 88(1), 130–147.
Chivers, C. J. (2003, April 27). Instruction and Methods from Al Qaeda took root in North Iraq with Islamic fighters. *The New York Times*, yt 14.
—— (February 1, 2009). Slain Exile Detailed Chechen Ruler's Cruelty. *The New York Times*, A1.
Choudhry, A. (1982). Principles of Islamic Economics. *Islamic Studies*, 21.
Christia, F. & M. Semple. (July/August 2009). Flipping the Taliban, How to Win in Afghanistan. *Foreign Affairs*, 88(4), 34–45.
Ciovacco, C. & H.G. Clark, J. Van de Velde. (July/August 2011). Ending al-Qaeda. *The American Interest*, VI(6), 40-49.
*Claiming the Future*. (1995). Washington, DC: The World Bank.
Clay, R. A. (June 2008). Science vs. Ideology. *Monitor on Psychology*, 39(6), 41–43.
Clarke, R. A. (Jan/Feb. 2005). Ten Years Later. *The Atlantic Monthly*, 61–77.
—— (2008). *Your Government Failed You, Breaking the Cycle of National Security Disasters*. New York: HarperCollins.
—— (May 3, 2011). Bin Laden's Dead. Al Qaeda's Not. *The New York Times*, A19.
*Cochran T. B. & M. G. McKinzie. (April 2008). Detecting Nuclear Smuggling.* Scientific American, *98–104*.
Cockburn, A. (2000). Libya, An End to Isolation? *National Geographic*, 198(5), 2–31.
Cohat, Y. (2004). *The Vikings, Lords of the Seas*. London: Thames and Hudson.
Cohen, R. (August 13, 2009). Iran: The Tragedy & the Future. *The New York Review of Books*, LVI, 13, 7–10.
Cole, D. (December 4, 2008). A Larger War on Terror? *The New York Review of Books*, 15–18.
Coll, S. (2005). *Ghost Wars, The Secret History of the CIA, Afghanistan, and Bin Laden, From the Soviet Invasion to September 10, 2001*. New York: Penguin Books.
*Condition of Education 2008 in Brief*. (June 2008). Washington, DC: National Center for Education Statistics, U.S. Department of Education.

Confer, J.C., J.A. Easton, D.S. Fleishman, C.D Goetz, D.M.G. Lewis, C. Perilloux, D. M. Buss. Evolutionary Psychology, *American Psychologist*, February/March 2010, 65(2), 110–126.

Cook, B. J. (2001). Islam and Egyptian Higher Education: Student Attitudes. *Comparative Education Review*, 45(3), 379-409.

—— (2000). Egypt's National Education Debate. *Comparative Education,* 36(4), 477-490.

Corbin, H. (February 1977). The Theory of Visionary Knowledge in Islamic Philosophy. Nouvelles de L'Institute Catholique de Paris, No 1.

Cox, A, (September 11, 2011). A 9/11 Tally: $3.3 Trillion. *The New York Times*, ny13.

Crenshaw, M. (2007). Explaining Suicide Terrorism: A Review Essay. *Security Studies*, 16(2), 133–162.

Crimp, S & J. Richardson. (2008). *Why We Left Islam, Former Muslims Speak Out.* Los Angeles: WND Books.

Crowley, R. (2008). *Empires of the Sea, The Siege of Malta, The Battle of Lepanto, and the Contest for the Center of the World.* New York: Random House.

Cudsi, A. S. & Ali, E. H. (1981). *Islam and Power.* London: Croom Helm.


Dalrymple, W. (2005, December 1). Inside the Madrassas. *The New York Review of Books*, 16-20.

—— (February 12, 2009). Pakistan in Peril. *The New York Review of Books*, 39–42.

Danner, M. (2005, Sept. 11). Taking Stock of the Forever War. *The New York Times Magazine*, 43ff.

Darwish, N. (2006). *Now They Call Me Infidel, Why I Renounced Jihad for America, Israel, and the War on Terror.* New York: Sentinel.

David, P. (July 25, 2009). Waking from Its Sleep, Special Report on the Arab World. *The Economist, 1–16.

Dawisha, A. (1999). Identity and Political Survival in Saddam's Iraq. *Middle East Journal,* 53(4), 553-67.

____ (2000). Arab Nationalism and Islamism: Competitive Past, Uncertain Future. *International Review of Education*, 46, 183-203.

DeAngelis, T. (November 2009). Understanding Terrorism. *APA Monitor on Psychology*, 40(10), 61–64.

Dekmejian, R. H. (1995). *Islam in Revolution, Fundamentalism in the Arab World.* (2nd Ed.) Syracuse, NY: Syracuse University Press.

Desai, M. (2007). *Rethinking Islamism, The Ideology of the New Terror.* New York: I. B. Tauris.

Dickey, C. (December 12, 2005). Women of Al Qaeda. *Newsweek*, 21-30.

Diner, D. (Spring 2006). In the Sphere of the Sacred, Modernity's Predicament in the Middle East. *The Berlin Journal*, 12, pp. 16-21.

Donohue, J. J. & Esposito, J. L. (1982). *Islam in Transition, Muslim Perspectives.* Oxford: Oxford University Press.

Durant, W. (1950). *The Age of Faith.* New York: Simon and Schuster.

—— (1957). *The Reformation.* New York: Simon & Schuster.


Ebrahim Z. (June 16, 2001). Ethnic Cleansing Feared in Balochistan. *The Jakarta Post*, p. 6.

Elliott, A. (January 31, 2010). The Jihadist Next Door. *The New York Times Magazine*, pp. 26ff.

—— (March 20, 2011). A Marked Man in America (Yashir Qadhi). *The New York Times Magazine,* 34ff.

250

Emerson, S. (2002). *American Jihad, The Terrorists Living Among Us*. New York: The
    Free Press.
Erlanger, S. (October 7, 2008). A Pro-Church Law Opens Doors to a French Mosque.
    *The New York Times*, A10.
—— (February 13, 2010). For a French Imam, Islam's True Enemy is Radicalism. *The
    New York Times*, p. A5.
—— (April 12, 2011). French Legislation Takes Effect Banning Fall-Face Coverings.
    *The New York Times*, A4.
Esposito, J. L. & Lalwani, S. B. (June 6, 2011). Getting It Right About Islam and Muslim
    Americans. *The Jakarta Post*, p. 13.
Evans, A. (2006). Understanding Madrassahs. *Foreign Affairs*, 85(1), 9-16.
Evans, H. (2008). Poisoning Minds in Bethlehem. *U.S. News and World Report*,
    145(14), 76.
Ewing, J. (May 1, 2011). Germany's Terrorism Arrests Disrupt A Broader Investigation
    of Al-Qaeda. *The New York Times*, A17.

Fair, C. C. (April 2008). Pakistan's Relations with Central Asia: Is Past Prologue? *The
    Journal of Strategic Studies*, 31(2), 201–227.
Farivar, M. (2009). *Confessions of a Mullah Warrior*. New York: Atlantic Monthly Press.
Feldman, N. (2004). *What We Owe Iraq, War and the Ethics of Nation Building*.
    Princeton: Princeton University Press.
Felter, J. & B. Fishman (October 13, 2008). *Iranian Strategy in Iraq, Politics and 'Other
    Means.'* West Point, NY: West Point Academy.
Festinger, L. (1959). *A Theory of Cognitive Dissonance*. Stanford, CA:
    Stanford University Press.
Filkins, D. (April 11, 2011). Letter from Yemen, After the Uprising. *The New Yorker*,
    pp. 39-51
Finkel, C. (2005). *Osman's Dream. The History of the Ottoman Empire*. New York:
    Basic Books.
Fischetti, M. (November 2007). Nuclear Weapons in a New World. *Scientific American*,
    74–85.
Fourest, C. (2008). *Brother Tariq, The Doublespeak of Tariq Ramadan*. New York:
    Encounter Books.
Fukuyama, F. (February 27, 2006). Europe vs. Radical Islam. *Slate*.
Fuller, T. (August 25, 2009). Malaysia Postpones Whipping of Woman Who Drank
    Beer. *The New York Times*, A6.
Fury, D. (2008). *Kill Bin Laden, A Delta Force Commander's Account of the Hunt for the
    World's Most Wanted Man*. New York: St. Martin's Press.

Gabriel, B. (2006). *Because They Hate, A Survivor of Islamic Terror Warns America*.
    New York: St. Martin's Griffin.
—— (2008). *They Must Be Stopped, Why We Must Defeat Radical Islam and How We
    Can Do It*. New York: St. Martin's Press.
Gall, C. & T. Shah (October 20, 2008). Taliban Insurgents in Afghanistan Stop Bus
    and Behead as Many as 30 Passengers. *The New York Times*, A5.
Gall, C. (September 27, 2011). Pakistanis Tied to 2007 Attack on Americans, *The New
    York Times*, A1ff.
Ganji, A. (2008), The Latter-Day Sultan, Power and Politics in Iran. *Foreign Affairs*,
    87(6), 45–66.
Gascoigne, B. (1971). *The Great Moghuls*. London: Jonathan Cape.

Gates, R. M. (2009). A Balanced Strategy, Reprogramming the Pentagon for a New
    Age. *Foreign Affairs,* 88(1), 28–40.

Geertz, C. (1968). *Islam Observed, Religious Development in Morocco and Indonesia.*
    New Haven: Yale University Press.

Gelling, P. (October 7, 2008a). Islamic Group Gains Power in Indonesia. *The*
    *New York Times*, A12.

—— (November 9, 2008b). 3 Executed for Attacks That Killed 202 in Bali. *The New*
    *York Times,* A6.

Gellman, B. (May 9, 2011). How the G-Man Got His Groove Back. *Time*, 22-32.

Gerecht, R. M. (February 11, 2010). Iran, Beacon of Liberty? *The New York Times*,
    A27.

Gerges, F. A. (2000). The End of Islamist insurgency in Egypt? Costs and Prospects.
    *Middle East Journal*, 4, 592-612.

Gettleman, J & M. Ibrahim. (April 15, 2008). 4 Teachers Are Killed in Raid
    By Islamists on Somali School. *The New York Times*, A5.

Ghazi, A. (1984). Problems of Religious Instruction in Textbooks in North
    America, *Journal of the Institute of Muslim Minority Affairs*, 5.

Gibbon, E. & S. Ockley (1873). *The Saracens, Their History and the Rise and Fall*
    *of Their Empire.* London: Rederick Warne and Co.

Gibbon, E. (1952). *The Decline and Fall of the Roman Empire.* New York: Penguin.

Gillani, W. (November 6, 2011). Pakistani Court Indicts 7 in Bhutto's Assassination.
    *The New York Times*, p. 11.

Gillespie, T. & J.A. Agnew (February 17, 2009). Finding Osama bin Laden: An
    Application of Biogeographic Theories and Satellite Imagery.
    MIT International Review web essay at http://web.mit.edu/mitir/.

Gladstone, R. (November 20, 2011). A Diplomatic Face Seeks to Counter Iran's Critics.
    *The New York Times*, A10.

Glazov, J. (February 26, 2008). Confronting Islam. FrontPageMagazine.com.

*Global Trends 2025: A Transformed World.* (November 2008). (Publication of the
    National Intelligence Council). Washington DC: US Government Printing
    Office.

Glubb, J. B. (1963). *The Great Arab Conquests.* Englewood Cliffs, NJ: Prentice-Hall.

Golberg, J. (June 2011). Danger: Falling Tyrants. *The Atlantic*, 307(5), 46-54.

Goodstein, L. (March 2, 2009). Poll Finds U.S. Muslims Thriving, But Not Content.
    *The New York Times*, A11.

Goodwin, J. (1998). *Lords of the Horizon, A History of the Ottoman Empire.* New York:
    Henry Holt and Company.

Goody, J. (2004). *Islam in Europe.* Cambridge, UK: Polity.

Gopal, A. (December 22, 2008). Who Are the Taliban? *The Nation*, 17–20.

Gordon, P. H. (November/December 2007). Can the War on Terror Be Won? *Foreign*
    *Affairs*, 86(6), 53–66.

Gorenberg, G. (July/August 2011). How to Open the Road. *The American Prospect*,
    pp. 12-17.

Gorman, S. (July 15, 2009). Goals of CIA Plan Emerge. *The Wall Street Journal.* p. 10.

*Guerilla Warfare and Special Forces Operations.* (September 1961). Washington, DC:
    Department of the Army.

Guevara, C. (1985). *Guerilla Warfare.* Lincoln: University of Nebraska Press.

Gunter, B. (Fall 2011). Ten Years After. *Intelligence Report*, 143, pp. 19-31.

Grose, T. K. (December 22, 2008). The Rise of Islamic Banking. *U.S. News and World*
    *Report*, 41–42.

Haass, R. N. & M. Indyk. (2009). Beyond Iraq, A New Strategy for the Middle East. *Foreign Affairs*, 88(1), 41–58.

Habib, I. (ed.) (1997). *Akbar and His India*. Delhi: Oxford University Press.

Hahn, G. M. (2007). *Russia's Islamic Threat*. New Haven: Yale University Press.

Halliday, F. (March 12, 2009). One Big Unhappy Family: The Bin Ladens. *The New York Review of Books*, 11–13.

Hamid, A. F. A. (1999). The Making of Nation-States in the Arab World: The Role of Oil, Islam and Arab Nationalism. *Jurnal Ikim*, 7(2), 19-43.

Hanushek, E. (2009). The Economic Value of Education and Cognitive Skills. In G. Sykes, B. Schneider, D. N. Plask, & T. C. Ford (eds). *Handbook of Education Policy Research*. New York: Routledge, pp. 39–56.

Haseman, J. B. & E. Lachia. (3rd Quarter 2009). Getting Indonesia Right, Managing a Security Partnership with a Non-allied Country. *Joint Force Quarterly*, V. 54, 89–91.

Hassan, F. (2001). Challenging the Stereotypes of Fundamentalism: An Islamic Feminist Perspective. *The Muslim World*, 91(1-2), 55-69.

Hassam, R. (1984). Iran's Revolutionaries. *Third World Quarterly*, 6.

Healy, J. March 11, 2012). Exodus from North Signals Iraqi Christians' Slow Decline. *The New York Times*, p. 6.

Hess, A. C. (1985). Islamic Civilization and the Legend of Political Failure. *Journal of Near Eastern Studies*, 44.

Hobsbawn, E. (1998). *On History*. London: Abacus.

Hockenos, P. (May 9, 2011). Europe's Rising Islamophobia. *The Nation*, 22-26.

Hodgson, M. (1974). *The Venture of Islam* (v.3). London: The University of Chicago Press.

Holmes, J. A. (2009). Where Are the Civilians? How to Rebuild the U.S. Foreign Service. *Foreign Affairs*, 88(1), 148–160.

Hopkins, T.C. F. (2006). *Confrontation at Lepanto, Christendom vs. Islam*. New York: Tom Doherty Associates.

Horton, S. (March 2010). The Guantanamo "Suicides," A Camp Delta Sergeant Blows the Whistle. *Harper's Magazine*, Vol. 320(1918), pp. 27–37.

Hosseini, K. (2007). *A Thousand Splendid Suns*. London: Bloomsbury.

Hovannisian, R. G. (1998). *Remembrance and Denial, The Case of the Armenian Genocide*. Detroit: Wayne State University Press.

Huntington, S. P. (1996). *The Clash of Civilizations and the Remaking of the World Order*. New York: Simon and Schuster.

Hurtzley, J. D. (2007). *Unmasking Terror, A Global Review of Terrorist Activities*. Washington DC: The Jamestown Foundation

Husain, S. S. & Ashraf, S. A. (1979). *Crisis in Muslim Education*. London: Hodder & Stoughton.

Hussain, M. F. (1984). The Islamization of Psychology. *The Islamic Quarterly*, 28.

Hyde, G. D. M. (1978). *Education in Modern Egypt, Ideals and Realities*. London: Routledge & Kegan Paul.

Ibn Arabi (1997). *Divine Governance of the Human Kingdom*. Louisville, KY: Fons Vitae.

—— (1976). *Whoso Knoweth Himself*. Abington, UK: Beshara Publications.

Ibn Taymiyya. (1984). *A Muslim Theologian's Response to Christianity*. (Ed. & Trans. T. F. Mitchell). Delmar, NY: Caravan Books.

Iqbal, A (March 11, 2002). Pakistan to Expel Foreign Seminary Students. *Gulf News*, 29.

*Implementation of the NPT Safeguards Agreement and relevant provisions of Security*

253

*Council resolutions in the Islamic Republic of Iran*, (November 9, 2011).
Vienna: International Atomic Energy Agency.

Jacobs, A. (July 23, 2009). China Fears Ethnic Strife Could Agitate Uighur Oasis. *The New York Times*, A6.

Jacobs, A., E. Wong, & K. Bradsher. (August 5, 2008). Attacks Adds to Chinese Concerns on Security. *International Herald Tribune*, 1

Jalal, A. (2008). *Partisans of Allah, Jihad in South Asia*. Cambridge, MA: Harvard University Press.

Juergensmeyer, M (1993). *The New Cold War? Religious Nationalism Confronts the Secular State*. Berkeley, CA: University of California Press.

Kakutani, M. (September 23, 2008). A Dialogue and a Discourse on America's Global Role. *The New York Times*, B7.

Kane, C. (May 2006). *Nuclear Decision-Making in Iran: A Rare Glimpse*. Brandeis University: Crown Center for Middle East Studies, No. 5.

Karimi, N. (November 24, 2009). Iran Begins Large-Scale War Games to Protect Nuclear Sites. *The Daily Star* (Beirut), p. 1.

Karlekar, H. (2005). *Bangladesh, The Next Afghanistan*? New Delhi: Sage.

Karsh, E. (2006). *Islamic Imperialism, A History*. New Haven: Yale University Press.

Keddie, N. (1972). *Sayyid Jamal ad-Din Al-Afghani*. Berkeley, CA: University of California Press.

Keller, B. (December 18, 2011). The Pakistanis Have a Point. *The New York Times Magazine*, pp. 44ff.

Kennedy, H. (1981). *The Early Abbasid Caliphate*. London: Croom Helm.

Kershaw, S. (January 10, 2010). The Terrorist Mind: An Update. *The New York Times*, wk1.

Kershner, I. (January 31, 2009). Israeli Advocacy Group Begins Campaign to Help Palestinians Sue Over Settlements. *The New York Times*, A8.

—— (December 20, 2011). Finding Fault in the Palestinian Messages That Aren't So Public. *The New York Times*, A14.

Khaldun, I. (1967). *The Muqaddimah, An Introduction to History*. Princeton: Princeton University Press.

Khomeini, R. (1981). *Islam and Revolution*. (Trans. H. Algar) Berkeley, CA: Mizan.

—— (no date). *Imam Khomeini's Last Will and Testament*. Washington, DC: Algerian Embassy.

Khosrokhavar, G. (2005). *Suicide Bombers, Allah's New* Martyrs. (Trans. D. Mace) Ann Arbor, MI: Pluto Press.

Kincheloe, J. L. & S. R. Steinberg, C. D. Stonebanks. (2010). *Teaching Against Islamophobia*. New York: Peter Lang.

King, C. & R. Menon. (July/August 2010). Prisoners of the Caucasus, Russia's Invisible Civil War. *Foreign Affairs*, 89(4), 20–34.

Kingsbury, A. (2008). Defeating al-Qaeda. *U.S. News & World Report*, 145(10), 42-43.

Kingsley, D. M. (January 2009). From Atoms to Traits. *Scientific American*, 300(1), 52–59.

Kirchick, J. (July/August 2011). Playing With Fire: Dispatch from Tajikistan. *The American Interest*, VI(6), 57-63.

Kirkpatrick, D. D. (January 24, 2012). Chaotic Start to Egypt's First Freely Elected Parliament. *The New York Times*, A4.

Kirkpatrick, D. D. & S. L. Myers, Overtures to Egypt's Islamist Reverse Longtime U.S. Policy, *The New York Times*, A1ff.

Kissinger, H. (October 12, 2009). Deployments and Diplomacy. *Newsweek*, 38–41.

254

Klein, J. (May 20, 2011). Obama 1, Osama 0. *Time*, pp. 30-35.

Klaussen, J. (2005). *The Islamic Challenge, Politics and Religion in Western Europe*. New York: Oxford University Press.

Knezevic, G. L. Stankov, G. Saucier. (2010). Militant Extremist Mind-Set: Proviolence, Vile World, and Divine Power. *Psychological Assessment*, 22(1), 70–86.

Kroenig, M. (January/February 2012). Time to Attack Iran, Why a Strike is the Least Bad Option. *Foreign Affairs*, 76-86.

Kober, A. (February 2008). The Israel Defense Forces in the Second Lebanon War: Why the Poor Performance? *Journal of Strategic Studies*, 31(2), 3–40.

Kokole, O. H. (1984). The Islamic Factor in African-Arab Relations. *Third World Quarterly*, 6.

Kovach, G. C. (November 15, 2008). U.S. Wins Convictions in Retrial of Terrorism-Financing Case. *The New York Times*, A13.

Kowalski, M. (March 2008). Global Insurgency or Global Confrontation? Counter-insurgency Doctrine and the 'Long War' on Terrorism. *Defense and Security Analysis*, 24(1), 65–71.

Kramer, A. E. (July 19, 2009). A Rattled Chechnya is Gripped by an Epidemic of Political Kidnappings. *The New York Times*, A12.

Kramer, M. (1980). *Political Islam*. London: Sage Publications.

Krasner, S. D. (January/February 2012). Talking Tough to Pakistan, How to End Islamabad's Defiance. *Foreign Affairs*, 87-96.


Lacey, R. (2009). *Inside the Kingdom, Kings, Clerics, Modernists, Terrorists, and the Struggle for Saudi Arabia*. New York: Viking.

Lamb, H. (1951). *Suleiman the Magnificent*. Garden City, NY: International Collectors Library.

Landau, R. (1959). *The Philosophy of Ibn 'Arabi*. London: George Allen & Unwin.

Lapidus, I. M. (2002). *A History of Islamic Societies* (2nd Ed.) New York: Cambridge University Press.

Latifa (2001). *My Forbidden Face, Growing Up Under the Taliban, A Young Woman's Story*. New York: Hyperion.

Lawler, A. (April 2009). Iran's Hidden Jewel. *Smithsonian*, 40(1), 36–46.

Lawrence, T. E. (1935). *Seven Pillars of Wisdom*. London: Jonathan Cape.

Lefkowitz, J. (May 5, 2008). Terrorists Behind Bars. www.nefafoundation.org.

Leverett F. & H. M Leverett (May 24, 2009). Have We Already Lost Iran? *The New York Times*, wk10.

Levi, M. (2008). Stopping Nuclear Terrorism, The Dangerous Allure of a Perfect Defence. *Foreign Affairs*, 87(1), 131–140.

Levy, C. J. (August 18, 2009). Central Asian Nations Sound alarm Over Seeping Islamic Radicalism. *The New York Times*, A4.

Lewis, B. (September 2006). Freedom and Justice in Islam. *Imprimis*, 35(9), 1–7.

—— (1993). Islam in History, Ideas, People and Events in the Middle East. Chicago: Open Court.

—— (2009). Free at Last? The Arab World in the Twenty-first Century. *Foreign Affairs*, 88(2), 77–88.

—— (2002). *What Went Wrong? The Clash Between Islam and Modernity*. New York: Harper Perennial Books

Limage, L. (2000). Education and Muslim identity: The Case of France. *Comparative Education*, 36(1), 73-94.

Lindsay, J. & R. Takeyh. (March/April 2010). After Iran Gets the Bomb. *Foreign Affairs*, 89(2), 33–49.

Long, A. (April-May 2008). The Anbar Awakening. *Survival*, 50(2), 67–94.

Luers, B., T. Pickering, & J. Walsh. (February 12, 2009). How to Deal with Iran. *The New York Review of Books*, 45–48.

Lynch, M. (July/August 2010). Veiled Truths, The Rise of Political Islam in the West. *Foreign Affairs*, 89(4), 138–147.


Maalouf, A. (2006). *The Crusades Through Arab Eyes*. London: Saqi Essentials.

MacFarquar, N. (October 19, 2001). Anti-Western and Extremist Views Pervade Saudi Schools. *The New York Times*, B1.

—— (November 12, 2008). Saudi Arabia, Missing Pluralism at Home, Seeks U.N. Platform to Promote It Abroad. *The New York Times*, A14.

Mackey, S. (1998). *The Iranians, Persia, Islam and the Soul of a Nation*. New York: Plume Books.

Macy, E. (August 2009). Apache, The Taliban vs. The World's Deadliest Helicopter. *Air & Space*, 24(3), 36–43.

McCants, W., J. Brachman, & J. Felter. (2006). *Militant Ideology Atlas*. West Point, NY: Combating Terrorism Center.

McFarlane, R. C. (October 23, 2008). From Beirut to 9/11. *The New York Times*, A27.

McClellan, S. (2008). *What Happened, Inside the Bush White House and Washington's Culture of Deception*. New York: PublicAffairs.

McVeigh, K. (July 27, 2007) Woman Arraigned 'Honor Killing' of Daughter-in-Law During Trip to India. *The Guardian*, 11.

Magnusson, M. (1992). *Vikings!* London: BBC Books.

Malandra, W. W. (1983). *An Introduction to Ancient Iranian Religion*. Minneapolis: University of Minnesota Press.

Manz, B. F. (1989). *The Rise and Rule of Tamerlane*. New York: Cambridge University Press.

Mayer, J. (2003, March 10). Lost in the Jihad. *The New Yorker*, 50–59.

Mead, R. M. (January/February 2009). Change They Can Believe In, To Make Israel Safe, Give Palestinians Their Due. *Foreign Affairs*, 88(1), 59–76.

Mearsheimer, J. J. & S. M. Walt. (2007). *The Israel Lobby and U.S. Foreign Policy*. New York: Farrar, Strauss and Giroux.

Meddeb, A. (2003). *The Malady of Islam*. New York: Basic Books.

Metz, S. (3rd Quarter 2009). Destroy the Taliban's Sanctuary. *Joint Force Quarterly*, V. 54(62).

Miller, J. (1997). *God has 99 names, Reporting from a Militant Middle East*. New York: Touchstone, Simon & Schuster.

Milton-Edwards, B. (2005). *Islamic Fundamentalism Since 1945*. London: Routledge.

Miner, M. (July/August 2011). The Americanization of Islamism. *The American Interest*, VI(6), 65-73.

Miniter, R. (2011). *Mastermind, The Many Faces of the 9/11 Architect, Khalid Shaikh Mohammed*. New York: Sentinel.

Mishra, P. (August 27, 2008). A Jihad Grows in Kashmir. *The New York Times*, A23.

Maloney, S. (April 2012). The Case for Containing a Nuclear Iran. *American Prospect*, 23(3), 12-19.

Mojeed, M. (January 23, 2012). Dozens Killed by Radical Islamic Group in Nigeria. *The New York Times*, A11.

Muller, J. Z. (2008). Us and Them, The Enduring Power of Ethnic Nationalism. *Foreign Affairs*, 87(2), 18–35.

256

Mulrine, A. (October 13, 2008). Heading Deeper into Afghanistan. *US News and World Report*. 20–24.

Naipaul, V. S. (1981). *Among the Believers, An Islamic Journey*. New York: Penguin Books.
Nagel, T. (2000). *The History of Islamic Theology, From Muhammad To the Present*. Princeton: Markus Wiener Publishers.
Nasr, S. H. (1968). *Science and Civilization in Islam*. New York: Barnes & Noble Books.
Nasr, V. & R. Takeyh. (2008) The Costs of Containing Iran, Washington's Misguided New Middle East Policy. *Foreign Affairs*, 87(1), 85–94.
Nasr, V. (2009). *Forces of Fortune, The Rise of the New Muslim Middle Class and What It Will Mean for our World*. New York: Free Press.
Norton, A. R. (2007). *Hezbollah, A Short History*. Princeton: Princeton University Press.
Norwich, J. J. (2003). *Byzantium, The Decline and Fall*. London: The Folio Society.

O'Balance, E. (1997). *Islamic Fundamentalist Terrorism, 1979–95*, The Iranian Connection. London: Macmillan.
O'Shea, S. (2006). *Sea of Faith, Islam and Christianity in the Medieval Mediterranean World*. New York: Walker and Company.
Oladosu, A. A. (2007). *Islam in Contemporary Africa, On Violence, Terrorism and Development*. Newcastle, UK: Cambridge Scholars Publishing.
O'Rourke, L. (August 5, 2008). The Woman Behind the Bomb. *International Herald Tribune*, 6.
Oufkir, M. (2000). *Stolen Lives, Twenty Years in a Desert Jail*. New York: Hyperion.
Ottaway, D. (May/June 2009). The King and Us, U.S.-Saudi Relations in the Wake of 9/11. *Foreign Affairs*, 88(3), 121–131.

Pamuk, O. (December 18, 2008). My Turkish Library. *The New York Review of Books*, 69.
Pantucci, R. (October 2009). Deep Impact, The Effect of Drone Attacks on British Counter-Terrorism, *The RUSI Journal*, Vol. 154(5), 72–75.
Payne, R. (1959). *The Holy Sword, The Story of Islam from Muhammad to the Present*. New York: Harper & Brothers.
Pedahzur, A. & A. Perlinger. (2006). The Changing Nature of Suicide Attacks: A Social Network Perspective. *Social Forces*, 84(4).
Pelham, N. & M. Rodenbeck. (November 5, 2009). Which Way for Hamas? *The New York Review of Books*, 57(17), 35–37.
Phares, W. (1994). The Intelligence Services in Lebanon During the War 1975–1990. *Journal of Intelligence and CounterIntelligence*, 7(3), 363–381.
Philby, H. St. John. (1934). *Harun Al Rashid*. New York: D. Appleton-Century Co.
Pierpont, C. R. (April 18, 2011). East is West, Freya Stark's Travels in Arabia. *The New Yorker*, pp.116-123.
Pillar, P. (2011). *Intelligence and U.S. Foreign Policy*. New York: Columbia University Press.
Piontkovsky, A. (June 3, 2011). The Caucasian Dark Circle. *The Jakarta Post*, p. 6.
Pipes, D. (2003). *Militant Islam Reaches America*. New York: W. W. Norton.
—— (1990). *Greater Syria, The History of an Ambition*. New York: Oxford University Press.
*Policy and Governance in Palestinian Refugee Camps*. (2009) Beirut, Lebanon: Issam Fares Institute, American University of Beirut.

Pollack, K. M. (July 15, 2008). How the Middle East Wastes Its Oil Wealth. *International Herald Tribune*, 8.

Polgreen, L. (December 1, 2008). Tense Calm Settles on Nigerian Town After Religious Clashes Kill Hundreds. *The New York Times*, A6.

Pryce-Jones, D. (2009). *The Closed Circle, An Interpretation of the Arabs*. Chicago: Ivan R. Dee.

Qutb, S. (2001). *Milestones*. New Delhi: Islamic Book Service.

Rahman, F. (1966). *Islam*. London: Weidenfield & Nicolson.

Rahman, H. U. (1995). *A Chronology of Islamic History, 570–1000 CE*. London: Ta–Ha Publishers.

Ramadan, T. (2010). *What I Believe*. Oxford: Oxford University Press.

Rashid, A. (2008). *Descent Into Chaos, The United States and the Failure of Nation Building in Pakistan, Afghanistan, and Central Asia*. New York: Viking.

—— (June 11, 2009). Pakistan on the Brink. *The New York Review of Books*, LVI(10), 12–16.

____ (September 8, 2009). The Afghanistan Impasse. *The New York Review of Books*, LVI (15), 42–45.

—— (September 11, 2011). And Hate Begat Hate. *The New York Times*, sr1ff.

*Report on Terrorism.* (April 30, 2009). Washington DC: National Counterterrorism Center.

Rich, P. (2009). *Creating the Arabian Gulf, The British Raj and the Invasions of the Gulf.* Lanham, MD: Lexington Books.

Riedel, B. (2011). *Deadly Embrace, Pakistan, America, and the Future of the Global Jihad*. Washington, DC: Brookings Institution Press.

Riley-Smith, J. (1997). *The Oxford Illustrated History of the Crusades*. New York: Oxford University Press.

Roberts, A. (February/March 2009). Doctrine and Reality in Afghanistan. *Survival*, 51(1), 29–60.

Roberts, J. M. (1993). *History of the World*. New York, Oxford University Press.

Robinson, D. (2004). *Muslim Societies in African History*. Cambridge, UK: Cambridge University Press.

Rodenbeck, M. (January 15, 2009). The Iran Mystery Case. *The New York Review of Books*, 35–38.

—— (2000). Witch Hunt in Egypt. *The New York Review of Books,* 47(18), 39–41.

Rougier, B. (2007). *Everyday Jihad, The Rise of Militant Islam Among Palestinians in Lebanon*. Cambridge, MA: Harvard University Press.

Rohde, D. (October 2, 2001). 12-year-olds take up arms against Taliban. *The New York Times*, A1.

Rosen, L. (2005) What We Got Wrong. *The American Scholar*, 74(1), 42ff.

Rosenberg, M (January 4, 2012). Taliban to Open Office and Maybe a Door to Talks. *The New York Times*, A3.

Roy, O. (2007). *Secularism Confronts Islam*. (Trans. G. Holoch). New York: Columbia University Press.

Rubin, A. (August 16, 2009). How Baida Wanted to Die. *The New York Times Magazine*, 38–43.

Rubin, E. (August 9, 2009). Karzai in His Labyrinth. *The New York Times Magazine*, 26ff.

Rubin, B. R., & A. Rashid. (2008). From Great Game to Grand Bargain, Ending Chaos in Afghanistan and Pakistan. *Foreign Affairs*, 87(6), 30–44.

Rudner, M. (1983). Higher Education and the Development of Science in Islamic Countries: A Comparative Analysis. *Canadian Journal of Development Studies*, 4.

Rudolph, K. (1978). *Manicheeism.* Leiden: E. J. Brill.

Runciman, S. (1965). *The Fall of Constantinople 1453.* Cambridge: The University Press.

Sabbagh, K. (2006). *Palestine, History of a Lost Nation.* New York: Grove Press.

Sageman, M. (2004). *Understanding Terror Networks.* Philadelphia: University of Pennsylvania Press.

Said, E. (1995). *Orientalism.* New York: Penguin Books.

Sanger, D. & W. J. Broad, (September 9, 2011). U.N Agency Says Iran Data Points to A-Bomb Work, *The New York Times*, p. A1ff.

—— (January 11, 2009), U.S. Rejected Aid for Israeli Raid on Nuclear Site. *The New York Times*, A1.

____ (December 5, 2011). Explosion Seen as Big Setback to Iran Missiles. *The New York Times*, A1ff.

Saunders, J. J. (1965). *A History of Medieval Islam.* New York: Barnes & Noble.

Saragih, (June 15, 2011). Conservative Youth Support Democracy. *The Jakarta Post*, A1.

Scheifer, S. (1984). Jihad: Sacred Struggle in Islam. *Islamic Quarterly*, 28.

Scheurer, M. (2004). *Imperial Hubris: Why the West is Losing the War on Terror.* Washington, DC: Brasseys.

—— (2008). *Marching Toward Hell, America and Islam After Iraq.* New York: Free Press.

Schmidle, N. (January 6, 2007). Next-Gen Taliban. *The New York Times Magazine*, 48 ff.

—— (February 15, 2009). The Saharan Conundrum. *The New York Times Magazine*, 34–39.

Schmidt, J. R. (June/July 2009). The Unraveling of Pakistan. *Survival*, 51(3), 29–54.

Schmidt, M.S. (January 23, 2012). Rising Strife Threatens Iraqi Stability. *The New York Times*, A4.

Schmitt, E. & R. F. Worth. (March 15, 2012). With Arms for Yemen Reels, Iran Seeks Wider Mideast Role. *The New York Times*, A1.

Schwartz, S. (2002). *The Two Faces of Islam, The House of Saud from Tradition to Terror.* New York: Doubleday.

Schwirtz, M. (June 3, 2009). Russia's Knotty Policies on Islam, Mirrored in a Trial. *The New York Times*, A14.

Seale, P. (1988). *Asad of Syria, The Struggle for the Middle East.* Berkeley: University of California Press.

Sen, A. (July 20, 2000). East and West: The Reach of Reason. *The New York Review of Books*, 33–38.

Sengupta, S. (July 26, 2008). Hindu-Christian Tension Turns Deadly in India, *International Herald Tribune*, p. A11.

Shah, T. (January 2, 2009). Militants Kill at Least 20 Bodyguards of Afghan Military Commander, *The New York Times*, A10.

Shane, S. & B. Weiser. (April 26, 2011). Dossier Paints Father and Son Tied to Militancy. *The New York Times*, A1.

Shane, S. (September 11, 2011). Al Qaeda's Outside Shadow. *The New York Times*, 10.

Shannon, V. P. & M. Dennis. (April-May 2007). Militant Islam and the Futile Fight for Reputation. *Security Studies*, 16(2), 287–317.

Sharpes, D. K. (Ed.) (2010). *Handbook of International Studies in Education.* Charlotte, NC: Information Age Publishing.

—— (2010). Cognitive Abilities of United Arab Emirates Female Education Students. *Handbook on International Studies in Education* Charlotte, NC: Information Age Publishing, pp. 95–105.

—— (2008). The Psychology of Radical Islam. Paper Presented at the Annual Meeting of the Rocky Mountain Psychological Association, April 12, 2008.

—— (December 30, 2006). To Win in Iraq, U.S. Must Join World Bazaar. *Scottsdale Tribune,* A17.

—— (January 10, 2003). Radical Islam: Martyrdom or Madness? *The Scottsdale Tribune,* A21.

—— (September 22, 2002). As Long as Saddam is Gone, 3 Iraqs are Much Safer Than 1. *The Arizona Republic,* V3.

—— (January 27, 1991). Saddam's Nuclear Ability Reason Enough for War. *The Salt Lake Tribune,* 16.

—— (1987). An Inquiry into Values of Islamic Fundamentalism. *The Journal of Value Inquiry,* XXI, 309-315.

—— (Oct.-Dec., 1986). Teacher Training and Higher Education in Selected Islamic Countries. *Journal of Education for Teaching,* 245-58.

Shorrock, T. (2008). *Spies for Hire, The Secret World of Intelligence Outsourcing.* New York: Simon and Schuster.

Shea, N. (June 24, 2006). This is a Saudi Textbook. *The Washington Post,* 13.

Shields S. A. & S. Bhatia (2009). Darwin on Race, Gender and Culture. *American Psychologist,* 64(2), 111–119.

Sinclair, S. (January 20, 2008). Inside a Female Circumcision Ceremony for Young Muslim Girls. *The New York Times Magazine,* 45-50.

Smith, N. (July 5, 2009). British Islamists Plot to Overthrow Pakistan Regime *The London Times,* p. 22.

Sokol, E. D. (1977). *Tamerlane.* Lawrence, KS: Coronado Press.

Sontag, D. (June 7, 2009). The Intersection of Islam, America and Identity. *The New York Times,* AR1.

Speckhard, A. (November 2008). The Emergence of Female Suicide Terrorists. *Studies in Conflict and Terrorism,* 31: 995–1023.

Spencer, R. (2002). *Islam Unveiled, Disturbing Questions About the World's Fastest Growing Faith.* San Francisco: Encounter Book.

Sperling, G. B. (2001). Toward Universal Education, Making a Promise and Keeping it. *Foreign Affairs,* 80(5), 7-14.

Stankov, l, & D. Higgins, G. Sucier, G. Knezevic. (2010). Contemporary Militant Extremism: A Linguistic Approach to Scale Development. *Psychological Assessment,* 22(2), 246–258.

Stark, F. (1934). *The Valleys of the Assassins.* London: John Murray.

Steele, R. D. (1994). Reinventing Intelligence: Holy Grail or Mission Impossible. *Journal of Intelligence and CounterIntelligence,* 7(2), 199–203.

Stern, E. (September 3, 2011). Don't Fear Islamic Law in America. *The New York Times,* A15.

Stewart, R. (January 14, 2010). Afghanistan: What Could Work. *The New York Review of Books,* LVII(1), 60–63.

Stoddard, P. H. (1981). *Change in the Muslim World.* Syracuse, NY: Syracuse University Press.

Stoye, J. (2007). *The Siege of Vienna, The Last Great Trial Between Cross and Crescent.* New York: Pegasus Books.

Sultan, W. (2009). *A God Who Hates*. New York: St. Martin's Press.

Sun-Tzu (1994). *The Art of War*. (Trans. R. D. Sawyer). New York: Barnes and Noble.

Suskind, R. (2008). *The Way of the World, A Story of Truth and Hope in an Age of Extremism*. New York: HarperCollins.

Tabaar, M. A. (December 7, 2008). Who Wrote the Koran? *The New York Times Magazine*, 24.

Taylor, B. (1892). *Travels in Arabia*. New York. Charles Scribner's Sons.

Thaib, L. (2005). *Islamic Political Representation in Malaysia*. Kuala Lumpur, Malaysia: University of Malaya Press.

Thomas, M. & R. Nayan. (2010). *Muslim Teenagers in Public Schools*. Paper Presented at the Annual Meeting of the American Educational Research Association, Denver, May 2, 2010.

Thompson, C. (August 16, 2009). Is Iran Going to Build a Bomb? *The New York Times Magazine*, pp. 22–25.

Thompson, G. (November 23, 2009). A Terror Suspect at Home in 2 Worlds. *International Herald Tribune*, p. 1.

—— (April 9, 2009). The Great Battle Against Islam. *The New York Review of Books*, LVI(6), 30–33.

Toynbee, A. (1949). *A Study of History*. London: Oxford University Press.

Traub, J. (April 5, 2009). Can Pakistan Be Governed? *The New York Times Magazine*, 26ff.

Tripp, C. (September/October 2009). All (Muslim) Politics is Local, How Context Shapes Islam in Power. *Foreign Affairs*, 88(5), 124–129.

Tritton, A. S. (1970). *The Caliphs and Their Non-Muslim Subjects*. London: Frank Cass & Co.

*UNESCO Statistical Yearbook* (1983). Paris: UNESCO.

Urquhart, B. (2008). The Middle East: What to Do? *The New York Review of Books*. 55 (17), 32–34.

Vaddy, C. (1982). *The Muslim Mind*. Harlow: Longman.

Van Natta, D. (May 17, 2011). Miami Imam Will Plead Not Guilty to Aiding Terror Group, Lawyer Says. *The New York Times*, A14.

Vinci, A. (February 2008). Becoming the Enemy: Convergence in the American and Al-Qaeda Ways of Warfare. *Journal of Strategic Studies*, 31(4), 69–88.

Visser, R. (April-May 2008). Historical Myths of a Divided Iraq. *Survival*, 50(2), 95–106.

Von Drehle, D. (May 20, 2011). Death Comes for the Terrorist, *Time*, 15-28.

Von Hippel, F. N. (May 2008). Rethinking Nuclear Fuel Recycling. *Scientific American*, 88–93.

Waddy, C. (1982). *The Muslim Mind*. London: Longman.

Wasdin, H. E. & S. Templin. (2011). *Seal Team Six, Memoirs of an Elite Navy Seal Sniper*. New York: St, Martin's Press.

Watt, W. M. (1979). *What is Islam?* London: Longman.

Weaver, M. A. (2005, Sept. 11). The War on Terror, Four Years On. *The New York Times Magazine*, 55-58.

—— (2003). Pharaohs in Waiting. *The Atlantic Monthly*, 292(3), 79–92.

——— (2000). *A Portrait of Egypt, A Journey through the World of Militant Islam.* New York: Farrar, Strauss and Giroux.

Weckes, R. V. (1978). *Muslim Peoples, a World Ethnographic Survey.* London: Greenwood Press.

Wetherford, J. (2004). *Genghis Khan and the Making of the Modern World.* New York: Three Rivers Press.

Wheatcroft, A. (2008). *The Enemy at the Gate, Habsburgs, Ottomans and the Battle for Europe.* New York: Basic Books.

Weiss, B. (April 2-3, 2011). The Tyrannies are Doomed. *The Wall Street Journal,* A13.

White, J. (July/August 2011). War With Iran. *The American Interest,* VI (6), 80-88.

Wiktorowicz, Q. (2005). *Radical Islam Rising, Muslim Extremism in the West.* Lanham, MD: Rowman and Littlefield.

Williams, C. (2000). Education and Human Survival: The Relevance of the Global Security Framework to International Education. *International Review of Education,* 46(3-4), 183–203.

Williams, T. (November 21-22, 2009). A Search for Blame in Reconstruction After War. *International Herald Tribune,* p. 4.

Wilson, G. W. (2005, July/August). The Show-Me Sheikh. *The Atlantic Monthly,* 40-44.

Witular, R.A. &H. Widhiarto (June 17, 2011) Can Prison Bars Put an End to Ba'asyir's Access to Jihadists? *The Jakarta Post,* A1 & A3.

Wong, E. (January 6, 2009). China Releases Arrest Report for Pre-Olympics Crackdown. *The New York Times,* A10.

——— (October 19, 2008). Wary of Islam, China Tightens a Vise of Rules. *The New York Times,* A1.

——— (December 4, 2008). Lack of Preparedness Comes Brutally to Light. *The New York Times,* A18.

Wright, R. (2008). *Dreams and Shadows, The Future of the Middle East.* New York: The Penguin Press.

Yamini, M. (November 24, 2009). Saudi Arabia Goes to War Against Houthi Rebels. *The Daily Star* (Beirut), p. 6.

Yousef, M. H. (2010). *Son of Hamas, A Gripping Account of Terror, Betrayal, Political Intrigue, and Unthinkable Choices.* Carol Stream, IL: SaltRiver, Tyndale House Publishers.

Zablon, A. B. (1981). *The Arab Brain Drain.* London: Ithaca Press.

Zaidi, S. M. A. (October 2009). The Taliban Organisation in Pakistan. *The RUSI Journal,* Vol. 154(5), 40–47.

Zakaria, F. (October 12, 2009). Containing a Nuclear Iran. *Newsweek,* 32–36.

——— (April 6, 2008). Bhutto and the Future of Islam. *The New York Times Book Review,* 16–17.

——— (2008b, May/June). The Future of American Power, How America Can Survive the Rise of the Rest. *Foreign Affairs,* (87(3), 18–43.

——— (June 29, 2009). Theocracy and Its Discontents. *Newsweek,* 30-38.

Zarate, J. C. (April 18, 2011). Al Qaeda Stirs Again. *The New York Times,* A21.

Zia-Elbrahini, R. (July 22, 2008). Mending a Muslim Divide, *International Herald Tribune,* 4.

Zoepf, K. (August 29, 2006). Women Lead an Islamic Revival in Syria, Testing Its Secularism. *The New York Times,* A1.

——— (November 9, 2008). Deprogramming Jihadists. *The New York Times Magazine,* 51-53.

# INDEX

**Donald K. Sharpes, Ph.D.** is Senior Visiting Fellow at Cambridge University, and Professor in the Emeritus College at Arizona State University, a former research associate at Stanford University and technical division director in the U.S. Department of Education in Washington DC. He has taught at the universities of Maryland, Maine, Virginia, Virginia Tech, Utah State, Weber State and Arizona State. He did postdoctoral studies at the University of Sussex, was a Visiting Scholar at Oxford University in 1998–1999, and has lived and worked in Asia and the Middle East. He has authored 21 books and over 240 articles in the social and behavioral sciences, humanities, and teacher education.

www.ingramcontent.com/pod-product-compliance
Lightning Source LLC
LaVergne TN
LVHW061222060426
835509LV00012B/1381